ROAD TRANSPORT LAW

TWENTY-NINTH EDITION

BY
JAMES DUCKWORTH

A summary of the legislation affecting the construction, equipment and use of commercial vehicles

British Library Cataloguing in Publication Data

A catalogue record of this book is
available from the British Library

ISBN 0 9519656 1 1

Published by Transport Law Services
              190 Goldsworth Road,
              Woking,
              Surrey,
              England,
              GU21 1NF

Typeset by Kerrypress (Typesetters) Ltd, Luton.
Printed and bound by Ashford Colour Press, Gosport.

Cover illustration—Leyland DAF FT85.360 tractor unit plated for 38 tonnes gtw.

Contents

Preface

Over the two years since the last edition of *Road Transport Law* many changes have been made to the legislation governing the operation of goods and passenger vehicles. So much so that, despite several pages of redundant material being removed from the book, such as the specimen pages of AETR record books and the rules on the old hgv driver's licence, the legislative changes and new material have added a further 24 pages to this edition.

The chapter on goods vehicle operators' licensing has been further improved by changes in presentation, the addition of the extensive rules governing public inquiries and the inclusion of many more judgments of the Transport Tribunal. *Road Transport Law* continues to be the leading work on this subject.

Opportunity has been taken to re-write and enlarge the chapter on PSV operator's licensing to make it far more comprehensive and easier to follow than before. A separate chapter has been created dealing with the registration of PSV services.

Many drafting changes to the chapter dealing with vehicle excise duty have been made due to the introduction of the Vehicle Excise and Registration Act 1994. The constant flow of changes to driver licensing law, including amendments to licence categories, test vehicles and medical disabilities, have been incorporated in this revision.

Explained in full are the regulations allowing 44-tonne vehicle combinations on road/rail transport operations and those dealing with the fitting of speed limiters to goods and passenger vehicles.

Changes to vehicle lighting legislation, including the compulsory use of reflective 'children' signs on school buses and revised reflective rear markings for goods vehicles, are included.

This edition contains the regulations governing the issue, use and removal of Community journey authorisations; changes in livestock transport; and the de-criminalised system of dealing with parking offences in London.

Also noted are the extra traffic signs which the Traffic Signs Regulations and General Directions 1994 have specified as being an offence to contravene and the legislation dealing with the use of cameras in speeding and traffic lights' prosecutions.

The recent EC Court rulings on drivers' hours regulations are referred to as well as relevant High Court decisions on other transport matters.

1st November, 1994   JD

System of reference

The purpose of this book is to enable the reader to understand more easily the various Acts and Regulations affecting the construction, equipment and operation of goods and large passenger vehicles. The legislation is presented in summarised form and, if it is desired to consult a particular Act, Regulation or Order, the special system of reference giving the official titles enables the particular legislation to be obtained for deeper study. Naturally, the extent to which the material is summarised in the book means that some of the more detailed points of law are omitted.

Each point of law is identified by reference to the appropriate Act, Regulation or Order. For example, 1078/86/12(1), means Regulation 12 of Statutory Instrument No. 1078 of 1986, the full title of which will be found at the head of the chapter. In succeeding references to the same Act or Regulation in the same or following sentences, the references are often abbreviated to, for example, [12(1)].

Copies of the Acts, Regulations and Orders referred to in this book may be ordered through any bookseller or obtained direct from HMSO Publications Centre, PO Box 276, London SW8 5DT (telephone orders 071–873 9090) or HMSO bookshops in London, Belfast, Birmingham, Bristol, Edinburgh and Manchester.

1 Definitions and general notes

Road Traffic Act 1988
Road Vehicles (Construction and Use) Regulations, **No. 1078/86**

Section 185 of the Road Traffic Act 1988 places motor vehicles into various basic classes according to their description and unladen weight.

A **motor car** is a mechanically propelled vehicle, not being a motor cycle or invalid carriage, which is constructed itself to carry a load or passengers and the unladen weight of which (a) if constructed solely for the carriage of not more than seven passengers and their effects does not exceed 3,050kg; (b) if constructed or adapted for the conveyance of goods or burden does not exceed 3,050kg; or (c) in any other case does not exceed 2,540kg.

A **heavy motor car** is a mechanically propelled vehicle, not being a motor car, which is constructed itself to carry a load or passengers and the unladen weight of which exceeds 2,540kg. A recovery vehicle towing a lorry and trailer by suspended tow was held not to be constructed to carry a load and, consequently, not a heavy motor car—*DPP v Yates* [1989] RTR 134.

A **motor tractor** is a mechanically propelled vehicle which is not constructed itself to carry a load, other than water, fuel, accumulators and other equipment used for the purpose of propulsion, loose tools and loose equipment, and the unladen weight of which does not exceed 7,370kg. In *LCC v Hays Wharf Cartage Co. Ltd* [1953] 2 All ER 34 it was held that ballast blocks on a haulage vehicle were part of its equipment and had to be included in its unladen weight.

A **locomotive** is a mechanically propelled vehicle, described in the same way as a motor tractor, and the unladen weight of which exceeds 7,370kg.

If a motor vehicle is constructed so that a trailer can be partially superimposed on it whereby a substantial part of the weight of the trailer is borne by the vehicle then that vehicle is deemed to be constructed itself to carry a load [186(2)].

1

For the above purposes a crane, dynamo, welding plant or other special appliance or apparatus which is a permanent or essentially permanent fixture on a motor vehicle does not constitute a load or goods or burden but is deemed to form part of the vehicle [186(3)].

A **motor vehicle** is a mechanically propelled vehicle intended or adapted for use on roads. A **trailer** is a vehicle drawn by a motor vehicle [185].

In the High Court Case of *Newberry v Simmonds* [1961] 2 QB 345, [1961] 2 All ER 318 it was held that a motor car from which the engine had been removed was still a mechanically propelled vehicle. A vehicle licence was required for a van with a defective engine which was being towed—*Cobb v Whorton* [1971] RTR 392. But in *Smart v Allan* [1962] 3 All ER 893 a vehicle was held not to be a mechanically propelled vehicle since it had no gearbox and the engine was so defective that there was no likelihood of it being repaired. Where a vehicle without engine and gearbox was alleged by police to be a mechanically propelled vehicle the burden of proof was on the police, it was ruled in *Reader v Bunyard* [1988] RTR 406.

In three cases, *MacDonald v Carmichael* 1941 SC(J) 27, *Daley v Hargreaves* [1961] 1 All ER 552 and *Chalgray v Aspley* (1965) 109 Sol Jo 394 it was decided that a dump truck, though used on a road, was not a motor vehicle because it was not 'intended or adapted for use on roads'. Similarly in *Burns v Currell* [1963] 2 QB 433, [1963] 2 All ER 297 a go-kart was held not to be a motor vehicle. On the other hand, in *Childs v Coghlan* (1968) 112 Sol Jo 175 a Euclid earth-scraper was held to be intended for use on roads since it was too large to be carried and to get from site to site had to be driven on the road.

A motor vehicle can change from one class to another if a reconstruction takes place. In *Keeble v Miller* [1950] 1 KB 601, [1950] 1 All ER 261, where a heavy motor car was converted into a locomotive, it was ruled that 'constructed' meant constructed at the material time and not originally constructed. A vehicle chassis on delivery was held not to be a motor tractor in *Millard v Turvey* [1968] 2 QB 390, [1968] 2 All ER 7 when it was said that 'constructed' meant constructed when completed.

An **articulated vehicle** (other than an articulated bus) is a motor car or heavy motor car with a trailer superimposed on it so that when the trailer is uniformly loaded not less than 20% of the weight of its load is borne by the drawing vehicle [1078/86/3(2)]. When coupled-up an artic is treated as a motor vehicle and trailer [Act 1988/187(1)]. An articulated bus is a passenger vehicle constructed that it can be divided into two parts, both being vehicles and one of which is a motor vehicle, but cannot be so divided without facilities normally found in a workshop, and passengers carried by the vehicle can at all times pass from one part to the other [1078/86/3(2)]. It is treated as a single vehicle [Act 1988/187(2)].

A **composite trailer** is a combination of a converter dolly and a semi-trailer [1078/86/3(2)]. A **converter dolly** is a trailer with two or more wheels designed to be used in combination with a semi-trailer without any part of its weight being borne by the drawing vehicle and which is not itself part of the semi-trailer or drawing vehicle. If used solely for agricultural, horticultural or forestry purposes part of the weight of the semi-trailer can be borne by the drawing vehicle [3(2)]. A **semi-trailer** is a trailer which is constructed to form part of an articulated vehicle including a vehicle which is not itself a motor vehicle but which has some or all of its wheels driven by the drawing vehicle [3(2)]. A composite trailer is to be treated as a single trailer for the purposes of Regulations 7 (overall length); 75 (gross weight); 76 (train weight); 78 (axle weight); and 83 (restriction on number of trailers) of the Road Vehicles (Construction and Use) Regulations 1986 [3(11)].

A **dual-purpose vehicle** is a vehicle not over 2,040kg unladen weight which is constructed or adapted to carry both passengers and goods and is either (a) so constructed that all its wheels can be power-driven or (b) constructed with a permanent roof, and behind the driver's seat has a row of transverse seats with backrests for two or more, in prescribed positions, and windows of minimum sizes [1078/86/ 3(2)].

A **goods vehicle** is a motor vehicle or trailer constructed or adapted for the carriage of goods. The carriage of goods includes the haulage of goods [Act 1988/192].

For particular purposes different definitions are given and these will be supplied in the relevant chapters. In *Plume v Suckling* [1977] RTR 271 a motor coach with most of its seats removed and adapted to carry domestic equipment and a stock car was, for speed limit purposes, held not to be a passenger vehicle but to be a goods vehicle.

The **unladen weight** of a vehicle is to be taken as its weight, inclusive of the body and all parts (the heavier being taken where alternative bodies or parts are used) necessary to or ordinarily used with the vehicle when working on a road but not including the weight of water, fuel or accumulators used to supply power for the propulsion of the vehicle, loose tools and loose equipment [Act 1988/190]. It was held in *Cording v Halse* [1955] 1 QB 63, [1954] 3 All ER 287 that a cattle container carried on a platform truck was not an alternative body and was excluded from unladen weight.

An **agricultural motor vehicle** is a motor vehicle constructed or adapted for use off roads for agriculture, horticulture or forestry and is primarily used for one or more of these purposes, but does not include a dual-purpose vehicle. An **agricultural trailer** is a trailer constructed or adapted for agriculture, horticulture or forestry and which is used only for one or more of these purposes, but does not include an agricultural trailed appliance. An **agricultural trailed appliance** is a trailer (a) which is an implement constructed or adapted for use off roads for agriculture, horticulture or forestry and is used only for one or more of these purposes and, except an appliance made before 1 December 1985 or a towed roller, its maximum gross weight is not more than twice its unladen weight; but (b) which is not certain living accommodation or certain mounted implements. An agricultural trailed appliance conveyor is an agricultural trailer not over 510kg unladen; with its unladen weight marked on it; with pneumatic tyres on all its wheels; and designed and constructed for conveying one agricultural trailed appliance or one agricultural, horticultural or forestry implement [1078/86/3(2)].

The majority of traffic offences can be committed only on a road. A **road** is defined as any highway and any other road to which the public has access, including bridges over which the road passes [Act 1988/192]. A paved shop frontage, part privately owned and part publicly owned, was held to be a road in *Price v DPP* [1990] RTR 413. Perimeter roads at Heathrow Airport, though subject to restrictions on the purposes for which they could be used, were held to be roads to which the public had access—*DPP v Cargo Handling Ltd* [1992] RTR 318. The inward freight immigration lane at Dover Eastern Docks was held to be a road to which the public had access even though it could only be accessed from the seaward side by persons arriving on a ferry—*DPP v Coulman* [1993] RTR 230.

Some traffic laws apply only to the '**driving**' of a vehicle and they are generally straightforward. In *McQuaid v Anderton* [1980] RTR 371 a person steering a vehicle being towed by another vehicle by means of a tow rope was held to be driving it. This was followed in *Caise v Wright* [1981] RTR 49 and in which the House of Lords refused leave to appeal against the High Court decision. But many others relate to a person who 'uses' or 'causes' or 'permits' a person to use it.

The person driving a vehicle '**uses**' it and an employer 'uses' it when it is driven on his business by an employee—*Green v Burnett* [1955] 1 QB 78, [1954] 3 All ER 273. Where a vehicle is driven by a person other than an employee of the owner the owner is not then using it—*Crawford v Haughton* [1972] 1 All ER 534, [1972] 1 WLR 572.

But in *NFC Forwarding Ltd v DPP* [1989] RTR 239 the owners of a semi-trailer were said to be using it though it was drawn by another company's tractor unit and driver. Where an owner-driver had a two-year contract with a heavy haulage company to provide traction for its trailers the company was held to be the 'user' of the vehicle because it was responsible for selecting the route; deciding the load; providing and loading the trailer, and giving an indemnity and notifying the movement—*Hallett Silberman Ltd v Cheshire CC* [1993] RTR 32.

A car-hire firm was not using a car which was hired out—*Carmichael & Sons v Cottle* [1971] RTR 11—and a truck operator was not using a vehicle driven by an agency driver on his business—*Howard v G. T. Jones & Co Ltd* [1975] RTR 150—nor when he hired a vehicle with a driver—*Balfour Beatty & Co Ltd v Grindley* [1975] RTR 156. In *Mickleburgh v BRS (Contracts) Ltd* [1977] RTR 389 the owners of a vehicle hired out with a driver for three years were held to be using it when overladen by the hirers who had control of its day-today operations. A 'sleeping' partner in a firm which employed the driver was held to be using the vehicle even though she took no active part in running the business—*Passmore v Gibbons* [1979] RTR 53.

In *Elliott v Grey* [1960] 1 QB 367, [1959] 3 All ER 733 it was ruled that a broken-down vehicle parked in the street was being 'used' and required insurance. But this case was not followed in *Hewer v Cutler* [1974] RTR 155 which involved an immobilised car parked without a test certificate. The court based its decision on the mischief aimed at by the test certificate requirement.

A passenger in a vehicle, who has no control over the driver, does not himself use it without insurance, or aid and abet uninsured use, merely by letting himself be driven even when he knows that the vehicle is uninsured—*B (a minor) v Knight* [1981] RTR 136.

A person '**causes**' a vehicle to be used if through some express or implied instruction, or through some position of authority, he causes another person to use it—*Houston v Buchanan* [1940] 2 All ER 179. To cause the use of an overloaded lorry a person must have knowledge of the facts constituting the offence and, in the case of a company, the knowledge had to be that of someone exercising a directing mind over the company's affairs—*Ross Hillman Ltd v Bond* [1974] QB 435, [1974] 2 All ER 287.

To '**permit**' use a person must have knowledge of what is alleged to have been permitted or must have been closing his eyes to the obvious not caring whether it happened or not—*James & Son v Smee* [1955] 1 QB 78, [1954] 3 All ER 273. Also, in *Grays Haulage Co Ltd v Arnold* [1966] 1 All ER 896, [1966] 1 WLR 534 it was held that the mere fact that an employer does not take steps to prevent an employee committing an offence does not mean that he has 'permitted' it. This was followed in *Knowles Transport Ltd v Russell* [1975] RTR 87 when it was held that knowledge of irregularities after they had occurred did not impute the knowledge required for permitting. Proof of knowledge by a responsible officer of a company of a vehicle's deficiency is required for permitting use of a vehicle with an insecure load—*P. Lowery & Sons Ltd v Wark* [1975] RTR 45. Because an employer had no knowledge of a vehicle's brake defect and there was no evidence he had been reckless or negligent he could not be guilty of 'permitting' the use of the vehicle with defective brakes—*Robinson v DPP* [1991] RTR 315. Whilst acquiescence can amount to permitting an offence it falls short of causing an offence—*Redhead Freight Ltd v Shulman* [1989] RTR 1.

If a person can be charged with causing or permitting an offence he should not be charged with aiding and abetting it—*Carmichael & Sons v Cottle* and followed in *Crawford v Haughton* [1972] 1 All ER 534, [1972] 1 WLR 572.

2 Construction of vehicles

Road Traffic Act 1988
Road Vehicles (Construction and Use) Regulations, **No.** 1978/86 as amended
by:
  Road Vehicles (Construction and Use) (Amendment) Regulations, **Nos.**
    1597/86, 676/87, 1478/89, 317/90, 1526/91, 352/92 and 1946/93
  Road Vehicles (Construction and Use) (Amendment) (No. 2) Regu-
    lations, **Nos. 1133/87, 1695/89, 1131/90, 422/92, 2199/93 and 329/94**
  Road Vehicles (Construction and Use) (Amendment) (No. 3) Regu-
    lations, **Nos. 1865/89, 1163/90, 2003/91, 646/92, 3048/93 and
    2192/94**
  Road Vehicles (Construction and Use) (Amendment) (No. 4) Regu-
    lations, **Nos. 1178/88, 2360/89, 1981/90, 2125/91 and 2016/92**
  Road Vehicles (Construction and Use) (Amendment) (No. 5) Regu-
    lations, **No. 1287/88, 2212/90, 2710/91 and 2137/92**
  Road Vehicles (Construction and Use) (Amendment) (No. 6) Regu-
    lations, **No. 1524/88 and 2902/92**
  Road Vehicles (Construction and Use) (Amendment) (No. 7) Regu-
    lations, **No. 1871/88 and 3088/92**
Road Vehicles (Marking of Special Weights) Regulations, **No. 910/83**
Road Vehicles (Marking of Special Weights) (Amendment) Regulations, **No.
  1326/87**

Brakes—new vehicles

Motor vehicles first used on or after 1 April 1983 and trailers made
on or after 1 October 1982 must comply with prescribed construction,
fitting and performance requirements for brakes specified in
Community Directive 79/489 or ECE Regulation 13.03, 13.04, 13.05
or 13.06 [1078/86/15(1) and (4)]. A motor vehicle first used before
April 1983 or a trailer made before 1 October 1982 can comply with
the above requirements instead of Regulations 16 and 17 given in the
next section [15(1) proviso].

  Buses over 5,000kg maximum gross weight and goods vehicles over
3,500kg maximum gross weight first used, in either case, from 1 April
1989; buses not over 5,000kg maximum gross weight and passenger

vehicles first used, in either case, from 1 April 1990; goods vehicles not over 3,500kg maximum gross weight and dual-purpose vehicles first used, in either case from 1 April 1992; and trailers made on or after 1 October 1988 must comply with prescribed requirements of Community Directive 85/647 or ECE Regulation 13.05 or 13.06 [15(1A), (1B) and (5)]. A motor vehicle first used or a trailer made before the above relevant dates can comply with this requirement instead of Regulation 15(1), 16 or 17 [15(1A) proviso].

A motor vehicle first used from 1 April 1992 or a trailer made on or after 1 October 1991 must comply with prescribed requirements of Community Directive 88/194 (which includes anti-lock brakes on inter-urban and long distance coaches over 12 tonnes gross weight and goods vehicles over 16 tonnes authorised to tow trailers over 10 tonnes gvw) or, if a trailer made before 1 April 1992, with ECE Regulation 13.05 or 13.06 or, if made on or after that date, ECE Regulation 13.06 [15(1C) and (5A)]. A motor vehicle first used or a trailer made before these dates can comply with this requirement instead of Regulation 15(1) or (1A), 16 or 17 [15(1C) proviso].

The Directives cover many pages of technical specifications and cannot be included in this work.

The above rules do not apply to an agricultural trailer or agricultural trailed appliance neither of which exceeds 20mph; a locomotive or motor tractor; an agricultural motor vehicle unless first used before 1 June 1986 and driven faster than 20mph; a vehicle which has a maximum speed not over 25km/h; a works truck or trailer; a public works vehicle; or a trailer designed, made or adapted to be drawn exclusively by one of the above motor vehicles; a street cleansing trailer; a trailer with axle weights not exceeding 750kg in total; certain agricultural trailers made before July 1947; an agricultural trailed appliance conveyor; a broken-down vehicle; a gritting trailer with a maximum gross weight not over 2,000kg; or a Leyland Atlantean bus first used before October 1984 [15(2)]. A public works vehicle for this purpose is a motor vehicle used by or on behalf of Central Scotland Water Development Board; a ferry or market undertaking; National Rivers Authority; public gas or electricity supplier; a telecommunications operator; a police, highway, local or water authority; Post Office; for works which that body has a duty or power to carry out, but excluding the carriage of persons other than crew and goods other than those needed for the vehicle's work [3].

Brakes—heavy motor cars used before 1 April 1983

A heavy motor car or motor car first used on or after 1 April 1938 and before 1 April 1983 (other than one which complies with the above

Directives or ECE Regulations) must be equipped with an efficient braking system with two means of operation, an efficient split braking system with one means of operation or two efficient braking systems with separate means of operation. In the case of a vehicle first used on or after 1 January 1968 no account will be taken of a multi-pull means of operation unless, on first application, it causes the application of brakes with an efficiency not less than 25%.

The brakes of a vehicle first used on or after 1 January 1968 must apply on all its wheels.

Except for vehicles with a split braking system and road rollers, in the event of failure of any part, other than a fixed member or brake shoe anchor pin, there must still be brakes capable of being applied to not less than half the number of the vehicle's wheels, sufficient under the most adverse conditions, to stop the vehicle within a reasonable distance. This requirement applies to both the braking systems of a trailer and its drawing vehicle, but if the brakes on the drawing vehicle fulfil Regulation 15, it applies only to the drawing vehicle.

The above two paragraphs do not apply to a works truck which has one braking system with one means of operation.

The braking system of a vehicle, when drawing a trailer which fulfils Regulation 15, must be constructed so that in the event of failure of any part, other than a fixed member or brake shoe anchor pin, the driver can still apply brakes to at least one wheel of a two-wheeled trailer or to at least two wheels of any other trailer, by using the drawing vehicle's secondary braking system.

The application of one means of operation of a braking system must not affect or operate the pedal or hand lever of any other means of operation.

Except for steam-propelled vehicles, the braking system must not be rendered ineffective by the non-rotation of the vehicle's engine or, in the case of a trailer, the drawing vehicle's engine.

At least one means of operation must be capable of applying brakes directly, not through the transmission gear, to at least half the number of wheels of the vehicle. This requirement does not apply to a works truck not over 7,370kg unladen weight; and industrial tractor; or a vehicle with more than four wheels if (a) the drive is transmitted to all wheels other than steering wheels without a differential between the axles carrying the driven wheels, (b) the brakes applied by one means of operation apply directly to two driving wheels on opposite sides of the vehicle and (c) the brakes applied by the other means act directly on all the other driven wheels.

On pre-1968 vehicles a parking brake must be designed and constructed so that (a) its means of operation is independent of the means of operation of any split braking system, (b) it can either be applied by direct mechanical action without the intervention of any hydraulic, electric or pneumatic device or brakes apply to all the wheels, and (c) it can be set to prevent at least two wheels—one in the case of a three-wheeler—from rotating.

All the above requirements, except that relating to brakes applying to at least half the numbers of wheels of the vehicle, also apply to heavy motor cars first used on or after 15 August 1928 and before April 1938. The requirements, except that relating to brakes not being rendered ineffective by the non-rotation of the engine, also apply to motor cars first used on or after 1 January 1915 and before 1938.

On vehicles first used on or after 1 January 1968, a parking brake must be designed and constructed so that (a) its means of operation is independent of the means of operating the service brake, and (b) it can be maintained in operation by direct mechanical action, without the intervention of any hydraulic, electric or pneumatic device, and can hold the vehicle stationary on a 16% gradient without the assistance of stored energy [1078/86/16 & Sch. 3]. The mechanical energy of a spring does not count as stored energy [3(2)].

None of the above requirements applies to a broken-down vehicle [16(3)].

Special provisions are made for heavy motor cars used before 15 August 1928 and motor cars used before 1915.

The engine of a steam-propelled heavy motor car or motor car will be deemed to be an efficient braking system with one means of operation if the engine is capable of being reversed and, in the case of a vehicle first used on or after 1 January 1927, is incapable of being disconnected from the driving wheels except by the sustained effort of the driver [Sch. 3(2)].

Brakes—locomotives and motor tractors used before 1 April 1983

All locomotives and motor tractors must be equipped with an efficient braking system.

Except for vehicles with a split braking system and road rollers, on locomotives first used on or after 1 June 1955 and all motor tractors (except industrial tractors), in the event of failure of any part, other than a fixed member or brake shoe anchor pin, there must still be brakes capable of being applied to not less than half the number of the vehicle's wheels, sufficient under the most adverse conditions, to stop the vehicle within a reasonable distance. This requirement applies to both the braking systems of a trailer and its drawing vehicle, but if the brakes on the drawing vehicle fulfil Regulation 15, it applies only to the drawing vehicle. The brakes of an industrial tractor must be designed and constructed so that in the event of failure of any part, a brake is still available which, under the most adverse conditions, will bring the vehicle to rest within a reasonable distance.

The braking system of a locomotive or motor tractor, when drawing a trailer which fulfils Regulation 15, must be constructed so that in the event of failure of any part, other than a fixed member or brake shoe anchor pin, the driver can still apply brakes to at least one wheel of a two-wheeled trailer or to at least two wheels of any other trailer, by using the drawing vehicle's secondary braking system.

On locomotives first used on or after 1 June 1955 and all motor tractors, the application of one means of operation of a braking system must not affect or operate the pedal or hand lever of any other means of operation.

On locomotives first used on or after 1 June 1955 and motor tractors first used on or after 1 April 1938, the braking system must not be rendered ineffective by the non-rotation of the engine. Steam-propelled motor tractors are excluded from this requirement.

On locomotives first used on or after 1 June 1955 and motor tractors first used on or after 14 January 1931, at least one means of operation must be capable of applying brakes directly, not through the transmission gear, to at least half the number of wheels of the vehicle. This requirement does not apply to a works truck not over 7,370kg unladen weight; an industrial tractor; or a vehicle with more than four wheels if (a) the drive is transmitted to all wheels other than steering wheels without a differential between the axles carrying the driving wheels, (b) the brakes applied by one means of operation apply directly to two driving wheels on opposite sides of the vehicle, and (c) the brakes applied by the other means act directly on all the other driving wheels.

The brakes on a locomotive used before 1 June 1955 must apply to all the wheels other than the steering wheels.

On locomotives used before 1 June 1955 and motor tractors used before 1 January 1968, a parking brake must be designed and constructed so that (a) its means of operation is independent of the means of operation of any split braking system, (b) it can either be applied by direct mechanical action without the intervention of any hydraulic, electric or pneumatic device or brakes apply to all the wheels, and (c) it can be set to prevent at least two wheels—one in the case of a three-wheeler—from rotating.

On locomotives first used on or after 1 June 1955 and motor tractors first used on or after 1 January 1968, a parking brake must be designed and constructed so that (a) its means of operation is independent of the means of operating the service brake, and (b) it can be maintained in operation by direct mechanical action, without the intervention of any hydraulic, electric or pneumatic device, and can hold the vehicle stationary on 16% gradient without the assistance of stored energy

[1078/86/16 & Sch. 3]. The mechanical energy of a spring does not count as stored energy [3(2)].

None of the above requirements applies to a broken-down vehicle or, apart from the parking brake requirement, to a steam-propelled locomotive used before 2 January 1933 which has an engine capable of being reversed [16(3)]. Neither do they apply to a vehicle which complies with Community Directives 79/489 or 85/647 or ECE Regulations 13.03, 13.04 or 13.05 [16(2)].

Brakes—trailers used before 1 April 1983

Trailers with maximum design axle weights which total more than 750kg must be equipped with an efficient braking system.

On such a trailer made before 1 January 1968 and an agricultural trailer whenever made, brakes must act automatically on its overrun, or be capable of being applied by a person on the drawing vehicle or on the trailer, to at least two wheels if it has no more than four wheels or to at least half its wheels if it has more than four wheels. It must also be fitted with a parking brake capable of being set to prevent at least two wheels from revolving when not being drawn.

Except for agricultural trailers, the braking system of a trailer made on or after 1 April 1938 must not be rendered ineffective by the non-rotation of the engine of the drawing vehicle (steam-propelled vehicles, other than locomotives and buses, excluded).

Except for agricultural trailers, a trailer made on or after 1 January 1968 must have brakes which act automatically on its overrun or be applied by the driver of the drawing vehicle when using its service brake. Apart from a trailer with overrun brakes, the brakes must apply to all the wheels of the trailer. Except for vehicles with a split braking system, in the event of failure of any part, other than a fixed member or brake shoe anchor pin, there must still be braking capable of being applied to not less than half the number of the trailer's wheels, sufficient under the most adverse conditions, to stop the vehicle within a reasonable distance. This requirement applies to both the braking systems of a trailer and its drawing vehicle, but if the brakes on the drawing vehicle fulfil Regulation 15, it applies only to the drawing vehicle.

Except for agricultural trailers, a trailer made on or after 1 January 1968 must have a parking brake so designed and constructed that the trailer's brakes can be applied and released by a person standing on the ground and by a means fitted to the trailer. It must also be capable of holding the trailer on a 16% gradient by direct mechanical action without the intervention of any hydraulic, electric or pneumatic device and without the assistance of stored energy [1078/86/16 & Sch. 3]. The mechanical energy of a spring does not count as stored energy [3(2)].

None of the above requirements applies to a street cleansing trailer carrying no load other than its necessary gear and equipment; an agricultural trailer made before 1 July 1947 when drawn by a motor tractor or agricultural motor vehicle if its unladen weight is not over 4,070kg, it is the only trailer drawn and it travels at not more than 10mph; an agricultural trailed appliance; an agricultural trailed appliance conveyor; a broken-down vehicle; a gritting trailer with a maximum gross weight not over 2,000kg; or a trailer which complies with Directives 79/489 or 85/647 or ECE Regulations 13.03, 13.04 or 13.05 [16(2)(3)].

Brakes—agricultural motor vehicles not driven over 20mph

An agricultural motor vehicle not driven at more than 20mph must be equipped with an efficient braking system. On such a vehicle used before 9 February 1980, other than one with a split braking system, in the event of failure of any part, other than a fixed member or brake shoe anchor pin, there must still be braking capable of being applied to not less than half the number of the vehicle's wheels, sufficient under the most adverse conditions, to stop the vehicle within a reasonable distance. On vehicles first used on or after 9 February 1980, in the event of a failure of any part of the system there must still be available a brake sufficient, under the most adverse conditions, to stop the vehicle within a reasonable distance.

The braking system of an agricultural motor vehicle, when drawing a trailer which fulfils Regulation 15, must be constructed so that in the event of failure of any part, other than a fixed member or brake shoe anchor pin, the driver can still apply brakes to at least one wheel of a two wheeled-trailer or to at least two wheels of any other trailer, by using the drawing vehicle's secondary braking system.

The application of one means of operation of a braking system must not affect or operate the pedal or hand lever of any other means of operation.

Except for steam-propelled vehicles, other than locomotives, the braking system must not be rendered ineffective by the non-rotation of the vehicle's engine or, in the case of a trailer, the drawing vehicle's engine.

On a vehicle used before 1 January 1968, a parking brake must be designed and constructed so that (a) its means of operation is independent of the means of operation of any split braking system, (b) it can either be applied by direct mechanical action without the intervention of any hydraulic, electric or pneumatic device or brakes apply to all the wheels, and (c) it can be set to prevent at least two wheels—one in the case of a three-wheeler—from rotating.

On vehicles first used on or after 1 January 1968, a parking brake must be designed and constructed so that (a) its means of operation is independent of the means of operating the service brake, and (b) it can be maintained in operation by direct mechanical action, without the intervention of any hydraulic, electric or pneumatic device, and can hold the vehicle stationary on a 16% gradient without the assistance of stored energy [1978/86/16 & Sch. 3]. The mechanical energy of a spring does not count as stored energy [3(2)].

Instead of complying with the above requirements, an agricultural motor vehicle may comply with Community Directives 76/432, 79/489 or 85/647 or ECE Regulations 13.03, 13.04 or 13.05 [16(2) (7)].

Brakes—pressure warning

If a vehicle first used on or after 1 October 1937 is equipped with a braking system which embodies a vacuum or pressure reservoir, there must also be a warning device so placed as to be readily visible to the driver from the driving seat in order to indicate any impending failure or deficiency in the vacuum or pressure system. This does not apply to a vehicle not exceeding 3,050kg unladen with a vacuum system dependent on engine induction provided that, despite a failure of the vacuum, the brakes are sufficient to bring the vehicle to rest within a reasonable distance; a vehicle to which Regulation 15(1) (1A) or (1C) applies or which complies with Community Directives 79/489, 85/647 or 88/194 or ECE Regulations 13.03, 13.04, 13.05 or 13.06; or an agricultural motor vehicle which complies with Community Directive 76/432 [1078/86/17].

Braking efficiency is defined as the maximum braking force capable of being developed by the brakes, expressed as a percentage of the weight of the vehicle including any persons or load carried in the vehicle [3(2)].

Coach strength and exits

The strength of the superstructure of a single deck coach equipped with a below-deck luggage compartment and first used on or after 1 April 1993 must comply with ECE Regulation 66 [1078/86/53A and 2360/89].

A double-deck coach first used on or after 1 April 1990 must be equipped with two staircases, one in each half of the vehicle [53B(1)(2)], but, instead of having two staircases, a vehicle may be equipped with a hammer or other device for breaking side windows in case of emergency. If a vehicle has a staircase in one half of the vehicle and an emergency exit in the same half of the upper deck of the vehicle, the hammer or device must be located in the other half of that deck [53B(3)(4)]. The hammer or other device must be in a conspicuous and readily accessible position on the upper deck and a notice of explaining its use must be displayed nearby [53B(5)]. A distance of at least half the length of the vehicle must be between the staircase and the other staircase or hammer for them to be regarded as being in different halves of the vehicle [53B(7)].

A coach is a vehicle with a maximum gross weight over 7.5 tonnes made to carry more than 16 seated passengers plus driver and at over 60mph [3(2)].

Compensator

Every motor vehicle or trailer with more than four wheels and every semi-trailer with more than two wheels must be provided with a compensating arrangement to ensure that all the wheels remain in contact with the road surface and will not be subject to abnormal variations of load. But a steerable wheel on which the load does not exceed 3,560kg is excluded and, in the case of an agricultural motor vehicle, any number of wheels in a transverse line on one side of the vehicle's longitudinal axis is to be treated for this regulation as one wheel [1078/86/23].

Exhaust and other emissions

Every motor vehicle must be so constructed and maintained that no avoidable smoke or visible vapour is emitted from it [1078/86/61(1)].

Any excess fuel device fitted to a diesel engine in any motor vehicle, other than a works truck, must be in such a position that it cannot readily be operated by any person on the vehicle. An excess fuel device which, after the engine has started, cannot feed the engine with excess fuel or increase smoke emission is, however, permitted [61(3) & Table I, Item 1].

Diesel-engined vehicles first used on or after 1 April 1973 must be constructed so that the engine is one of a type for which there has been issued, on behalf of the Secretary of State, a type test certificate in accordance with a prescribed British Standard Specification indicating that the smoke emitted does not exceed specified limits. The requirement does not apply to vehicles made before 1 October 1972; vehicles made before 1 April 1973, and propelled by a Perkins 6.354 engine; or to an agricultural motor vehicle, industrial tractor, works truck or engineering plant which, in each case, is propelled by a diesel engine having not more than two cylinders 61(3) & Table I, Item 2.

Crankcase vapours on a petrol-engined vehicle first used on or after 1 January 1972 must not escape into the atmosphere otherwise than through the engine's combustion chamber. This does not apply to vehicles with a two-stroke engine, to vehicles made before 1 July 1971 or vehicles to which any item in Table II applies [61(3) & Table I, Item 3].

Vehicles using solid fuel must have an efficient appliance to prevent the emission of sparks or grit, and ashes must not be allowed to fall on to the road [61(2)].

Instead of complying with Regulation 61(1) or Items 1, 2 or 3 in Table I, a vehicle may comply with specified Community Directives or ECE Regulations [61(3A),(3B),(3C) and (4)].

Both petrol- and diesel-engined vehicles first used after various specified dates must comply with EC Directives or ECE Regulations on the emission of carbon monoxide, hydrocarbon, nitrous oxide and particulates [61(7)–(11) and Table II]. They are too extensive and detailed to include in this work and are of more interest to the vehicle manufacturer.

Other emission restrictions are specified for vehicles propelled by a four-stroke petrol engine (including a rotary engine) first used on or after 1 August 1975 and on or after 1 August 1983 [61(10A), (10B), (10C)].

Fuel tanks

Every fuel tank fitted to a wheeled vehicle to supply its engine, an ancillary engine or any other equipment forming part of the vehicle, must be constructed and maintained so that leakage of any liquid or vapour from the tank is adequately prevented, apart from vapour through a pressure-relief valve.

If a tank fitted to a vehicle first used on or after 1 July 1973 contains petrol it must be made only of metal and must be fixed and maintained in a position to be reasonably secure from damage.

Instead of complying with the above requirement a vehicle can comply with Community Directive 70/221, ECE Regulations 34 or 34.01 or, in the case of an agricultural motor vehicle, Community Directive 74/151 [1078/86/39].

Gas-powered vehicles

A motor vehicle first propelled by gas as a fuel before 19 November 1982 and a trailer made on or after that date which is fitted with a gas container must comply with prescribed conditions as to the fitting of the gas container, pipes, unions, etc. [1078/86/40(1) & Sch. 4 or 5].

In the case of a motor vehicle first propelled by gas as a fuel on or after 19 November 1982, a trailer made on or after that date and a motor vehicle first used on or after 1 May 1984 stricter requirements are prescribed for gas containers, filling systems, pipelines, unions, pressure relief valves and gauges. A gas propulsion system has to have automatic stop valves and special safety provisions are made for buses. Conditions are also prescribed for gas-fired appliances (i.e. a device in a motor vehicle or trailer which consumes gas other than the engine of the motor vehicle, Gas Board detecting equipment or an acetylene lamp) [40(2) & Sch. 5].

Ground clearance

A goods trailer made on or after 1 April 1984 must have a minimum ground clearance of at least 160mm if its axle interspace is between 6m and 11.5m and at least 190mm if the axle interspace is 11.5 m or more. Axle interspace means (a) in the case of a semi-trailer, the distance between its king pin and, if it has only one axle, the centre of that axle, or if it has more than one axle, the centre of the bogie and (b) in the case of any other trailer, the distance between the centre of its front axle or if it has more than one front axle, the centre point of the bogie, and the centre of the rear axle or, if it has more than one rear axle, the centre of the bogie. Ground clearance is defined as the distance between that part of the trailer (excluding suspension, brake or steering parts attached to an axle, any wheel or air skirt) contained in the area formed by the width of the trailer and the middle 70% of the axle interspace and the ground. The measurement to be taken when tyres are properly inflated and the trailer is as near as may be to horizontal on ground which is reasonably flat.

This requirement does not apply where a trailer has suspension which can be raised or lowered while that system is being operated to enable the trailer to pass under a bridge or other obstruction over a road as long as the trailer does not, and is not likely to, touch the ground. Neither does the requirement apply to a trailer while it is being loaded or unloaded [1078/86/12].

Height

The overall height of a bus must not exceed 4.57m [1078/86/9(1)].

Overall height is the vertical distance from the ground to the point on the vehicle farthest from the ground when unladen, with tyres properly inflated and on reasonably flat ground [3(2)]. A bus is a motor vehicle adapted to carry more than eight seated passengers in addition to the driver [3(2)].

No part of the structure of a semi-trailer must be more than 4.2m from the ground if the total laden weight of the semi-trailer and its drawing vehicle exceeds 35,000kg. Where a motor vehicle draws a trailer (other than a semi-trailer) no part of the structure of the motor vehicle or trailer must be more than 4.2m from the ground if the total laden weight of the combination exceeds 35,000kg.

For this purpose the structure of a vehicle includes any detachable structure attached to the vehicle for the purpose of containing a load, but does not include any load which is not a detachable structure or any means of covering or securing a load. This height restriction does not apply while the vehicle is being loaded or unloaded [9(2)(3)].

Certain vehicles over 3.66m high must carry a height warning notice—see page 354.

Horns, gongs, sirens, bells

Every motor vehicle which has a maximum speed of more than 20mph must be fitted with a horn, not being a reversing alarm or two-tone horn, and, except in the case of a horn fitted to a vehicle first used before 1 August 1973 and a reversing alarm, the sound must be continuous and uniform and not strident [1078/86/37(1)(2)(3)]. Gongs, sirens, two-tone horns and bells are prohibited except on motor vehicles used solely for fire-brigade, ambulance, salvage corps or police purposes, motor vehicles owned by the Forestry Commission or local authorities and used sometimes for fire-fighting, vehicles used for bomb disposal, blood-transfusion service vehicles, vehicles used for coastguard service, mine rescue vehicles owned by the National Coal Board; RAF mountain rescue vehicles and RNLI lifeboat-launching vehicles [37(4)(5)].

In addition to a horn, a vehicle may be fitted with sound instruments (e.g. chimes on an ice-cream van) to inform members of the public that goods are on the vehicle for sale [37(6)].

A vehicle may be fitted with a gong, bell or siren if its purpose is to prevent the theft of the vehicle or its contents or, in the case of a bus, its purpose is to summon help. Where a gong, bell, siren, or the horn of a vehicle first used on or after 1 October 1982 is used as an anti-theft measure, a device must be fitted to stop noise being emitted for a continuous period of more than 5 minutes. The device must be maintained in good working order [37(7)(8)].

Instead of complying with the above requirements a vehicle may comply with Community Directive 70/388 or ECE Regulation 28 or, in the case of an agricultural motor vehicle, Community Directive 74/151 [37(9)].

Length limits

Type of vehicle	Max length in metres
1. Motor vehicle drawing 1 trailer, other than a semi-trailer, if Reg. 7(5A) is not complied with	18
1A. Motor vehicle drawing 1 trailer, other than a semi-trailer, if Reg. 7(5A) is complied with	18.35
2. Articulated bus	18
3. Articulated vehicle with a semi-trailer which does not comply with Reg. 7(6) and is not a low loader	15.5
3A. Articulated vehicle with a semi-trailer which does comply with Reg. 7(6)	16.5
3B. Articulated vehicle which is a low loader	18
4. Wheeled motor vehicle not included above	12
5. Track-laying motor vehicle	9.2
6. Agricultural trailed appliance made on or after 1 December 1985	15
7. Semi-trailer made on or after 1 May 1983 which does not comply with Reg. 7(6) and is not a low loader	12.2
7A. Composite trailer drawn by a goods vehicle over 3,500kg maximum gross weight or by an agricultural motor vehicle	14.04
8. Trailer (other than a semi-trailer or composite trailer) with at least 4 wheels which is (a) drawn by a goods vehicle over 3,500kg maximum gross weight or (b) an agricultural trailer	12
9. Any other trailer, not being an agricultural trailed appliance or a semi-trailer	7

[1078/86/7(1)]

Regulation 7(5A), referred to in the Table above, requires that one of the vehicles in the combination is not a goods vehicle or, if both are goods vehicles,

(a) the distance from the foremost point of the loading area behind the driver's cab to the rear of the trailer minus the distance between motor vehicle and trailer does not exceed 15.65m (except where both vehicles are car transporters), and

(b) the distance from the foremost point of the loading area behind the driver's cab to the rear of the trailer does not exceed 16m

In Regulation 7(5A), if the forward end of the motor vehicle's loading area is bounded by a wall, the thickness of the wall is counted as loading area and coupling equipment is disregarded when measuring the distance between motor vehicle and trailer [7(6A)].

Regulation 7(6), referred to in the Table above, requires that on the semi-trailer

(a) the distance from the kingpin to the rear of the semi-trailer does not exceed 12.5m in the case of a car transporter or 12m in any other case; and

(b) no part of the trailer is more than 4.19m forward of the kingpin in the case of a car transporter, or 2.04m in any other case.

Where a semi-trailer has more than one king-pin or is constructed to be used with a king-pin in different positions, distances are measured from the rearmost king-pin or position [7A].

A car transporter is a trailer constructed and normally used for carrying at least two other wheeled vehicles [3(2)].

A low loader is a semi-trailer constructed and normally used for carrying engineering equipment with the major part of its load platform not over or between the wheels and its upper surface below the height of the top of the trailer's tyres when any adjustable suspension is at normal height, tyres are properly inflated and the trailer is unladen [3(2)].

Where a showman's vehicle draws one trailer which is used primarily as living accommodation and not also used for the carriage of goods, other than those needed for residence, the length can be 22m instead of 18m and item 1A in the Table does not apply [7(2)].

Items 1, 1A, 3, 3A, and 3B in the Table do not apply to:

(a) a vehicle combination which includes a trailer constructed and normally used for the conveyance of indivisible loads of exceptional length. An indivisible load is one which cannot, without undue expense or risk of damage, be divided into two or more loads [3(2)]. A load which can be carried within a vehicle of standard length is not of exceptional length—*Cook v Briddon* [1975] RTR 505. Where a container is carried, it is the contents which have to be considered as indivisible and not the container itself—*Patterson v Redpath Brothers Ltd* [1979] RTR 431;

(b) a vehicle combination consisting of a broken-down vehicle (including an articulated vehicle) being drawn by a motor vehicle in consequence of a breakdown;

(c) an articulated vehicle, the semi-trailer of which is a low-loader made before 1 April 1991 [7(3)].

Item 6 to 9 in the Table do not apply to

(a) a trailer constructed and normally used for the conveyance of indivisible loads of exceptional length;

(b) a broken-down vehicle (including an articulated vehicle) being drawn in consequence of a breakdown; or

(c) a trailer which is drying or mixing plant for producing asphalt, bitumen or tarmacadam and used mainly for the construction, repair or maintenance of roads, or a road planing machine so used [7(3A)].

Item 7 does not apply to a semi-trailer which is a car transporter or to a semi-trailer which is normally used on international journeys any part of which takes place outside the UK [7(3B)].

If a motor vehicle draws two trailers only, one of them may exceed 7m. If three trailers are drawn none of them may exceed 7m [7(4)].

Where a motor vehicle is drawing two or more trailers, or one trailer constructed and normally used for indivisible loads of exceptional length, the length of the motor vehicle must not exceed 9.2m and, unless police notice is given and an attendant employed, the length of the combination must not exceed 25.9m [7(5)].

For the purposes of Regulation 7(4) and (5), above, a broken-down articulated vehicle drawn by a motor vehicle in consequence of a breakdown is treated as if it were a single trailer and the reference in Regulation 7(5) to one indivisible load trailer did not apply to it [7(8)].

A trailer with an overall length over 18.65m must not be used on a road unless police have been given two days' notice of the movement of the vehicle and an attendant is employed [7(9)].

For the purposes of Regulation 7 and 13A, the overall length of a trailer (other than an agricultural trailed appliance) does not include any parts for attaching it to another vehicle and the overall length of a semi-trailer excludes the thickness of any front or rear wall and any part forward of the front wall or rearward of the rear wall which does not increase the vehicle's load-carrying capacity [3(2)].

Overall length is the distance between a vehicle's extreme projecting points including any receptacle which is of a permanent character and strong enough for repeated use, and any fitting on or attached to the vehicle but excluding:

a. any driving mirror, extending part of a turntable fire escape, front snow plough, container to hold a Customs seal;
b. sheeting or other readily flexible means of covering or securing a load;
c. an empty receptacle which is itself a load;
d. a receptacle which contains an indivisible load of exceptional length or width;
e. a receptacle with an external length not over 2.5m;
f. a fitting attached to a vehicle or receptacle on the vehicle which does not increase the carrying capacity of the vehicle or receptacle but enables it to be transferred to or from a railway vehicle, be secured to the railway vehicle or carried on the railway vehicle by means of stanchions;
g. a tailboard let down on a stationary vehicle to facilitate loading or unloading;
h. a tailboard let down to facilitate the carriage of, but which is not essential to the support of, a load which is so long as to extend as far as the tailboard;
i. a plate fitted to a car-transporter trailer for bridging the gap between it and the drawing vehicle;
j. a receptacle made before 30 October 1985 which is not a maritime container (i.e. a container designed primarily for carriage on sea transport without an accompanying road vehicle);
k. a special appliance or apparatus, such as a crane, which is a permanent or essentially permanent fixture but which does not itself increase the carrying capacity of the vehicle. [1078/86/3(2)]

Maker's plate

A maker's plate must be fitted to:

(a) heavy motor cars and motor cars first used on or after 1 January 1968, except dual-purpose vehicles, agricultural motor vehicles, works trucks, pedestrian-controlled vehicles and passenger vehicles;
(b) buses, including articulated buses, first used on or after 1 April 1982;
(c) locomotives and motor tractors first used on or after 1 April 1973, except agricultural motor vehicles, industrial tractors, works trucks, engineering plant and pedestrian-controlled vehicles;
(d) trailers over 1,020kg unladen made on or after 1 January 1968, except plant trailers not over 2,290kg unladen, pneumatic-tyred living van trailers not over 2,040kg unladen, works trailers, trailers

made and used abroad before being used in Britain and pre-April 1983 trailers not required to have brakes (page 13);

(e) a converter dolly made on or after 1 January 1979.

[1078/86/66(1)].

The plate must contain information required under (a) Schedule 8 of the Construction and Use Regulations, (b) the Annex to Community Directive 78/507, or (c) in the case of a vehicle used before October 1982, the Annex to Community Directive 76/114. The information required in these Annexes is modified to correspond to that required in Schedule 8 [66(2)(3)].

Schedule 8 states that the plate on a motor vehicle must contain the maker's name, vehicle type, engine type and power (not for vehicles made before 1 October 1972, or for petrol-engined vehicles), chassis or serial number, number of axles, maximum design weight for each axle, maximum design gross weight, maximum design train weight (only if constructed to draw a trailer), maximum permitted axle and gross weights (not for vehicles made before 1 October 1972, locomotives or motor tractors). The plate on a trailer must contain the maker's name, chassis or serial number, number of axles, maximum design axle weight, maximum weight designed to be imposed on drawing vehicle (semi-trailers), maximum design gross weight, maximum permitted axle weight (not for trailer made before 1 October 1972), maximum permitted gross weight (not the trailer made before 1 October 1972, or a semi-trailer), year of manufacture (except trailer made before 1 April 1970).

An agricultural trailed appliance made on or after 1 December 1985 must be equipped with a plate showing the maker's name; year of manufacture; design maximum gross weight; unladen weight; and maximum load imposed on the drawing vehicle [68].

Certain passenger and dual-purpose vehicles made on or after 1 October 1979 and first used on or after 1 April 1980 must be fitted with a plate which contains the maker's name, vehicle identification number and the approval reference number of either the vehicle's type approval certificate or the Minister's approval certificate [67].

The weights at which a vehicle manufacturer considers a vehicle can be used at a speed authorised under the Motor Vehicles (Authorisation of Special Types) General Order can be marked on a plate securely fixed in a conspicuous position on the vehicle [910/83 & 1326/87]. Such a plate must be fitted to a Category 2 or 3 Special Types vehicle made on or after 1 October 1989—see page 342.

Minibuses

Except for Land Rovers and prison vehicles, the following construction requirements apply to a minibus first used on or after 1 April 1988 [1078/86/41 & Sch. 6]. A minibus is a vehicle made to carry 8 but not more than 16 seated passengers in addition to the driver [3(2)].

The exhaust pipe outlet must be at the rear or offside of the vehicle; there must be no tanks or apparatus for supplying fuel in the driver's or passengers' accommodation; and there must be lamps to illuminate steps in a gangway or passenger exit.

There must be a service door on the nearside and an emergency door at the rear or offside (in addition to the driver's door) but an emergency door is not required if the vehicle has a service door at the rear in addition to the one on the nearside. Only a driver's door and emergency doors may be on the offside. Emergency doors must be marked as such, open outwards if hinged, be capable of being operated manually and have an aperture at least 1,210mm high and 530mm wide.

Power-operated doors must incorporate transparent panels; be capable of being operated by the driver when in his seat; in an emergency or power failure be capable of being opened from inside and outside by controls on or adjacent to the door which override others and are marked with their method of operation and that they are not for the normal use of passengers; have soft edges so that a trapped finger is unlikely to be injured; and when the closing door meets a resistance of 150 Newtons it will stop. A failure of the power supply for the doors must not adversely affect the vehicle's braking system.

A door which can be locked from outside must be capable of being opened from inside; inside door handles must be designed and protected to prevent the accidental opening of doors; doors must be capable of being opened by a single movement of the handle or other device; there must be a device to hold doors closed to prevent passengers falling out; a rear-hinged outward-opening side door must have more than one rigid panel; except for power-operated doors, a door must have a two-stage slam lock or a device to warn the driver when the door is not properly closed. Some of these requirements do not apply to the nearside door of a pair of rear doors.

There must be mirrors or other means to enable the driver to see the inside and outside of every service door, except for a rear service door if a person 1.3m tall and standing 1m behind the vehicle can be seen by the driver when in his seat.

There must be unobstructed access from every passenger seat to at least two doors, one on the nearside and the other at the rear or offside, but exception is made for lifting seats and platforms.

Every side service door must be provided with a grab handle or hand rail to assist passengers to get on or off the vehicle.

Seats must not be fitted to doors; seats and wheelchair anchorages must be fitted to the vehicle; except for wheelchairs, seats must be 400mm wide (excluding armrests); wheelchair anchorages must not cause a wheelchair to face the side of the vehicle; a side-facing seat immediately forward of a rear door must have armrests or similar to prevent a passenger falling through the doorway; other seats must be protected to prevent passengers being thrown through a doorway or down any steps.

Provisions are made as to electrical circuits, fuses, circuit breakers and isolating switches.

All bodywork and fittings must be soundly and properly constructed of suitable materials, maintained in good and serviceable condition and capable of withstanding normal loads and stresses.

A minibus first used on or after 1 April 1988, other than a Land Rover, must carry a prescribed type of fire extinguisher which is readily available for use, marked with a British Standards numbers and maintained in good and efficient working order [42, Sch. 7 and 2360/89]. It must also carry prescribed first aid equipment (same as a psv, page 288) in a prominently marked receptacle which is readily available for use [43 & Sch. 7].

No highly inflammable or dangerous substance may be carried in a minibus (of any age), other than a Land Rover, unless it is carried in containers and packed so that, even in an accident, it is unlikely to damage the vehicle or injure passengers [44].

Mirrors

Rear view mirrors are not required on:

(a) a vehicle drawing a trailer if a person is carried on the trailer who can tell the driver about traffic to the rear;
(b) an agricultural motor vehicle used before 1 June 1978 if (i) over 7,370kg unladen, or (ii) the driver can obtain a view to the rear;
(c) a works truck if the driver can obtain a view to the rear;
(d) a pedestrian-controlled vehicle;
(e) a chassis being driven from its maker to its bodybuilder.
                              [1078/86/33, Table, Item 1].

A vehicle not included above which is a locomotive or motor tractor first used on or after 1 June 1978, an agricultural motor vehicle not over 7,370kg unladen, an agricultural motor vehicle first used after 1

June 1986 and not driven at over 20mph, or a works truck, must have at least one mirror fitted externally on the offside [Item 2].

A vehicle first used on or after 1 April 1983 which is a bus or a goods vehicle over 3,500kg maximum weight (not being one driven at more than 20mph or an agricultural motor vehicle) must have mirrors complying with Community Directives 71/127, 79/795 or 86/562 [Item 3].

A goods vehicle over 12,000kg maximum weight, other than an agricultural motor vehicle, first used on or after 1 October 1988, must have mirrors complying with Community Directive 86/562 [Item 4].

A motor vehicle not within Items 1 to 4 above and first used on or after 1 June 1978 or, in the case of a Ford Transit, 10 July 1978, must have (i) at least one mirror externally on the offside, (ii) at least one interior mirror unless it would give no view to the rear, and (iii) at least one mirror externally on the nearside unless an interior mirror gives an adequate view to the rear. Mirrors must comply with Community Directive 71/127, 79/795, 80/780 or 86/562 [Item 6].

A motor vehicle or Ford Transit used before the above dates and which is a bus, dual-purpose vehicle or goods vehicle must have at least one exterior mirror on the offside and either at least one interior mirror or at least one exterior mirror on the nearside [Item 7].

A motor vehicle not included in any of the above requirements must have at least one interior or exterior mirror [Item 8].

The edges of any interior mirror fitted to a vehicle referred to in Items 1, 2, 7 or 8 and first used on or after 1 April 1969 must be surrounded by some material to make severe cuts unlikely if an occupant struck the mirror [33(3)].

No offence is committed where a mirror is temporarily obscured by a load—*Mawdsley v Walter Cox (Transport) Ltd* [1965] 3 All ER 728, [1966] 1 WLR 63.

Mirrors fitted to a vehicle first used on or after 1 June 1978 or, in the case of a Ford Transit, 10 July 1978, must (a) be fixed to remain steady under normal driving conditions; (b) an exterior mirror must be visible through a side window or through a part of the windscreen swept by the windscreen wiper; (c) where the bottom edge of an exterior mirror is less than 2m above the road it must not project more than 20cm beyond the width of the vehicle or, if the vehicle draws a wider trailer, 20cm beyond the width of the trailer; (d) an interior mirror must be capable of being adjusted by the driver in his seat; (e) except for a spring-back mirror, an exterior mirror on the driver's side must be capable of being adjusted by the driver in his seat, but this does not prevent a mirror being locked in position from outside the vehicle [33(4)].

Instead of complying with any of the above requirements, a goods vehicle over 3,500kg maximum gross weight first used on or after 1

April 1985 and before 1 August 1989 may comply with Community Directives 79/795, 85/205 or 86/562. Goods vehicles first used on or after 1 August 1989 over 3,500kg but not over 12,000kg maximum gross weight can comply with Directives 79/795, 85/205 or 86/562 and a vehicle over 12,000kg can comply with Directives 85/205 or 86/562. Agricultural motor vehicles can comply with Directives 71/127, 74/346, 79/795, 85/205 or 86/562. Excluding motor cycles, any other vehicle can comply with Directives 71/127, 79/795, 85/205 or 86/562 [33(5) and 1178/88].

A mirror is to assist the driver to become aware of traffic, in the case of an interior mirror, to the rear of the vehicle, and, in the case of an exterior mirror, rearwards on that side of the vehicle [33(7)].

Noise

Every motor vehicle, first used on or after 1 April 1970 and before 1 October 1983, must be constructed to pass the appropriate noise measurement test undertaken by prescribed noise meter and used in specified conditions.

Excluding motor cycles, maximum sound levels, in decibels are:

Class of vehicle	*Decibels*
Goods vehicles first used on or after January 1, 1968 and plated by the maker for a gross weight over 3,560kg	89
Goods vehicles not over 3,050kg unladen, other than above	85
Motor tractors, locomotives, agricultural motor vehicles, works trucks and engineering plant	89
Passenger vehicles for more than 12 passengers	89
Any other passenger vehicles	84
Any other vehicle not listed above	85

[1078/86/58(1)]

Exceptions are motor vehicles which at the time of first use complied with specified Community Directives; road rollers; type-approved diesel-engined vehicles; airport fire vehicles over 220 kW engine power; and agricultural motor vehicles made on or after 7 February 1975 which comply with Regulation 56 below [58(2)].

Lower limits are specified for certain vehicles made on or after 1 April 1983, and first used on or after 1 October 1983 [55]. By incorporating Community Directives they are extremely complicated and are best left for the vehicle manufacturer to comply with when building the vehicle.

A vehicle first used on or after 1 April 1983 which is an agricultural motor vehicle (except one first used on or after 1 June 1986 and driven at more than 20mph) or an industrial tractor (other than a road roller) must be constructed so that its sound level does not exceed (a) 89 dB(A) if its engine power is less than 65 kW, (b) 92 dB(A) if used before 1 October 1991 and its engine power is 65 kW or more, or (c) 89 dB(A) if first used on or after 1 October 1991 and its engine power is 65 kW or more [56].

A vehicle is not subject to any of the above requirements if it is going to a place, by previous arrangement, to be noise tested or mechanically adjusted, modified or equipped so that it complies or returning from such a place immediately after noise has been measured [59].

Overhang

'Overhang' of a vehicle (not to be confused with overhang of a load) is the distance between the rearmost point of the vehicle (excluding any luggage carrier on a motor car seating not more than eight passengers excluding the driver or any expanding or extensible contrivance forming part of a turntable fire-escape fixed to a vehicle), and (a) in the case of a two-axled or twin-steered three-axle vehicle, the centre of the rear axle, (b) if it has three or four axles (the front one or two of which respectively are steering axles), a point 110mm behind a line midway between the two rear axles, (c) in any other case, a point on the longitudinal axis of the vehicle, being the point from which a line, if projected at right angles, will pass through the centre of the minimum turning circle of the vehicle [1078/86/3(2)].

For heavy motor cars and motor cars, overhang is limited to 60% of the wheelbase, measured from the centre of the front wheels to (a), (b), or (c) above, as the case may be. Overhang on vehicles with a wheelbase not exceeding 2.29m and used before 1 January 1966 may be increased by up to 76mm.

The above overhang limit does not apply to buses; refuse vehicles (including street cleansing, gully and cesspool emptying vehicles); agricultural motor vehicles; motor cars which are ambulances; rear-tipping vehicles if the overhang does not exceed 1.15m; and vehicles used before 2 January 1933.

In calculating the overhang of vehicles which are special road-repair machines, incorporating road-heating plant, the length of such plant may be ignored.

The overhang of a motor tractor must not exceed 1.83m and on an agricultural motor vehicle the distance from the centre of the rearmost axle to the rear of the vehicle must not exceed 3m [1078/86/11].

No overhang limit is prescribed for a locomotive or a trailer.

In *Hawkins v Harold A. Russett Ltd* [1983] RTR 406 it was held that a demountable body which could be lifted on and off a vehicle was not a load but part of the vehicle and had to be included when measuring the vehicle's overhang. See also *Bindley v Willett* (page 185) where it was ruled that a container was not a load but part of the vehicle. And in *Carey v Heath* [1952] 1 KB 62 it was ruled that a four-wheeled vehicle did not cease to be a four-wheeled vehicle because two wheels were raised from the ground.

Power to weight ratio

Diesel-engined locomotives, motor tractors, heavy motor cars and motor cars first used on or after 1 April 1973, and which are required to be fitted with a maker's plate, must be so constructed that the engine power figure given on the plate indicates that the engine produces at least 4.4 kilowatts for every 1,000kg (i.e. 6 bhp per ton) of the design train weight given on the plate or, if not shown, the permitted gross weight. This does not apply to heavy motor cars or motor cars used before 1 April 1973, to any vehicle made before 1 April 1973 and which is powered by a Perkins 6.354 engine, or to a bus [1078/86/45(1)(2)].

If the vehicle's engine also drives ancillary equipment which is designed for use, or is likely to be used, when the vehicle is moving on a road faster than 5mph the engine power must not fall below the minimum ratio when the equipment is being used [45(3)].

Safety glass

The glass of windscreens and all other outside windows of passenger vehicles and dual-purpose vehicles first used on or after 1 January 1959 must be of safety glass. On goods vehicles (other than dual-purpose vehicles, locomotives and motor tractors) first used on or after 1 January 1959 the glass of windscreens and all windows in front and on either side of the driver's seat must be of safety glass. In all other cases, except for glass fitted to the upper deck of a double-decker, the glass of windscreens and other outside windows facing to the front of any motor vehicle must be of safety glass. If the inside surface of any glass at the front of the vehicle is at an angle of more than 30 degrees to the longitudinal axis of the vehicle, it is deemed to be facing to the front. 'Safety glass' is glass so constructed or treated that if broken it does not fly into fragments likely to cause severe cuts [1078/86/31].

More stringent requirements apply to (a) caravan trailers first used from 1 September 1978 and (b) motor vehicles and other trailers first used from 1 June 1978 [32(1)]. Apart from the following exceptions, such vehicles must meet the requirements that (a) on vehicles first used on or after 1 April 1985, the windscreen and all other windows which are wholly or partly in front of or on either side of the driver's seat must be made of specified safety glass, (b) on vehicles used before 1 April 1985, such windscreens and windows must be made of either specified safety glass or safety glazing and (c) all other windows must be made of specified safety glass, specified safety glass (1980) or safety glazing [32(2)]. Specified safety glass is glass which complies with British Standard Specification No. 857 or No. 5282 and safety glazing is material, other than glass, which is so constructed or treated that if broken it does not fly into fragments likely to cause serious cuts. Specified safety glass (1980) is glass which complies with BS No. 857 as amended [32(13)].

The windscreen and other windows in security vehicles may be made of either safety glass or safety glazing [32(3)]. The windscreens of motor cycles not fitted with an enclosed driver's cab may be fitted with safety glazing [32(4)]. Windscreens or other windows in front of or alongside the driver's seat which are fitted temporarily to replace broken windows need not be of specified safety glass but must be of safety glazing and be fitted only while the vehicle is driven or towed to a place where new windows are to be permanently fitted or to complete the journey involved [32(5)]. Windows in a screen or door inside a bus first used on or after 1 April 1988 must be of safety glazing or specified safety glass (1980) [32(6)]. The windows, other than windscreens, of engineering plant, industrial tractors, agricultural motor vehicles (unless first used on or after 1 June 1986 and driven at over 20mph) wholly or partly in front of or alongside the driver's seat may be of specified safety glass, specified safety glass (1980) or safety glazing. So also may the windows in the roof of a vehicle and windows in the upper deck of a double-decked bus [32(7)]. Motor vehicles and trailers which have not been fitted with permanent windows and are being taken to a place where they are to be fitted may have temporary windscreens or windows of specified safety glass, specified safety glass (1980) or safety glazing [32(8)]. Glass fitted to vehicles must generally meet technical requirements as to light transmission [32(10)]. The requirements of Regulation 32 do not apply to vehicles fitted with certain French glass [32(9)]. Exceptions from some requirements are provided for windows marked with a designated approval mark [32(12A),(12B)].

Seat belts and anchorage points

A motor car first used on or after 1 January 1965 and a heavy motor car first used on or after 1 October 1988 must be equipped with seat belt anchorage points [1978/86/46(1)(3)].

Exempt are:
a. a goods vehicle (other than a dual-purpose vehicle) first used
    (i) before 1 April 1967,
    (ii) on or after 1 April 1980 and before 1 October 1988, in the
          case of a vehicle with a maximum gross weight over 3,500kg,
          or
    (iii) before 1 April 1980 or, if the vehicle is of a model
           made prior to October 1979, used before 1 April 1982, and
           in either case the vehicle has an unladen weight over 1,525kg;
b. a bus, which is
    (i) a minibus used before 1 October 1988 and constructed to
         carry more than 12 passengers or, first used on or after 1
         October 1988 with a maximum gross weight over 3,500kg;
    (ii) a large bus other than a coach first used on or after 1 October
          1988; (a minibus is made to carry more than 8 but not more
          than 16 seated passengers in addition to the driver, a large bus
          is made to carry more than 16 such passengers and a coach is
          a large bus with a maximum gross weight over 7.5 tonnes and
          a maximum speed over 60mph);
c. an agricultural motor vehicle;
d. a motor tractor;
e. a works truck;
f. an electrically-propelled goods vehicle used before 1 October 1988;
g. a pedestrian-controlled vehicle;
h. a vehicle used abroad and imported into Great Britain, while driven
    from its place of entry to the owner or driver's residence and then
    to a place for anchorage points and seat belts to be fitted;
i. a vehicle with a maximum speed not over 16mph;
j. a locomotive.
                                                        [46(2)].

On a vehicle used before 1 April 1982, the anchorage points must
be for seat belts for the driver's and specified passenger's seat (if any)
[46(3)]
On a vehicle first used on or after 1 April 1982, the anchorage points
must:
(a) be made to hold securely seat belts for
     (i) in the case of a minibus, ambulance or caravan
          (A) the driver's and specified passenger's seat on a vehicle
          used before 1 October 1988,
          (B) the driver's seat and any forward-facing front seat on a
          vehicle first used on or after 1 October 1988,
     (ii) on any other passenger or dual-purpose vehicle, every
           forward-facing seat made to accommodate one adult,

(iii)   in any other case, every forward-facing seat and every non-protected seat; and
(b) comply with Community Directives 76/115, 81/575, 82/318 or 90/629 or ECE Regulation 14 [46(4)].

The above requirement does not apply to:
(a) a goods vehicle with a maximum gross weight over 3,500kg first used on or after 1 October 1988 but the vehicle must be equipped with two belt anchorages for lap belts on the driver's and each forward-facing front seat;
(b) a coach equipped with anchorage points for all exposed forward-facing seats and which comply with the above Community Directives or ECE Regulation or form part of a seat and do not become detached from it before the seat becomes detached from the vehicle [46(4A)].

Instead of complying with Regulation 46(4), a vehicle can comply with the Directives or Regulation specified in it [46(4B)].

The specified passenger's seat is (a) the forward-facing front seat alongside the driver's seat or, where there is more than one such seat, the one furthest from the driver, or (b) if there is no seat alongside the driver's, the foremost forward-facing front passenger seat furthest from the driver unless there is a fixed partition separating that seat from the space in front and alongside the driver [47(8)].

A forward-facing seat is one which has an axis at an angle of no more than 30 degrees to the longitudinal axis of the vehicle. A forward-facing front seat is any forward-facing seat alongside the driver's seat or, if there is no such seat, each forward-facing passenger seat which is foremost in the vehicle [47(8)].

The seat belt requirements apply to vehicles which have to be fitted with anchorage points [47(1)].

A vehicle used before 1 April 1981 must have a body-restraining belt for the driver's and specified passenger's seat (if any). A vehicle first used on or after 1 April 1981 must have a three-point belt for those seats [47(2)(a)(b)].

A vehicle first used on or after 1 April 1987 to which Regulation 46(4)(a)(ii) or (iii) applies must:
(a) in addition to the above, be fitted with a three-point, lap or disabled person's belt for any other forward-facing seat alongside the driver's seat (e.g. centre seat of a Land Rover);
(b) in the case of a passenger or dual-purpose vehicle with not more than two forward-facing seats behind the driver's seat, be fitted with either an inertia reel belt for at least one of those seats or a three-point, lap or disabled person's belt for each of them;

(c) in the case of such a vehicle with more than two forward-facing seats behind the driver's seat, be fitted with
  (i) an inertia reel belt for at least one of them and a three-point, lap, disabled person's or child's belt for at least one other,
  (ii) a three-point belt for one of the seats and a child's or disabled person's belt for at least one other, or
  (iii) a three-point, lap, disabled person's or child's belt of them [47(2)(c)].

A minibus, ambulance or motor caravan first used on or after 1 October 1988 must have three-point belts for the driver's and specified passenger's seats and a three-point or lap for any other forward-facing front seat [47(2)(d)].

A coach must be equipped with three-point, lap or disabled person's belts [47(2)(e)].

Where a lap belt is fitted to a forward-facing front seat of a minibus, ambulance or motor caravan, or an exposed forward-facing front seat of a coach (other than the driver's or crew seat), either padding must be provided (with specified exceptions) as prescribed on any bar or the top edge of any screen or partition likely to be struck by the head of a passenger wearing the lap belt in an accident or requirements of ECE Regulation 21 are met [47(2)].

The above requirements to fit seat belts do not apply to:

a. a vehicle while used under a trade licence;
b. a vehicle, to which type approval regulations do not apply, while driven from its maker or a dealer to premises of a dealer or of the purchaser or hirer of the vehicle;
c. seats provided with seat belts marked with BS AU 183:1983, BS 3254:1960 or BS 3254: Part 1: 1988;
d. the driver's or specified passenger's seat of a car adapted for a disabled person where a disabled person's seat belt is provided for that seat;
e. a goods vehicle over 3,500kg gross weight first used on or after 1 October 1988 [47(4)].

For the complulsory use of seat belts see page 385

Selling defective vehicles or parts

It is unlawful to sell, offer to sell or supply or expose for sale, any vehicle not complying with the C and U Regulations respecting brakes, steering gear or tyres or construction, weight or equipment of vehicles or maintenance of parts or accessories, or its condition would involve a danger of injury to any person [Act 1988/75 and Act 1991]. Nor must a vehicle be altered so that its use on a road would entail a breach of the regulations regarding construction, weight or equipment [75(4)] or be supplied in that altered condition [75(5)].

A person will not be convicted of any of these offences if he proves that a vehicle was for export, or that he had reasonable cause to believe it would not be used on a road in Great Britain, or that it would not be used until it had been put into proper condition [75(6)]. The last of these defences does not apply where a person who, in the course of a trade or business, (a) exposes a vehicle for sale unless he proves he took all reasonable steps to ensure any prospective purchaser was aware it was unroadworthy or (b) offers to sell a vehicle, unless he proves he took all reasonable steps to ensure the offeree was made aware it was unroadworthy [75(6A) and Act 1991].

A contract of sale will not be invalidated merely because these provisions are contravened [75(7)]. (But an innocent buyer may be able to discharge the contract through the seller's breach of condition or claim damages for breach of condition or warranty.)

It is an offence for a person to fit, or cause or permit the fitting of, a part to a vehicle if by such fitting the vehicle would involve a danger of injury to any person or contravene the C and U Regulations [76(1)]. If a person who sells or supplies, or offers to sell or supply a vehicle part (or causes or permits the same) believes that it is to be fitted to a vehicle he commits an offence if the part could not be fitted without the vehicle contravening the C and U Regulations or involving a danger of injury to any person [76(3)]. It is a defence to both offences for a person to prove that the vehicle was to be exported or he had cause to believe that the vehicle would not be used on British roads or would not be so used until put into a proper condition [76(2), (5)].

The provisions of this Section do not affect the validity of a contract (e.g. sale or repair) or rights under it [76(10)].

Sideguards

A goods vehicle being either (i) a motor vehicle with a plated gross weight over 3,500kg, made on or after 1 October 1983 and first used on or after 1 April 1984, (ii) a trailer over 1,020kg unladen weight and made on or after 1 May 1983 or (iii) a semi-trailer made before 1 May 1983 plated for over 26,000kg gross weight and which forms part of an articulated vehicle with a plated gross train weight over 32,520kg must be fitted with a sideguard on both sides if, in the case of a semi-trailer the distance between the centres of the king pin and the front axle exceeds 4.5m or, in the case of any other vehicle, the distance between the centres of any two consecutive axles exceeds 3m [1078/86/51(1)(3)].

The following vehicles are exempt from sideguards:
- (a) a motor vehicle incapable of exceeding 15mph on the level;
- (b) an agricultural trailer;
- (c) engineering plant;
- (d) a fire engine;
- (e) an agricultural motor vehicle;
- (f) a vehicle constructed to unload by tipping sideways or rearwards;
- (g) a vehicle owned by the Defence Secretary and used for naval, military or air force purposes;
- (h) a vehicle without bodywork and which is driven or towed
    - (i) for a quality check by its manufacturer or a dealer or distributor of such vehicles;
    - (ii) to a place where, by previous arrangement, bodywork is to be fitted or work preparatory to the fitting of bodywork is to be carried out, or
    - (iii) by previous arrangement, to premises of a dealer in, or distributor of, such vehicles;
- (i) a vehicle which is being driven or towed to a place where by previous arrangement a sideguard is to be fitted so that it complies with the Regulation;
- (j) a vehicle designed solely for use and used solely for street cleansing or the collection or disposal of refuse or the contents of gullies or cesspools;
- (k) a trailer specially designed and constructed, not merely adapted, to carry round timber, beams or girders of exceptional length;
- (l) a motor car or heavy motor car constructed or adapted to form part of an articulated vehicle;
- (m) a vehicle specially designed and constructed, not merely adapted, to carry other vehicles loaded on it from front or rear;
- (n) a trailer with a load platform no part of the edge of which is more than 60mm inboard of the outer face of a tyre on that side at the rear and the upper surface of the platform is not more than 750mm from the ground in the area where a sideguard would normally have to be fitted;
- (o) a trailer based outside Great Britain provided a period of not more than 12 months has elapsed since the vehicle was last brought into Great Britain;
- (p) an agricultural trailed appliance

[51(2)]

None of the above exemptions applies to a semi-trailer if any of its wheels is driven by the drawing vehicle [51(2A)].

A sideguard must comply with the following specification:
1. the outermost surface must be smooth, essentially rigid and either flat or horizontally corrugated, but any part of the surface may

overlap another part as long as the overlapping edge faces rearwards or downwards; a gap of 25mm may exist between adjacent parts as long as the forward edge of the rearmost part does not protrude beyond the rearmost edge of the rearmost part; and domed bolt or rivet heads may protrude not more than 10mm;

2. the lowest edge must be no more than 550mm above ground when the vehicle is on level ground and, in the case of a semi-trailer, when its load platform is horizontal;

3. the highest edge must be
   (i) where the vehicle's floor extends sideways beyond the outermost rear wheel, it is not over 1.85m above ground, it extends over the whole length of the sideguard and has a side-rave the lower edge of which is not more than 150mm below the underside of the floor, not more than 350mm below the lower edge of the side rave;
   (ii) where the vehicle's floor extends sideways beyond the outermost rear wheel, but does not comply with any of the other conditions in (i) above, and any part of the vehicle below 1.85m extends sideways beyond the outermost rear wheel, not more than 350mm below the structure which so extends;
   (iii) where no part of the vehicle's structure below 1.85m extends sideways beyond the outermost rear wheel and the upper surface of the load carrying structure is less than 1.5m above ground, not less than the height of that surface;
   (iv) a vehicle specially designed, not merely adapted, for the carriage and mixing of liquid concrete, not less than 1m above ground;
   (v) in any other case, not less than 1.5m above ground;

4. the distance between its rearmost edge and the tyre nearest to it must not exceed 300mm;

5. in the case of a semi-trailer, the distance between the front edge of the sideguard and a point at right angles to the centre of the king pin must not exceed 3m;

6. in the case of a semi-trailer with landing legs, the distance is as in 5 above and front edge of sideguard to be not over 250mm from leg centre;

7. in the case of a vehicle other than a semi-trailer, the sideguard's front edge must not be more than 300mm from the nearest front tyre where the vehicle is a motor vehicle or 500mm if the vehicle is a trailer;

8. its external edges must be rounded to a radius of at least 2.5mm;

9. it must not be more than 30mm inboard of the outer face of the outer most tyre at the rear of the vehicle;

10. it must not add to the vehicle's normal width;
11. it must extend downwards at least 100mm from its highest edge, 100mm upwards from its lowest edge and 100mm rearwards and inwards from its front edge. It must not have a vertical gap more than 300mm nor any vertical surface less than 100mm;
12. except for trailers made before 1 May 1983, if a force of 2 kilonewtons (almost 200kg static pressure) is applied at right angles to any side of the sideguard no part of it has to deflect more than 150mm and no part within 250mm of the rear edge must deflect more than 30mm.   [51(5)].

Paragraphs 4 to 7 above do not apply to the additional length attributed to the extending of an extendible trailer beyond its minimum length. In the case of a vehicle constructed to carry a demountable body or lift-off container (of at least 8 cubic metres), paragraphs 1 to 12 apply when it is not carrying a body or container in the same manner as if it were carrying such a body or container. The specification applies only as far as is practicable in the case of (a) a vehicle fitted with a tank for carrying fluid and which is provided with valves and hose or pipe connections for loading and unloading, and (ii) a vehicle with extending stabilisers required for stability during loading, unloading or while used for operations for which it is designed or adapted[51(6)].

In the case of a vehicle which was required to be type approved before 1 October 1983, if the vehicle's bodywork covers the whole of the area mentioned in paragraphs 2, 3, 4 and 7 of the fitting specification (given above) the other paragraphs do not apply to that vehicle. If the bodywork covers only part of that area, the part not covered must have sideguards which comply with the specification except that there must not be a gap between (a) the rearmost edge of the sideguard or the rearmost part of the bodywork (whichever is furthest to the rear) and the front of the nearest tyre of more than 300mm; (b) the foremost edge of the sideguard or the foremost part of the bodywork (whichever is furthest to the front) and rear of the nearest tyre of more than 300mm; and (c) any vertical or sloping edge of any part of the bodywork and the edge of the sideguard immediately forward or rearward of it of more than 25mm [51(7)].

Instead of complying with the above provisions a vehicle can comply with Community Directive 89/297 [51(9) and 1695/89].

Silencer

A vehicle propelled by an internal combustion engine must be fitted with an exhaust system including a silencer suitable and sufficient for reducing noise caused by the escape of exhaust gases from the engine [1078/86/54](1). But, instead, a vehicle may comply with Community Directives 77/212, 81/334, 84/372 or 84/424 [54(3)].

Speed limiter—coaches

A coach first used on or after 1 April 1974 and before 1 January 1988 which would, apart from a speed limiter, have a maximum speed exceeding 70mph, must be fitted with a speed limiter [1078/86/36A(1)]. The limiter must be calibrated to a set speed not over 70mph [36A(6)].

A coach is a motor vehicle constructed or adapted to carry more than 16 seated passengers (in addition to the driver), with a maximum gross weight over 7.5 tonnes and a maximum speed exceeding 60mph [3(2)].

A bus first used on or after 1 January 1988, which has a maximum gross weight exceeding 7.5 tonnes and would, apart from a limiter, have a maximum speed exceeding 65mph, must be fitted with a speed limiter [36A(2)]. The limiter must be adjusted so that the stabilised speed of the vehicle does not exceed 65mph [36A(7)].

A bus is a motor vehicle constructed or adapted to carry more than 8 seated passengers in addition to the driver [3(2)]. (Note that the definition of a bus covers vehicles within the definition of a coach).

The above requirements are modified as follows:
(a) until 1 January 1996, in relation to vehicles used exclusively on transport operations within the UK, or
(b) until 1 January 1995 in relation to any other vehicles,
the dates of 1 January 1988 in the above paragraphs are substituted by 1 January 1994 [36A(3)].

A speed limiter is a device to limit maximum speed by controlling a vehicle's engine power [36A(14)].

A speed limiter must be sealed by an authorised sealer to prevent improper interference or adjustment or interruption of power supply and be maintained in good and efficient working order [36A(5)]. But a limiter fitted before 1 August 1992 to a vehicle first used before that date or a limiter sealed outside the United Kingdom does not have to be sealed by an 'authorised' sealer [36A(10)].

A speed limiter fitted-
a. at any time to any coach within Regulation 36A(1), or
b. before 1 October 1994 to a bus within Regulation 36A(2) first used before that date,
must comply with BS AU 217: Part 1: 1987 as amended or EC Directive 92/24 [36A(8)]. But this requirement does not apply to a speed limiter fitted before 1 October 1988 or if the limiter complies

with an equivalent standard [36A(11),(12)]. A limiter fitted in a bus within Regulation 36A(2) first used on or after 1 October 1994 or fitted on or after that date to a vehicle used before that date must comply with EC Directive 92/24 [36A(9)].

The above requirements do not apply to a vehicle-

a. being taken to a place where a limiter is to be installed, calibrated, repaired or replaced; or
b. completing a journey on which the limiter has accidentally ceased to function [36A(13)].

Speed limiter—goods vehicles

A goods vehicle first used on or after 1 August 1992 with a maximum gross weight over 7,500kg but not over 12,000kg and capable of exceeding 60mph on the level (without a speed limiter) must not be used on a road unless it is fitted with a speed limiter [1078/91/36B(1)]. The limiter must be calibrated to a set speed not over 60mph [36B(8)]. Until 1 January 1996, in relation to vehicles used exclusively on transport operations within the UK, or until 1 January 1995 in relation to any other vehicles, the above weight criteria is modified to refer to either a maximum gross weight exceeding 7,500kg in the case of a vehicle first used before 1 January 1994 or a maximum gross weight over 7,500kg but not over 12,000kg in the case of a vehicle first used on of after 1 January 1994 [36B(5)].

A goods vehicle first used on or after 1 January 1988 with a maximum gross weight over 12,000kg and capable of exceeding 56mph on the level (without a speed limiter) must not be used on a road unless it is fitted with a speed limiter [1078/91/36B(2)]. The limiter must be calibrated to a set speed not over 56mph [36B(9)]. Until 1 January 1996, in relation to vehicles used exclusively on transport operations within the UK, or until 1 January 1995 in relation to any other vehicles, the date of 1 January 1988 is substituted by 1 January 1994 [36B(5)].

Until 1 January 1996, in relation to vehicles used exclusively on transport operations within the UK, or until 1 January 1995 in relation to any other vehicles, a speed limiter is required in a goods vehicle first used on or after 1 January 1988 but before 1 August 1992 which is capable of exceeding 60mph on the level (without a speed limiter), has a maximum gross weight over 16,000kg and is either

(a) constructed to form part of an articulated vehicle, or
(b) is a rigid vehicle constructed to draw a trailer and the difference between its plated gross weight and gross train weight exceeds 5,000kg, must not be used on a road unless it is fitted with a speed

limiter [36B((3),(4) & (16)]. The limiter must be calibrated to a set speed not over 60mph [36B(8)].

A speed limiter must be sealed by an authorised sealer to prevent improper interference or adjustment or interruption of power supply and be maintained in good and efficient working order [36B(7)]. But a limiter fitted before 1 August 1992 to a vehicle first used before that date or a limiter sealed outside the United Kingdom does not have to be sealed by an 'authorised' sealer [36B(12)].

A speed limiter fitted-

a. at any time to a vehicle within Regulation 36B(1),
b. before 1 October 1994 to a vehicle within Regulation 36B(2) first used before that date, or
c. at any time to vehicle within Regulation 36B(3)

must comply with BS AU 217: Part 1: 1987 as amended or EC Directive 92/24 [36B(10)]. But this requirement does not apply to a speed limiter if it complies with an equivalent standard [36B(13)]. A limiter fitted in a vehicle within Regulation 36B(2) first used on or after 1 October 1994 or fitted on or after that date to a vehicle used before that date must comply with EC Directive 92/24 [36B(11)].

The above requirements do not apply to a vehicle:

a. being taken to a place where a limiter is to be installed, calibrated, repaired or replaced;
b. completing a journey on which the limiter has accidentally ceased to function;
c. owned by the Defence Secretary and used for naval military or air force purposes;
d. used for naval, military or air force purposes while driven by a person subject to armed forces' orders;
e. while used for fire brigade, police or ambulance purposes;
f. while exempt vehicle excise duty due to not travelling more than 6 miles a week on public roads [36B(12)].

Speed limiter plate

A coach, bus or goods vehicle required to be fitted with a speed limiter must also be fitted with a plate in a conspicuous position in the driving compartment and be clearly and indelibly marked with the speed at which the limiter has been set [1078/86/70A].

Speedometers

A motor vehicle first used on or after 1 October 1937 must be fitted with a speedometer which, in the case of a vehicle first used on or after

1 April 1984, must be capable of indicating speed in miles per hour and kilometres per hour either simultaneously or, by operating a switch, separately [1078/86/35(1)]. None of the above requirements applies to a works truck first used before 1 April 1984; a vehicle which it is unlawful to drive over 25mph; a vehicle incapable by its construction of exceeding 25mph; a vehicle fitted with an approved tachograph; or an agricultural motor vehicle not driven over 20mph [35(2)].

Instead of complying with the above, a vehicle may comply with Community Directive 75/443 or ECE Regulation 39 [35(3)].

Spray suppression

These requirements apply to goods vehicles being (a) motor vehicles made on or after 1 October 1985 and first used on or after 1 April 1986 which have a design maximum gross weight of over 12 tonnes; (b) trailers made on or after 1 May 1985 which have a maximum design gross weight of over 3.5 tonnes; and (c) trailers, whenever made, which have a design maximum gross weight over 16 tonnes and have two or more axles [1078/86/64(1)].

Such a vehicle must be fitted, in relation to all its wheels, with spray containment devices which meet British Standards specification BS AU 200: 1984 or, in the case of a device fitted on or after 1 May 1987, BS AU 200: 1986. A device fitted before 1 January 1985 will be deemed to comply with the requirements if it substantially conforms to the specification [64(3)].

Exempt are:
a. a motor vehicle which can be driven by a front and rear axle together;
b. a motor vehicle which has a ground clearance of at least 400mm along its length and for the middle 80 per cent of the shortest distance between two opposite wheels;
c. a works truck and a works trailer;
d. a broken-down vehicle;
e. a motor vehicle incapable of exceeding 30mph;
f. a vehicle exempt from sideguards under paragraphs (b), (c), (d), (f), (g), (h), (j), (k), (o) or (p) of Regulation 51(2) (given on page 35);
g. a vehicle specially designed for carrying and mixing liquid concrete;
h. a vehicle driven or towed to a place where, by previous arrangement, a spray suppression device is to be fitted [64(2)].

The requirement does not apply to a vehicle fitted with spray suppression devices in accordance with EC Directive 226/91 [64(2A)]

The duty to fit spray suppression devices does not derogate from the requirements for a vehicle to be fitted with mudwings [64(5)].

Springs

Motor vehicles and trailers must have 'suitable and sufficient' springs between each wheel and the chassis frame, but the following are exempt: (a) a vehicle first used on or before 1 January 1932, (b) a motor tractor not exceeding 4,070kg unladen, if fitted with pneumatic tyres, (c) an agricultural trailer or agricultural trailed appliance; (d) a trailer used solely for the haulage of felled trees, (e) a rail-shunting motor tractor not exceeding 4,070kg unladen, used on the road only when crossing from one part of the rail track to another, (f) motor cycles, (g) mobile cranes, (h) works trucks or works trailers, (i) a pneumatic-tyred vehicle not exceeding 4,070kg unladen, designed and mainly used for work on rough ground or unmade roads, provided it is not driven or drawn at more than 20mph, (j) pneumatic or solid-tyred vehicles, not exceeding 4,070kg unladen, used only for road sweeping and not driven or drawn at more than 20mph, (k) pneumatic-tyred pedestrian-controlled vehicles, (l) a broken-down vehicle, and (m) road rollers [1078/86/22].

Turning circle—articulated vehicles

Except where its semi-trailer—

(a) was made before 1 April 1990 and has an overall length not exceeding the length it had on that date;
(b) is a car transporter;
(c) is a low loader;
(d) is a stepframe low loader; or
(e) is constructed and normally used for the conveyance of indivisible loads of exceptional length,

an articulated vehicle with an overall length exceeding 15.5m must be able to move on either lock so that no part of it projects outside the area contained between two concentric circles of 5.3m and 12.5m radii. Items excluded from overall width (page 49) can project outside the circles [1078/86/13A].

An articulated vehicle over 15.5m overall length with a car

transporter semi-trailer must be able to move on either lock so that, apart from items excluded from overall width, no part of the motor vehicle and no part of the trailer to the rear of the kingpin projects outside the above area.

This requirement does not apply to an articulated vehicle of which the semi-trailer—

(a) was made before 1 April 1990 and the distance from the front of the trailer to its rearmost axle is no greater than on that date;
(b) is a low loader; or
(c) is a stepframe low loader [1076/86/13B].

A car transporter is a trailer constructed and normally used for carrying at least two other wheeled vehicles [3(2)].

A low loader is a semi-trailer constructed and normally used for carrying engineering equipment with the major part of its load platform not over or between the wheels and its upper surface below the height of the top of the trailer's tyres when on the level and any adjustable suspension is at normal height, tyres are properly inflated and the trailer is unladen [3(2)].

A stepframe low loader is a semi-trailer (other than a low-loader) constructed and normally used for carrying engineering equipment with the upper surface of the major part of its load platform less than 1 metre above the ground when on the level and any adjustable suspension is at normal height, tyres are properly inflated and the trailer is unladen [3(2)].

Turning circle—buses

A bus used on or after 1 April 1982 must be able to move on either lock so that no part of it projects outside the area contained between concentric circles of 5.3 and 12m radius. When the vehicle is stationary and is turned so that its outermost part would describe a 12m radius circle the side of the vehicle opposite to the direction of turn must not swing out more than 0.8m in the case of a rigid vehicle or 1.2m in the case of an articulated vehicle [1078/86/13].

In the case of an articulated bus first used on or after 1 April 1982, the section connecting both parts has to comply with paragraph 5.9 of ECE Regulation 36 and the bus must be constructed so that when moving in a straight line the centre line of each section forms a continuous line without any deflection [14]. Paragraph 5.9 deals with the floor levels and the gaps between the two sections.

Tyres

Locomotives, motor tractors and agricultural motor vehicles (not driven over 20mph) must have pneumatic or resilient tyres. Smooth-soled tyres of different material are allowed on an agricultural motor vehicle in prescribed circumstances. Recut pneumatic tyres must not be used on a motor tractor or agricultural motor vehicle under 2,540kg unladen unless the wheel has a rim diameter of at least 405mm.

Heavy motor cars must have pneumatic tyres, but resilient tyres can be used on vehicles used before 3 January 1933; vehicles used mainly on rough ground; vehicles used solely for street cleansing or the collection or disposal of refuse or contents of gullies or cesspools; turntable fire escapes; tower wagons; and works trucks.

Motor cars must have pneumatic tyres, but resilient tyres can be used on vehicles not over 1,020kg unladen; work trucks; electrically propelled vehicles not over 1,270kg unladen; vehicles used solely for street cleansing or the collection and disposal of refuse or contents of gullies or cesspools; turntable fire escapes; tower wagons; and vehicles used before 3 January 1933. Recut pneumatic tyres must not be fitted to a motor car other than an electric goods vehicle or a goods vehicle of 2,540kg unladen weight and with a wheel rim diameter of at least 405mm.

Trailers, except for water carts used for road rollers, agricultural trailers made before 1 December 1985 and agricultural trailed appliances, must have pneumatic tyres; but pneumatic (recut or otherwise) or resilient tyres can be used on works trailers, vehicles used solely for street cleansing or the collection and disposal of refuse or contents of gullies and cesspools, trailers drawn by resilient-tyred heavy motor cars, trailers drawn by locomotives or motor tractors, and broken-down vehicles. Apart from these latter vehicles, recut pneumatic tyres must not be fitted to any trailer not exceeding 1,020kg unladen, any trailer constructed to carry only plant or apparatus permanently affixed to it and which, in total, does not weigh more than 2290kg or any trailer which is a living van and does not exceed 2040kg unladen weight [1078/86/24(1)].

Except for 'home-made' vehicles, a wheel of a vehicle may not be fitted with a temporary use spare tyre unless the vehicle is a passenger vehicle (other than a bus) used before April 1987 or a vehicle which complies, at the time of its first use, with ECE Regulation 64 [24(4)].

Tyres are not required on a road roller [24(2)].A pneumatic tyre is defined as a tyre which is provided with, or together with the wheel forms, a continuous closed chamber inflated to a pressure substantially exceeding atmospheric pressure, capable of being inflated and deflated without removal from the wheel or vehicle and, when deflated and under load, the sides collapse [3(2)]. A resilient tyre is a tyre, other than pneumatic, of soft or elastic material [3(2)] but a tyre will not be deemed to be such unless the material is continuous, around the wheel's circumference or is fitted in sections so that as far as reasonably practicable no space is left between the ends and, in either case it is thick enough to minimise vibration and is free from defects which might damage the road [3(5)].

Tyre loads and speeds

A tyre fitted to the axle of
1. a goods vehicle, trailer, bus, agricultural vehicle or works trailer; or
2. if first used on or after 1 April 1991, engineering plant, a track-laying vehicle, a vehicle equipped with speed category Q tyres, works truck or a vehicle (other than an agricultural or electrically propelled vehicle) with a maximum speed not over 30mph,

must, as respects strength, be designed and manufactured adequately to support the maximum permitted axle weight for the axle [25(1), (5)].

The tyres of vehicles in item 1 above must also be designed and manufactured adequately to support the maximum permitted axle weight when the vehicle is driven at the speed shown in the following table. If a vehicle comes within more than one category the lowest speed applies:

Vehicle	*Speed*
Vehicle (other than agricultural) for which a maximum speed is given in Schedule 6 of the Road Traffic Regulation Act 1984 (see page 354)	The highest permitted speed
Electrically propelled vehicle with a maximum speed not over 50mph	Its maximum speed
A local service bus or restricted speed vehicle	50mph
A low-platform trailer, agricultural vehicle, municipal vehicle or multi-stop local collection and delivery vehicle (excluding an electrically propelled vehicle capable of exceeding 40mph)	40mph
A trailer with a maximum gross weight not over 3,500kg or any trailer with tyres of speed category F or G	60mph
A trailer not described above	60mph
A motor vehicle not described above	70mph

[25(1),(6)].

Vehicles in the above Table first used on or after 1 April 1991 must not be used if the load applied to any tyre exceeds, or exceeds a permitted variation of, the tyre's load capacity index [25(8)].

A tyre fitted to a vehicle in Item 1 (but excluding vehicles in Item 2) first used on or after 1 April 1991 must, when first fitted, have complied with ECE Regulation 30, 30.01, 30.02 or 54, unless it is a re-treaded tyre [25(7)]. A tyre supplied for test or trial by a manufacturer and fitted to a vehicle first used on or after 1 April 1991 is exempt this requirement while used for those purposes [25(4)].

Regulations 25(6) and (7) do not apply to agricultural vehicles driven or drawn at not more than 20mph or works trailers drawn at not more than 18mph [25(7A)].

Regulations 25(5), (6) and (7) do not apply to any tyre fitted to an axle of a vehicle which is broken down or going to a place to be broken up and is being drawn at a speed not over 20mph [25(3)].

The above references to the date of the first use refer, in the case of a trailer, to a date six months after its date of manufacture [25(10)].

A low-platform trailer has tyres with a rim diameter size code of 20 or less and which carries a rectangular plate 225mm by 175mm bearing two letters 'L' 125mm high and 90mm wide in black on a white background. A municipal vehicle is a motor vehicle or trailer used only by a local authority or person under contract with such authority, for road cleansing or watering; collection and disposal or refuse, night soil or cesspool contents; or enactments relating to weights and measures or food and drugs. A multi-stop collection and delivery vehicle is used only within a 25-mile radius of the permanent base at which it is normally kept. A restricted speed vehicle is one which displays a 50mph plate at its rear [3(2) and 25(9)].

For maintenance of tyres see page 183.

Under-run protection

A goods vehicle which is (a) a motor vehicle with a design gross weight over 3,500kg and which is made on or after 1 October 1983 and first used on or after 1 April 1984 or (b) a trailer over 1,020kg unladen and made on or after 1 May 1983, must be fitted with a rear under-run protective device which complies with Community Directive 79/490 [1078/86/49(1)].

This requirement does not apply to:
a. a motor vehicle incapable of exceeding 15mph on the level;
b. a motor car or heavy motor car made to form part of an articulated vehicle;
c. an agricultural trailer;
d. engineering plant;
e. a fire engine;

f. an agricultural motor vehicle;
g. a vehicle fitted at the rear with apparatus specially designed for spreading material on a road;
h. a vehicle that can be unloaded by tipping rearwards;
i. a vehicle owned by the Defence Secretary and used for naval, military or air force purposes;
j. a vehicle with no bodywork and which is driven or towed
   (i) for a quality or safety check by its manufacturer, or a dealer or distributor in such vehicles;
   (ii) to a place where, by previous arrangement, bodywork is to be fitted or work preparatory to the fitting of bodywork is to be carried out, or
   (iii) by previous arrangement to premises of a dealer in, or distributor of, such vehicles;
k. a vehicle being driven or towed to a place where, by previous arrangement, a device is to be fitted so that it complies with the requirements;
l. a vehicle specially designed and constructed, and not merely adapted, to carry other vehicles loaded on it from the rear;
m. a trailer specially designed and constructed, and not merely adapted, to carry round timber, beams or girders, being items of exceptional length;
n. a vehicle with a tail lift of which the platform forms part of the vehicle floor which has a length of at least 1m;
o. a trailer based outside Great Britain provided a period of not more than 12 months has elapsed since the vehicle was last brought into Great Britain;
p. a vehicle specially designed, not merely adapted, for the carriage and mixing of liquid concrete;
q. a vehicle designed and used solely for the delivery of coal by a conveyor fitted at the rear which renders the fitting of a rear under-run device impracticable;
r. an agricultural trailer appliance

[49(2)].

If a vehicle has a tail lift, bodywork or other part which makes its being equipped with a rear under-run protective device impracticable it must instead be fitted with one or more devices which comply with specified modifications to the EEC rules [49(4)].

Unleaded petrol

Petrol-engined vehicles first used on or after 1 April 1991 must be designed and constructed for running on unleaded petrol [1078/86/39A(1), (2)].

Excluded, subject to specified conditions being met, are:

(a) vehicles less than 1,400 cc first used before 1 April 1992;
(b) vehicles of 1,400 cc but not over 2,000cc first used before 1 April 1994;
(c)   passenger vehicles for not more than 8 passengers (excluding driver) first used before 1 April 1993 which are (i) made to carry not more than 5 passengers (excluding driver) or (ii) have a maximum gross weight not over 2,500 kg, in either case not being off-road vehicles [39A(4) and Sch 3A].

A vehicle subject to this Regulation must not be used on a road if it has been altered to run on leaded petrol and, as a result, is incapable of running on unleaded petrol [39A(2)] because prolonged continuous running on that petrol would damage the engine [39A(6)].

The fuel tank fitted to a vehicle to which Regulation 39A applies must be constructed and fitted so that it cannot be filled from a petrol pump nozzle with an outside diameter of 23.6mm or more [39B(1)]. Exemption is made for a vehicle so constructed that prolonged running on leaded petrol would not cause an emission control device to malfunction and it is marked to show that unleaded petrol can be used [39B(2)].

Vehicles first registered or first used

Some regulations refer to a date of first registration and others to a date when the vehicle was first used. The date a vehicle is first used is the earlier of (a) the date it was first registered under the Vehicles (Excise) Acts and (b) the date it was manufactured in the case of vehicles previously owned by the crown or by visiting forces, vehicles used abroad before being imported into Great Britain, vehicles used on land before being registered and vehicles used on trade plates (except demonstration and delivery) [1078/86/3(3)].

View to the front

The design and construction of every motor vehicle must be such that while controlling the vehicle the driver can have a full view of the road and traffic ahead [1078/86/30].

A vehicle may, instead, comply with Community Directives 77/649, 81/643, 88/366, 90/630 or, in the case of an agricultural motor vehicle, 79/1073 [30(2)].

Wheels

A minimum rim diameter of 670mm is laid down for wheels not fitted with pneumatic tyres, but this limit does not apply to special municipal vehicles, agricultural trailed appliances, works trucks, works trailers, mobile cranes, pedestrian-controlled vehicles, vehicles first used on or before 2 January 1933, and trailers built before 1 January 1933; to any wheel of a motor car first used on or before 1 July 1936, if the diameter of the wheel plus tyre is not less than 670mm; to any broken-down vehicle which is being drawn by a motor vehicle as a result of the breakdown nor to an electrically propelled goods vehicle not over 1,270kg unladen [1078/86/21].

Twin wheels are counted as one for the purpose of the Regulations (except Regulation 26 and 27—tyre mixing and maintenance) if the distance between the centres of the areas of contact between such wheels and the road surface is less than 460mm [3(7)].

'Close-coupled', in relation to a trailer, means that the wheels on the same side are unsteerable when in motion and that the distance between their areas of contact with the road surface is not more than 1m [3(2)].

Width

Type of vehicle	Max. width metres
Locomotive (except agricultural motor vehicle)	2.75
Refrigerated vehicle	2.6
Any other motor vehicle	2.5
Trailer drawn by a motor vehicle with a maximum gross weight over 3,500kg	2.5
Agricultural trailer	2.5
Any other trailer drawn by a vehicle other than	2.5
a motor cycle	2.3

[1078/86/8(1) and 1871/88].

The width limits do not apply to a broken-down vehicle being drawn in consequence of the breakdown [8(2)].

The overall width of a combination of an agricultural motor vehicle and any trailer it draws must not exceed 2.5m [8(3)].

A refrigerated vehicle is especially designed to carry goods at low temperatures and which has sidewalls at least 45mm thick [8(4)].

'Overall width' includes any part of the vehicle or any receptacle of a permanent character but excludes a driving mirror, any lamp or reflector, any snow-plough fixed in front of the vehicle, any tyre distortion caused by weight, front position or side marker lamps, containers to hold seals for Customs clearance, and, the items listed b. to k. in the definition of overall length on page 21 [3(2)].

Windscreen wipers and washers

One or more automatic windscreen wipers must be fitted to every vehicle unless the driver can see clearly to the front of the vehicle without looking through the windscreen, such as by opening the windscreen or looking over it. The wipers must clean the windscreen to enable the driver to see clearly the road in front on both sides of the vehicle as well as ahead [1078/86/34(1)].

On vehicles required to have wipers there must also be windscreen washers capable of clearing, with the wipers, the area of windscreen swept by the wipers. Agricultural motor vehicles, (unless first used on or after 1 June 1986 and driven over 20mph), vehicles providing a local bus service and vehicles incapable of exceeding 20mph are exempt [34(1)].

Instead of complying with the above requirements, a vehicle may comply with Community Directive 78/318 or, in the case of an agricultural motor vehicle, 79/103 [34(4)(5)].

Wings

Heavy motor cars and motor cars (other than agricultural motor vehicles and pedestrian-controlled vehicles); agricultural motor vehicles driven at more than 20mph; and trailers, must be equipped with wings or similar fittings to catch, so far as practicable, mud or water thrown up by the rotation of the wheels [1078/86/63(1)(2)].

If a trailer has more than two wheels, wings are required only on the rearmost two wheels [63(3)].

Exempt are works trucks; living vans; water carts; agricultural trailers drawn at not over 20mph; agricultural trailed appliances; agricultural trailed appliance conveyors; broken-down vehicles; an unfinished vehicle going to a workshop for completion; trailers used for carrying round timber and the rear wheels of a motor vehicle drawing a semi-trailer so used; trailers drawn by vehicles restricted to 20mph or less [63(4)].

Instead of complying with the above requirements a vehicle may comply with Community Directive 78/549 [63(5)].

Exemptions

A vehicle being used on a statutory test by a person authorised to carry out the test is exempt from construction requirements, weight limits and certain maintenance regulations [1078/86/4].

A British motor vehicle bought by a visitor from abroad or by a person about to be resident abroad and which is exempt from car tax or is zero-rated for value added tax purposes is exempt from Regulations 11 to 39, 41 to 52, 54 to 56, 58 to 69 and 71 provided it complies with specified requirements of an international convention.

Vehicles proceeding to a port for export are exempt from Regulations 7 to 15, 17 to 19, 21 to 29, 31 to 33, 35, 36, 38 to 52, 54 to 56, 58 to 69 and 71 [4].

A wheeled towing implement attached only to its drawing vehicle and not used during the hours of darkness or drawn at over 20mph is exempt from Regulations 7 to 65. So too is a vehicle being drawn in the exercise of a statutory power of removal [4].

Exemptions are also made for vehicles in the service of a visiting force or headquarters and certain pre-1906 motor cars [4].

Exemptions for vehicles temporarily in Great Britain are given on page 453.

3 Dangerous goods

Radioactive Substances (Carriage by Road) (Great Britain) Regulations, **No. 1735/74**

Poisons Rules, **No. 218/82**

International Carriage of Dangerous Goods by Road (Fees) Regulations, **Nos. 370/88** and **3067/93**

Road Traffic (Carriage of Explosives) Regulations, **No. 615/89**

Packaging of Explosives for Carriage Regulations, **No. 2097/91**

Road Traffic (Carriage of Dangerous Substances in Packages) Regulations, **No. 742/92**

Road Traffic (Carriage of Dangerous Substances in Road Tankers and Tank Containers) Regulations, **No. 743/92**

Road Traffic (Training of Drivers of Vehicles Carrying Dangerous Goods) Regulations, **No. 744/92**

Road Traffic (Carriage of Dangerous Goods and Substances) (Amendment) Regulations, **No. 1213/92**

Road Traffic (Training of Drivers of Vehicles Carrying Dangerous Goods) (Amendment) Regulations, **No. 1122/93**

Carriage of Goods by Road and Rail (Classification, Packaging and Labelling) Regulations, **No. 669/94**

Danger loads in road tankers and tank containers

The transport of specified dangerous substances—including petroleum-spirit—in tankers is subject to the Road Traffic (Carriage of Dangerous Substances in Road Tankers and Tank Containers) Regulations 1992.

The dangerous substances to which the Regulations apply are (a) those specified in an approved list, unless so diluted to be of no risk, or (b) any other substance which because of prescribed characteristics creates a risk comparable to substances in the approved list [743/92/2(1)].

The 'approved list' is published by the Health and Safety Commission under the title 'Road Tanker Approved List' [4(1)]. The Commission can approve a revision of the list but such a revision will not take effect till six months after its approval date. During that period an operator may mark a tanker in accordance with the revision [4(2)].

A road tanker is a goods vehicle with a tank which is structurally attached to, or is an integral part of, the frame of the vehicle and includes a tube trailer, which is a trailer with more than one gas cylinder structurally attached to it and intended to be used for the carriage of compressed gases. A tank container is defined as a tank (with or without compartments) having a total capacity of more than 3 cubic metres, other than the tank of a road tanker and includes a tube container. A tube container is a liftable framework containing a group of gas cylinders connected together and with a capacity of more than 3 cubic metres. A tank is defined as a tank which is (a) used to carry by road a liquid, gaseous, powdery or granular material or a sludge, in bulk; and (b) except for pressure relief, can be securely closed during conveyance by road [2(1)].

In these Regulations a combination of a motor vehicle and one or more trailers is treated as one vehicle as long as they are attached, but a trailer not forming part of a combination is not regarded as being engaged in carriage [2(2)].

Carriage by road means, in the case of a road tanker, the period from the start of its loading for the purpose of carriage by road until it is cleaned out of substances or vapours sufficient to create a risk to health or safety. In the case of a vehicle carrying a tank container it is the period from (a) the time a loaded container is placed on the vehicle or (b) the start of the loading of a tank already on the vehicle, in either case for the purpose of carriage by road, until (c) the tank container is removed from the vehicle or (d) the tank or compartment is cleaned out of substances or vapours sufficient to create a risk to health or safety, whether the road tanker or vehicle is on a road is not relevant [3(2)]. The operator of a road tanker or other vehicle carrying a tank container is described as the person who holds its operator's licence or, if such a licence is not required, the vehicle's keeper or, in the case of a foreign-registered vehicle, the driver. If a vehicle is on hire, the hirer is treated as its keeper and if the hirer is an employee, his employer will be regarded as the vehicle operator [5(1)]. The operator of a tank container is either (a) the owner if he has a place of business in Great Britain and is identified on the tank container or a document on the vehicle as the owner; (b) if not within (a), the agent of the owner if he has a place of business in Great Britain and is identified as the agent on the tank container or a document on the vehicle; or (c) if not within (a) or (b), the operator of the vehicle carrying the tank container [5(2)]. A person to whom a tank container is leased or hired is deemed to be its owner unless otherwise agreed [5(3)].

EXEMPTIONS

The Regulations apply to the carriage by road of a dangerous substance in a road tanker or tank container except where:

1. the substance is used solely in connection with the operation of the vehicle;
2. in the case of tank container, the dangerous substance is used solely in connection with the operation of the tank container, except for liquid nitrogen in a tank jacket used for insulating liquid helium or liquid hydrogen in the container;
3. the substance is radioactive and within other Regulations;
4. except for Regulations 12 and 26 the vehicle is on an international transport operation within the meaning of the Convention concerning International Carriage by Rail (COTIF) and the carriage conforms entirely with the Regulations concerning the International Carriage of Dangerous Goods by Rail(RID);
5. the vehicle is on an international transport operation within the European Agreement (ADR) and conforms to the conditions in that Agreement;
6. the carriage is a transport operation subject to a special bilateral or multilateral agreement, provided for under Article 4.3 of ADR, to which the UK is a signatory and the carriage conforms to any conditions of the agreement;
7. the vehicle is not subject to the ADR agreement because it is controlled by the armed forces of the Crown or a visiting force;
8. the vehicle is used on a road only in passing from one part of private premises to another part in the immediate vicinity;
9. the vehicle is a road construction vehicle other than a road tanker used for liquid tar (including road asphalt and oils, bitumen and cutbacks) which has the identification number 1999 or 7033;
10. petroleum fuel carried in a volumetric prover in specified circumstances;
11. the vehicle designed for servicing aircraft is carrying aircraft fuel on an aerodrome or outside when passing from one part of the aerodrome to another, but specified regulations still apply;
12. the dangerous substance is a pesticide (other than dilute sulphuric acid or wood preservative) and is diluted or otherwise ready for use and an approval has been given for it under the Control of Pesticides Regulations.

CONSTRUCTION AND TESTING

An operator must not use a vehicle or tank container for the carriage by road of a dangerous substance unless:

(a) it is properly designed, of adequate strength and of good construction from sound and suitable material;

(b) it is suitable for the purpose having regard to the journey, the characteristics and quantity of the substance (including any non-dangerous substance);

(c) the tank or tank container and any fittings are designed, constructed and maintained to prevent the contents escaping (except for suitable safety devices) and one made of materials not liable to be adversely affected by the substance or to react with the substance; and

(d) in the case of a tanker or tank container first used on or after 1 June, 1992 for the carriage of a dangerous substance, he has sufficient written information about its design, construction, examination and maintenance and any repairs or modifications made to it (6).

The construction requirements for road tankers are contained in four Codes of Practice:

Design and construction of vented non-pressure road tankers used for the carriage of flammable liquids;
Design and construction of road tankers used for the carriage of carbon disulphide;
Design and construction of vacuum-operated road tankers used for the carriage of hazardous waste;
Design and construction of vacuum insulated road tankers used for the carriage of non-toxic deeply refrigerated gases.

A dangerous substance must not be carried in a tanker or tank container unless it has been certified as suitable for the purpose it is to be used, there is a written inspection and maintenance scheme and there is a current report of the last examination [7(1)]. A dangerous substance must not be carried in a tanker or tank container which has been damaged, repaired or modified in a way which might affect its safety since the last examination report or test [7(3)]. A tank must have a plate fastened to it which gives details of its manufacturer, serial number, date of last examination and, if a pressure vessel, the maximum working pressure [7(6)].

The carriage of petrol from one site to another site of a used underground storage tank from the place it is removed from the ground at the first site for cleaning, demolition or disposal at the second site is exempt Regulations 6 and 7, subject to specified conditions [8(1)]. The references in Regulation 6 to suitability and contents not escaping do not apply where a tanker or tank container has been damaged and is being moved to the nearest suitable safe place, steps have been taken to make it as secure from leaks as is reasonable and it is escorted by police or fire brigade [8(2)].

The documents referred to in Regulations 6 and 7 must be kept by a tanker operator at the premises the vehicle operates from or his principal place of business in Great Britain and by a tank container operator at the address in Great Britain from which the use of the container is controlled [9(1)]. If a tank container owner has no place of business in Great Britain it will suffice if a photocopy of the documents is kept by the operator or the documents are readily available from the owner [9(2)]. When the operator of a tanker or tank container changes, the previous operator must, if he is based in Great Britain, give the documents to the new operator [9(3)].

INFORMATION OF LOAD

The consignor of a dangerous substance must ensure that each operator who is to carry it receives information to enable him to comply with the Regulations and be aware of the hazards created by the substance [10(1)]. The information must be accurate, sufficient and, as far as practicable, in writing [10(3)]. An operator must not carry the substance unless he has possession of that information and, if he does not receive the information in writing, he must put it in writing or enter it into a computer (if it can be produced in written form when required, is secure from interference and can be authenticated only by the person entering it) [10(2), (4), (6)]. The operator must keep the information for at least two weeks after completion of the journey [10(5)].

The operator of a road tanker or a vehicle carrying a tank container carrying a dangerous substance must ensure that the driver has received adequate written information about the identity of the substance, the quantity carried, the hazards which could arise and the action to be taken in emergency [12(1)]. The driver must ensure that information is kept in the cab of the vehicle and is readily available while the substance is being carried [12(2)]. If a tanker or tank container is not carrying a dangerous substance or when a tank has been emptied and cleaned out the information must be destroyed, removed from the vehicle or placed in a securely closed container marked to show the information does not relate to a substance being carried [12(3), (4)].

Where the tractor unit of an articulated vehicle carrying a dangerous substance is detached from the trailer on a road or in premises, the driver must attach the written information to the trailer in a readily visible position or, if detached in premises, give the information to the occupier of the premises who must ensure it is readily available

[12(6)]. In an emergency the driver must produce the information to police, fire or ambulance staff [12(7)].

SAFETY PRECAUTIONS

An operator must ensure that:

(a) any organic peroxide which is a dangerous substance is not carried in a road tanker or tank container unless it is named in Part I of the approved list and any specified conditions are complied with;
(b) where a dangerous substance is not specified in Part I of the approved list it is not carried in a road tanker or tank container unless its characteristics create no greater risk to health or safety than specified substances with similar characteristics; and
(c) where a maximum concentration or other condition is prescribed for a substance in Part I of the approved list that limit or condition is complied with [11].

The operator of a vehicle carrying a dangerous substance must provide the vehicle with adequate fire-fighting equipment. Every driver and every person repairing, maintaining, examining, inspecting, loading, unloading or otherwise dealing with a tanker or vehicle carrying a tank container containing a dangerous substance must observe all precautions necessary for preventing fire or explosion [13].

The operator of a tanker or tank container which is to be loaded with a dangerous substance must ensure the substance will not, in conjunction with any substance already in the tank, increase risks to health [14]. He must also ensure that no tank or compartment is overfilled with a dangerous substance [15].

The driver of a tanker or vehicle carrying a tank container carrying a dangerous substance must ensure, as far as practicable, that all openings, valves and caps in the tank are securely closed before the start of a journey [16].

Except where tanks are nominally empty, the driver of a road tanker or tank container vehicle which is required to display hazard warning panels with an emergency code ending with the letter 'E' must ensure that the vehicle, when not being driven, is parked in a safe place or is supervised at all times by a person over 18 years of age. Nominally empty means that as much of the dangerous substance as is reasonably practicable has been discharged [17].

HAZARD WARNING PANELS

The operator of a road tanker being used to convey a dangerous substance must ensure that it displays a hazard warning panel at each side and at the rear. Each panel must be rigid or fixed so as to be rigid; be substantially vertical; have its lower edge at least one metre above the ground or, if not possible, as high as reasonably practicable; the forward edge of each side panel must be as close as reasonably practicable to the front of the tank or foremost tank; and it must be weather resistant and indelibly marked with prescribed information. The tanker driver must ensure the hazard warning panels are displayed [18].

The operator of a tank container over 6 cubic metres in which a dangerous substance is carried must ensure that four hazard warning panels are displayed, one on each side and one at each end, and on a container of 6 cubic metres or less, two panels are displayed, one on each side. Each panel must be rigid or fixed so as to be rigid; be substantially vertical and midway along the side of the tank; be weather resistant and indelibly marked with prescribed information. The operator and driver must ensure the hazard warning panels are displayed [19].

Where a multi-load is carried in compartments or separate tanks the operator of the road tanker or tank container must ensure that each tank or compartment containing a dangerous substance displays two labels, one on each side. Each label must be marked or securely attached midway along the side of the tank or compartment; it must be weather resistant and indelibly marked with prescribed information [20].

The requirement to display hazard warning panels and labels does not apply where a road tanker or tank container is being used solely to carry a dangerous substance from:

(a) another tanker or tank container which has been damaged due to an accident on a road or has broken down on a road; or
(b) a rail tanker which has been damaged, derailed or broken down other than on a siding where it was loaded; and either,
(c) the vehicle is escorted by police or fire brigade; or
(d) the vehicle displays a hazard warning sign at the rear [21(1)].

Also exempt from the marking requirements is (a) the carriage of a dangerous substance to a port for carriage by sea, or from a port having been carried by sea, and (b) a tanker or tank container used in (a) which has discharged its load but not been cleaned out or re-loaded if, in either case, the road tanker or tank container is labelled in accordance with the International Maritime Dangerous Goods Code [21(3)]. Neither are hazard warning panels required on a tanker or tank container (a) which has been used for the carriage of a dangerous substance in an international transport operation subject to ADR or RID if the tank is labelled under ADR or RID and has not been cleaned out or re-loaded, or (b) which is used to carry a dangerous substance under RID to a railhead for the international transport by rail of the tanker or container or from a railhead where it has been brought by international rail transport (21(3)].

The marking requirements do not apply to vehicles in the service of the armed forces of the Crown or of visiting forces while the vehicle conveying the dangerous substance is being used on authorised manoeuvres or training [21(4)].

The form a hazard warning panel and label should take, their size and the information to be given on them is laid down in Schedule 3 of the Regulations. See the accompanying diagrams. A warning panel must generally contain the emergency action code; the substance identification number (its trade name may be included); the hazard warning sign for the class of substance (specified in Schedule 1); the telephone number or other permitted information indicating where specialist advice can be obtained from; the name of the manufacturer or owner of the substance. A warning label must give the substance identification number (its name may be included) and the hazard warning sign. Except for the space for the hazard warning sign, the panel and label are to be coloured orange [Sch. 3].

A tanker or tank container being used solely to carry a substance which is not dangerous or is empty must not display, or be provided with, hazard warning panels or labels [22(1)]. Nothing must be displayed on a tanker or tank container which would be likely to confuse emergency services if read in conjunction with hazard warning panels or labels [22(2)]

Where a tank or all compartments have been emptied and cleaned out so that any substance or vapour remaining is not sufficient to create a risk to health or safety, the operator and driver must ensure that warning panels and labels are completely covered or removed, covered except for the specialist-advice telephone number or placed in a secure container marked to show they do not relate to a substance then being carried [23(1)]. Warning panels for petrol or kerosene can be displayed on a vehicle regularly carrying these substances but which is, for the time being, conveying gas oil or derv or both [23(3)]. In the case of a multi-load, where one or more tanks or compartments are emptied and cleaned out, as above, the driver and operator must ensure that the label referring to the removed substance is completely covered, removed or placed in a secure container marked to show they do not relate to a substance then being carried and the warning panel is changed to suit the remaining load [23(2)].

An operator and driver must ensure that while a dangerous substance is conveyed the warning panels and any labels are displayed, kept clean and (apart from a light rear ladder) kept free from obstruction [24].

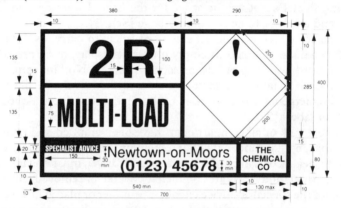

The specification for hazard warning panels for single loads with dimensions in millimetres. The specimen information shows the emergency action code (top left), the substance identification number (centre left), the place where specialist advice can be obtained (bottom left), the hazard warning sign and maker's name.

The hazard warning panel specification for a multi-load tanker.

The specification for a compartment label with the dimensions in millimetres. The specimen information shows the substance identification numbers and the hazard warning sign

[743/92/Sch. 3.]

The specification for hazard warning panels for single loads with dimensions in millimetres. The specimen information shows the emergency action code (top left); the substance identification number (centre left); the place where specialist advice can be obtained (bottom left); and the hazard warning sign and maker's name.

OTHER PROVISIONS

Where petroleum-spirit is unloaded at (a) a petroleum filling station or (b) other premises licensed to store not more than 100,000 litres of petroleum-spirit, the Regulations impose duties on the tanker driver and the person in charge of the storage tank in relation to the unloading [25 and Sch. 4].

The Health and Safety Executive may exempt, by written certificate, any person or class of persons, dangerous substance or class of dangerous substances, from all or any of these requirements or prohibitions [28].

When requested a driver must give to a police officer or traffic examiner any documents required to be carried under these Regulations and any other information about the identity and quantity of the dangerous substance being carried [27].

In a prosecution under the Regulations it is a defence for a person to prove that he took all reasonable precautions and exercised all due diligence to avoid the commission of the offence [29].

A Code of Practice on the operational provisions of these regulations has been published by the Health and Safety Commission.

ADR fees

The fee charged for providing inspection facilities and administrative work in connection with an application for an ADR certificate is £98.80 when the inspection is carried out on the same day as an examination under the Plating and Testing Regulations. If the inspection is to be carried out at any other time the fee is £98.80 plus the plating and testing fee [370/88/3 and 3067/93].

If a vehicle fails the inspection but arrangements are made for a further inspection to be made within 14 days the fee for the second inspection is £49.40 [4(2)].

A copy of an ADR certificate lost or destroyed costs £5.70 [6]

A fee can be refunded under the same circumstances as a plating and testing fee—see page 251 [8] but is otherwise not generally refundable even if the vehicle is not inspected [5(1)].

If a single ADR certificate for a motor vehicle and trailer is applied for, the fee payable is that for two vehicles [9].

Danger loads in packages

The Road Traffic (Carriage of Dangerous Substances in Packages, etc) Regulations 1992 apply to the carriage of:

(a) any quantity of a dangerous substance in bulk;
(b) any quantity of an organic peroxide or an inflammable solid which has a self-accelerating decomposition temperature of 50 or 55 degrees C respectively or less;
(c) any other organic peroxide, flammable or toxic gas, or dangerous substance allocated a specified packing group in a receptacle with a capacity of 5 litres or more;
(d) asbestos or asbestos waste which is a dangerous substance in a receptacle with a capacity of 5 litres or more;
(e) any dangerous substance listed in the approved list as hazardous waste and designated special waste which is in a receptacle with a capacity of 5 litres or more;
(f) any other dangerous substance in a receptacle with a capacity of 200 litres or more;
(g) any other dangerous substance in a transformer or capacitor regardless of its capacity;
(h) Regulation 15(2) (production of information) applies to carriage on a vehicle, in receptacles of less than 5 litres, of a substance in (c), (d) or (e) above or, in a receptacle of less than 200 litres, a substance in (f) above; and
(i) Regulation 16 (restrictions on food vehicles) applies to the carriage of any toxic or harmful substance in bulk or in a receptacle of any capacity [742/92/3(1)].

A dangerous substance is any explosives; radioactive material; goods named in the approved carriage list (unless diluted or treated to be not hazardous); or any other goods which have specified hazardous properties [2(1) and 669/94]. The approved carriage list is a list published by the Health and Safety Commission entitled 'Information Approved for the Classification, Packaging and Labelling of Dangerous Goods for Carriage by Road and Rail' and which contains lists of dangerous substances and other information [2(1)].

The Regulations do not apply where:
  (i) the substance is used solely in connection with the operation of the vehicle;

(ii) the substance is radioactive and within the Ionising Radiations Regulations 1985;

(iii) the substance is a Class 1 explosive within the Classification and Labelling of Explosives Regulations 1983;

(iv) the vehicle is on an international transport operation within the COTIF rail convention and conforms to RID rules specified in CIM;

(v) the vehicle is on an international transport operation within the ADR agreement and complies with its conditions;

(vi) the transport of a dangerous substance subject to a special bilateral or multilateral agreement, provided for under Article 4.3 of ADR, to which the UK is a signatory and the carriage conforms to any conditions of the agreement;

(vii) the vehicle is not for the time being subject to the ADR agreement because it is under the orders of the armed forces of a contracting party;

(viii) the vehicle is only used on roads to deliver goods between private premises and a vehicle in the immediate vicinity or in passing from one part of premises to another in the immediate vicinity;

(ix) the vehicle goes from one part of agricultural land to another and the dangerous substance is diluted or ready for use;

(x) the substance is specified in Regulation 3 (1)(c) to (i) of the Classification, Packaging and Labelling of Dangerous Substances Regulations 1984 (these include food, animal feed, raw materials for cosmetics, medicinal products, controlled drugs, disease-producing micro-organisms and samples taken for enforcement purposes);

(xi) the substance is commercial butane or commercial propane, or a mixture of them, in a cylinder carried in connection with the operation of a vehicle or as part of the equipment of a vehicle and not more than two cylinders (including a spare) are carried;

(xii) vehicles carrying ammonium nitrate fertiliser in specified circumstances are exempt Regulations 7, 10(1) and 12 [3(2)].

A vehicle is deemed to be used for the carriage of a dangerous substance (a) in the case of a vehicle carrying a dangerous substance in bulk, from the start of loading to the time the vehicle has been unloaded and, where necessary, cleaned out so that any substance remaining in the vehicle is not a risk to health or safety, or (b) in the case of carriage in a freight container, receptacle, transformer or capacitor, from the time it is placed on a vehicle already loaded or is loaded while on a vehicle until it is removed from the vehicle or it has been emptied and cleaned out, and in any case, whether or not the vehicle is on a road at the material time [3(3)].

The operator of a vehicle is defined in the same way as the operator of a road tanker [4]—see page 53.

The vehicle operator must ensure the vehicle and any freight container:

a. is properly designed, of adequate strength and of good construction from sound and suitable materials and adequately maintained;
b. is suitable for the purpose to which it put having regard to the nature of the journey and the properties and quantity of the dangerous substances, and any other substances, carried;
c. in the case of bulk loads, the vehicle and its fittings which come into contact with the substances are made of materials not liable to be affected by the substance or, with the substance, create any other hazardous substance [5].

The consignor of a dangerous substance must ensure the vehicle operator receives information to enable him to comply with the Regulations and be aware of the hazards created by the substance [6(1)]. The information must be accurate, sufficient and, as far as practicable, in writing [6(3)]. An operator must not carry the substance unless he has possession of that information [6(2)]. The operator must keep the information for at least two weeks after completion of the journey either in written form or in a computer under his control [6(4)]. Information may only be kept in a computer if it can be produced in written form when required, is secure from interference and can be authenticated only by the person entering it [6(5)].

The operator of a vehicle carrying a dangerous substance must ensure the driver has received adequate written information about the identity of the substance, the quantity carried, the hazards which could arise and the action to be taken in emergency [7(1)]. The driver must ensure the information is kept on the vehicle and is readily available while the substance is being carried. Any information relating to a substance not being carried must be destroyed, removed from the vehicle or placed in a securely closed container marked to show the information does not relate to a substance being carried, unless a substance calling for identical emergency action is still being carried [7(2), (3)].

Where the tractor unit of an articulated vehicle carrying a dangerous substance is detached from the trailer on a road or in premises, the driver must attach the written information to the trailer in a readily visible position or, if detached in premises, give the information to the occupier of the premises, who must ensure it is readily available [7(4)]. In an emergency the driver must produce the information to police, fire or ambulance staff [7(5)].

The vehicle operator and any person engaged in the carriage of a dangerous substance must take reasonable steps to ensure that the loading, stowage or unloading of the substance is not likely to create a hazard to health or safety [9]. The operator of a vehicle carrying a dangerous substance must ensure the vehicle carries adequate fire-fighting equipment. Every driver and every person repairing, maintaining, examining, inspecting, loading, unloading or otherwise dealing with a vehicle carrying a dangerous substance must take all precautions necessary for preventing fire or explosion [10].

If the approved list specifies a maximum concentration or some other condition for a substance, it must not be carried at a higher concentration or contrary to the condition [11(1)]. If a vehicle is used to carry an organic peroxide or flammable solid which has a self-accelerating decomposition temperature of 50 or 55°C respectively or below, the operator and driver must ensure the peroxide or solid is kept below its decomposition temperature at all times while it is carried [11(2), (3)].

If a vehicle is carrying a total of 500kg of one or more dangerous substances, the operator must ensure that the vehicle displays clearly, at front and rear in a substantially vertical plane, two reflectorised orange plates 400mm wide and 300mm high with a 15mm black border. Plates complying with these rules can be fitted voluntarily where less than 500kg is carried. The operator and driver must ensure the plates are displayed at all times when required by Regulations, they are kept clean and unobscured (except the rear plate when loading or unloading) and only used on a vehicle carrying a dangerous substance [12].

A vehicle not being used to carry a dangerous substance must not display the plates. When a vehicle is displaying plates, nothing should be displayed on it which would be likely to confuse emergency services if read in conjunction with those plates [13].

The orange-plate requirements do not apply:

(a) to the carriage of a substance to a port for carriage by sea, or from a port having been carried by sea, if the vehicle or any freight container on it is marked in accordance with the Maritime Dangerous Goods Code;

(b) where the vehicle is carrying the substance from (i) another road vehicle which has been damaged in an accident or has broken-down, or (ii) from a rail vehicle which has been damaged in an accident or has broken-down on a railway other than the siding where it was loaded;

(c) armed forces vehicles on manoeuvres or training [12(6), (7) and 1213/92].

If a vehicle carries 3 tonnes or more of a dangerous substance(s), or any quantity of specified organic peroxides or flammable solids, the driver must ensure that when the vehicle is not being driven it is parked in a safe place or is supervised by him or competent person over the age of 18 years, unless he has left the vehicle to seek assistance in case of damage or breakdown [14].

When requested, a driver must give to a police officer or goods vehicle examiner any documents required to be carried under these Regulations and any other information about the identity and quantity of dangerous substances being carried [15].

The vehicle operator and driver must ensure that specified dangerous substances which are toxic are not carried in any vehicle in which food is carried unless the food is carried in a part of the vehicle effectively separated from that containing the substance or it is adequately protected from risks of contamination [16].

In any proceedings for an offence under these Regulations it is a defence for a person to prove that he took all reasonable precautions and exercised all due diligence to avoid the commission of the offence [17].

A Code of Practice on the operational provisions of these regulations has been published by the Health and Safety Commission.

The Chemicals (Hazard Information and Packaging) Regulations 1993 place a duty on suppliers and consignors of specified dangerous goods to ensure that they are properly packaged and labelled. See also the Carriage of Dangerous Goods by Road and Rail (Classification, Packaging and Labelling) Regulations 1994.

Driver training

The Road Traffic (Training of Drivers of Vehicles Carrying Dangerous Goods) Regulations 1992 apply to:

(a) the carriage of any dangerous substance or radioactive material in
    (i) a road tanker with a capacity of more than 3,000 litres or a permissible maximum weight over 3.5 tonnes, or
    (ii) in a tank container carried by a vehicle regardless of its permissible maximum weight;
(b) the carriage in a vehicle with a permissible maximum weight over 3.5 tonnes of:
    (i) any dangerous substance in bulk;
    (ii) any organic peroxide with a self-accelerating decomposition temperature of 50°C or below;
    (iii) any flammable solid with a self-accelerating decomposition temperature of 55°C or below;
    (iv) any other organic peroxide, flammable or toxic gas, or other

dangerous substance in packing Group 1, in each case in a receptacle of over 5 litres;
- (v) any asbestos or special waste containing asbestos in a receptacle of over 5 litres;
- (vi) any hazardous waste which is special waste in a receptacle of over 5 litres;
- (vii) any dangerous substance not in (ii) to (vi) above and in a receptacle of over 200 litres;
- (viii) any dangerous substance not in (ii) to (v) above if in a transformer or capacitor regardless of its capacity;
- (c) the carriage of any explosives in a vehicle not also being used to carry passengers for hire or reward;
- (d) the carriage of any radioactive material in a vehicle with a permissible maximum weight over 3.5 tonnes [744/92/2(1) and 1122/93].

General exemptions from the Regulations are provided where:

1. the dangerous goods are carried in connection with the operation of the vehicle;
2. the vehicle is being moved by a breakdown vehicle under police or fire brigade escort to the nearest safe place for repair, cleaning, etc;
3. the vehicle is being driven on test by a fitter or vehicle tester and he understands the nature of the dangers of the goods carried and the emergency action to be taken;
4. the vehicle is driven by a policeman in an emergency and he understands the nature of the danger of the goods carried and the appropriate action to take in emergency;
5. the vehicle is delivering dangerous goods between private premises and another vehicle in the immediate vicinity or between parts of the same premises in the immediate vicinity of each other;
6. except for explosives' carriage, the vehicle is on an international journey within and conforming to ADR, or the transport is under a special bilateral or multilateral agreement provided for in ADR, or the vehicle is used by the armed forces of an ADR contracting party [2(1) and Sch. 1].

Further exemptions are provided for carriage of specified dangerous substances in road tankers, tank containers and receptacles and for specified explosives [Sch. 2].

A vehicle is deemed to be engaged in the carriage of a dangerous substance or radioactive material in the same way as a road tanker or vehicle carrying a tank container—see page 51 [2(3)]. The operator of a vehicle is also defined in the same way as in the tanker regulations—see page 53 [3].

The operator of any vehicle (regardless of its capacity or permissible maximum weight) registered in the United Kingdom and engaged in the carriage of dangerous goods must ensure the driver has received adequate instruction and training to enable him to understand the nature of the dangers which might arise with the particular goods carried, the emergency action to be taken, his duties under the Health and Safety at Work Act and his duties under the particular Regulations governing the operation [4(1)].

The operator must keep a record of the training he provides to a driver who is his employee and make a copy of it available to him [4(2)].

The operator of a vehicle engaged in the carriage of dangerous goods in paragraphs a. and c. above (and b. and d. from 1 January 1995) must ensure the driver holds a vocational training certificate applicable to that carriage [5(1)]. A certificate will be issued only where the driver has successfully completed an approved training course, passed an examination and paid a fee of £2.50 [5(2)]. The training must be a theoretical course accompanied by practical exercises covering specified subjects [5(4) and Sch. 3]. A certificate will be valid for five years but can be renewed for five years if, in the 12 months preceding its expiry date, the holder can show he has successfully completed an approved refresher course, passed an examination and paid a fee of £2.50 [5(5)]. An ADR training certificate issued in Northern Ireland or an EC country other than the UK is deemed to be a vocational training certificate for the goods to which it relates [5(7)].

Until 1 January 1995 it is sufficient compliance with Regulation 5 if a driver holds a provisional vocational training certificate. It can be issued to a person who shows he has been working as a driver of vehicles engaged in carrying goods to which the certificate relates for the period of five years preceding 1 January 1992 and who pays a fee of £5 [6(1), (2) and (4)]. In this period no account is taken of seasonal lay-offs or holidays, or breaks between employment up to six months in any 12-month period or totalling up to 18 months [6(3)]. A provisional certificate issued in Northern Ireland is valid in Great Britain [6(5)].

Existing training certificates, issued under national legislation in an EC country and confirmed by the EC Commission as meeting the EC Directive, for the type of goods carried will be acceptable until the earlier of (1) their expiry date, (2) 1 July 1997 in respect of operations in (a) or (c) above; and (3) 1 January 2000 in respect of operations in (b) or (d) above [7].

The driver of a vehicle engaged in the carriage of dangerous goods must ensure his certificate is with him and immediately available [9] and he must produce it on request of a policeman or goods vehicle examiner [10].

In any proceedings for an offence under Regulation 4 or 5(1) it is a defence for the operator to prove he took all reasonable precautions and exercised all due diligence to avoid the commission of the offence [13].

Compressed gases

The provisions of the Petroleum (Consolidation) Act 1928, referring to the labelling and conveyance of petroleum spirit, have been adapted to apply to the carriage of the following gases when compressed in metal cylinders: air, argon, carbon monoxide, coal gas, hydrogen, methane, neon, nitrogen, oxygen [34/30]. All cylinders used for the conveyance by road of any of these gases must comply with the provisions of 679/31, 1594/47 and 1919/59.

Recommendations have been made by the Home Office as regards the carriage of other gases, such as sulphur dioxide and ammonia. Details are obtainable from the Health and Safety Executive, Baynards House, 1 Chepstow Place, Westbourne Grove, London, W2 4TF.

Poisons

Poisons must be packed by consignors sufficiently stoutly to avoid leakage arising from the ordinary risks of handling and transport [218/82/22].

Poisons must have their contents conspicuously labelled on their package with an indication that the package must be kept separate from food and empty food containers [218/82/23]. Protection for food against contamination must be afforded by the carrier.

Radioactive substances

Restrictions are placed on the carriage by a road vehicle of any radioactive substance whose specific gravity exceeds 0.002 of a microcurie per gramme of substance. Among general prohibitions are that a radioactive substance must not be carried on a public service vehicle or any vehicle carrying explosives. Packages containing radioactive material and vehicles carrying them must be labelled in a prescribed manner. It is an offence to remove or damage such labels. Only the carrier or his employees may travel in a vehicle carrying radioactive material and they must be in a compartment separate from the material. Restrictions are placed on the amount of radioactive material which can be carried on a vehicle; the action to be taken when a package is lost or damaged is prescribed and particular obligations affecting vehicle drivers are laid down [1735/74].

The transport of radioactive materials to which the above requirements do not apply may be subject to the Ionising Radiations Regulations 1985.

The Radioactive Material (Road Transport) Act 1991 provides for regulations to be made dealing with safety aspects of handling, transporting, storing, delivering, placarding of vehicles, keeping records, etc. At the date of this book no regulations had been made.

Explosives

In the following requirements a vehicle is deemed to be used for the carriage of explosives from the start of their loading until they have been unloaded, whether or not the vehicle is on a road [615/89/2(6)]. But a trailer or semi-trailer containing explosives is deemed not be used for their carriage when not attached to a motor vehicle. If the trailer or semi-trailer is loaded when detached from a motor vehicle, the carriage begins when the motor vehicle is attached and ends when it is detached or all explosives unloaded, whichever is the earlier [2(7)].

Explosives of compatibility group K are not allowed to be carried in a vehicle [615/89/4(1)] and unclassified explosives may not be carried except in connection with their classification and in accordance with written conditions of the Health and Safety Executive or Secretary of State for Defence [4(2)].

Explosives must not be carried on a vehicle used to carry passengers for payment except where the only explosives carried by a person are a prescribed kind (e.g. cartridges, fireworks, flares, etc), gunpowder or smokeless powder; the total does not exceed 2kg; they are properly packed and kept with that person; and he takes all reasonable precautions to prevent accidents from them [5(1), (2)]. Where explosives are carried by a passenger, the driver and operator are not treated as carrying them [5(3)].

The operator of a vehicle carrying explosives must ensure that it and any freight container are safe and secure having regard to the type and quantity of explosives carried [6(1)]. The operator must ensure that restrictions on the quantities of specified explosives are not exceeded [6(2), (3)] and that conditions on the carriage of explosives in different compatibility groups are complied with [7].

The operator and driver of a vehicle must ensure that at all times when explosives are carried:

(a) an orange reflectorised plate, 300mm by 400mm, with a 15mm black border, is fixed at the front and rear of the vehicle, and

(b) on each side is an orange placard, at least 250mm square, with a black border and, generally, a pictograph of a bomb blast in the upper half and a division number, compatibility letter and class number in the lower half.

The plates and placards must be clearly visible, kept clean and free from obstruction and be removed or covered when all explosives have been removed from the vehicle or container.

Exemptions are provided for the carriage of certain quantities of explosives in specified compatibility groups and for explosives carried in connection with sea or air transport in accordance with appropriate international codes [8 and Sch. 4].

The vehicle operator must ensure that he has obtained from the explosives' consignor, or a person acting for him, information to enable him to comply with the Regulations [9(1)]. The consignor must ensure it is provided to the operator in writing and it is accurate and sufficient [9(2)]. An operator must not remove explosives from a consignor's premises unless he is ready to take them immediately to the consignee or other authorised place (see Regulations 13(1)(c) below) [9(3)].

The vehicle operator must ensure that the driver or any attendant of the vehicle has the following information in writing at the start of the journey:

(a) the division and compatibility group of classified explosives;
(b) the metric net weight of each type of explosive carried, but a total can be given if he does not know and could not reasonably ascertain the net weights;
(c) whether any explosives in compatibility groups C, D or G are substances or articles;
(d) the name and address of the consignor, vehicle operator and consignee; and
(e) information to enable the driver and any attendant to know the dangers the explosives may present and the action to be taken in emergency.

A driver and attendant must not carry explosives unless (i) this written information is kept on the vehicle from the start of the journey and is readily available while the explosives are carried and (ii) any information relating to explosives not being carried at that time is deleted, destroyed, removed from the vehicle or put in a secure container clearly marked to show that it does not relate to the present load.

A driver or attendant must show the written information to police or traffic examiners when required.

This written information is not required for the carriage of specified explosives (e.g. certain cartridges and fireworks, flares, etc); no more than 5kg total of gunpowder or smokeless powder; or not more than 50kg of other specified explosives (other types of cartridges, fireworks and signalling devices) [10 and Sch. 1].

The vehicle operator and any person engaged in the carriage, or having custody or control of explosives during carriage, must take reasonable steps to prevent accidents; minimise harm from any accident; and prevent unauthorised access to, or removal of, all or part of the load [11(1)]. The operator and driver of a vehicle used for carrying explosives must ensure that a competent person is constantly in attendance with it whenever the driver is not present, except (a) during stops in a safe and secure place in premises controlled by the Explosives Act or Ministry of Defence or (b) the vehicle is on a site where some or all of the explosives are to be used for blasting, only specified quantities of explosives and detonators are carried and adequate security precautions are taken [11(2), (3)].

The driver or, in his absence, the person having custody or control of the explosives, must, in the event of:

(a) spillage or explosives constituting a risk to safety;
(b) damage to the explosives or their packaging constituting a risk to safety;
(c) the vehicle overturning; or
(d) a fire or explosion on the vehicle;

ensure that the police, fire brigade and vehicle operator are informed by the quickest practicable means [12(1)]. The vehicle operator and driver (or other person in custody or control of it) must take all precautions for the security of the explosives and safety of persons likely to be affected by explosion [12(3)].

On being informed of such occurrence, the vehicle operator must inform the Health and Safety Executive by the quickest practicable means [12(2)].

The operator and driver must ensure:

(a) the carriage of explosives is completed within a reasonable length of time;
(b) explosives are unloaded as soon as reasonably practicable at the delivery point;
(c) the explosives are delivered to:
  (i) the consignee or his agent, or
  (ii) any other person who accepts their custody for onward despatch, provided they are delivered to a safe and secure place (referred to above) or a designated parking area in an airport, rail depot or siding, harbour or harbour area,

and, if they cannot be so delivered, they are returned to the consignor or his agent; and

(d) any trailer, semi-trailer or freight container containing explosives is not detached except at a place in (c)(ii) above or in case of emergency [13(1)].

Except for the carriage of explosives of a specified kind or quantity, the vehicle operator must ensure that drivers and attendants have received adequate training and instruction to enable them to understand the dangers which the explosives might present, action to be taken in emergency and their duties under these Regulations and the Health and Safety at Work Act [14(1), (3)]. The operator must keep a record of training and instruction received by himself (if a driver or attendant) and by drivers and attendants in his employment to whom a copy must be available [14(2)].

A person under 18 years of age must not use a vehicle for the carriage of explosives; be employed as the driver or attendant of such a vehicle; be made responsible for the security of explosives; or be allowed to go in or on such a vehicle except in the presence and supervision of a person at least 18 years of age. Exemption is made for the carriage of explosives of a specified kind or quantity [15].

Regulations 6 to 15 do not apply to the carriage of explosives in a vehicle carrying passengers for hire or reward [3(2)] and Regulations 4(1), 6 to 10, and 11(2) to 15 do not apply to members of armed or visiting forces in the course of their duties [3(3)]. Regulations 4, 6 to 10, and 11(2) to 15 do not apply to explosive ordnance disposal under the direction of army, police or a person authorised by the Defence Secretary [3(4)]. Regulations 8 to 10 do not apply to (a) a vehicle exempt from excise duty under Section 7(1) of the Vehicles (Excise) Act 1971 (no more than 6 miles a week) or (b) a vehicle used on a road only for delivering goods between private premises and, in the immediate vicinity, a vehicle or another part of the premises [3(5)].

A person must not knowingly carry explosives unless they are in packages which comply with the Packaging of Explosives for Carriage Regulations 1991. Explosives are deemed to be carried on a vehicle from the time they are placed on it to the time they are removed [2097/91/2(2)].

4 Driver licensing

Road Traffic Act 1988
Road Traffic Offenders Act 1988
Road Traffic (Driver Licensing and Information Systems) Act 1989
Road Traffic Act 1991
Motor Vehicles (International Circulation) Order, No. 1208/75
Motor Vehicles (Minimum Age for Driving) (Community Rules) Regulations, No. 2036/75
Goods Vehicles (Ascertainment of Maximum Gross Weights) Regulation, No. 555/76
Motor Vehicles (International Circulation) (Amendment) Order, 1095/80
Driving Licences (Exchangeable Licences) Order, Nos. 672/84 and 65/85
Driving Licences (Exchangeable Licences) (No. 2) Order, No. 1461/85
Motor Vehicles (Driving Licences) Regulations, No. 1378/87
Motor Vehicles (Driving Licences) (Amendment) Regulations, Nos. 965/88, 1062/88, 842/90, 1396/90, 2493/91, 485/91, 1318/92, 3090/92, 1602/93, 638/94 and 1862/94
Motor Vehicles (International Circulation) (Amendment) Order, No. 993/89
Driving Licences (Community Driving Licence) Regulations, No. 144/90
Motor Vehicles (Driving Licences) (Heavy Goods and Public Service Vehicles) Regulations, No 2611/90
Motor Vehicles (Driving Licences) (Heavy Goods and Public Service Vehicles) Amendment) Regulations, Nos. 2491/91 and 3085/92
Motor Vehicles (Driving Licences) (Large Goods and Passenger-Carrying Vehicles) Regulations, No. 2612/90
Motor Vehicles (Driving Licences) (Large Goods and Passenger-Carrying Vehicles) (Amendment) Regulations, Nos. 515/91, 1122/91, 1541/91, 2492/91, 166/92, 538/92, 1356/92, 1761/92, 3089/92, 1603/93 and 639/94
Driving Licences (Designation of Relevant External Law) Order, Nos. 3281/92 and 116/94

A person must not drive, on a road, a motor vehicle of any class otherwise than in accordance with a licence granted under Part III of the 1988 Act which authorises him to drive a vehicle of that class [Act 1988/87(1) & Act 1991]. A person must not cause or permit that to happen [87(2)]. In *Ferry Masters Ltd v Adams* [1980] RTR 139 a company was held to have permitted its driver to drive without a licence where it had no system for checking that drivers renewed their licences.

A steersman of a motor vehicle limited to 5mph does not require a licence when he acts under the orders of the driver who is the holder of a Part III licence and a large goods vehicle drivers' licence and a person may cause or permit such an unlicensed person to act as steersman [88(7)].

A person may drive a vehicle of any class if he has held a licence, a Northern Ireland licence, a British external licence, a British Forces licence or an exchangeable licence for that class; a qualifying application for a licence covering that period has been received by the Secretary of State or his licence to drive that class has been revoked or surrendered other than due to disqualification or being granted in error; and any conditions attached to a provisional licence are complied with [88(1)]. This exception ends when the licence is granted or, if not granted, one year after the date of the application or, if refused, when the applicant receives notice of refusal [88(2)].

A person who becomes resident in Great Britain will, during the 12-month period after he becomes resident, be treated as the holder of a licence authorising him to drive vehicles of any class for which he holds a permit as long as the permit is valid and he is not disqualified from holding a licence in Great Britain [88(5) and 1378/87/25].

Groups to categories

Driving licence categories are shown overleaf.

In licences issued before 1 June 1990 a reference to a group in column 1 of the Table below is to be construed as a reference to the category opposite in column 2 and a person can drive a vehicle in that category in addition to motor vehicles in that group, but this provision does not authorise a person to drive passenger vehicles with more than 16 seats on or after 1 October 1992.

A person who passed a test before 1 June 1990 to drive a vehicle in a group in column 1 is regarded as having passed a test to drive a vehicle in the category opposite in column 2.

1 Group	2 Category
A	B
B	B, limited to automatics
C	B1
D	A
E	P

F	F
G	G
H	H
J	B1, limited to invalid carriages
K	K
L	L
M	Trolley vehicles with more than 16 seats
N	N

[1378/87/33, 842/90 and 485/91]

DRIVING LICENCE CATEGORIES

Category	Vehicle	Additional categories covered
A	Motor bicycle	B1, P
B	Motor vehicle with permissible maximum weight not over 3.5 tonnes and not more than 8 seats (excluding driver's) and including such a vehicle drawing a trailer with a permissible maximum weight not over 750kg	B+E, B1, C1, C1+E, D1, D1+E. F, K, L, N, P
B+E	Category B vehicle and a trailer with a permissible maximum weight over 750kg	—
B1	Motor tricycle not over 500kg unladen and maximum design speed not over 50km/h	K, L, P
C	Motor vehicle used for the carriage of goods, over 3.5 tonnes permissible maximum weight including such a vehicle drawing a single-axled trailer not over 5,000kg permissible maximum weight or any other trailer not over 750kg permissible maximum weight, but excluding a vehicle in Category C1	—
C+E	Category C vehicle and a trailer with a permissible maximum weight over 5,000kg or any other trailer over 750kg permissible maximum weight	—
C1	Motor vehicle used for the carriage of goods with a permissible maximum weight over 3.5 tonnes but not over 7.5 tonnes and including such a vehicle drawing a trailer not over 750kg permissible maximum weight	B, B+E, B1, C1+E, D1, D1+E, F, K, L, N, P

Category	Vehicle	Additional categories covered
C1+E	Category C1 vehicle and a trailer with a permissible maximum weight over 750kg and where the permissible maximum weight of the combination does not exceed 8.25 tonnes	—
D	Motor vehicle used for the carriage of passengers with more than 8 seats (excluding driver's), including such a vehicle drawing a single-axled trailer with a permissible maximum weight not over 5,000kg or, in the case of any other trailer, not over 750kg permissible maximum weight, but excluding a vehicle in Category D1	—
D+E	Category D vehicle and a single-axled trailer with a permissible maximum weight over 5,000kg or any other trailer over 750kg permissible maximum weight	—
D1	As D but not more than 16 seats, not used for hire or reward and including such a vehicle drawing a trailer not over 750kg maximum gross weight	B, B+E, B1, C1, C1+E, D1+E, F, K, L, N, P
D1+E	Category D1 vehicle and a trailer with a maximum gross weight over 750kg	—
F	Agricultural tractor	K
G	Road roller	—
H	Track-laying vehicle	—
K	Mowing machine or pedestrian-controlled vehicle	—
L	Electrically-propelled vehicle	K
N	Vehicle exempt duty by not going more than 6 miles a week on public roads	—
P	Moped	—

[1378/87/Sch. 3, 842/90, 3090/92, 2612/90/Sch.1 and 3089/92]

Qualification for holding a licence

A person cannot be granted a licence for a class of vehicle unless he satisfies the Secretary of State:

1 (a) that at some time during the two years before the application and on or after 1 April 1991 he has passed
    (i)   a test of competence to drive,
    (ii) a corresponding Northern Ireland driving test, or
    (iii) a test on another class of vehicle which covers driving of the vehicle in question; or
  (b) except for vehicles in categories C, C+E, D and D+E, that at some time before 1 April 1991 and in the 10 years preceding the application he has passed a test as in (a) above; or
  (c) for vehicles in categories C, C+E, D or D+E, that at some time before 1 April 1991 and in the 5 years preceding the application he has passed a test (including a Northern Ireland test) to drive an hgv or psv corresponding to the class of vehicle to which the application relates; or

2 (a) that at some time on or after 1 April 1991 he has held
    (i)   a full licence for that class of vehicle, or
    (ii) a full Northern Ireland licence for that class of vehicle or a corresponding class; or
  (b) except for vehicles in categories C, C+E, D and D+E, that at some time between 1 January 1976 and 1 April 1991 he has held a full licence for that class of vehicle or a full Northern Ireland licence for a corresponding class; or
  (c) for vehicles in categories C, C+E, D or D+E, that at some time in the 5 years preceding 1 April 1991 he has held a full hgv or psv licence (including a Northern Ireland licence) for a class corresponding to the class to which the application relates; or

3 that in the two years preceding the application he has passed a test to drive that or a corresponding class of vehicle under a relevant external law or to obtain a British Forces licence: or

4 (a) that at some time on or after 1 April 1991 he has held a full British external licence or full British Forces licence to drive that or a corresponding class of vehicle, or
  (b) that at some time before 1 April 1991 and in the 10 years preceding the application he has held a full licence as in (a); or

5 that at some time during the two years preceding the application he has passed a test to drive that or a corresponding class of vehicle in another EC State, Gibraltar, a designated country or territory;or

6 that, at the time of the application, he holds an exchangeable licence for that or a corresponding class of vehicle and is normally resident in Great Britain (or the UK in the case of a Community licence) but has not been resident for more than five years.

[Act 1988/89 and 89A, 1378/87/5 and 29, 2612/90/8, 14 and 25, and 1602/93]

A British Forces licence is granted in Germany by the British authorities to British forces' members, civilians or their dependents [Act 1988/88(8)]. A relevant external law is one in force in the Isle of Man or Channel Islands which corresponds to the British licence law and a British external licence is one granted under such a law. But an Isle of Man or Channel Islands test or licence for goods or passenger-carrying vehicles is disregarded until approved by Secretary of State [88 and 89(2)]. This approval has been given [3281/92 and 116/94].

An exchangeable licence is a Community licence or a document equal to a Community licence issued in Gibraltar, Australia, Kenya, New Zealand, Norway, Singapore, Sweden, Switzerland, Hong Kong, Barbados, Cyprus, Finland, Malta, Austria, Japan, Zimbabwe or British Virgin Islands [Act 1988/108, 672/84, 65/85 and 1461/85]. A Community licence is a document issued by another Member State authorising the holder to drive a motor vehicle but which is not (a) a licence issued in exchange for a non-Member State driving licence or (b) an international driving permit [108].

Provisional licences

With a view to passing a driving test a person can apply for a provisional driving licence [Act 1988/97(2)]. Conditions attached to a provisional licence are that the driver must not drive otherwise than under the supervision of a qualified driver, 'L' plates are displayed so as to be clearly visible within a reasonable distance from the front and rear of the vehicle and a trailer is not drawn [1378/87/9(1)]. However, the licence holder may drive without supervision (a) on a driving test, (b) if the vehicle (not being a motor car) is not constructed to carry another person, (c) an electrically propelled goods vehicle not over 815kg unladen and constructed to carry only one person, (d) a goods-carrying road roller not over 3,050kg unladen, or (e) on a road in an exempted island [9(2)]. The definition of exempted island excludes the main off-shore islands of Great Britain [9(6)]. The ban on drawing a trailer does not apply to the driving of an agricultural tractor or in the case of an articulated vehicle [9(3)].

The above conditions do not apply where a provisional licence is held by a visitor to or new resident in Britain during the 12 months following his arrival if he holds a valid foreign driving licence [9(5)].

A qualified driver for these purposes is the holder of a full licence authorising him to drive the class of vehicle driven by the provisional licence holder including a person whose full licence is restricted due to a leg disability and who, in either case (except for armed forces on duty) is at least 21 years of age and has held a full licence for at least three years [1378/87/9(6) and 1396/90]. If an applicant for a provisional licence cannot perform the driving test eyesight requirements (reading a number plate at prescribed distances) he can be granted a licence for category K only (pedestrian-controlled vehicles) [10].

A full licence can serve as a provisional licence to enable the holder to drive vehicles of a different class but if he does so he is subject to the same conditions as a provisional licence holder [Act 1988/98(2)]. However, this provision does not entitle a person to drive a vehicle of another class if he is not old enough to drive that class [98(3)(a)] or the full licence relates to specially adapted vehicles or to vehicles in category K and full licences granted from 1 October 1982 which do not include category B, B+E, B1, C1, C1+E, D1, D1+E or P do not authorise the driving of category A motor cycles [1378/87/11 and 842/90].

Medical disabilities

An applicant for a licence must declare whether he suffers or has suffered from a relevant disability, which is a prescribed disability or any other disability likely to cause his driving to be a source of danger. He must also declare any prospective disability, which is any other disability which at the time of the application is not a prescribed disability but due to its intermittent or progressive nature or otherwise may become a relevant disability [92(1)]. Driving a motor vehicle on a road after obtaining a licence by making a false declaration is an offence [92(10) and Act 1991/18].

The prescribed disabilities are epilepsy, severe mental handicap, liability to sudden giddy or fainting attacks (including such attacks caused by a heart defect for which a cardiac pacemaker is fitted), and inability to read a number plate at the specified distance [1378/87/24(1)]. If the Secretary of State is satisfied that a person suffers from a disability he must generally refuse to grant a licence [92(3)].

But a licence will not be refused

(a) if the applicant has passed a test and a specified disability has not become more acute since then;
(b) in the case of a person suffering from epilepsy, if he has had no attacks in the preceding one year or, if he has had an attack only while asleep during that period he shall have had an attack more than 3 years before the licence is granted and none while awake since that attack, and his driving is not likely to be a danger;

(c) in the case of a person who has sudden attacks of fainting or giddiness due to a heart defect for which he has a cardiac pacemaker if his driving will not cause danger and he has medical supervision by a cardiologist; or,

(d) in the case of an applicant for a provisional licence, if his disability is a specified disability [92(4), 1378/87/24(2)-(4) and 1862/94].

The disability specified for (a) and (d) above is one which is not progressive in nature and consists solely of (i) the absence of one or more limbs, (ii) deformity of one or more limbs and/or (iii) loss of use of one or more limbs. A reference to a limb includes part of a limb [24(4)].

If the Secretary of State finds that a licence holder suffers from a relevant or prospective disability he can revoke that licence [93]. If a person drives a motor vehicle on a road after being refused a licence, or having a licence revoked, on medical grounds he commits an offence. The penalty for this offence is far greater than simply driving without a licence [Act 1988/94A and Act 1991].

If a licence holder finds that he is suffering from a relevant or prospective disability not previously disclosed or that a disclosed disability has become worse he must notify the Secretary of State, unless he has not previously suffered from the disability and he believes the condition will not last for more than 3 months [Act 1988/94(1),(2)].

If an applicant for a licence or a licence holder has been disqualified for drink/driving and was two and a half times over the limit; or refused to provide a specimen; or has been disqualified for drink/driving twice or more in any period of 10 years or if the Secretary of State believes that an applicant for, or the holder of, a licence suffers from a relevant or prospective disability he may (a) require that person to supply him with an authorisation enabling him to obtain medical information from that person's doctor, or (b) require him to submit to a medical examination or (c) in the case of a full licence, require that person to take a test. If a person does not comply with these requirements the Secretary of State may refuse or revoke the licence [94(4)-(6), 1378/87/24(7) and 842/90].

A person who is refused a licence, granted a 'disability' licence for three years or less or whose licence is revoked can, after giving the Secretary of State notice of his intention to do so, appeal to a magistrates' court [100].

If in court proceedings for a motoring offence it appears to the court that the accused may be suffering from a prescribed or prospective disability it must notify the Secretary of State [RTO Act 1988/22]. If an insurer refuses to issue a third-party insurance policy on health grounds it must give details to the Secretary of State [Act 1988/95].

Duration and cost

Except for lgv and pcv licences (dealt with later), a full driving licence or provisional licence (except for a motor cycle) will last till the holder's 70th birthday or for 3 years, whichever is the longer. A full licence issued to a person suffering from a relevant or prospective disability will last for not more than 3 years nor less than one year [99(1)]. If the name or address specified on the licence ceases to be correct, its holder must forthwith send it to the Secretary of State with particulars of the alteration to be made and a replacement will be issued free of charge [99(4)]. The fee for a full or provisional licence is £21 or, for a person over 70 years of age £6. The fee for the first licence after a drink/drive disqualification or a provisional licence when required to take a driving test after such a conviction is £20. The fee for a licence after disqualification for any other offence or a provisional licence when required to take a test after such a conviction is £12. The fee for a first full licence after passing a test following a court order or for an exchange or duplicate licence is £6 [1378/87/7, 1602/88 and 2493/91].

If a licence holder satisfies the licensing authority that his licence has been lost or defaced, that he is entitled to continue to hold the licence and he pays the above fee, he will be issued with a duplicate licence. The original, if found, must be returned to the licensing authority [1378/87/13].

Tests

Driving tests may be conducted by (a) examiners appointed by the Licensing Authority, (b) the Secretary of State for Defence as respects service personnel, (c) a fire chief as respects employees of the fire service, (d) a police chief as respects policemen and employees of the police authority, (e) the Metropolitan Police Commissioner as respects taxi drivers or psv drivers (who reside in the Metropolitan Traffic Area), and (f) operators of large vehicle fleets, if appointed to do so by the Licensing Authority, as respects their own staff [1378/87/14(1)]. The above bodies, except for (e), and authorised training establishments may also conduct the Part I motor cycle test [14(2)]. A fleet operator may apply to be appointed to conduct tests of his employees if he ordinarily employs over 250 drivers, proper arrangements are made for the conduct of tests and records are made [15]. A person referred to in (b) to (f) above can delegate the function to a suitable person [17].

Driving tests of members of the public are normally carried out by an examiner appointed under Regulation 14(1)(a) and an applicant for such a test should apply to the licensing authority [18(1)].

Except for an lgv or pcv, the fee for taking a test between 0830 and 1630 Monday to Friday is £27.50 or, if taken at any other time, £35 (an invalid carriage driver's test is free) [19 and 638/94]. The fee for an extended driving test is £55 or, if conducted on a Saturday, £77.50 [19A, 1318/92 and 638/94]. The fee can be refunded only if no appointment is made or it is cancelled by the Secretary of State; if the applicant gives 10 clear days' notice cancelling the appointment; if the test does not take place due to some fault other than his or his vehicle's; or a court orders it to be repaid because the test was not properly conducted [Act 1988/91, 1378/87/18 and 965/88].

A person taking a test must satisfy the examiner that he is fully conversant with the Highway Code, that he is competent to drive the vehicle without danger to others and that he can perform specified movements with the vehicle [1378/87/20]. The person taking a test must provide a vehicle which is suitable and on which only the driver can operate the accelerator. He must produce evidence of his identity to the satisfaction of the examiner and sign a declaration that the vehicle is insured. On failure to do any of these things the examiner can refuse to conduct the test [21, 1396/90 and 638/94]. A person who passes the test is given a certificate and a person who fails is given a statement of failure [22]. If a person fails the test he cannot submit himself for another test on the same category of vehicles for at least one month [23].

A person who considers that his test was not properly conducted can appeal to a magistrates' court or sheriff who, if satisfied that the test was not properly conducted, can order that the applicant may take another test without waiting the statutory one month and that the test shall be free [Act 1988/90].

A person from abroad who becomes resident in Great Britain may drive without holding a British Part III licence for a period of one year following his taking up residence provided he holds an international driving permit, a domestic driving permit of his own country or a British Forces driving licence which, in each case, authorises the driving of the class of vehicle being driven and he is not disqualified from holding a British licence [1378/87/25].

Endorsement and disqualification

Schedule 2 of the Road Traffic Offenders Act 1988 sets out the offences which involve obligatory or discretionary disqualification and licence endorsement and specifies the penalty points involved.

If disqualification is obligatory the court must order the offender to be disqualified for at least 12 months unless there are special reasons for not doing so [RTO Act 1988/34(1)]. This minimum period is 3 years for a second drink/driving offence in 10 years [34(3)] and 2 years for causing death by reckless driving; causing death by careless driving while under the influence of drink or drugs; and where a person has been disqualified for more than one period of at least 56 days each in the three years preceding the offence [34(4) and Act 1991].

If a person is convicted of an offence involving obligatory or endorsement penalty points are attributed to the offence [28(1)]. If a person is convicted of two or more such offences committed on the same occasion the penalty points to be awarded are the highest number for one of the offences [28(4)]. In *Johnson v Finbow* [1983] RTR 363 it was held that a driver who had failed to stop after an accident and who had failed to report it within 24 hours had committed the two offences on the same occasion and only one set of penalty points should be awarded.

When a person is convicted of a disqualification offence and the penalty points to be taken into account total 12 or more the court must order a specified minimum period of disqualification unless it is satisfied, having regard to all the circumstances (except those excluded), that there are mitigating grounds for imposing a shorter disqualification or none at all [35(1)].

The penalty points to be taken into account are any to be ordered by the court on that occasion (except where obligatory or discretionary disqualification is ordered) and on any previous occasion unless, since that occasion, the offender had been disqualified under the totting-up procedure. The penalty points for an offence committed more than three years before another are not to be included [29]. In *R v Yates* [1986] RTR 68 it was held that penalty points are not to be imposed at the same time as a disqualification.

If a person is convicted of an endorsable offence and his licence is liable to be endorsed for a fixed penalty offence committed on the same occasion, the number of points to be attributed to the first offence is the normal figure less the fixed penalty points[30].

The minimum disqualification period is 6 months if no previous disqualification period is to be taken into account; 12 months if one and 24 months if more than one such disqualification is to be taken into account. A previous disqualification is to be taken into account if it was for 56 days or more and was imposed in the 3 years preceding the latest offence [35(2)].

If a person is convicted on the same occasion of more than one offence involving disqualification all the offences shall be taken into account and not more than one disqualification shall be imposed [35(3)].

The circumstances for mitigating a disqualification are not to include facts suggesting the offence is not a serious one; hardship, other than exceptional hardship; and any circumstances during the preceding three years already used in mitigating a disqualification order [35(4)].

A disqualification takes effect as soon as it is ordered and a court has no power to make a disqualification period consecutive to one imposed by the same or a different court—*R v Meese* [1973] 2 All ER 1103, [1973] 1 WLR 675 and *R v Sandwell* [1985] RTR 45.

When a person is convicted of manslaughter, causing death by dangerous driving or dangerous driving the court must order him to be disqualified until he passes a driving test [36(1) and Act 1991]. Provision is made for such an order to be made in relation to other disqualifications to be prescribed by the Secretary of State [36(3)]. In other cases involving obligatory endorsement the court may disqualify a person until he passes a driving test [36(4) and Act 1991]. In *R v Donnelly* [1975] All ER 1103 the High court said that discretionary disqualification should not be ordered unless the competence of the driver was in question.

The driving test for a person convicted of an offence involving obligatory disqualification or who is disqualified under the totting-up system is an extended driving test [36(5)]. It involves at least one hour's driving and the test fee is £47 (£75 on a Saturday) [1378/87/19A, 20(2) and 1318/92].

A person disqualified under Section 36 can hold a provisional licence and drive in accordance with conditions attached to the licence [37(3)].

A disqualified person can apply to the court which imposed the disqualification to have it removed. An application cannot be made before 2 years have passed in the case of a disqualification of less than 4 years; one half of the period in the case of a disqualification of 4 to 10 years; or 5 years in any other case [42].

If a person is convicted of an offence involving obligatory endorsement, particulars of the conviction must be endorsed on the licence together with particulars of the disqualification or penalty points awarded [44(1)]. If the person is not disqualified the court need not endorse the licence if there are special reasons for not doing so [44(2)]. A special reason is one special to the facts of the particular case and is a mitigating or extenuating circumstance, not amounting in law to a defence to the charge, but is directly connected with the commission of the offence and one which a court ought properly to take into consideration when imposing a punishment—*Whittall v Kirby* [1947] KB 194; *Agnew v DPP* [1991] RTR 144. If a person is convicted of an offence involving disqualification the court may take into account any conviction recorded on the licence [31]. Particulars of an endorsement and penalty points must be entered on any new licence obtained [45(2)] but a person can obtain a licence free from that endorsement (a) 4 years after a conviction when disqualification was ordered; (b) 4 years after the offence if disqualification was not ordered; (c) 11 years after certain drink/driving convictions [45(4)-(7)]. References here to a licence include its counterpart [144/90/3].

Disqualification and endorsement will not be ordered in the case of a person convicted (a) under Section 40A of the 1988 Act of using a vehicle in dangerous condition or with an insecure load if he proves that he did not know, and had no reasonable cause to suspect, that the use of the vehicle involved a danger of injury to any person, or (b) under Section 41A of a Construction and Use offence relating to tyres, steering or brakes if he proves that he did not know, and had no reasonable cause to suspect, that the facts were such that an offence would be committed [48]. (An offence of dangerous condition or insecure load under Regulation 100 of the Construction and Use Regulations is punishable under Section 42 which does not carry licence endorsement.)

A court which makes a disqualification order can suspend it pending an appeal against the order [39].

When a disqualified driver appeals against conviction or sentence to the Crown Court or Court of Appeal that court may suspend the disqualification order. Also, if a disqualified driver appeals to the House of Lords, appeals by case stated to the Divisional Court or applies to that court for an order of certiorari the High Court may suspend the disqualification. The court may suspend a disqualification on its own terms. Similar provision is made for appeals to the High Court of Justiciary in Scotland [40, 41].

Minimum age

Minimum ages for driving different classes of motor vehicles are contained in Section 101 of the Road Traffic Act 1988 and modified by Regulations.

Class of vehicle	Age
1. Invalid carriage	16
2. Motor cycle	17
(other than mopeds, mowing machines and pedestrian-controlled vehicles for which the age is 16)	17
3. Small passenger vehicle or small goods vehicle	
4. Agricultural tractor	17
5. Medium-sized goods vehicle	18
6. Other motor vehicles	21

The age for driving an agricultural tractor is reduced to 16 years where the vehicle is not over 2.45m wide, draws no trailer other than a two-wheeled or close-coupled four-wheeled trailer not over 2.45m wide and is taxed as an agricultural machine [1378/87/4(1)(c)]. 'Close-coupled' for this purpose means that the centres of two wheels on the same side of the trailer are not more than 840mm apart [4(2)]. A road roller not over 11,690kg unladen, not steam driven and not fitted with soft tyres can be driven at 17 years [4(1)(d)]. At item 6 in the table the age of 18 years can be substituted for 21 years for an employee of a Health Authority or, in Scotland, the Common Services Agency, when driving a vehicle for the ambulance service of the Authority [4(1)(e)]. The age for driving an lgv is reduced from 21 years to 18 years in the case of a driver registered under a training scheme if the vehicle is owned or operated by his registered employer or by a registered training establishment [4(1)(f)].

At item 6 in the above table the age of 18 years can be substituted for 21 years in the case of a large passenger vehicle where

(a) the driver is not engaged in carrying passengers and he either holds a psv or pcv driver's licence, is undergoing a pcv driving test or is acting under the supervision of such a licence holder; or

(b) the driver holds a psv licence and is engaged in carrying passengers on a regular service on a route not over 50km or on a national transport operation with a vehicle constructed to carry not more than 17 persons including the driver,

and, in either case, the vehicle operator holds a psv operator's licence, a community bus permit or a minibus permit. A large passenger vehicle, for this purpose, is a motor vehicle constructed solely to carry passengers and their effects and is constructed to carry more than 9 passengers including the driver [1378/87/4(1)(g) and 485/91].

At items 5 and 6 in the table the age of 17 years can be substituted for 18 and 21 years in the case of members of the armed forces doing urgent work of national importance in accordance with an order of the Defence Council [952/81/4(1)(h)] or when receiving instruction in driving large goods vehicles in preparation for the lgv driving test or when taking, going to or from, such a test [4(1)(i)].

For the purposes of the above table, an agricultural tractor is a tractor used primarily for work on land in connection with agriculture. A small passenger vehicle is a motor vehicle constructed solely to carry passengers and their effects and is adapted to carry not more than 9 persons inclusive of the driver. A small goods vehicle is a motor vehicle constructed or adapted to carry or haul goods, is not adapted to carry more than 9 persons (including the driver) and its permissible maximum weight does not exceed 3.5 tonnes. A medium-sized goods vehicle is a like-constructed vehicle which exceeds 3.5 tonnes but does not exceed 7.5 tonnes permissible maximum weight [Act 1988/108]. Motor vehicles for more than 9 passengers and goods vehicles over 7.5 tonnes permissible maximum weight are 'other motor vehicles' for which the minimum age is 21 years.

The permissible maximum weight of a goods vehicle is obtained by reference to a number of involved definitions. They are given in the next section.

The provisions of Article 5 of EC Regulation 3820/85 relating to minimum ages of goods vehicle drivers and minimum ages and other qualifications of passenger vehicle drivers have been suspended in specified cases. They are suspended in the case of carriage in Great Britain by a driver resident in the United Kingdom and who, immediately before 1 January 1976, held a licence or but for a court disqualification would be entitled to hold a licence or another provisional licence or who is a resident from abroad treated as the holder of such a licence [2036/75].

Permissible maximum weight

'Permissible maximum weight' for driver licensing and minimum age purposes means:

(a) in the case of a motor vehicle which neither is an articulated goods vehicle nor is drawing a trailer, the relevant maximum weight of the vehicle;

(b) in the case of an articulated goods vehicle—
   (i) when drawing only a semi-trailer, the relevant maximum train weight of the combination;
   (ii) when drawing a trailer as well as a semi-trailer, the total of the relevant maximum train weight of the articulated combination and the relevant maximum weight of the trailer;
   (iii) when drawing a trailer but not a semi-trailer, the total of the relevant maximum weight of the articulated goods vehicle and the relevant maximum weight of the trailer;
   (iv) when drawing no trailer, the relevant maximum weight of the vehicle;

(c) in the case of a motor vehicle (not being an articulated goods vehicle) which is drawing a trailer, the total of the relevant maximum weights of the motor vehicle and trailer.

'Relevant maximum weight' in relation to a motor vehicle or trailer means:

(a) if the vehicle is fitted with a Department of Transport plate, the maximum gross weight marked on that plate;
(b) if the vehicle does not have a DoT plate but is required to be fitted with a manufacturer's plate, the maximum gross weight on that plate;
(c) if the vehicle has a manufacturer's plate though not required to be fitted with one, the maximum gross weight on that plate;
(d) if the vehicle does not have a plated gross weight, the notional maximum gross weight produced by multiplying the vehicle's unladen weight by a prescribed figure.

'Relevant maximum train weight' in relation to an articulated combination means:

(a) if the motor vehicle is fitted with a DoT plate, the maximum train weight marked on that plate;
(b) if the motor vehicle does not have a DoT plate but is required to be fitted with a manufacturer's plate, the maximum train weight marked on that plate;
(c) if the motor vehicle has a manufacturer's plate though not required to be fitted with one, the maximum train weight marked on that plate;
(d) if the motor vehicle does not have a plated train weight, the notional maximum gross weight of the combination obtained by multiplying the sum of the unladen weights of the motor vehicle and semi-trailer by a prescribed figure.

'Maximum gross weight' means the weight of the vehicle laden with the heaviest load it is constructed or adapted to carry and 'maximum train weight' means the weight of an articulated combination laden with the heaviest load it is constructed or adapted to carry
[Act 1988/108].

The tables on the preceding page and below give the multipliers for obtaining a notional gross or train weight from a vehicle's unladen weight. The notional weight figure is obtained by multiplying the unladen weight of a vehicle in a specified class by the corresponding number in the right hand column [555/76]. It must be noted that the notional gross weights are of relevance only to driving licence provisions and are to be used only where a vehicle had no plated gross or train weight.

MULTIPLIERS FOR MOTOR VEHICLES AND TRAILERS

(1) Class of vehicle	(2) Number
Part A—Motor vehicles	
1. Dual-purpose vehicles not constructed or adapted to form part of an articulated goods vehicle combination	1.5
2. Breakdown vehicles	2
3. Works trucks and straddle carriers used solely as works truck	2
4. Electrically propelled motor vehicle	2
5. Vehicles constructed or adapted for, and used solely for, spreading material on roads to deal with frost, ice or snow	2
6. Motor vehicles used for no other purpose than the haulage of lifeboats and the conveyance of the necessary gear of the lifeboats which are being hauled	2
7. Living vans	1.5
8. Vehicles constructed or adapted for, and used primarily for the purpose of, carrying equipment permanently fixed to the vehicle, in a case where the equipment is used for medical, dental, veterinary, health educational, display or clerical purposes and such use does not directly involve the sale, hire or loan of goods from the vehicle	1.5
9. Three-wheeled motor vehicles designed for the purpose of street cleansing, the collection or disposal of refuse or the collection or disposal of the contents of gullies	2
10. Steam propelled vehicles	2
11. Vehicles designed and used for the purpose of servicing, controlling loading or unloading aircraft on an aerodrome	2
12. Motor vehicles of a class not mentioned above where equipment, apparatus or other burden is permanently attached to and forms part of the vehicle and where the vehicle is only used on a road for carrying, or in connection with the use of, such equipment, apparatus or other burden	1
13. Motor vehicles of a class not mentioned above which are either (a) heavy motor cars or motor cars first used before 1 January 1968 or (b) locomotives or tractors first used before 1 April 1973	2
14. Any motor vehicles not mentioned above 4	4
Part B—Trailers	
1. Engineering plant	1
2. Trailers which consist of drying or mixing plant designed for the production of asphalt or of bituminous or tar macadam	1
3. Agricultural trailers	1
4. Works trailers	1
5. Living vans	1.5
6. Any trailers not mentioned above	3

MULTIPLIERS FOR ARTICULATED GOODS VEHICLE COMBINATIONS

(1) Class of combination	(2) Number
1. Articulated goods vehicle combination where the semi-trailer is a trailer of a kind mentioned in paragraph 1, 2, 3, 4 or 5 of Part B above	1.5
2. Any other articulated goods vehicle combination	2.5

Large goods and passenger-carrying vehicles

DEFINITIONS

A large good vehicle (lgv) is defined as:

(a) an articulated goods vehicle, or
(b) a motor vehicle (not being an articulated goods vehicle) which is constructed or adapted to carry or to haul goods and the permissible maximum weight of which exceeds 7.5 tonnes [Act 1988/121].

A passenger-carrying vehicle (pcv) is defined as:

(a) a large passenger-carrying vehicle, which is a vehicle used for carrying passengers and is constructed or adapted to carry more than 16 passengers, or
(b) a small passenger-carrying vehicle, which is a vehicle carrying passengers for hire or reward and constructed or adapted to carry more than 8 but not more than 16 passengers [Act 1988/121].

An lgv driver's licence is a licence under Part III of the Road Traffic Act 1988 in so far as it authorises a person to drive large goods vehicles of any class. A pcv driver's licence is a licence under Part III in so far as it authorises a person to drive passenger-carrying vehicles of any class [Act 1988/110(2)].

EXISTING PSV LICENCES

A psv licence in force immediately before 1 April 1991 remains valid while it is current [Act 1989/1(2)]. It entitles the holder to drive the corresponding EC categories of vehicles listed on page 106 [2611/90/16]. Appeals pending on 1 April 1991 against the conduct of an hgv driving test or the refusal, suspension or revocation of a psv licence, could be continued. Any licence issued as a result is treated as a pre-April licence [Act 1989/1(3) & 2611/90/13].

EXEMPTIONS

The law on lgv driver licensing does not apply to vehicles of the following classes:
a. track laying vehicles;
b. steam propelled vehicles;
c. road rollers;
d. road construction vehicles used or kept on the road solely for conveying built-in road construction machinery (with or without articles or materials used for that machinery):
e. engineering plant;
f. works trucks;
g. industrial tractors;
h. agricultural motor vehicles;
i. digging machines;
j. vehicles exempt excise duty because used less than 6 miles a week on public roads;
k. an artic drawing unit not over 3,050kg unladen weight and without a trailer attached;
l. vehicles used only for haulage of lifeboats and necessary gear;
m. vehicles made before 1960, used unladen and not drawing a laden trailer;
n. vehicles of a visiting force or headquarters;
o. wheeled armoured vehicles owned or controlled by the Defence Secretary;
p. a vehicle driven by a policeman for removing or avoiding obstruction to others, for protecting life or property (including the vehicle and its load) or similar purposes;
q. an articulated vehicle with a permissible maximum weight not over 7.5 tonnes or the tractor unit of which does not exceed 2.05 tonnes unladen;
r. a rigid vehicle with a relevant maximum weight not over 3.5 tonnes to which a trailer is attached;
s. rigid vehicles not over 10.2 tonnes unladen, operated by the holder of a psv licence and driven by the holder of a psv or pcv licence and used for
   (i) going to or from a place to assist or having assisted a disabled pcv or
   (ii) giving assistance to or moving a disabled pcv or moving a wreck which was a pcv;

t. vehicles fitted with apparatus for lifting a vehicle partly from the ground and for drawing it when so raised and which are
   (i) used solely for dealing with disabled vehicles,
   (ii) not used to carry any load other than a disabled vehicle, water fuel and accumulators and articles required for the apparatus or dealing with disabled vehicles, and
   (iii) with an unladen weight not over 3.05 tonnes;
u. vehicles originally constructed to carry passengers but adapted to carry goods
   (i) when carrying children's play equipment and not more than 8 passengers to or from a place where the equipment is to be, or has been, made available for such use, or, when carrying display or exhibition articles and not more than 8 passengers to or from the display or exhibition, or
   (ii) when a vehicle in (i) above is driven to or from a place for repair or pre-arranged compulsory test;
v. fire fighting or fire salvage vehicles owned or controlled by the Defence Secretary and driven by a member of the armed forces;
w. a vehicle driven by a member of the armed forces on urgent work of national importance in accordance with a Defence Council order [2612/90/27(1)].

A person may drive a vehicle in a. to w. above if he holds a full licence to drive vehicles in categories B and C1 and may drive a vehicle in 1. or 2. below if he holds a full licence to drive vehicles in categories B and D1 [2612/90/27(3)].

A pcv licence is not required for:

1. vehicles made more than 30 years ago and not used for hire or reward or to carry more than 8 passengers;
2. a vehicle driven by a policeman for removing or avoiding obstruction to others, for protecting life or property (including the vehicle and its passengers) or similar purposes [2612/90/27(2)].

Pcv requirements do not apply to a category C lgv, adapted to carry up to 24 passengers, driven by a member of the armed forces and used to carry passengers for naval, military or air force purposes [27(5)]. Otherwise, lgv requirements do not apply to vehicles which are passenger-carrying vehicles as well as large goods vehicle [27(4)].

CHANGES AFFECTING BUS LICENCES

A person who held a full licence to drive category B and D1 vehicles on 31 May 1990 and who satisfied the Secretary of State he had been regularly driving a category D vehicle with more than 16 seats (excluding the driver's seat) during the 3 years immediately preceding his licence application and who made his application before 1 October 1992 was, regardless of not having passed a test for that category, entitled to the grant of a category D licence but limited to vehicles not used for hire or reward [2612/90/28(1) & 538/92].

A person who holds a full category C licence, may also drive vehicles, used for the carriage of passengers, with more than 16 seats which are not being used for hire or reward or to carry more than 8 passengers [28(2)].

A person who, before 1 April 1994, takes a test for category D vehicles in a vehicle less than 8.5m long or, on or after that date, in a vehicle less than 9m long, will have his licence limited to vehicles with not more than 16 seats (excluding the driver's) [29].

APPLICATIONS—LGV & PCV

A person who wants an lgv or pcv licence must

(a) make his application not more than 3 months before it is to take effect; and
(b) send with it
  (i)   if required, a medical certificate in a form specified by the Secretary of State and signed by a registered medical practitioner not more than 4 months before the licence is to take effect,
  (ii) if required, his ordinary driving licence, Northern Ireland driving licence or existing hgv or psv licence,
  (iii) a test pass certificate for the category of vehicle the licence is applied for, except for a provisional licence applicant or a person who has held a previous full licence, and
  (iv) in the case of an applicant for a category D licence based on 3 years' previous experience, a certificate as to that experience [2612/90/4].

When a licence is granted an applicant must have the following qualifications:

(a) he must not be a person who
  (i)   holds an lgv or pcv licence which has been suspended, except that a person can apply for an lgv licence even though his pcv licence is suspended if the suspension is for reasons other than his conduct as a driver;
  (ii) is disqualified from holding an lgv or pcv licence, except that

a person can apply for an lgv licence even though disqualified from holding a pcv licence if the disqualification is for reasons other than his conduct as a driver;

(iii) is disqualified from holding an ordinary licence;

(iv) is disqualified by reason of age for the category of licence; or

(v) would hold more than one licence to drive an lgv or pcv, including hgv, psv, Northern Ireland, British external, British Forces or exchangeable licences;

(b) except for a full-time member of the armed forces, he must hold a full ordinary driving licence for category B vehicles, be authorised to drive category B by Section 88 of the 1988 Act (licence applied for or surrendered) or have passed a test for category B; and

(c) an applicant for an lgv trainee driver's licence must be a registered employee of a registered employer and his ordinary licence must be free from penalty points or relevant endorsements [2612/90/3].

If an applicant for a provisional licence holds an ordinary licence (including a Northern Ireland ordinary licence) limited to vehicles of a particular design, construction or class any licence granted to drive an lgv or pcv must contain a corresponding limitation [2612/90/7].

MEDICAL DISABILITIES—LGV & PCV

The following disabilities are relevant disabilities prescribed for the purposes of Section 92 of the 1988 Act for lgv and pcv licences—in addition to those prescribed for an ordinary licence—which means that if the Secretary of State is satisfied that an applicant is suffering from such a disability he must refuse the licence:

(a) liability to epileptic seizures;

(b) abnormal sight in one or both eyes where

(i) in the case of a person who held a licence on 1 January 1983 and who held it on 1 April 1991, the visual acuity is worse than 6/12 with the better eye and worse than 6/36 with the other eye and, if corrective lenses are worn, the uncorrected acuity in each eye is worse than 3/60, or

(ii) in the case of a person not within (i) above but who held a licence on 1 March 1992, the visual acuity is worse than 6/9 in the better eye and worse than 6/12 in the other eye and, if corrective lenses are worn, the uncorrected acuity in each eye is worse than 3/60, or

(iii) in any other case, the visual acuity is worse than 6/9 in the better eye or worse than 6/12 in the other eye or, if corrective lenses have to be worn to ensure the acuity in one or both eyes is no worse than 6/9 in the better eye and 6/12 in the other eye, the uncorrected acuity in each eye is worse than 3/60;

(c) sight in only one eye unless

   (i) in the case of a person who held a licence on 1 January 1983 and who held it on 1 April 1991, the traffic commissioner in whose area he lives or who granted the licence knew of the disability before 1 January 1991 and the visual acuity in that eye is no worse than 6/12, or

   (ii) in the case of a person who did not hold a licence on 1 January 1983 but did on 1 April 1991, the traffic commissioner in whose area he lives or who granted the last licence knew of the disability before 1 January 1991 and the visual acuity in that eye is no worse than 6/9;

(d) diabetes subject to insulin treatment, unless the person held a licence on 1 April 1991 and the traffic commissioner in whose area he lives or who granted the licence knew of the disability before 1 January 1991 [2612/90/6(1), 166/92 and 3089/92].

CONDUCT OF APPLICANTS

The Secretary of State cannot grant an lgv or pcv licence unless satisfied, having regard to his conduct, that the applicant is a fit person to hold it [Act 1988/112].

Conduct means, in relation to an applicant for an lgv licence, his conduct as a driver of a motor vehicle and, in relation to a pcv licence, his conduct both as a driver and in any other way relevant to his holding a pcv licence [121(1)].

Any question relating to an applicant's conduct may be referred by the Secretary of State to the traffic commissioner of the area in which the applicant lives [113(1)]. The traffic commissioner must determine whether, having regard to his conduct, the applicant is a fit person to hold a licence to drive an lgv or pcv [113(2)].

A traffic commissioner can require the applicant to supply him with information and may require the applicant to appear before him, at a time and place he specifies, to give the information and to answer questions relating to his application [113(3)].

If the applicant fails, without reasonable excuse, to supply information, appear before or answer questions properly put to him, the commissioner may decline to proceed further with the application and, if he does so, he must notify the Secretary of State who must refuse the licence [113(4)].

Unless he has declined to proceed further with an application, the traffic commissioner must notify the Secretary of State and the applicant of his determination in the matter and his decision is binding on the Secretary of State [113(5)].

DURATION

An existing psv licence remains in force for 5 years unless it is previously revoked, suspended or surrendered. If, when a person applies for a licence to drive a pcv, he is the holder of a psv licence, that licence will not expire under these time limits but will remain in force until the application is disposed of [Act 1989/Sch.1/par 4].

A licence to drive an lgv or a pcv remains in force (unless it is previously revoked, suspended or surrendered) until the holder's 45th birthday or for five years, whichever is the longer and, where the licence holder exceeds 65 years of age, for one year [Act 1988/99(1A)]. It is the intention of DVLA to require a medical certificate on each renewal.

An exchange licence is granted for the period outstanding on the original licence. Subject to any shorter period mentioned above, the Secretary of State can grant a licence for one to three years to a person appearing to suffer from a relevant or prospective disability [99(1A)].

LICENCE FEES

A full licence costs £21 but the first full licence granted (a) after a period of disqualification costs £12 or (b) after a person has taken a test he was ordered to take costs £6 unless, in either case, the previous licence would have less than 3 months left to run. A provisional licence costs £21 but the first provisional licence of a person ordered to take a driving test costs £12. A full lgv trainee's licence for category C or an lgv trainee's provisional licence for category C+E costs £6. When more than one licence or an ordinary licence is applied for at the same time only the highest single fee is payable [2612/90/9 & 2492/91].

LEARNERS

Whilst a full ordinary licence can be used, under Section 98(2) of the 1988 Act, as a provisional to drive other classes of vehicle, a category B licence cannot be used under that Section to drive category C, C+E, D or D+E vehicles. Similarly, a licence of category C or C+E cannot be used as a provisional to drive vehicles of category D or D+E, and vice versa [2612/90/10]. This means that a learner must hold a provisional lgv or pcv licence of the appropriate category.

A provisional lgv or pcv licence, including a full licence treated as a provisional (i.e. C for C+E and D for D+E), is subject to conditions that he does not drive an lgv (a) otherwise than under the supervision of a person in the vehicle who holds a full standard lgv licence to drive the vehicle; (b) unless there is clearly displayed in a conspicuous manner on the front and back of the vehicle (i) before 1 April 1996, an hgv 'L' plate or an ordinary 'L' plate of (ii) from 1 April 1996, an ordinary 'L' plate; and (c) in the case of a pcv, while carrying any person other than the supervisor in (a); a driving test examiner or person authorised by the Secretary of State; or the holder of a psv or pcv licence who is a learner or instructor. Condition (a) does not apply when undergoing a driving test and (a),(b) and (c) do not apply when a person has passed a test for the category of vehicle being driven or while driving a passenger vehicle he is entitled to drive as a pre-June 1990 group A or B licence holder [Act 1988/114, 2612/90/10 & 515/91].

The above requirements do not apply to lgv trainee drivers [2612/90/10(6)].

LGV LICENCES FOR PERSONS UNDER 21

An lgv licence issued to a person under 21 years of age is subject to conditions that:
(a) a full-time member of the armed forces must not drive an lgv other than for naval, military or air force purposes;
(b) the holder of an lgv trainee driver's licence must not drive an lgv unless he is the registered employee of a registered employer and either
    (i) the vehicle is a category of lgv to which his training agreement applies and is owned or operated by that employer or a registered lgv driver training establishment, or
    (ii) the holder is a part-time member of the armed forces and the vehicle is owned by the Secretary of State for Defence and used for naval, military or air force purposes;
(c) the holder of a trainee's full licence does not drive a vehicle of any category if it is drawing a trailer, except under the supervision of a person in the vehicle who holds a full standard lgv licence to drive the vehicle [Act 1988/114(1) & 2612/90/11(1)].

An lgv trainee driver's full licence to drive category C vehicles can be used as a provisional for category C+E vehicles two years after he passes the category C test [11(2)].

An lgv trainee's provisional licence, including a trainee's full licence which is treated as a provisional, is also subject to the following conditions that the holder must not drive an lgv under the licence

(i) otherwise than under the supervision of a person in the vehicle who holds a full licence to drive the vehicle (except when undergoing a driving test);

(ii) unless there is clearly displayed in a conspicuous manner on the front and back of the vehicle (A) before 1 April 1996, an hgv 'L' plate or an ordinary 'L' plate and (B) from 1 April 1996, an ordinary 'L' plate; and

(iii) if the vehicle is drawing a trailer unless the   combination   is category C+E.

Conditions (i)–(iii) do not apply where the licence holder has passed a test for an lgv of a category for which the licence is, or is treated as, a provisional, but if a trailer is drawn or the vehicle is in Category C+E the supervision condition applies [11(4)–(6)].

DRIVING TESTS

Tests can be conducted by:

(a) examiners appointed by the Secretary of State;

(b) examiners appointed by the Defence Secretary for testing armed forces personnel;

(c) fire chiefs for fire brigade drivers;

(d) police chiefs for police drivers;

(e) in the case of pcv tests, an examiner who is, or is employed by, the holder of a psv operator's licence and authorised by the Secretary of State to conduct tests of employees or prospective employees of the psv business [1612/90/19(1),(3) & 1541/91].

Fire and police chiefs can, subject to the Secretary of State's approval, delegate testing to a suitable person [19(2)].

A person who wants to take a test conducted by an examiner in (a) above must apply for an appointment to any office of the Driving Standards Agency, specify the category of test vehicle and pay a fee of £62 or, for a Saturday test, £80 [15 and 639/94].

A test applicant must be the holder of a provisional lgv or pcv licence, provisional hgv licence or a full licence which is treated as a provisional entitling him to drive the test vehicle [16].

The test must be carried out on a vehicle of the category for which a full licence is sought and the examiner must be satisfied that the candidate is fully conversant with the Highway Code; that he has sufficient mechanical knowledge of the vehicle and the effects of load distribution; he is competent to drive without danger to others; and he can safely and competently carry out specified manoeuvres [17 & Sch.5].

A test candidate must comply with the following or the test may be refused:

(a) supply a suitable, unladen vehicle fitted with a seat (protected against bad weather) for the examiner and the vehicle must be such that the accelerator can be operated by the driver only. A pcv must be constructed so that the examiner can, from the same deck as the driver, have a clear view to the rear of the vehicle without the use of an optical device, except where the vehicle's construction makes that impracticable or the examiner agrees otherwise;
(b) sign a declaration that the vehicle is insured; and
(c) produce evidence of identity to the satisfaction of the examiner in the form of another specified driving licence or permit which bears his signature, a passport which bears his signature or an employment identity card which bears his photo and signature [18 and 639/94].

A pcv is not suitable for taking a test unless it is capable of a speed of at least 80km/h and
(a) a category D vehicle (not limited to 16 seats) has an overall length of at least 9m;
(b) a category D vehicle limited to 16 seats has an overall length of less than 9m;
(c) a category D+E vehicle comprises a category D vehicle in (a) above and a trailer with a permissible maximum weight of at least 1.25 tonnes [18(3)(b) and 3089/92].

Before 1 July 1996 a lgv is not suitable for taking a test unless:
(a) a category C vehicle has a permissible maximum weight exceeding 7.5 tonnes;
(b) a category C+E vehicle is either
    (i)   an articulated vehicle; or
    (ii) a category C vehicle and a trailer with at least two axles and the combination's permissible maximum weight is at least 15 tonnes [18(3A)(a) & 3089/92].

From 1 July 1996 a lgv is not suitable for taking a test unless it is capable of a speed of at least 80km/h and
(a) a category C vehicle has a permissible maximum weight of at least 10 tonnes and an overall length of at least 7m;
(b) a category C+ E vehicle is either
    (i)   an articulated vehicle with a permissible maximum weight of at least 18 tonnes and an overall length of at least 12m; or
    (ii) a combination of vehicles with a permissible maximum weight of at least 18 tonnes and an overall length of at least 12m comprising a category C vehicle with a permissible maximum weight of at least 10 tonnes and an overall length of at least 7m and a trailer with an overall length of at least 4m [18(3A)(b) & 3089/92].

A person who has passed tests to drive a vehicle in category C+E and in category D is deemed to be competent to drive vehicles in category D+E which correspond to the vehicle in category D [22].

A person taking a test must allow the examiner and any person authorised by the Secretary of State to travel in the vehicle [18(5)].

SUSPENSION AND REVOCATION—PSV

A psv licence must
(a) be revoked
  (i) if its holder develops a prescribed disability. These are the same as those listed in paragraphs (a) to (d) in the Medical Disabilities section above [2611/90/7(1) and 3085/92]; or
  (ii) if prescribed circumstances come into existence in relation to the holder. They are, in the case of an hgv licence holder who is under 21 years of age, that (A) his ordinary licence has more than 3 penalty points endorsed on it; or (B) his Northern Ireland ordinary driving licence has more than one relevant endorsement [2611/90/7(2)].
(b) be suspended or revoked if the holder's conduct or a physical disability makes him unfit to hold the licence [Act 1989/ Sch.1./paragraph 5(1)].

If a person comes within both paragraphs (a) and (b) action must be taken under paragraph (a) [5(2)].

SUSPENSION AND REVOCATION—LGV & PCV

An lgv or pcv licence must:
(a) be revoked if prescribed circumstances relating to the holder's conduct come into existence. They are that, in the case of an lgv licence holder under 21, his ordinary driving licence bears more than 3 penalty points [2612/90/12(1)].
(b) be revoked or suspended if the holder's conduct makes him unfit to hold the licence [Act 1988/115(1)].

If a person comes within paragraphs (a) and (b) action must be taken under (a) [115(2)].

DISQUALIFICATION

If the Secretary of State revokes a psv licence for a prescribed disability he must order the holder to be disqualified indefinitely. If he revokes the licence for prescribed circumstances he must disqualify the holder until he is 21 years of age or, at his discretion, for a longer period [Act

1989/Sch.1/par 6(1) & 2611/90/9]. If the circumstances cease to exist the Secretary of State must remove the disqualification if asked to do so [par 6(3)].

If he revokes a psv, lgv or pcv licence because the holder is unfit due to his conduct or, in the case of a psv licence, a physical disability he may:

(a) order the holder to be disqualified indefinitely or for a period he thinks fit, or

(b) except for the holder of a provisional licence, order him to be disqualified from holding a full licence until he passes a test to drive an lgv or pcv [Act 1989/Sch.1/par 6(2) & Act 1988/117(2)].

If a person is disqualified by a court from holding a licence the Secretary of State may also disqualify him from holding an lgv or pcv licence or disqualify him until he passes a lgv or pcv driving test [2612/90/12A & 1356/92]. If an lgv licence holder under 21 is disqualified by a court and his lgv licence would, under Section 115(1) above, have to be revoked because it bears more than 3 penalty points, the Secretary of State must also disqualify the holder until he is 21 years of age or for whatever longer period he decides [12A(3)].

Disqualification, in a case of licence revocation due to the holder's conduct as a driver, means being banned from holding or obtaining a licence to drive vehicles of categories C, C+E, D and D+E. And, where a psv or pcv licence is revoked for conduct other than as a driver, disqualified means being banned from holding a licence to drive passenger-carrying vehicles of categories D and D+E [Act 1989/Sch.1/paragraph 6(7) & 2611/90/9(3)—Act 1988/117(7) & 2612/90/14].

CONDUCT OF LICENCE HOLDERS

The question of a person's fitness to hold a psv, lgv or pcv licence by reason of his conduct may be referred, by the Secretary of State, to the traffic commissioner of the area in which the person lives [Act 1989/Sch.1/paragraph 5(4)—Act 1988/116(1)].

Conduct, in relation to the holder of an lgv licence, means his conduct as a driver and, in relation to the holder of a psv or pcv licence, conduct both as a driver and in any other way relevant to his holding such a licence [Act 1989/Sch.1/paragraph 1—Act 1988/121(1)].

A traffic commissioner may require the licence holder to supply him with information and may require the licence holder to appear before him, at a time and place specified, to give the information and to answer questions relating the matter referred by the Secretary of State [Act 1989/Sch.1/paragraph 5(6)—Act 1988/116(3)].

If the licence holder fails, without reasonable excuse, to supply information, appear before or answer questions properly put to him, the commissioner may notify the failure to the Secretary of State who may revoke or suspend the licence [Act 1989/Sch.1/paragraph 5(7)— Act 1988/116(4)].

If the traffic commissioner finds that a person is not fit to hold the licence he must also determine whether the conduct warrants revocation or suspension of the licence. If he favours revocation he must then decide whether or not the licence holder should be disqualified and, if so, whether indefinitely, for a fixed period or until the holder passes a test [Act 1989/Sch.1/paragraph 5(5)]—Act 1988/116(2)].

Except where he has notified a failure to co-operate, the traffic commissioner must notify the Secretary of State and the licence holder of his determination in the matter and his decision is binding on the Secretary of State [Act 1989/Sch.1/paragraph 5(8)— Act 1988/116(5)].

If the Secretary of State, without referring to the traffic commissioner, decides to revoke or suspend a licence he must notify the licence holder and, in a case of suspension, the traffic commissioner [Act 1989/Sch.1/paragraph 5(9)—Act 1988/116(6)].

APPEALS

A licence applicant aggrieved at its refusal or a licence holder aggrieved at suspension or revocation of his licence or disqualification can, after notifying his intention to do so to the Secretary of State and any traffic commissioner to whom the matter was referred, appeal to a magistrates court or, in Scotland, a sheriff in whose area he lives. An order by the court or sheriff is binding on the Secretary of State [Act 1989/ Sch.1/paragraph 7—Act 1988/119].

A driver can apply to the Secretary of State for a disqualification, imposed for reasons of fitness, to be removed as long as he has incurred no further penalty points or, in Northern Ireland, a relevant endorsement. The driver's application can be made after 2 years if the ban is for less than 4 years; after half the ban period if it is for 4 years or more but less than 10; and five years in any other case, including an indefinite ban [Act 1989/Sch.1/paragraph 6(4) & 2611/90/10—Act 1988/117(4) & 2612/90/13]. In the case of an lgv or pcv licence, the Secretary of State must consult the traffic commissioner if the matter was referred to him originally [Act 1988/117(4)].

When an application to remove a ban is refused, another such application cannot be considered if made within three months of the refusal [2611/90/10 & 2612/90/13].

Appeals against the conduct of a driving test can be made to a magistrates court in the same way as appeals relating to ordinary driving tests.

PRODUCTION, SURRENDER, ETC OF LICENCE

When required to do so by a certifying officer, vehicle examiner or a person authorised by a traffic commissioner (in each case, on production of his authority if required) or by a police constable the holder of a hgv or psv licence must produce it for examination. If production is required by police, the licence holder may produce it in person within the next 7 days at a police station he specified at the time of the request. If production was required by anyone else, the licence can be made available for examination within the next 10 days at an office specified by the person requiring production [2611/90/6].

Production of an lgv or pcv licence to police, examiners, etc. is governed by the law relating to ordinary driving licences.

If, during the currency of a driver's psv licence, his ordinary driving licence is revoked or surrendered, he must surrender his psv licence to the traffic commissioner of the area in which he resides [Act 1989/1(4)].

The holder of a psv licence who is disqualified from holding an ordinary driving licence (including a ban until a test is passed) or is refused an ordinary licence due to physical fitness must surrender his hgv or psv licence (or both) to the traffic commissioner in whose area he lives [2611/90/4].

The holder of a psv licence which has been suspended or revoked must, within 7 days of notice of that decision, send or deliver the licence to the traffic commissioner in whose area he lives for endorsement or cancellation. Northern Ireland licences go to the North Western traffic commissioner. If the holder fails to deliver the licence, a police constable or vehicle examiner may require production of it and seize it for endorsement or cancellation [2611/90/6(3)].

If a psv licence holder changes his name or address he must notify the Secretary of State of the new details and surrender his licence for replacement by a lgv or pcv licence [2611/90/3].

When an lgv or pcv licence is revoked the holder must return it to the Secretary of State when required to do so. On receipt of the licence the Secretary of State must issue to the holder a licence for the classes of vehicles not affected by the revocation [Act 1988/118(4)].

When an lgv or pcv licence is suspended the holder must, when required to do so, deliver it to the traffic commissioner of the area in which he lives. On receipt of a suspended licence the traffic commissioner must endorse it with particulars of the suspension and return it to the holder [Act 1988/118(5)].

LOST OR DAMAGED LICENCES

When a psv licence is lost the holder must notify the traffic commissioner who, if satisfied it has been lost and a fee is paid, will issue a duplicate. If the licence is subsequently recovered by the holder he must return it to the traffic commissioner. If a licence becomes defaced the holder must return it to the traffic commissioner who will, on payment of a fee, issue a duplicate. The fee for a duplicate licence is £6 and the holder must sign the licence in ink [2611/90/5 & 2491/91].

The loss of an lgv or pcv licence is governed by the law relating to the loss of ordinary licences.

NORTHERN IRELAND LICENCES

A psv, lgv or pcv licence granted under the law of Northern Ireland may, as respects Great Britain, be revoked or suspended by the Secretary of State who may also disqualify the licence holder. References to the traffic commissioner of the area in which the licence holder lives are to be taken as references to the traffic commissioner of the North Western traffic area. The magistrates court or sheriff to whom a Northern Ireland licence holder can appeal is (a) one he nominates when starting his appeal or (b) in the absence of such a nomination, the court in which the North Western traffic commissioner has his office [Act 1989/Sch.1/paragraph 9 & 2611/90/15—Act 1988/122 & 2612/90/24].

CLASSES OF EXISTING PSV LICENCES

Class	Psv
1	Double-decked vehicle without automatic transmission
1A	Double-decked vehicle with automatic transmission
2	Single-decked or half-decked vehicle without automatic transmission and over 8.5m overall length
2A	As 2 but with automatic transmission
3	Single-decked or half-decked vehicle without automatic transmission, over 5.5m but not over 8.5m overall length
3A	As 3 but with automatic transmission
4	Single-decked or half-decked vehicle without automatic transmission not over 5.5m overall length
4A	As 4 but with automatic transmission
4B	As 4 or 4A but restricted to uses specified in the licence

[2611/90/Sch.1]

ENTITLEMENT TO PCV CATEGORIES

The holder of an existing psv licence to drive vehicles of a class in column 1 below is authorised, during the currency of the licence, to drive vehicles of the categories in column 2.

Class of psv	Category of pcv
1 or 2	D and D+E
1A or 2A	As for 1 but limited to vehicles with automatic transmission
3	D
3A	D but limited to vehicle with automatic transmission
4	D but limited to vehicles not over 5.5m long
4A	As for 4 but limited to vehicles with automatic transmission
4B	B

[2611/90/16 and Sch.3]

International permits

A person over 18 years of age can obtain an international driving permit for use outside the United Kingdom if he holds a full licence or has passed a driving test and is a resident of the UK [1208/75/1 and 1095/80]. Permits are issued on behalf of the Secretary of State by the Royal Automobile Club, the Royal Scottish Automobile Club and the Automobile Association [1(8)]. The fee for a permit is £3 [Schedule 2 and 993/89].

A person who resides outside the United Kingdom, is temporarily in Great Britain and who holds an international driving permit, a domestic driving permit of a foreign country or a British Forces driving licence does not require a British driving licence during the 12-month period following his last entry into the UK. For full details see page 445.

Driving instruction

No instruction in the driving of a motor car for which payment of money or money's worth is, or is to be, made by, or in respect of, the person instructed may be given unless the instructor is registered as an approved driving instructor in a register maintained by the Secretary of State [Act 1988/123]. The only exceptions, apart from persons in Crown services, are police instructors [124].

The Motor Cars (Driving Instruction) Regulations 1989 control the examinations and tests of instructors.

5 Drivers' hours

Transport Act 1968
European Communities Act 1972
Road Traffic (Drivers' Ages and Hours of Work) Act 1976
Transport Act 1978
EC Regulation 3820/85
EC Regulation 599/88
European Agreement concerning the Work of Crews of Vehicles engaged in
    International Road Transport (AETR), Command papers 4858 and 9037
Drivers' Hours (Passenger Vehicles) (Exemptions) Regulations, **No. 145/70**
Drivers' Hours (Goods Vehicles) (Modifications) Order, **No. 257/70**
Drivers' Hours (Passenger Vehicles) (Exemptions) (Amendment) Regu-
    lations, **No. 649/70**
Drivers' Hours (Passenger and Goods Vehicles) (Modifications) Order, **No.
    818/71**
Community Drivers' Hours and Recording Equipment (Exemptions and
    Supplementary Provisions) Regulations, **No. 1456/86**
Drivers' Hours (Harmonisation with Community Rules) Regulations, **No.
    1458/86**
Drivers' Hours (Goods Vehicles) (Modifications) Order, **No. 1459/86**
Drivers' Hours (Goods Vehicles) (Exemptions) Regulations, **No. 1492/86**
Community Drivers' Hours and Recording Equipment (Exemptions and
    Supplementary Provisions) (Amendment) Regulations, **Nos. 1669/86,
    805/87** and **760/88**

Drivers of goods and passenger vehicles are generally subject to the
EC hours' law contained in EC Regulation 3820/85 but a large
number of exemptions from those rules are provided.

A driver who comes within one of the exemptions will be subject to
the British hours' law contained in Section 96 of the Transport Act
1968, as varied by regulations, unless he comes within exemptions
from the British law.

Drivers on international journeys to or through countries which are
not in the EC but which are parties to the European Agreement on
the Work of Crews of Vehicles engaged in International Road
Transport (AETR for short) have to comply with the AETR rules for

the whole of the journey instead of the EC Regulation. However, following major amendments in 1992, the AETR rules are now the same as the EC rules on international transport.

On a journey to, from or through a country which is neither in the EC nor a party to the AETR agreement (such as Switzerland) the driver of a vehicle registered in a Member State must comply with the EC law, the EC Court ruled in the case of *Van Swieten*, Case C313/92. That third country might also apply its own hours' rules to visiting vehicles.

EC hours' law

The EC Regulation applies to 'carriage by road' within the Community and 'carriage by road' is defined as any journey on roads open to the public of a vehicle, whether laden or not, used for the carriage of passengers or goods [3820/85/2].

The AETR rules apply, instead of the EC Regulation, to international road transport operations (a) to, from or through non-EC countries which are parties to AETR by vehicles registered in an EC or AETR country for the whole of the journey, and (b) in EC countries by a vehicle registered in a non-EC country which is not party to AETR [2].

DEFINITIONS

For the purposes of the Regulation a vehicle is a motor vehicle, tractor, trailer or semi-trailer. A motor vehicle is defined as 'any mechanically self-propelled vehicle circulating on the road, other than a vehicle running on rails, and normally used for carrying passengers or goods'. A tractor is 'any mechanically self-propelled vehicle circulating on the road, other than a vehicle running on rails, and specially designed to pull, push or move trailers, semi-trailers, implements or machines'. A trailer is 'any vehicle designed to be coupled to a motor vehicle or tractor' and a semi-trailer is 'a trailer without a front axle coupled in such a way that a substantial part of its weight and of the weight of its load is borne by the tractor or motor vehicle'.

A driver is any person who drives the vehicle even for a short period or who is carried in the vehicle to be available for driving if necessary.

A week is the period from 00.00 hours on Monday to 24.00 hours on Sunday and 'rest' means any uninterrupted period of at least one hour during which the driver may freely dispose of his time.

Permissible maximum weight is the maximum authorised weight of the vehicle fully laden [3820/85/1]. In *Small v DPP* [15 March 1994 and reported in *Commercial Motor* of 24 March 1994] the High Court ruled that the definitions in Section 108 of the Road Traffic Act 1988 should be used to interpret this provision and the permissible maximum weight of a van towing a drawbar trailer was the sum of the plated gross weights of each vehicle, not the plated train weight of the van.

DRIVING TIME

The driving period between any two daily rest periods, or between a daily rest period and a weekly rest period, (referred to as the daily driving period) must not exceed nine hours, but twice a week it may be extended to 10 hours [3820/85/6(1)].

After not more than 6 daily driving periods a driver must take a weekly rest period, but it may be postponed until the end of the 6th day if his total driving time over the 6 days does not exceed the maximum corresponding to 6 daily driving periods. (The key to understanding this small concession is appreciating that 6 daily driving periods can be completed in less than 6 days.) In the case of international passenger services, other than regular services, 6 and 6th can be replaced by 12 and 12th [6(1)]. Member States can extend the 12-day provision to national passenger services, other than regular services, and the Secretary of State for Transport has taken this action [1456/86/3].

The total period of driving in any fortnight must not exceed 90 hours [3820/85/6(2)].

In *Kelly v Shulman* [1989] RTR 84 it was ruled that a 'day' in Article 6(1) meant successive periods of 24 hours beginning with the driver's resumption of driving after his last weekly rest period.

BREAKS

After 4½ hours' driving a driver must take a break of 45 minutes unless he is then beginning a daily rest period [7(1)]. The 45 minute break can be replaced by breaks of at least 15 minutes each spread out over the driving period or immediately after it so that the requirement is complied with [7(2)]. In *Charlton v DPP* [1994] RTR 133 the European Court ruled (1) where a driver has taken a 45-minute break, either as a single break or several breaks of at least 15 minutes during or at the end of a 4½ period, the calculation provided in Article 7(1) should begin afresh, without taking into account the driving time and breaks previously completed by the driver and (2) the calculation provided for in Article 7(1) begins at the moment the driver sets in motion the tachograph equipment and he begins driving.

In the case of regular national passenger services, Member States can change the break requirement to one of 30 minutes after 4 hours' driving where taking a 45 minute break could hamper urban traffic flows [7(3)]. The Secretary of State has used this power in relation to specified services in four London Boroughs and in the cities of Birmingham, Bristol, Leeds, Leicester, Nottingham and Oxford [1456/86/3 & 1669/86/3].

During a break a driver may not carry out any other work but waiting time and non-driving time spent in a moving vehicle, a ferry or a train will not be regarded as other work [3820/85/7(4)].

Breaks taken under Article 7 may not be regarded as daily rest periods [7(5)].

DAILY REST PERIOD

In each period of 24 hours a driver must have a daily rest period of at least 11 consecutive hours but it may be reduced to 9 hours three times a week as long as an equivalent compensatory period of rest is taken before the end of the following week [8(1)]. Rest taken to compensate for a reduced daily rest period must be attached to a rest period of at least 8 hours and must be granted, at the driver's request, at the vehicle's or driver's base [8(6)].

The period of 24 hours commences at the time the driver activates his tachograph following a weekly or daily rest period and, where the daily rest is taken in two or three separate periods, the calculation must commence at the end of the period of not less than eight hours, the EC Court ruled in the case of *Van Swieten*, Case C313/92.

On days when the rest period is not reduced it can be taken in 2 or 3 separate periods within the 24 hours. Each period must be at least 1 hour, one of them must be at least 8 hours and when a daily rest period is split in this way it must be increased to 12 hours [8(1)].

If a vehicle is manned by 2 drivers, each driver must have a daily rest period of 8 consecutive hours within a 30-hour period [8(2)]. *Williams v Boyd* [1986] RTR 185 decided that to meet this provision two drivers must be on the vehicle while it is in motion. In that case, where four coaches each had a driver with a fifth driver acting as relief for each, it was held that none of the vehicles was double-manned.

A daily rest period may be taken inside a vehicle if it is fitted with a bunk and is stationary [8(7)].

Where a driver accompanies a goods or passenger vehicle which is carried by ferry or train the daily rest period may be interrupted once on condition that:

(a) the part of the rest period taken on land is taken before or after that part taken on the boat or train;
(b) the period between the two parts is as short as possible and does not exceed 1 hour before embarkation or after disembarkation (customs formalities being included in the embarkation or disembarkation operation);
(c) during both parts of the rest period the driver is able to have access to a bunk or couchette; and
(d) a daily rest period interrupted in this way is increased by 2 hours [9].

WEEKLY REST PERIOD

During each week one of the daily rest periods must be extended into a weekly rest period of 45 consecutive hours, but this period may be reduced to 36 hours, if taken at the vehicle's or driver's base, or to 24 hours if taken elsewhere. Any reduction in the weekly rest period must be compensated for by an equivalent rest being taken en bloc before the end of the third week following the week in question [8(3)].

A weekly rest period which begins in one week and continues into the following week may be attached to either of those weeks [8(4)].

Where, under Article 6 above, drivers on passenger services are allowed 12 days between weekly rest periods, the weekly rest period may be postponed until the week following that in which it is due and added to that second week's weekly rest [8(5)].

Rest taken to compensate for a reduced weekly rest period must be attached to a rest period of at least 8 hours and must be granted, at the driver's request, at the vehicle's or driver's base [8(6)].

BONUS BAN

Payments to wage-earning drivers, even in the form of bonuses or wage supplements, related to distances travelled and/or the amount of goods carried are prohibited, unless the payments are of such a kind as not to endanger road safety [10].

DELAY RELIEF

Provided road safety is not jeopardised and to enable him to reach a suitable stopping place, a driver may depart from the requirements of the Regulation to the extent necessary to ensure the safety of persons, of the vehicle or its load. The reason for any such departure must be recorded by him on his tachograph disc or duty roster [12].

In *Geldart v Brown* [1986] RTR 106, a case under a similar provision in the AETR agreement, it was decided that in order for the exception to come into operation there had to be a real emergency.

PASSENGER VEHICLE CONTROLS

The driver of a passenger vehicle on (a) a national regular service, or (b) an international regular service not over 100 km and which has terminals within 50 km of a frontier between two Member States, must carry a copy of the duty roster and service timetable. The undertaking must preserve the duty roster for at least 12 months. However, these requirements do not apply where a tachograph is fitted and used in a vehicle [14].

OPERATORS' DUTIES

Transport undertakings must organise drivers' work so that they are able to comply with the hours' and tachograph law and they must make periodic checks to ensure that these rules are complied with. If breaches are found the undertaking has to take appropriate steps to prevent their repetition [15].

Exemptions from EC hours' law

Exemptions are given both in the EC Regulation and, for national operations within the United Kingdom, in regulations made by the Secretary of State.

Vehicles exempt by Article 4 of EC Regulation 3820/85 are as follows:

1. Goods vehicles with a permissible maximum weight, including any trailer, not over 3.5 tonnes;
2. Passenger vehicles which, by their construction and equipment, are suitable for carrying not more than 9 persons including the driver;
3. Passenger vehicles on regular services where the service route is not over 50km;
4. Vehicles with a maximum authorised speed not over 30km/h;
5. Vehicles used or controlled by armed forces, civil defence, fire service or forces responsible for maintaining public order;
6. Vehicles used in connection with sewage, flood protection, water, gas and electricity services, highway maintenance and control, refuse collection and disposal, telegraph and telephone services,

carriage of postal articles, radio and television broadcasting, and the detection of radio or television transmitters or receivers.

In *DPP v Ryan* [1992] RTR 13 it was said that this exemption was capable of wide construction and was available to private contractors as well as public authorities. A contractor's vehicle used in connection with drilling water wells was held to be exempt;

7. Vehicles used in emergencies or rescue operations;
8. Specialised vehicles used for medical purposes;
9. Vehicles transporting circus and fun-fair equipment;
10. Specialised breakdown vehicles.

In *Hamilton v Whitelock* [1988] RTR 23 the European Court ruled that 'specialised breakdown vehicle' means a vehicle 'whose construction, fitments or other permanent characteristics are such that it will be used mainly for removing vehicles that have recently been involved in an accident or have broken down for another reason. Such a vehicle is not subject to (the tachograph requirements) whatever use is actually made of it by its owner'. In that case a vehicle fitted with lifting equipment was towing a trailer and both were carrying unroadworthy cars bought at an auction.

11. Vehicles undergoing road tests for technical development, repair or maintenance purposes, and new or re-built vehicles not yet put into service;
12. Vehicles used for non-commercial carriage of goods for personal use; and
13. Vehicles used for milk collection from farms and the return to farms of milk containers or milk products intended for animal feed.

The following vehicles, listed in the Schedule of the Community Drivers' Hours and Recording Equipment (Exemptions and Supplementary Provisions) Regulations 1986, as amended, are exempt the EC hours' law while on national transport operations:

1. A passenger vehicle which, by its construction and equipment, is suitable for carrying not more than 17 persons including the driver;
2. A vehicle used by a public authority to provide public services otherwise than in competition with professional road hauliers; but a vehicle does not come within this paragraph unless it is being used by:
   a. a health authority to provide ambulance services or to carry staff, patients, medical supplies or equipment;
   b. a local authority to provide social services for old persons or

welfare arrangements for physically and mentally handicapped persons;

c. HM Coastguard, a general or local lighthouse authority;

d. a harbour authority within the limits of a harbour for the improvement, maintenance or management of which it is responsible;

e. an airports authority within the perimeter of an airport owned or managed by it;

f. the British Railways Board, London Regional Transport and any wholly-owned subsidiary, a Passenger Transport Executive or a local authority for maintaining railways; or

g. the British Waterways Board for maintaining navigable waterways;

3. A vehicle used by agricultural, horticultural, forestry or fishery undertakings for carrying goods within a 50km radius of the vehicle's normal base, including local administrative areas the centres of which are situated within that radius. A vehicle used by a fishery undertaking does not come within this paragraph unless it is used to carry (a) live fish, or (b) a catch of fish from the place of landing to a place where it is to be processed;

4. A vehicle used for carrying animal waste or carcases which are not intended for human consumption.

The European Court, in the case of *W. Weddel & Co Ltd, Exeter Hide and Skin Co Ltd v F.A. Leyland* No. 90/83, ruled that 'waste' was those parts of an animal not intended for oral human consumption;

5. A vehicle used for carrying live animals between a farm and a local market or from a market to a local abattoir.

In *DPP v Sidney Hackett Ltd* [1985] RTR 209 the European Court ruled that 'local market' meant "the market which, having regard to geographical circumstances, is the nearest to a particular farm and at which it is possible to buy or sell, as the case may be, according to the needs of the normal, average-sized farms which may be considered typical of the area in question";

6. A vehicle used as a shop at a local market; for door-to-door selling; for mobile banking, exchange or savings transactions; for worship; the lending of books, records or cassettes; or for cultural events or exhibitions; and, in each case, specially fitted for such use.

The European Court, in *R v Thomas Scott and Sons (Bakers) Ltd* [1984] RTR 337, held that 'specialised vehicle', in this exemption's predecessor, meant a vehicle whose construction, fitments or other permanent characteristics guaranteed that it was used primarily for one of the listed operations. The same case also decided that door-to-door selling could include calls on potential wholesale customers such as shops, works' canteens, old people's homes and supermarkets provided that the activity of selling was characterised by frequent stops by the specialised vehicle.

In *DPP v Digby* [1992] RTR 204 it was held that a vehicle delivering miners' coal entitlements was not used for door-to-door selling because no sale was involved;

7. A goods vehicle, not over 7.5 tonnes permissible maximum weight, carrying material or equipment for the driver's use in the course of his work within a 50km radius of the vehicle's normal base, but excluding a vehicle if driving it constitutes his main activity.

In *DPP v Aston* [1989] RTR 198 it was held that fruit and vegetables carried by a greengrocer from a wholesale market to a retail market were not 'material for the driver's own use';

8. A vehicle operating exclusively on an island not over 2,300 square kilometres in area and not linked to the rest of Great Britain by a bridge, ford or tunnel open for use by motor vehicles;

9. A goods vehicle, not over 7.5 tonnes permissible maximum weight, propelled by gas produced on the vehicle or by electricity;

10. A vehicle being used for driving instruction with a view to obtaining a driving licence, as long as it or any trailer drawn is not being used to carry goods for hire or reward or in connection with a trade or business;

11. A tractor used exclusively for agricultural and forestry work;

12. A vehicle being used by the Royal National Lifeboat Institution for the purpose of hauling lifeboats;

13. A vehicle made before 1 January 1947;

14. Any vehicle propelled by steam.

15. A passenger vehicle over 25 years old, not carrying more than 9 persons including the driver, not used for profit and being driven in, to or from a vintage rally, to or from a museum or display or to or from repair, maintenance or testing.

The UK has been authorised by the EC Commission to grant a national exemption from the hours' and tachograph regulations to:

a. vehicles which, because of the dimensions of their load or their gross weight are required to have their movement notified to police; and

b. vehicles used exclusively within airports in connection with the operation of airports and which are not authorised or technically approved for travel on public highways outside airports.

No regulations have yet been made to implement these exemptions.

British hours' law

The British hours' law, contained in Part VI of the Transport Act 1968, applies to goods vehicles, described as:
(a) locomotives, motor tractors and articulated tractor units, and
(b) motor vehicles constructed or adapted to carry goods other than the effects of passengers;
and to passenger vehicles, described as:
(a) public service vehicles, and
(b) other motor vehicles constructed or adapted to carry more than 12 passengers [Act 1968/95(2)].

It does not apply to driving or work to which the EC hours' law applies [1458/86/2(1)], but where, during a working day, the driver of a vehicle to which the British law applies also spends time in driving a vehicle to which the EC law applies, the time spent on driving or work subject to the EC rules must be included when applying the British law. Time spent on EC-controlled driving or work is not to be regarded as a rest period under the British law [2(2)-(4)].

Therefore, the only drivers who can be subject to the British hours' law are those exempt from the EC law.

A driver is either an employee-driver or an owner-driver. An employee-driver is defined as a person who drives a Part VI vehicle in the course of his employment and an owner-driver is a person who drives such a vehicle for the purposes of a trade or business carried on by him [Act 1968/95(3)]. In *Alcock v G.C. Griston Ltd* [1981] RTR 34 it was held that an employer was the person who wanted the driver to drive for him and consequently an agency driver was an employee-driver of the vehicle operator and not the agency.

Driving means being at the driving controls of the vehicle for the purpose of controlling its movement, whether it is in motion or is stationary with the engine running [103(3)].

'On duty' in the case of an employee-driver means being on duty, whether for driving a vehicle or other purposes, in his employment as an employee-driver or in any other employment under the same employer. In the case of an owner-driver it means driving a Part VI vehicle in connection with the vehicle or its load [103(4)]. It is a question of fact in each case whether a driver is on duty or off duty during a 30-minute break—*Carter v Walton* [1985] RTR 378.

A working week is a week beginning at midnight between Sunday and Monday [103(1) & 1458/86].

GOODS VEHICLES

Where, during a working day, a driver spends all or most of the time he spends in driving Part VI vehicles in driving goods vehicles, he must not drive such goods vehicles for a total of more than 10 hours and his working day must not exceed 11 hours [96(1) & (3), 1459/86].

A working day is defined as (a) any working period which does not fall to be added to another such period, and (b) where a working period is followed by one or more such periods in the 24 hours beginning with the start of the first working period, the total of the work periods falling within that 24 hours. A working period is any period during which the driver is on duty [103(1) & 1459/86]. For example, if a driver working from 8am to 6pm every day, without an off-duty break in the middle, that 10 hours would come within paragraph (a) of the definition and be his working day. If he worked 7am to 12 noon and then 2pm to 6pm and did not start work again until 7am the next day, those two 4-hour periods would be a working day of 8 hours under paragraph (b); but if on the next day he started work before 7am, that time would have to be added to the 8 hours worked the previous day since it would fall within the 24-hour period beginning at 7am on that previous day.

If a driver does not drive Part VI vehicles for more than 4 hours on each calendar day of a working week he is exempt from the British law for the whole of that week [96(7)].

If, on a working day, a goods vehicle driver does not drive a Part VI vehicle, the working-day limit does not apply to him on that day [96(8) & 1459/86/2].

Site work

In counting the 10 hours daily driving in sub-section 96(1) and the 4 hours in sub-section 96(7) no account is to be taken of driving a vehicle in the course of agriculture or forestry operations when it is not on the road [96(9)]. Also discounted is off-road driving in quarrying, construction, reconstruction, alteration, extension or maintenance of a building or other fixed works of construction or civil engineering, including the construction, maintenance or improvement of roads. Time spent driving in connection with the improvement or maintenance of a road shall be regarded as if it were spent off the road [257/70/4 & 818/71/5].

Light goods vehicles

If a driver, in a working week, and apart from social, domestic and pleasure driving, spends all of the time when he is driving Part VI vehicles in driving a light goods vehicle:
(a) solely in connection with carrying on the profession of medical practitioner, nurse, midwife, dentist or veterinary surgeon;
(b) wholly or mainly in connection with carrying out any service of inspection, cleaning, maintenance, repair, installation or fitting;

(c) solely while acting as a commercial traveller and the only goods carried (apart from personal effects) are those for soliciting orders;
(d) solely while acting in employment of the AA, RAC or SRAC; or
(e) solely in connection with cinematography, radio or television broadcasting;

he is exempt from the limit of 11 hours on any working day falling wholly within that working week [1459/86/3(1)].

A light goods vehicle, for the above purpose, is a goods vehicle with a permissible maximum weight not over 3.5 tonnes or a dual-purpose vehicle and, in either case, is a vehicle to which Part VI applies [3(2)]. Permissible maximum weight has the same meaning as in driver licensing law on page 88.

Emergency work

Where, on a working day, a goods vehicle driver spends time on duty to deal with one of the emergencies listed below, he is exempt from the daily driving and working day limits on that working day as long as he does not spend time on such duty (except to deal with an emergency) for more than 11 hours.

The emergencies are:
(1) events which cause or are likely to cause such
  (a) danger to life or health of one or more individuals or animals;
  (b) a serious interruption in the maintenance of public services for the supply of water, gas, electricity or drainage or of telecommunication or postal services; or
  (c) a serious interruption in the use of road, railways, ports or airports;
  as to necessitate taking immediate action to prevent the occurrence or continuance of such danger or interruption;
(2) events likely to cause such serious damage to property as to necessitate taking immediate action to prevent the occurrence of such damage [1492/86/2].

PASSENGER VEHICLES

Where, during any working day or, as the case may be, working week, all or most of the time spent by a driver in driving Part VI vehicles is spent in driving passenger vehicles, the basic hours' law of Section 96 of the Transport Act 1968 has been modified [818/71] to provide the following limits and requirements:

Driving time must not exceed 10 hours in a working day [Act 1968/96(1)].

When a driver has been driving for 5½ hours and during that period he has not had a 30-minute break for rest and refreshment he must then take such a break unless the end of the 5½ hours marks the end of the working day; but this requirement does not apply if, in any continuous period of 8½ hours, a driver does not drive for more than a total of 7¾ hours, between the driving periods there are periods totalling at least 45 minutes in which no driving is performed and the last of his driving periods marks either the end of the working day or the start of a 30-minute break [96(2) & 818/71/4(2)].

The working day must not exceed 16 hours [96(3) & 818/71/4(3)].

Between any two successive working days a driver must have a rest period of at least 10 hours but, on three occasions in a working week, it may be reduced to 8½ hours [96(4) & 818/71/4(4)].

In every period of two successive working weeks a driver must have a period of 24 hours off duty. It may start in the second of the two weeks and end in the first of the next two successive weeks but, apart from any period which exceeds the minimum 24 hours, the overlap cannot be counted as part of a 24 hour rest period in those next two weeks [96(6) & 818/71/4(6)].

If a driver does not drive Part VI vehicles for more than 4 hours on more than two calendar days of a working week (and on those two days he complies with the above hours' rules) he is exempt from Section 96(1) to (4) on the other days of that week. If this situation arises in two successive working weeks the driver is exempt from Section 96(6) in relation to those weeks [96(7) & 818/71/4(7)].

If, on a working day, a driver does not drive a Part VI vehicle, Section 96(2) & (3) does not apply to him on that day [96(8) & 818/71/4(5)].

A working day, for passenger vehicle drivers, is defined as the total period of time the driver is on duty, together with breaks between on-duty periods, until a 10 hour or, where permitted, an 8½ hours rest period is taken [103(1) & 818/71/4(8)].

Emergency work

The driver of any passenger vehicle who spends time on duty to deal with an emergency is given liberal exemptions from the hours' law. An emergency here means 'an event which

(a) causes or is likely to cause such
    (i)   danger to the life or health of one or more individuals, or
    (ii) a serious interruption in the maintenance of public services for the supply of water, gas, electricity or drainage or of telecommunications or postal services, or
    (iii) a serious interruption in the use of roads, or
    (iv) a serious interruption in private transport or public transport (not being an interruption caused by a trade dispute

involving persons who carry passengers for hire or reward),
or

(b) is likely to cause such serious damage to property' in any of these cases 'as to necessitate the taking of immediate action to prevent the occurrence or continuance of such danger or interruption or the occurrence of such damage'.

Time spent by a driver on emergency work is deemed not to be driving time for the purposes of sub-section 96(1) and for sub-sections 96(1) to 96(6) be deemed to be time spent off duty [145/70/3].

Special needs

Twice a week a driver who works solely in connection with the carriage of blood for transfusions or the carriage of physically or mentally disabled people can have a working day of 14 hours provided that he is able to obtain rest and refreshment for periods which are at least equal to the time by which his day exceeds 10 hours [145/70/4 and 649/70/2]. This provision has been overtaken by the introduction of the 16-hour working day.

AETR rules

The European Agreement concerning the Work of Crews of Vehicles engaged in International Road Transport—known as the AETR agreement—applies, instead of the EC Regulation, to road transport operations by goods and passenger vehicles:

(a) to, from or through non-EC countries which are parties to AETR by vehicles registered in an EC or AETR country and for the whole of the journey; and

(b) in EC countries by a vehicle registered in a non-EC country which is not party to AETR [3820/85/2].

Paragraph (a) applies, therefore, to journeys involving Austria, the former Czechoslovakia, Norway, Sweden, Yugoslavia and the former USSR because these countries are not in the EC but are parties to AETR.

Paragraph (b) applies to vehicles from Switzerland, Poland, Hungary, Rumania, Bulgaria and Turkey because they are in neither the EC not AETR.

The AETR requirements are now virtually the same as the EC law hours' law in EC Regulation 3820/85.

Prosecutions and defences

It is an offence for the British hours' law to be contravened by (a) a driver and (b) any other person, being the driver's employer or a person to whose orders he was subject, who caused or permitted the contravention. But a person will not be liable to be convicted 'if he proves to the court that the contravention was due to unavoidable delay in the completion of a journey arising out of circumstances which he could not reasonably have foreseen'. It is also a defence for a person, described at (b), to prove that the contravention was due to the driver being on duty otherwise than in his employment and that he was not and could not reasonably have become aware of that fact [Act 1968/96(11) and Act 1976].

A company was held to have permitted hours' offences through the knowledge of its transport manager even though he was not an employee of the company—*Worthy v Gordon Plant (Services) Ltd* [1989] RTR 7.

If there is a contravention in Great Britain of EC Regulation 3820/85 regarding periods of driving, distance driven or periods on or off duty then the driver, his employer and any other person to whose orders he was subject who caused or permitted the contravention commits an offence [Act 1968/96(11A) and Acts 1972 and 1976]. The statutory defences to contraventions of the British law (described in the preceding paragraph) are also available to a person contravening the EC law in Britain [Act 1968/96(11B) and Act 1978/10].

Since Section 96(11A) deals only with contraventions of the EC law committed in Great Britain a driver cannot be prosecuted in Britain for a contravention of the EC law which arises entirely in another EC country. But, in the House of Lords case of *Fox v Lawson* [1974] WLR 247, it was held that in deciding whether an offence had been committed in Britain it was right to take into account work, driving and rest periods taken outside Great Britain which, if done or taken in Great Britain, would be taken into account when computing a driver's hours.

Vehicles used for police or fire-brigade purposes are exempt from the British hours' law [Act 1968/102(4)].

Except for naval, military and air force purposes, the British hours' law applies to Crown vehicles [102(1), (2)].

A court has jurisdiction to deal with an hours' or records offence under Part VI of the Transport Act 1968 as if the offence has been committed at the place:

(a) where the defendant was driving when evidence of the offence first came to the attention of a policeman or vehicle examiner;

(b) where the defendant lives or is believed to live at the time when proceedings are commenced; or

(c) where the defendant, his employer or, in the case of an owner-driver, the person for whom he was driving, has his principal place of business or his operating centre for the vehicle in question [Act 1968/103(7) and Act 1976].

In the case of *R v Abergavenny Justices* [1994] RTR 98 a check by police in Gwent on a driver's tachograph records revealed summary offences committed elsewhere by his employer and another driver. The High Court ruled that magistrates in Abergavenny had no jurisdiction under Section 103(7) above or under the Magistrates' Courts Act to deal with those offences.

EC standard enforcement procedure

Member States must organise regular checks, at the roadside and at operators' premises, covering each year a large and representative cross section of drivers, operators and vehicles. Each year, checks must cover at least 1% of days worked by drivers subject to the EC hours' law and at least 15% of the days checked must be at the roadside and at least 25% at the operator's premises [599/88/2].

Roadside checks must be at different places and cover an extensive part of the road network to make it difficult to avoid checkpoints and they must be carried out without discrimination of vehicles and drivers, whether of that country or foreign. When checking the driver of a vehicle registered in another Member State, the competent authorities in each Member State must assist each other [3].

At least twice a year Member States must undertake concerted operations to check drivers and vehicles at the roadside and, where possible, should be undertaken by two or more Member States at the same time [5]. Member States must exchange information ever year about breaches of the hours and tachograph regulations and the penalties imposed on non-residents and, for offences committed in another Member State, on their own residents [6].

6 Drivers' records

Transport Act 1968
EC Regulations 3820/85 and 3821/85
European Agreement concerning the Work of Crews of Vehicles engaged in International Road Transport (AETR), Command papers 4858 and 9037
Passenger and Goods Vehicles (Recording Equipment) Regulations, **No. 1746/79** and **2121/89**
Passenger and Goods Vehicles (Recording Equipment) (Amendment) Regulations, **Nos. 144/84** and **2076/86**
Community Driver's Hours and Recording Equipment (Exemptions and Supplementary Provisions) Regulations, **No. 1456/86**
Community Drivers' Hours and Recording Equipment Regulations, **No. 1457/86**
Passenger and Goods Vehicles (Recording Equipment) (Approval of fitters and workshops) (Fees) Regulations, **Nos. 2128/86** and **713/92**
Community Drivers' Hours and Recording Equipment (Exemptions and Supplementary Provisions) (Amendment) Regulations, **No. 805/87**
Drivers' Hours (Goods Vehicles) (Keeping of Records) Regulations, **No. 1421/87**

EC tachograph law

Recording equipment (the tachograph) must be installed and used in vehicles registered in a Member State and which are used for the carriage of passengers or goods by road [3821/85/3(1)].

Definitions in the EC hours' law of Regulation 3820/85—given in the preceding chapter—also apply to terms in the tachograph law [3821/85/2].

Exempt from the tachograph law are those vehicles exempt from the EC hours' law under both Regulation 3820/85 and British derogations [3821/85/3(1) & 1456/86/4]. They are listed on pages 113 to 116.

Also exempt are vehicles (a) on regular national passenger services, and (b) regular international passenger services with a route not over 100km and with terminals within 50km of a frontier between two Member States [3821/85/3].

Exemption is also made for a vehicle which is being used for collecting sea coal [1456/86 & 805/87].

Notwithstanding the exemption from the hours' and tachograph law given to vehicles used for 'carriage of postal articles', the Secretary of State has, under powers in Article 3(4) of Regulation 3821/85, applied the tachograph law to vehicles used for the carriage of postal articles on national transport operations, except for (a) vehicles with a permissible maximum weight not over 3.5 tonnes, and (b) vehicles used by the Post Office in connection with the carriage of letters [1456/86/5(1)]. Permissible maximum weight had the same meaning as in driver licensing law—page 88.

A tachograph may be installed in a vehicle or repaired only by fitters or workshops approved by a Member State. The fitter or workshop must place a special mark on the seals which it uses and lists of the fitters, workshops and marks have to be circulated between Member States. An installation plaque certifying that it has been properly installed must be fixed on or beside the tachograph [3821/85/12].

Employers and drivers are responsible for seeing that the equipment functions correctly [13].

An employer must issue a driver with sufficient record sheets to cover his period of work and having regard to sheets being damaged or being taken by an inspecting officer. They must be of an approved type suitable for use in the vehicle's tachograph. The employer must keep record sheets in good order for a year after their use and give copies to drivers who request them. The sheets must be produced or handed over at the request of an inspecting officer [14]. In the case of an agency driver, it was held in *Alcock v Griston* [1981] RTR 34 that the driver's employer for this purpose was the operator of the vehicle— not the agency which paid his wages—and the operator should have issued him with a record book.

A driver must not use dirty or damaged record sheets. If a sheet bearing recordings is damaged it must be attached to the spare sheet used to replace it [15(1)].

A driver must use a record sheet every day on which he is driving, starting from the moment he takes over the vehicle. A record must not be withdrawn before the end of the daily working period unless its withdrawal is authorised. A record sheet must not be used to cover a period longer than that for which it is intended. When a driver is away from the vehicle and unable to use the tachograph, periods of work and rest must be entered on the sheet in a legible manner. If there is more than one driver on the vehicle the record sheets have to be 'amended' so that the distance, speed and driving time recorded relates to the person who is driving [15(2)].

The EC Court has ruled, in the case of *M. Michielsen v Geybels Transport Service NV*, Case No. C394/92, that a 'daily working period' for the purposes of Article 15(2) above comprises the driving time, all other periods of work, the period of availability, breaks in work and, where the driver divides his daily rest into two or three separate periods, such a period, provided it does not exceed one hour. The 'daily working period' commences when the driver activates the tachograph following a weekly or daily rest period or, if the daily rest period is divided into separate periods, following the rest period of at least 8 hours. It ends at the beginning of a daily rest period or, if that is divided into separate periods, at the beginning of the period of at least 8 consecutive hours.

A driver must ensure that the time recorded on the sheet is the official time of the vehicle's country of registration. He must operate the switches enabling driving time, other working time and rest breaks to be recorded [15(3)].

A crew member must enter on the tachograph sheet:

(a) his full name;
(b) the date and place where use of the sheet starts and ends;
(c) the registration number of the vehicle and any other vehicle to which he changes;
(d) the odometer reading at the start of the first and end of the last journey recorded on the sheet and, if there is a change of vehicle, the same readings for the other vehicle or vehicles;
(e) the time any change of vehicle takes place [15(5)].

The tachograph must be designed so that an inspecting officer can read the recordings (if necessary by opening the instrument) relating to the preceding 9 hours without damaging the sheet. It must also be designed that it is possible, without opening the instrument, to verify that recordings are being made [15(6)].

A driver has to be able to produce record sheets for 'the current week' plus the last day of the previous week on which he drove [15(7)]. The European Court, in the case of *M. Nijs v NW Transport Vanshoonbeck Matterne*, Case C–158/90 (OJ C15 21.1.92), ruled that 'drove' meant drove a vehicle subject to the EC hours' law.

Where a tachograph breaks down or becomes defective an employer must have it repaired as soon as circumstances permit and, if the vehicle is unable to return to 'the premises' within one week of the breakdown or its discovery, the repair must be carried out en route [16(1)]. While the instrument is defective, the driver must mark on the record sheet—or a temporary sheet attached to it—the information not being correctly recorded by the tachograph [16(2)].

The construction of tachographs, their installation, use and testing are prescribed in Annex 1 to Regulation 3821/85. The following is a summary of the more day-to-day requirements.

The tachograph must be capable of recording the distance travelled and speed of the vehicle, driving time, other periods of work, breaks from work and daily rest periods, and the opening of the part of the equipment which contains the record sheet. If a vehicle has more than one driver the instrument must be capable of recording simultaneously, but distinctly and on separate sheets, the driving, work and breaks of both drivers. The tachograph must include a distance recorder, speedometer and clock which can all be seen by the driver. The distance recorder can measure either forward or reverse movements or forward movements only, but if reverse movements are shown they must not interfere with the clarity of other recordings.

The control for re-setting or winding the clock must be inside that part of the tachograph which contains the record cards, so that each time the instrument is opened a mark is made on the card. Where the clock controls the forward movement of the record sheet it must be capable of running 10% longer than the time value of the record sheets in use at the time. All internal parts of the tachograph must be protected against damp and dust, and the casing must be capable of being sealed to prevent tampering. The speedometer, odometer and clock must be provided with lighting. The odometer has to be able to record 99,999.9 kilometers in units of 0.1km. The speedometer must be calibrated in units of 1, 2, 5 or 10km/h.

Whether the tachograph records on either a strip or disc record sheet, there must be provision on the sheet to ensure that times on the sheet and tachograph correspond. A record sheet must cover a period of at least 24 hours. The part of the tachograph containing the record sheet and clock winder must be provided with a lock. The equipment must be fitted so that the driver has a clear view of it and, in the case of a vehicle with a two-speed rear axle, the tachograph must have an adaptation which operates automatically with selection of the different axle ratio.

Seals must be fitted to both ends of the speedometer drive cable, the adaptor and compensator for the two-speed axle, and the casing of the tachograph. If seals are broken a written statement of the reason must be available to the authorities.

A periodic inspection of the tachograph must be made every two years and may be carried out in conjunction with a roadworthiness test. The inspection must include a check that the equipment is working correctly, that it carries a type approval mark, that the installation plaque is fitted, that seals are intact and on the actual circumference of the tyres. A check that the distance and speed recorders and the clock are operating within the maximum tolerances allowed must be made at least once every six years and this check must include replacement of the installation plaque.

Application of EC law

Sections 97, 97A, 97AA and 97B of the Transport Act 1968, as amended, enable the EC tachograph law to be enforced in Great Britain. The vehicles to which the tachograph law applies are those goods and passenger vehicles which are subject to the British hours' law (listed on page 117) if, at the time, EC Regulation 3821/85 requires a tachograph to be installed and used in the vehicle [Act 1968/97(6)].

In such a vehicle a tachograph must be installed in accordance with EC Regulation 3821/85; it must comply with Annexes I and II of that Regulation; and it must be used as provided in Articles 13 to 15 of that Regulation [97(1), 144/84 and 1457/86]. A tachograph must not be repaired otherwise than in accordance with the EC Regulation [97(1) and 2121/89].

A tachograph is used under the EC law only if all the requirements of Articles 13 to 15 of EC Regulation 3821/85 are complied with [97(5)].

The British rules require that the driver must, unless he has a reasonable excuse, return a completed record sheet to his employer within 21 days of its completion [97A(1)(a)]. If two or more persons employ him as a driver he must supply each with the name and address of the other [97A(1)(b)]. An employer must, unless he has reasonable cause, secure that record sheets are returned by the driver within 21 days of completion [97A(2)]. Where a driver has two or more employers it is the one who employed him first to whom he must return the record sheets and who must ensure that they are returned [97A(3)].

In *Pearson v Rutterford* [1982] RTR 54 it was decided that a goods vehicle driving instructor who had an evening job driving goods vehicles for a different employer should have recorded his full-time job as work and not a rest period on the record sheet he kept for the part-time employer.

It is an offence for a person to forge, alter or use, with intent to deceive, any seal on a tachograph installed in, or designed for installation in, a vehicle to which the tachograph law applies [97AA and 2121/89].

In any proceedings under Part VI of the Act for an offence against the hours, records or tachograph law any record produced by a tachograph or any entry made on a record sheet by a crew member is evidence of the matter appearing on the sheet [97B].

British records' law

The requirements to keep a driver's record book, under the Drivers' Hours (Goods Vehicles) (Keeping of Records) Regulations 1987, apply to drivers of goods vehicles, and to employers of employee-drivers of such vehicles, in relation to journeys or work to which the EC rules do not apply [1421/87/4].

A driver's record book must contain a front sheet; instructions to drivers for completion of sheets; notes for guidance on use of the book; and weekly record sheets in duplicate together with carbon paper or other means of making simultaneous duplicates. Each page must be at least A6 format (105x148mm) and conform to the model prescribed (pages 135 to 138) [5].

Where an employee-driver is required to enter information in a record book the employer must issue him with a record book. If an employee-driver has more than one employer it is the one for whom he first acted these Regulations came into operation who must issue the book. Where an employee-driver ceases to be employed by the employer who issued him with a record book he must return the book to that employer and, if he has more than one employer, the one he next works for must issue him with a record book [6]. If a driver drives goods and passenger vehicles for different employers, it is the goods vehicle employer who must issue the record book [13(2)].

Before a record book is issued or used, an employer or owner-driver must enter or secure there is entered the information in items 4 and 6 of the front sheet. A driver must enter, and the employer of an employee-driver must cause him to enter, in accordance with the instructions to drivers for completing sheets, the other information on the front sheet and on the weekly record sheets. When making an entry on a record sheet a driver must ensure that a duplicate is made simultaneously [7].

If a driver, in a working week, drives both goods and passenger vehicles the information to be entered in his record book must include both employments [13(1)].

When a record sheet has been completed by an employee-driver he must deliver the book (including the duplicate sheet) to the employer who issued it within 7 days or earlier if the employer so requires. The employer must examine the completed sheet, sign it and its duplicate; detach the duplicate sheet; and return the book to the driver before he is next on duty. When all the sheets in a book have been used the driver must retain the book for 14 days after it was returned to him and he must then return it to the employer as soon as reasonably practicable [8(1) to (3)].

When a record sheet has been completed by an owner-driver he must, within 7 days, detach the duplicate and deliver it to the address given at item 4 of the front sheet [8(4)].

An employee-driver or an owner-driver will not be treated as having failed to deliver the duplicate record sheet within 7 days if he can show it was not reasonably practicable for him to comply with the requirement and that the duplicate was delivered as soon as was reasonably practicable [8(5)].

If a driver makes an entry in a record book he must not, until all the sheets in that book have been completed, make an entry in any other record book [8(6)]. An employee-driver must not make entries in a record book not supplied to him by his employer unless such a book was not available [8(7)].

An entry in a record book must not be erased or obliterated. A correction may only be made by striking the original entry through so that it can still be read and writing the correction nearby along with the maker's initials [8(8)].

Where an employee-driver has more than one employer for whom he drives vehicles subject to the hours' law, each employer who did not issue the driver's record book must require the driver to produce the book and enter on the front sheet the information required at item 5. An employee-driver must produce his record book for inspection whenever required to do so by such an employer or the employer who issued the book [9].

A driver must have his current record book in his possession at all times when he is on duty [10] including any time spent in driving passenger vehicles [13(1)].

Used record books must be preserved intact along with duplicate record sheets for 12 months starting, in the case of an owner-driver, from the time the book ceased to be used and, in the case of an employer, from the time the record book is returned by the driver under Regulation 8(3) [11].

EXEMPTIONS

Where a driver does not, on a working day, drive a goods vehicle other than one exempt from operators' licensing, or a Crown vehicle which would be so exempt, he and his employer are exempt from keeping records on that day [12(1)].

Where a driver does not, on a working day, drive a goods vehicle for more than 4 hours and outside a radius of 50 km of the vehicle's operating centre, he and his employer are exempt from keeping records on that day. The 4 hours does not include driving, when not on a road, for the purpose of agriculture, forestry or quarrying or in connection with construction, reconstruction, alteration, extension or maintenance of a building or other fixed works of construction or civil engineering, including road works. Driving on a road in the course of carrying out road works shall be treated as not being on a road [12(2)].

If, during a working day, a driver does not spend the greater part of his time driving goods and passenger vehicles, to which the British hours' law applies, in driving goods vehicles, he and his employer are exempt from record keeping on that day [12(3)].

The driver of a vehicle carrying postal articles on national transport operations to which the EC tachograph law has been applied, and his employer, are exempt from keeping a British record book when the vehicle is used in those circumstances [12(4)].

A tachograph can be fitted and used voluntarily at any time. If its fitting and use comply with the EC law the operator and crew member need not keep record books. This relief is not presented as an exemption but as a defence to a charge under the records law. The defendant has to prove that the tachograph was fitted and properly used under the EC law [Act 1968/98(4A) and 1746/79/3].

AETR rules

British or foreign drivers and drivers' mates who have to comply with AETR hours' rules (explained on page 121) must use a tachograph in the way described in the EC rules but, until 24 April 1995, the old-style individual control book can be used instead [AETR, Art. 10 and 13].

Prosecutions and defences

It is an offence to use, or cause or permit to be used, a vehicle to which EC Regulation 3821/85 applies unless it has a tachograph (a) installed under the Regulation, which complies with Annexes I and II of that Regulation and is being used in accordance with Articles 13 to 15 of that Regulation or (b) which has been repaired otherwise than in accordance with that Regulation [Act 1968/97(1), 1746/89, 144/84 and 2121/89].

In *Redhead Freight Ltd v Shulman* [1989] RTR 1 it was held that acquiescence in a driver's regular failure to complete tachograph records correctly could amount to permitting an offence but fell short of causing an offence.

It is a defence for a person charged under Section 97(1) to prove that he neither knew nor ought to have known that a tachograph had not been installed or repaired in accordance with EC Regulation 3821/85 [97(1A) and 2121/89].

A person will not be convicted of using or causing or permitting the use of a vehicle which is not fitted with a tachograph or in which it is not used if he proves that at the time the vehicle was going to a place where an EC approved tachograph was to be installed [97(2)]

It is also a defence to a charge of using a vehicle with a defective tachograph to prove that (a) it had not been reasonably practicable for it to be repaired by an approved fitter or workshop and (b) while it was unserviceable the crew member had kept a record of the information not properly recorded by the instrument [97(3)].

A person will not be convicted of using a vehicle with tachograph seals broken if he proves that (i) the breaking or removal of the seal could not have been avoided, (ii) it had not been reasonably practicable for the seal to be replaced by an approved fitter or workshop and (iii) the equipment was otherwise being used in accordance with Articles 13 to 15 of the EC Regulation [97(4)].

It is an offence for any person to contravene the British records' regulations but the employer of an employee-driver will not be convicted of failing to cause records to be kept if he proves to the court that he has given proper instructions to his employees regarding the keeping of records and has from time to time taken reasonable steps to secure that those instructions are being carried out [Act 1968/98(4)]. Neither will a person be convicted of contravening the record book law if he proves to the court that the vehicle in question was fitted with a tachograph and tachograph records were properly kept [98(4A) and 1746/79].

Where a tachograph is installed in a vehicle to which Part VI of the Transport Act applies, any record produced by the equipment is evidence of the matters appearing from the record [Act 1968/97B(1)]. Any entry made on a record sheet by a driver for the purposes of the EC Regulation is evidence of the matters appearing from that entry [97B(2)]. An entry made by an employee-driver in a British or EC record is admissible in evidence against his employer [98(5)].

The place where a records' offence can be brought before a court is the same as that for an hours' offence and is given on page 122/123.

Production of records, etc.

An officer may, on production of his authority if required (except that police in uniform do not have produce an authority), require any person to produce and permit him to inspect and copy—

(a)   any book or register which that person is required, under Section 98 (i.e. record books for drivers on national work exempt the EC rules), to carry or have in his possession;

(b)   any book or register as in (a) which that person is required to preserve;

(bb) any record sheet the person is required under the EC tachograph rules to retain or be able to produce;

(c)   if the person is the owner of a vehicle to which the hours' and records' law applies, any other document which the official may reasonably require to inspect to check that the Transport Act hours' and records' law is being complied with;

(d) any book, register or other document required to be kept by the EC rules or which the official may reasonably require to inspect to check that the EC hours' and records' rules are being complied with.

The officer can also require, by written notice, that any record sheet, book, register or other document referred to above, shall be produced at the office of the Traffic Commissioner by a specified time, but not within 10 days of the notice [Act 1968/99(1)].

In exercising his powers under (a) and (d) above an officer can detain a vehicle during the time required for inspecting and copying the records, books, etc [99(3)].

An 'officer' for the above and following purposes is a Ministry examiner; a person authorised for the purpose by a Traffic Commissioner; and a police officer.

Section 99(2) provides that an officer may—

(a) at any time enter any vehicle to which Part VI of the Transport Act applies and inspect the vehicle and any tachograph installed in it and inspect and copy any record sheet on the vehicle on which a record has been made by the equipment or an entry has been made;

(b) at any time which is reasonable in the circumstances, enter any premises on which he has reason to believe that such a Part VI vehicle is kept or any such record sheet, books, registers or other documents (listed in Section 99(1) above) are to be found, and inspect any such vehicle and inspect and copy any record sheet, book, register of other document he finds there [99(2)]. **The Order (SI 259/70) which brought this sub-section into force on 1 March 1970 specifically excluded those parts which 'relate to the entry and inspection of any vehicle or to any equipment installed on any vehicle for the purpose of Section 97 or any record mentioned in that Section'. Therefore, the only parts of Section 99(2) in force are those in paragraph (b) dealing with the entry into premises and the inspection of British record books or 'other documents'.**

It is an offence for a person to fail to comply with Section 99(1) or obstruct an officer acting under Section 99(2) or (3), but it is a defence to a charge of failing to produce British records to prove that the vehicle was fitted with a tachograph and records were being properly kept [99(4) and (4A)].

It is an indictable offence for a person to make, or cause to be made, any record or entry on a record sheet kept or carried for the purpose of the EC rules or any entry in a book, register or other document kept or carried for the purpose of the British records' law which he knows to be false or, with intent to deceive, alters or causes to be altered [99(5)].

If an officer has reason to believe an offence against Section 99(5) has been committed in relation to any record or document inspected by him, he may seize that record or document [99(6)].

Under Section 19(2) of the Police and Criminal Evidence Act 1984 a police officer has power to seize anything which is on premises (which includes a vehicle) if he has reasonable grounds for believing that (a) it is evidence in relation to an offence which he is investigating or any other offence and (b) it is necessary to seize it in order to prevent the evidence being concealed, lost, altered or destroyed. Ministry examiners do not have this power.

Calibration

In Great Britain the Secretary of State for Transport is the competent authority for approving fitters and workshops for the purposes of installing and repairing tachographs and for nominating bodies for carrying out periodic checks and inspections of tachographs [1746/79/4 and 144/84]. The fee for issue of an approval is £254 and, for its renewal, £103 [2128/86/3 and 713/92].

An approval or nomination must be in writing, specify its scope and may contain conditions as to fees; the places where the work is to be carried out; the procedure to be adopted in carrying out the work; records to be kept; training of persons carrying out the work; and the display of signs indicating that such work is carried out at approved places [4(2), (3)].

The Secretary of State must publish, from time to time, lists of approved fitters and workshops and the bodies nominated by him for checking and inspecting tachographs [4(4)].

MODEL FOR BRITISH DRIVER'S RECORD BOOK

RECORD BOOK FOR DRIVERS IN ROAD TRANSPORT

1. Date book first used ....

2. Date book last used ....

3. Surname, first name(s), and address of holder of book ....

4. Name, address, telephone number and stamp (if any) of employer/undertaking...

5. Name, address, telephone number and stamp (if any) of any other employer(s)...

6. Operator's Licence No. (Nos.)...

INSTRUCTIONS TO DRIVERS FOR COMPLETION OF SHEETS

FRONT SHEET

1. Enter your surname, first name(s) and address (item 3). Owner-drivers need not make any entry in item 3 unless their personal address is different from the address of their place of business.

2. Enter the date on which you first use the book (item 1).

3. Immediately after you have completed all the weekly sheets enter in item 2 the date on which you last made an entry in weekly sheet. If you cease to be employed by the employer who issued you with a record book enter the last date on which you were employed in item 2.

WEEKLY RECORD SHEET

4. Use a new sheet each week. A week runs from midnight on Sunday/Monday to midnight the next Sunday/Monday.

5. Complete boxes 1 and 2 at the beginning of each week in which you work as a driver.

6. Each day on which you do work as a driver complete boxes 3-9 in accordance with the instructions below.

7. Enter in box 3 for the day in question the registration number of any vehicle used during that day.

8. Complete boxes 4 and 5 at the beginning of each day on which you do work as a driver.

9. Complete boxes 6, 7 and 8 and 9 at the end of the day's work.

NOTES FOR GUIDANCE ON THE USE OF RECORD BOOKS

FOR EMPLOYERS

1. After completing items 4 and 6 on the front sheet, issue a record book to the drivers employed by you.

2. Give the holder the necessary instructions for correct use of the book.

3. When the record book is handed in to you by the drivers employed by you within seven days of the end of each week of driving, examine and sign the weekly record sheet (including the duplicate sheet) for the week to which it relates. Tear out and keep the duplicate sheets, leaving the top sheets in the book and return the book to the driver before he is next on duty.

4. When the used books have been handed back to you by the drivers employed by you preserve them together with the duplicate sheets for not less than one year.

FOR EMPLOYEE-DRIVERS

5. Ensure that items 1 and 3 on the front sheet are completed before you use the book.

6. This record book is personal. Carry it with you when on duty and produce it to any authorised inspecting officer on request. Hand it over to your employer when you leave the undertaking.

7. Produce this record book to your employer within 7 days of the end of each week of driving, so that he can check and countersign your entries. Keep the top sheets in the book.

8. When the book is completed, complete item 2 on the front sheet and keep the book for 2 weeks so that it can be produced at any time to an authorised inspecting officer and then hand it to your employer.

FOR OWNER-DRIVERS

9. Ensure that items 1, 3 (if applicable) 4 and 6 on the front sheet are completed before you use the record book. Enter your business address in item 4.

10. This record book is personal. Carry it with you when on duty and produce it to any authorised inspecting officer on request.

11. Tear out and keep the duplicate of each weekly record sheet at the end of the week to which it relates.

12. When the book is completed, complete item 2 on the front sheet. Preserve the used books and the duplicate sheets for not less than a year.

GENERAL

13. All entries must be made in ink or with a ball-point pen.

14. If you have to correct an entry, strike the incorrect entry through, write the correct entry near it and initial the correction.(These notes are for guidance only and reference should be made to Part VI of the Transport Act 1968 and, the Drivers' Hours (Keeping of Records) Regulations 1987 for particulars of the statutory provisions).

WEEKLY SHEET

1. DRIVER'S NAME

2. PERIOD COVERED BY SHEET ....
   WEEK COMMENCING (DATE) ....
   TO WEEK ENDING (DATE) ....

DAY ON WHICH DUTY COMMENCED	REGISTRATION NO. OF VEHICLE(S) 3	PLACE WHERE VEHICLE(S) BASED 4	TIME OF GOING ON DUTY 5	TIME OF GOING OFF DUTY 6	TIME SPENT DRIVING 7	TIME SPENT ON DUTY 8	SIGNATURE OF DRIVER 9
MONDAY							
TUESDAY							
WEDNESDAY							
THURSDAY							
FRIDAY							
SATURDAY							
SUNDAY							

10. CERTIFICATION BY EMPLOYER

I HAVE EXAMINED THE ENTRIES IN THIS SHEET
SIGNATURE ....
POSITION HELD ....

7 Lighting

International Carriage of Dangerous Goods (Rear Markings on Motor
   Vehicles) Regulations, **No. 2111/75**
Road Vehicles Lighting Regulations, **No. 1796/89**
Road Vehicles Lighting (Amendment) Regulations, **No. 2280/94**

Front position lamps

A front position lamp is used to indicate the presence and width of a
vehicle when viewed from the front [1796/89/3(2).

Except for a trailer with an overall width not over 1.6m, a trailer
made before 1 October 1985 with an overall length (excluding any
drawbar) not over 2.3m and a trailer for carrying and launching a boat,
every motor vehicle with three or more wheels and every trailer must
be equipped with front position lamps [18 and Sch. 1].

Two front position lamps must be carried so that the maximum
distance from the side of the vehicle to a lamp is 400mm in the case
of a motor vehicle first used on or after 1 April 1986; 150mm in the
case of a trailer made on or after 1 October 1985; 400mm in the case
of any other vehicle made on or after 1 October 1985; 510mm in the
case of a motor vehicle first used before 1 April 1986 and a trailer made
before 1 October 1985.

The maximum height above ground for a lamp is 1.5m, or if the
vehicle structure makes this impracticable, 2.1m. In the case of a
motor vehicle first used before 1 April 1986 and a trailer made before
1 October 1985 it is 2.3m. For a motor vehicle first used on or after
1 April 1986 and which has a maximum speed of 25mph the maximum
height is 2.1m. There is no minimum height requirement.

In the case of a motor vehicle first used on or after 1 April 1986 and
a trailer made on or after 1 October 1985 a front position lamp must
be visible through 80° outwards and 45° inwards (5° inwards in the
case of a trailer) and through 15° above and below the horizontal,
except that where a lamp is not more than 750mm above the ground
the latter angles are 15° above and 5° below the horizontal. On any
other vehicle the lamps must simply be visible to the front.

Front position lamps must show a white light but, if the lamp is incorporated in a headlamp capable of emitting only a yellow light, the light may be yellow.

The front position lamps on a motor vehicle first used on or after 1 January 1972 and a trailer made on or after 1 October 1985 must have an approval mark. On vehicles made on or after 1 October 1995 lamps must have an approval mark or British Standard mark. Lamps which do not have an approval mark must be visible from a reasonable distance. Except in the case of a trailer made before 1 October 1985, where two front position lamps are fitted they must form a pair, i.e. same height above ground and same distance from the centre line of the vehicle [18, Sch. 2 and 2280/94].

Any number of additional front position lamps may be fitted and of the requirements given above the only one which applies to them is that they show a white light or, where permitted, a yellow light [20 and Sch. 2].

A trailer made before 1 October 1985 does not require front position lamps when drawn by a passenger vehicle [6(2)] and a broken-down vehicle when being drawn does not require such lamps [6(7)].

See also section 'General exemptions' on page 167D.

Dipped-beam headlamps

A dipped beam is a beam of light emitted by a lamp which illuminates the road ahead of the vehicle without causing undue dazzle or discomfort to oncoming drivers or other road users [1796/89/3(2)]. A headlamp is a lamp used to illuminate the road in front of a vehicle and which is not a front fog lamp [3(2)].

A motor vehicle with three or more wheels first used on or after 1 January 1931 must be equipped with dipped-beam headlamps, but the requirement does not apply to a vehicle with a maximum speed of 15mph or to a vehicle first used before 1 April 1986 which is an agricultural vehicle or a works truck [18 and Sch. 1].

Two dipped-beam headlamps must be fitted, except that only one such lamp is required on a vehicle for more than 8 seated passengers (in addition to the driver) first used before 1 October 1969; a three-wheeled vehicle first used before 1 January 1972; and a three-wheeled vehicle first used on or after 1 January 1972 not over 400kg unladen weight and not over 1.3m wide.

Except for agricultural vehicles, engineering plant, industrial tractors and any vehicle first used before 1 January 1972 a dipped-beam headlamp, where two are required, must not be more than 400mm from the side of the vehicle. Where one such lamp is required it must, except for a bus with more than 8 seats first used before 1 October 1969, be fitted on the centre line of the vehicle or at any distance from the side provided a duplicate is fitted on the other side so they form a matched pair. In this latter case both lamps will be regarded as obligatory.

The maximum height above ground of a dipped-beam headlamp is 1,200mm but this does not apply to a vehicle first used before 1 January 1952; an agricultural vehicle; a road clearance vehicle; an aerodrome fire tender or runway sweeper; an industrial tractor; engineering plant; or an armed forces' vehicle. The minimum height above ground for a lamp is 500mm, except for vehicles first used before 1 January 1956.

Except for a three-wheeled vehicle with a maximum speed of 50mph, a dipped-beam headlamp fitted to a vehicle first used on or after 1 April 1986 must bear an approval mark or a British Standard mark.

A dipped-beam headlamp must be white or yellow and, in the case of a vehicle with at least four wheels first used before 1 April 1986, it must be 30 watts minimum, 15 watts minimum in the case of three-wheeled vehicle first used on or after 1 April 1986 which has a maximum speed of 50mph and 24 watts minimum for a three-wheeled vehicle first used before 1 April 1986.

When a vehicle is at its kerbside weight, a 75kg weight is in the driver's seat and any manual headlamp levelling device is set at the stop position, the alignment of a dipped-beam headlamp must, as near as practicable, be as follows:

(a) in the case of a vehicle with a maximum speed over 25mph,
   (i) if the lamp bears an approval mark, its aim must be set so that the horizontal part of the beam cut-off pattern is inclined downwards as indicated by the vehicle maker's marking or, where no marking is provided, 1.3% if the headlamp centre is not more than 850mm above ground or 2% if it is more than 850mm;
   (ii) if the lamp has no approval mark and it can also emit a main beam, its aim must be set so that the centre of the main beam pattern is horizontal or inclined slightly below the horizontal;
   (iii) if the lamp has no approval mark and it does not emit a main beam, its aim must be set so as not to cause undue dazzle or discomfort to other road users;
(b) in the case of a vehicle with a maximum speed not over 25mph, and regardless of approval marks, if the lamp can also emit a main beam its aim must be set as in (a)(ii) above, or, if not, as in (a)(iii) above.

A vehicle first used on or after 1 April, 1991 which is capable of exceeding 25mph and has dipped-beam headlamps bearing an approval mark must be marked, near the headlamps or maker's plate, with the maker's recommended setting for the downward inclination of the horizontal part of the cut-off of the lamp beam pattern when the vehicle is at its kerbside weight and a weight of 75kg is on the driver's seat. The setting must be a single figure (a) between 1 and 1.5% if the centre of the lamp is not more than 850mm above ground or (b) between 1 and 2% if more than 850mm.

The lamp must be constructed so that it can be adjusted while the vehicle is stationary and, where two dipped-beam headlamps are required, they must form a matched pair and be capable of being switched on and off simultaneously and not otherwise. On vehicles first used on or after 1 April 1986 dipped-beam headlamps must be designed for a vehicle intended to be driven on the left-hand side of the road [18 and Sch. 4].

Any number of additional dipped-beam headlamps may be fitted as long as they comply with the maximum and minimum heights (if specified), they are yellow or white, properly aligned and they can be adjusted while the vehicle is stationary. But a vehicle first used on or after 1 April 1991, with three or more wheels and a maximum speed over 25mph, may have only two additional dipped-beam headlamps which must form a matched pair, be designed for a vehicle intended to be driven on the right-hand side of the road and are wired up so that only one pair of dipped-beam headlamps can be lit at a time. They must also comply with height, colour, adjustment, alignment and single-switching requirements [20 and Sch. 4].

A dipped-beam headlamp must not be used as to cause undue dazzle or discomfort to other persons using the road or be lit while the vehicle is parked [27].

A dipped-beam headlamp is not required on a broken-down vehicle being drawn [6(7)].

Main-beam headlamps

A main beam is a beam of light emitted by a lamp which illuminates the road over a long distance ahead of the vehicle [1796/89/3(2)]. A headlamp is a lamp used to illuminate the road in front of a vehicle and which is not a front fog lamp [3(2)].

A motor vehicle first used on or after 1 January 1931 must be equipped with main-beam headlamps, but the requirement does not apply to a vehicle with a maximum speed of 25mph or a vehicle first used before 1 January 1986 which is an agricultural vehicle or a works truck [18 and Sch. 1].

Two main-beam headlamps must be fitted except that only one such lamp is required on a three-wheeled vehicle first used before 1 January 1972 and a three-wheeled vehicle first used on or after 1 January 1972 not over 400kg unladen weight and not over 1.3m wide.

Where two main-beam headlamps are fitted the outer edges of their illuminated areas must not be nearer to the side of the vehicle than the outer edges of the illuminated area of the obligatory dipped-beam headlamps. Where one main-beam headlamp is fitted it must be on the vehicle's centre line or at any distance from the side provided a duplicate lamp is fitted on the other side so they form a matched pair. In this latter case both lamps will be treated as obligatory. No maximum or minimum height is specified.

Except for a three-wheeled vehicle with a maximum speed of 50mph, a main-beam headlamp fitted to a vehicle first used on or after 1 April 1986 must bear an approval mark or a British Standard mark.

A main-beam headlamp must be yellow or white and, in the case of a vehicle first used before 1 April 1986, must be 30 watts minimum.

A main-beam headlamp must be made so that its direction of light can be adjusted while the vehicle is stationary and, except for a bus with more than 8 seats first used before 1 October 1969, where two such lamps are required they must form a matched pair and be capable of being switched on and off simultaneously and not otherwise.

Every such lamp must be constructed so that the light can (a) be deflected at the will of the driver to become a dipped beam, or (b) be extinguished by a device which at the same time either (i) causes the lamp to emit a dipped beam, or (ii) causes another lamp to emit a dipped beam. A motor vehicle first used on or after 1 April 1986 must be equipped with circuit-closed tell-tale for the main-beam headlamps [18 and Sch. 5].

Any number of additional main-beam headlamps may be fitted as long as they are yellow or white, they comply with the dipping requirements of the above paragraph, they can be adjusted while the vehicle is stationary and, in the case of a vehicle first used on or after 1 April 1991, have an approval mark [20 and Sch. 5].

A main-beam headlamp must not be lit when the vehicle is parked or be used so as to cause undue dazzle or discomfort to other persons using the road [27].

A main-beam headlamp is not required on a broken-down vehicle being drawn [6(7)].

Front fog lamps

A front fog lamp is a lamp used to improve the illumination of the road in front of a motor vehicle in conditions of seriously reduced visibility [1796/89/3(2)].

Any number of front fog lamps, which must show a white or yellow light, may be fitted to a motor vehicle except a vehicle first used on or after 1 April 1991 which can have only two such lamps. Where a pair of front fog lamps is used in conditions of seriously reduce visibility in place of obligatory dipped-beam headlamps they must be not more than 400mm from the side of the vehicle. The maximum height above ground is 1.2m, except for agricultural vehicles, road clearance vehicles, aerodrome fire tenders and runway sweepers, industrial tractors, engineering plant and armed forces vehicles. No minimum height is specified. A front fog lamp fitted to a vehicle first used on or after 1 April 1986 must bear an approval mark. No requirement is made as to the wattage of the lamp. It must show to the front and be so aimed that the top edge of the beam is, as near as practicable, 3% below the horizontal when the vehicle is at its kerbside weight and with a 75kg weight on the driver's seat [20 and Sch. 6].

A front fog lamp must not be used as to cause undue dazzle or discomfort to other persons using the road; it must not be lit otherwise than in conditions of seriously reduced visibility; and it must not be lit when the vehicle is parked [27].

Dim-dip devices and running lamps

A dim-dip device causes a dipped-beam headlamp to operate at reduced intensity and running lamps (other than front position lamps, end-outline marker lamps, headlamps and front fog lamps) are used to make a moving vehicle readily visible from the front [1796/89/3(1)].

Except for the armed forces, motor vehicles with three or more wheels first used from 1 April 1987 and capable of exceeding 40mph must be fitted with a dim-dip device or running lamps. Following the European Court ruling that the dim-dip requirement was in breach of EC Directive 756/76—which does not require such devices—and the UK had failed to fulfil its Treaty obligations, exemption has been made for a vehicle which complies with that Directive.

A dim-dip device must cause light to be emitted from the dipped-beam filament of each obligatory dipped-beam headlamp so that each light has, as far as practicable, an intensity of 10 to 20% of the normal dipped beam.

Running lamps must be a matched pair of front lamps each fitted where an obligatory front lamp may be fitted and capable of emitting white light of not less than 200 candelas directly to the front and not more than 800 candelas in total.

A dip-dim device or running lamps must operate automatically when the vehicle's engine is running or the starter key is in the normal position for driving the vehicle; the obligatory headlamps and any front fog lamp are switched off; and the obligatory position lamps are switched on (18, Sch. 3 and 2280/94].

These requirements do not apply to a broken-down vehicle being drawn [6(7)].

Rear position lamps

A rear position lamp is a lamp used to indicate the presence and width of a vehicle when viewed from the rear [1796/89/3(2)].

Rear position lamps are required on any motor vehicle with three or more wheels and any trailer [18 and Sch. 1].

A motor vehicle first used before 1 April 1986 and a trailer made before 1 October 1985 does not require any rear position lamp while a trailer fitted with such a lamp is attached to its rear [6(1)]. A broken-down vehicle being drawn does not require rear position lamps except between sunset and sunrise [6(7)]. See section on 'General exemptions' page 167D.

Two such lamps are required, except that only one is required on a bus with more than 8 seats first used before 1 April 1955. A motor vehicle with three or more wheels and a maximum speed of 25mph, and any trailer drawn thereby, requires four rear position lamps if the structure of the vehicle makes it impractical to comply with the following positioning and visibility requirements.

Lamps must be fitted at or near the rear of the vehicle and where only one lamp is required it must be fitted on the vehicle's centre line or offside. Where two lamps are required on a motor vehicle first used on or after 1 April 1986 or any other vehicle made on or after 1 October 1985 they must not be more than 400mm from the side of the vehicle and, in any other case, not more than 800mm. The minimum separation distance between a pair of lamps fitted to a motor vehicle first used on or after 1 April 1986 or any other vehicle made on or after 1 October 1985 is 500mm, or 400mm in the case of a vehicle less than 1.4m wide. Where four rear position lamps are required one pair must comply with the distance-to-side measurements and one pair with the minimum separation distance measurements given above.

Where one or two rear position lamps are required they must not be more than 1.5m above ground but, if the vehicle's structure makes it impractical, they may be up to 2.1m. But, in the case of a bus with more than 8 seats first used before 1 April 1986 there is no maximum height and in the case of any other motor vehicle first used before that date, a trailer made before 1 October 1985, an agricultural vehicle, an industrial tractor and engineering plant, the maximum height is 2.1m. Where four rear position lamps are required one pair of them must comply with the appropriate height limit above. On a motor vehicle first used on or after 1 April 1986 and any other vehicle made on or after 1 October 1985 the lamps must be at least 350mm above ground.

On a motor vehicle first used on or after 1 April 1986 and a trailer made on or after 1 October 1985 the lamps must be visible through a horizontal angle 45° inwards and 80° outwards. If four lamps are required on a vehicle the inner pair must be visible through the above angles and the outer pair through 80° outwards only. Rear position lamps on such a vehicle must also be visible through 15° above and below the horizontal except that where a lamp is less than 750mm above ground the lower angle is 5° below the horizontal and, where it is less than 1,500mm above ground, that angle is 10°. Where four rear lamps are required one pair must comply with the above angles and the other pair must be visible to the rear.

In the case of a motor vehicle first used before 1 April 1986 and any other vehicle made before 1 October 1985 no angles of visibility are specified but the lamps must be visible to the rear.

Except for a motor vehicle first used before 1 January 1974 and a trailer made before that date, rear position lamps must bear an approval mark. The lamps must be red and those which do not bear an approval mark must be visible from a reasonable distance. Rear position lamps fitted to a motor vehicle first used on or after 1 April 1986 and any other vehicle made on or after 1 October 1985 must form a matched pair and, if four lamps are required, they must form two matched pairs [18, Sch. 10 and 2280/94].

Any number of additional rear position lamps may be fitted as long as they are red. The above positioning and other requirements do not apply to such additional lamps [20 and Sch. 10].

Rear position lamps must not be used to cause undue dazzle or discomfort to other road users [27].

Number-plate lamp

Except for a works truck and a vehicle not required to be fitted with a rear registration plate, every motor vehicle with three or more wheels and every trailer must be fitted with a rear registration plate lamp [1796/89/18 and Sch. 1]. A broken-down vehicle being drawn does not require such a lamp [6(7)].

The number and position of lamps must be such that it or they are capable of adequately illuminating the rear registration plate. A lamp fitted to a motor vehicle first used on or after 1 April 1986 and a trailer made on or after 1 October 1985 must bear an approval mark [18 and Sch. 15]. The lamp must not be used so as to cause undue dazzle or discomfort to other road users [27].

Use of lamps

It is an offence for a person-
(a) to use, or cause or permit to be used, a vehicle in motion on a road between sunset and sunrise;

(b) to use, or cause or permit to be used, a vehicle in motion on a road between sunrise and sunset in seriously reduced visibility; or

(c) to allow to remain at rest, or cause or permit to be allowed to remain at rest, on a road a vehicle between sunset and sunrise,

unless every front position lamp, rear position lamp, rear registration plate lamp, end-outline marker lamp and side marker lamp with which the vehicle is required to be fitted is kept lit and unobscured [1796/89/24(1)].

If a trailer, not required to be fitted with front position lamps, is parked between sunset and sunrise without a vehicle attached at the front, it must be fitted with a pair of front position lamps which must be kept lit and unobscured [24(3)].

The requirements of Regulation 24(1) and (3) above do not apply to a vehicle which is parked in an area outlined by amber lamps or traffic signs to prevent the presence of the vehicle, its load or equipment being a danger to other road users [24(9)(c)].

Neither does Regulation 24(1) or (3) apply to a goods vehicle not over 1,525kg unladen weight or a passenger vehicle, other than a bus with more than 8 seats and, in either case, the vehicle is not drawing a trailer or carrying a projecting load which requires extra lights and it complies with specified conditions. The conditions are that the road must be subject to a speed limit of 30mph or less and the vehicle is parked in a statutorily authorised parking place; in a lay-by which is marked as such by a traffic sign, by a different surface or a different strip of surface; or in any other place if the vehicle is parked with its nearside close to and parallel with the nearside kerb (in a one-way street its offside may be against the offside kerb) and no part of the vehicle is within 10m of a road junction. The points at a junction from which the 10m is to be measured are shown in the diagram overleaf [24(5), (7)].

No person must use, or cause or permit to be used, on a road a vehicle fitted with obligatory dipped-beam headlamps unless every such lamp is kept lit (a) during the hours of darkness, except when on a road equipped with lighted street lamps not more than 200 yards apart (in Scotland 185m apart and on a Class C or unclassified road), and (b) in seriously reduced visibility [25(1)]. These requirements do not apply to: (i) a vehicle fitted with one obligatory dipped-beam headlamp if the main-beam headlamp or front fog lamp is lit; (ii) a vehicle with a pair of main-beam headlamps lit or, in seriously reduced visibility, a pair of fog lamps, not more than 400mm from the side of the vehicle, is lit; (iii) a vehicle being drawn by another vehicle; (iv) a vehicle propelling a snowplough; or (v) a parked vehicle [25(2)]. A light provided by a dim-dip device is deemed not to satisfy these requirements [25(3)].

The hours of darkness is the time between half an hour after sunset and half an hour before sunrise and daylight hours is the remaining time [3(1)]. Seriously reduced visibility is not defined in the Regulations.

Areas where unlit parking is not permitted near a junction

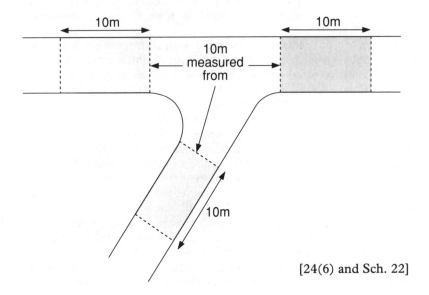

[24(6) and Sch. 22]

Restrictions on colour of lamps

No vehicle shall be fitted with a lamp or retro reflecting material capable of showing a red light to the front, except a red light from an authorised traffic sign, a red and white lamp fitted to a fire service control vehicle, a side marker lamp or side retro reflector [1796/89/11(1) and 2280/94].

A vehicle must not be fitted with a lamp or retro reflecting material capable of showing to the rear any light other than a red light, except an amber direction indicator or side marker lamp; a white reversing lamp; a white work lamp; a light to illuminate a vehicle's interior; a light from an illuminated rear registration plate; a taxi-meter light; a route indicator on a bus with more than 8 seats; a blue and white light from a lamp fitted to a police control vehicle; a white light from a red and white lamp fitted to a fire service control vehicle; a green and white light from an ambulance control vehicle; a light from a warning beacon (listed on pages 156 and 157); amber retro reflecting material on a road clearance vehicle; yellow retro reflective registration plates; yellow retro reflective material of a rear marking on a vehicle required or allowed to be fitted with the marking under Schedule 19 or fitted to a load carried by such a vehicle; light of any colour from an authorised traffic sign fitted to the vehicle; orange retro reflective material in a danger-load sign; or yellow reflective material in a children sign fitted to the rear of a bus [11(2) and 2280/94]. A road clearance vehicle is a vehicle used for dealing with frost, ice or snow on roads [3(2)].

Movement of lamps

A vehicle must not be used on a road if it, or any load or equipment, is fitted with a lamp, reflector or marking which is capable of being moved by swivelling, deflecting or otherwise while the vehicle is moving. This restriction does not apply to a headlamp which can be dipped only by movement of the headlamp or its reflector; a headlamp which can be adjusted to compensate for the effects of its load; a lamp or reflector which can be deflected to the side by the action of steering the vehicle; a headlamp or front fog lamp which can be wholly or partially retracted or concealed; a direction indicator fitted to a motor vehicle first used before 1 April 1968; a work lamp; or a warning beacon [1796/89/12].

A vehicle must not be fitted with a lamp which automatically emits a flashing light, except a direction indicator; a warning beacon or special warning lamp; a lamp or sign fitted to a vehicle used for police purposes; a green lamp used as an anti-lock brake indicator; a headlamp fitted to an emergency vehicle; or lamps forming part of a traffic sign [13].

Front retro reflectors

A trailer made on or after 1 October 1990, except an agricultural vehicle or a works trailer, must be fitted with a pair of white front retro reflectors not less than 350mm and not more than 900mm above ground level or, if the structure of the trailer makes that impracticable, not more than 1,400mm [1796/89/18 and Sch. 21].

A reflector must be not more than 150mm from the side of the trailer and the minimum separation distance between the pair must be at least 600mm or, if the trailer is less than 1,400mm wide, 400mm. They must be visible through a horizontal angle 30° outward and 5° inward and a vertical angle of 15° above and 15° below the horizontal. If a reflector is less than 750mm above ground the lower angle can be 5°.

A reflector must not be triangular shaped and must bear an approval mark.

Extra front retro reflectors can be fitted as long as they are not triangular and not red [Sch. 21].

Rear retro reflectors

A rear retro reflector is a retro reflector used to indicate the presence and width of a vehicle when viewed from the rear [1796/89/3(2)].

A motor vehicle with three or more wheels and any trailer must be equipped with rear retro reflectors [18 and Sch. 1]. A motor vehicle first used before 1 April 1986 or a trailer made before 1 October 1985 does not require rear reflectors while a trailer with such reflectors is attached to its rear [6(1)] and a broken-down vehicle being drawn does not require rear reflectors except between sunset and sunrise [6(7)]. See also section 'General exemptions' page 167D.

A vehicle must be fitted with two rear reflex reflectors but four are required on a motor vehicle with a maximum speed of over 25mph, or any trailer it draws, if the structure of the vehicle makes it impractical to comply with the following positioning requirements.

A rear reflector must not be more than 400mm from the side of the vehicle but on a vehicle for carrying round timber it may be up to 765mm and on a motor vehicle first used before 1 April 1986 or any other vehicle made before 1 October 1985, it may be up to 610mm from the side of the vehicle. No such distance is specified for a bus with 8 or more seats first used before 1 October 1954. On a motor vehicle first used on or after 1 April 1986 and any other vehicle made on or after 1 October 1985 the minimum separation distance between two reflectors forming a pair is 600mm or, if the vehicle is less than 1.3m, wide, 400mm. Where four reflectors are fitted one pair must satisfy the above distance-to-side requirements and one pair the separation distance requirement.

Rear reflectors should not be more than 900mm above ground level or, if the structure of the vehicle makes this impractical, 1,200mm. But, on a motor vehicle first used before 1 April 1986 or any other vehicle made before 1 October 1985, the maximum height is 1,525mm. If four rear reflectors are required one pair must comply with the above height requirements and the other pair must not be higher than 2,100mm. The minimum height for reflectors on a motor vehicle first used on or after 1 April 1986 or any other vehicle made on or after 1 October 1985 is 350mm.

The reflectors must be fitted at or near the rear of the vehicle, face to the rear and be red in colour.

On a motor vehicle first used on or after 1 April 1986 and any other vehicle made on or after 1 October 1985 the reflectors must be visible through a horizontal angle 30° outwards and inwards and a vertical angle 15° above and below the horizontal, but if a reflector is not more than 750mm above ground the latter angle can be 15° above and 5° below the horizontal. If four reflectors are required one pair must comply with the above visibility requirements and the other pair must be plainly visible to the rear. For a motor vehicle first used before 1 April 1986 and a trailer made before 1 October 1985 no visibility angles are specified but the reflectors must be plainly visible to the rear.

Reflectors fitted to motor vehicles first used on or after 1 July 1970 and before 1 April 1991 must bear an approval mark or a British Standard mark. Reflectors on a motor vehicle first used on or after 1 April 1991 must bear an approval mark. Reflectors on a motor vehicle first used on or after 1 April 1991 must bear an approval mark. Reflectors on trailers made on or after 1 October 1989 must bear an approval mark and trailers made before this date but on or after 1 July 1970 must bear an approval mark, British Standard mark or, if made in Italy, an Italian approval mark.

On a motor vehicle first used on or after 1 April 1986 and a trailer made on or after 1 October 1985 the two reflectors must form a pair or, if four reflectors are required, two pairs.

No vehicle, other than a trailer or a broken-down motor vehicle being towed, may be fitted with triangular-shaped reflectors [18 and Sch. 18].

Any number of additional reflectors may be fitted as long as they are red and, except where permitted, are not triangular [18, Sch. 18 and 2280/94].

Reversing lamps

A reversing lamp is a lamp used to illuminate the road to the rear of a vehicle for the purpose of reversing and to warn other road users that the vehicle is reversing or about to reverse [1796/89/3(2)]. Not more than two reversing lamps may be fitted, they must show a white light and the total wattage of any one lamp must not exceed 24 watts. The reversing lamp fitted to a motor vehicle first used on or after 1 April 1986 or to a trailer made on or after 1 October 1985 must bear an approval mark. Where a reversing lamp is fitted to a motor vehicle first used on or after 1 July 1954 the vehicle must be fitted with a circuit-closed tell-tale light to show when the reversing lamp is switched on unless the lamps electrical connections are such that it cannot be lit otherwise than by selection of reverse gear [20 and Sch. 14]. A reversing lamp must not be used when lit except for the purpose of reversing the vehicle [27].

Rear fog lamps

A rear fog lamp is a lamp used to render a vehicle more readily visible from the rear in conditions of seriously reduced visibility [1796/89/3(2)].

A motor vehicle with at least three wheels first used on or after 1 April 1980 and a trailer made on or after 1 April 1980 must be fitted with at least one rear fog lamp [1796/89/18 and Sch. 11]. On such motor vehicles and any other vehicle made on or after 1 October 1979 not more than two rear fog lamps may be fitted and, where two lamps are fitted on a motor vehicle first used on or after 1 April 1986 or a trailer made on or after 1 October 1985, they must form a matched pair [Sch. 11].

Exempt from rear fog lamps are vehicles with an overall width not over 1.3m; a motor vehicle with a maximum speed of 25mph; a motor vehicle first used before 1 April 1986 which is an agricultural vehicle or a works truck; a works trailer; and a trailer which is an agricultural vehicle [Sch. 1].

A motor vehicle first used before 1 April 1986 or trailer before 1 October 1985 is not required to be fitted with rear fog lamps while a trailer fitted with such lamps is attached to its rear [6(1)]. A trailer made before 1 October 1985 is not required to be fitted with rear fog lamps when drawn by a motor vehicle which is not required to have such lamps [6(3)].

A rear fog lamp to which the above provisions apply must be at or near the rear of the vehicle and, where one lamp is fitted, it must be on the vehicle's centre-line or offside. A lamp's minimum height above ground is 250mm and its maximum height 1m, except on an agricultural vehicle, engineering plant and a motor tractor the maximum height is 2.1m. There must be a minimum separation distance of 100mm between a rear fog lamp and a stop lamp and a fog lamp must not be fitted so that it can be lit by the application of the vehicle's brakes. A lamp must show a red light visible through 5° above and below the horizontal and through 25° inwards and outwards, but if two lamps are fitted this latter requirement is satisfied if any one of the lamps can be seen throughout the 50° sector. A rear fog lamp must bear an approval mark and a circuit-closed tell-tale light must be fitted to show when a rear fog lamp is in use [Sch. 11].

In the case of a motor vehicle first used before 1 April 1980 and any other vehicle made before 1 October 1979 any number of rear fog lamps may be fitted and the only requirements listed above which apply to them are the 100mm separation distance, that they do not operate by the application of the vehicle's brakes and that they are red [20 and Sch. 11].

No rear fog lamp must be used to cause undue dazzle or discomfort to the driver of a following vehicle; it must not be lit at any time other than in conditions of seriously reduced visibility; and, except in emergency, it must not be lit when a vehicle is parked [27].

Side marker lamps

A side marker lamp is a lamp fitted to the side of a vehicle or its load and used to render the vehicle more visible to other road users [1796/89/3(2)]. They must be used between sunset and sunrise and in seriously reduced visibility during daytime hours [22].

Side marker lamps must be fitted where the overall length of a vehicle or vehicles, inclusive of any load, is more than 18.3m and be placed on each side so that (a) one lamp is not more than 9.15m from the front of the outfit or load and (b) one lamp is within 3.05m of the rear of the outfit or load. Additional lamps must be fitted between (a) and (b) so that there is no space of more than 3.05m without a lamp.

Where a combination of two or more vehicles (excluding an articulated vehicle) carries a load supported by any two of the vehicles and the overall length of the outfit, including the load, is over 12.2m but not over 18.3m, side marker lamps must be fitted to each side so that a lamp is not forward of nor more than 1,530mm to the rear of, the rearmost part of the motor vehicle. Also, if the supported load extends more than 9.15m behind the rear of the motor vehicle, a lamp must be fitted in a position not in front of, and not more than 1,530mm to the rear of, the centre point of the length of the load.

The above requirements do not apply when a vehicle being drawn is broken-down or when a single vehicle fitted with a projecting special appliance or carrying a projecting load has the required illuminated marker boards on the projection [22 (2)].

Any trailer made before 1 October, 1990 not covered by the above requirements and which exceeds 9.15m in length (excluding its drawbar) must be fitted on each side with a side marker lamp so that it is not forward of, or more than 1,530mm to the rear of, the centre point of the trailer [Sch. 1 and 9].

Motor vehicles first used on or after 1 April 1991, with a maximum speed over 25mph and over 6m long must be fitted with side marker lamps. Exempt are passenger vehicles; an incomplete vehicle going for completion, storage or sale; and vehicles first used before 1 April 1996 complying with EC Directive 756/76. Trailers over 6m long made on or after 1 October 1990 must also be fitted with side marker lamps.

Exempt are incomplete trailers going for completion, storage or sale; an agricultural or works trailer; a caravan; a trailer for carrying and launching a boat; and a trailer made before 1 October 1995 complying with EC Directive 756/76. On these vehicles side marker lamps must be at each side, not more than 4m from the front nor more than 1m from the rear. The distance between adjacent lamps must be not more than 3m or, if not practicable, 4m [Sch. 1 and 9 and 2280/94].

Side marker lamps must show an amber light (or red within 1m of the rear of the vehicle) but on a pre-October 1990 trailer they may show white to the front and red to the rear. The light should be visible through 45° each side of a line at right angles to the vehicle's length and which passes through the centre of the lamp. The light must be visible from a reasonable distance and the lamps must be fitted not more than 2.3m above ground level [Sch. 9].

Additional side marker lamps may be fitted and the only conditions relating to such optional lamps is that they comply with the colour requirements [20 and Sch. 9].

Side retro reflectors

A side retro reflector is a reflector fitted to the side of a vehicle or its load and used to render the vehicle more visible from the side [1796/89/3(2)].

A motor vehicle with three or more wheels must be equipped with side reflectors but exempt is a vehicle with a maximum speed of 25mph; a goods vehicle first used on or after 1 April 1986 with an overall length not over 6m; a goods vehicle first used before 1 April 1986 with an overall length not over 8m; an incomplete vehicle going to a place for completion, storage or sale; a dump truck authorised under the Special Types Order; a mobile crane; and engineering plant [18 and Sch. 1].

A trailer over 5m overall length (excluding any drawbar) must be fitted with side retro reflectors but exempt is an incomplete trailer going to a place for completion, storage or sale; engineering plant; and a dump trailer authorised under the Special Types Order [18 and Sch. 1].

A motor vehicle first used on or after 1 April 1986 and a trailer made on or after 1 October 1985 must be fitted with at least two reflectors on each side so that the distance from the foremost reflector to the front of the vehicle does not exceed 4m, the distance from the rearmost reflector to the rear of the vehicle does not exceed 1m and the distance between two adjacent reflectors does not exceed 3m or, if not practicable, 4m. On such a vehicle, when viewed from the side, a reflector has to be visible through 45° to left and right; and be visible through 15° above and below the horizontal, except that a reflector fitted less than 750mm high has to be visible 15° above and 5° below the horizontal.

A motor vehicle first used before 1 April 1986 and a trailer made before 1 October 1985 must have two reflectors on each side with the rearmost one not more than 1 m from the rear of the vehicle and the other 'towards the centre' of the vehicle. On such a vehicle it has to be plainly visible to the side.

On any vehicle a reflector must face to the side; be at least 350mm and not more than 1,500mm above the ground; carry an approval mark; and not be triangular. Reflectors must be amber or, if within 1m of rear of vehicle, may be red [Sch. 17].

Additional side reflex reflectors maybe fitted and the only conditions relating to such optional reflectors is that they be amber in colour (or red where permitted) and not triangular in shape [20 and Sch. 17].

See section on projecting loads (below) in a case where a load obscures a side reflex reflector.

Projecting trailers, loads and equipment

(1) If a trailer not fitted with front position lamps projects on any side more than 400mm beyond the obligatory front lamp fitted on that side to a preceding vehicle in the combination, a lamp showing a white light to the front must be fitted to the trailer so that the trailer does not project laterally more than 400mm beyond it.

(2) If a trailer not fitted with front position lamps carries a load or equipment which projects on any side more than 400mm beyond the obligatory front position lamp fitted on that side to a preceding vehicle in the combination, a lamp showing a white light to the front must be fitted to the trailer, load or equipment so that the load or equipment does not project laterally more than 400mm beyond it.

(3) If a motor vehicle or trailer carries a load or equipment which projects on any side more than 400mm beyond the obligatory front or rear position lamp on that side either (a) the obligatory front or rear position lamp must be transferred to the load or equipment to which a white front or a red rear reflector must also be attached, or (b) an additional front or rear position lamp and a white front or a red rear reflector must be fitted to the vehicle, load or equipment.

(4) If a vehicle carries a load or equipment which projects beyond the rear of the vehicle or, in the case of a combination of vehicles, beyond the rear of the rearmost vehicle, more than 1m or, in the case of an agricultural vehicle or a vehicle carrying a fire escape, 2m an additional lamp showing a red light to the rear and a red reflector, both

visible from a reasonable distance, must be fitted not more than 1m or 2m respectively from the end of the projection.

(5) If a vehicle carries a load or equipment which projects beyond the front of the vehicle more than 1m or, in the case of an agricultural vehicle or a vehicle carrying a fire escape, 2m, an additional lamp showing a white light to the front and a white reflector, both visible from a reasonable distance, must be fitted not more than 1m or 2m respectively from the end of the projection.

(6) If a motor vehicle or trailer carries a load or equipment which obscures any obligatory lamp, reflector or rear marking either (a) the lamp, reflector or rear marking must be transferred to a position on the vehicle, load or equipment where it is not obscured, or (b) an additional lamp, reflector or rear marking must be fitted to the vehicle, load or equipment.

The installation and performance requirements relating to obligatory front and rear position lamps and rear retro reflectors do not apply to the additional lamps and reflectors required in paragraphs 1, 2, 4 and 5 above and apply only in modified form to those in paragraph 3. Such requirements apply in full to the lamps mentioned in paragraph 6.

The requirements of paragraph 6 in relation to obligatory stop lamps and direction indicators apply at all times whereas those in paragraphs 1 to 6 relating to other lamps, reflectors and rear markings apply only between sunset and sunrise or, except for obligatory reflectors, in seriously reduced visibility. It is an offence for a person to use, or cause or permit to be used, a vehicle on a road in contravention of the above requirements [1796/89/21].

Warning beacons and special warning lamps

A warning beacon is a lamp that is capable of emitting a flashing or rotating beam of light throughout 360° in the horizontal plane [1796/89/3(2)].

A special warning lamp is a lamp fitted to the front or rear of a vehicle, capable of emitting a blue flashing light and not any other kind of light [3(2)].

No vehicle, other than an emergency vehicle, can be fitted with a blue warning beacon or special warning lamp, or a device resembling either whether or not the beacon, lamp or device is in working order [16].

An emergency vehicle is defined as:

(a) a motor vehicle used for fire brigade or police purposes;
(b) an ambulance, being a motor vehicle constructed or adapted for

conveying sick, injured or disabled persons and which is used for such purposes;

(c) a motor vehicle owned by a fire salvage body and used for that purpose;

(d) a motor vehicle owned by the Forestry Commission or a local authority and used for fighting fires;

(e) a motor vehicle owned by the Secretary of State for Defence and used for bomb disposal; used by the Naval Emergency Monitoring Organisation in connection with nuclear accidents, etc. or used by Royal Air Force Mountain Rescue Service for rescue operations or emergencies; or used by the Royal Air Force Armament Support Unit;

(f) a motor vehicle used primarily by the Blood Transfusion Service;

(g) a motor vehicle used by H. M. Coastguard or Coastguard Auxiliary Service for giving aid to persons in danger or vessels in distress on or near the coast;

(h) a motor vehicle owned by the British Coal Corporation and used for rescue at mines;

(i) a motor vehicle owned by the RNLI and used for launching lifeboats; and

(j) a motor vehicle primarily used for conveying human tissue for transplant. [3(2)]

The following warning beacons or special warning lamps can be fitted to the vehicles mentioned as exemptions from the rule that no vehicle be fitted with a lamp capable of showing a light to the rear other than a red light:

(1) a blue beacon or special warning lamp on an emergency vehicle or from any device fitted to a police vehicle;

(2) an amber beacon fitted to a road clearance vehicle; a refuse collection vehicle; a breakdown vehicle; a vehicle with a maximum speed of 25mph; a vehicle with an overall width over 2.9m; a vehicle used for testing, maintaining, improving, cleansing or watering roads; a vehicle used for inspecting, cleansing, maintaining, adjusting, renewing or installing any apparatus on, under or over a road; a vehicle authorised under the Special Types Order; a vehicle used for escort purposes when not travelling over 25mph; a vehicle used by Customs and Excise for testing fuel; a vehicle used for surveying; and a vehicle used for statutory removal or immobilisation of vehicles;

(3) a green beacon fitted to a vehicle used by a medical practitioner;

(4) a yellow beacon fitted to a vehicle used at airports.

[1796/89/11(2)]

Blue warning beacons and special warning lamps may be used only at the scene of an emergency or when it is necessary or desirable to indicate to others the urgency of the vehicle's purpose or to warn persons of the presence of the vehicle or a hazard on the road [27].

Amber beacons may be used only at the scene of an emergency; when it is required, necessary or desirable to warn persons of the presence of the vehicle; and, in the case of a breakdown vehicle, while it is used in the immediate vicinity of an accident or breakdown or while drawing a broken-down vehicle [27]. A breakdown vehicle is a vehicle used to attend an accident or breakdown or to draw a broken-down vehicle [3(2)].

A green beacon may be used only on a vehicle while it is occupied by a medical practitioner and is used for the purpose of an emergency [27].

A yellow warning beacon may not be used on a vehicle while it is on a road [27].

There is no restriction on the number of warning beacons a vehicle may be fitted with. Any warning beacon must be fitted to the vehicle so that the centre of the lamp is not less than 1.2m above the ground. The light shown from at least one beacon (not necessarily the same beacon) must be visible from any point at a reasonable distance from the vehicle and the light must be displayed between 60 and 240 equal times a minute with the intervals between each display of light being constant [1796/89/20 and Sch. 16].

Obligatory warning beacons

A motor vehicle with four or more wheels and incapable of exceeding 25mph must not be used on an unrestricted dual-carriageway unless it, or any trailer drawn, is fitted with at least one amber warning beacon which is lit. This does not apply to a vehicle used before 1947 or to a vehicle crossing the dual-carriageway in the quickest practicable manner. An unrestricted dual-carriageway is a dual-carriageway with a central reservation and on which vehicles may lawfully be driven over 50mph [1796/89/17 and 3(1)].

The beacon must comply with the requirements described in the last paragraph of the preceding section [17 and Sch. 16].

Stop lamps

A stop lamp is a lamp used to indicate to road users that the brakes of a vehicle or combination of vehicles are being applied [1796/89/3(2)].

A motor vehicle with three or more wheels and any trailer drawn by a motor vehicle must be fitted with stop lamps. Exempt are a motor vehicle with a maximum speed of 25mph; a motor vehicle first used before 1 April 1986 which is an agricultural vehicle or a works truck; a motor vehicle first used before 1 January 1936; a trailer which is an agricultural vehicle or a works trailer [1796/89/18 and Sch. 1]. No motor vehicle first used before 1 April 1986 and no trailer made before 1 October 1985 is required to be fitted with stop lamps while a trailer fitted with stop lamps is attached to its rear [6(1)]. A trailer does not require stop lamps if it is drawn by a motor vehicle which is not required to be fitted with stop lamps [6(3)]. Stop lamps are not required on a trailer made before 1 October 1990 which is drawn by a motor vehicle fitted with one or two stop lamps if the dimensions of the trailer are such that when it is squarely behind the motor vehicle that vehicle's stop lamp(s) are visible from a point 6m behind the trailer whether it is loaded or not [6(5)]. A broken-down vehicle which is being drawn does not require stop lamps [6(7)]. See also the section 'General exemptions' on page 167D.

A vehicle to which stop lamp requirements apply must be fitted with two stop lamps, except that a motor vehicle first used before 1 January 1971 and a trailer made before that date require only one stop lamp. The lamps must face to the rear of the vehicle; where only one lamp is fitted it must be on the centre line or offside of the vehicle; and where two lamps are fitted they must form a pair at each side of the centre-line and be at least 400mm apart. In the case of a motor vehicle first used on or after 1 January 1971 and a trailer made on or after that date the minimum height above ground for stop lamps is 350mm; the maximum height is 1,500mm or, if the structure of the vehicle makes this impracticable, 2,100mm; each lamp must be visible through 45° to the left and right; and generally be visible through 15° above and below the horizontal. No minimum and maximum height is specified for the stop lamps of a motor vehicle first used before 1 January 1971 or a trailer made before that date and the only visibility requirement is that they are visible to the rear. A stop lamp fitted to a motor vehicle first used on or after 1 February 1974 or trailer made on or after that date must bear an approval mark. All stop lamps must be red and, except for a stop lamp fitted to a motor vehicle first used before 1 January 1971, a trailer made before that date and a lamp bearing an approval mark, a stop lamp must be between 15 and 36 watts. A stop lamp shall be operated by the application of the vehicle's service braking system or, in the case of trailer, the drawing vehicle's service braking system [18 and Sch. 12].

Any number of additional stop lamps can be fitted but they must comply with all the above requirements except those relating to position and angles of visibility. And, on a motor vehicle first used on or after 1 April 1991, a stop lamp fitted centrally or to project light through the rear window must not be less than 20 nor more than 60 candelas [20 and Sch. 12].

A stop lamp must not be used as to cause undue dazzle or discomfort to other persons using the road [27].

Direction indicators

A direction indicator is a lamp on a vehicle used to indicate to other road users that the driver intends to change direction to the left or to the right [1796/89/3(2)].

Direction indicators must be fitted to motor vehicles with three or more wheels and to trailers drawn by motor vehicles. Exempt are motor vehicles first used before 1 January 1936; a motor vehicle with a maximum speed of 15mph; a motor vehicle which is an agricultural vehicle with an unladen weight not over 255kg; a motor vehicle first used before 1 April 1986 which is an agricultural vehicle, industrial tractor or works truck; a trailer made before 1 September 1965; a trailer made before 1 October 1990 which is an agricultural vehicle or a works trailer [18 and Sch. 1].

Rear direction indicators are not required on a motor vehicle first used before 1 April 1986 or a trailer made before 1 October 1985 while a trailer fitted with such lamps is attached to its rear [6(1)]. Direction indicators are not required on a trailer made before 1 October 1985 while it is drawn by a motor vehicle not required to be fitted with such lamps [6(3)]. Direction indicators are not required on a trailer made before 1 October 1990 if it is drawn by a motor vehicle which is fitted with two or more direction indicators if the dimensions of the trailer are such that when it is squarely behind the motor vehicle at least one indicator on each side of that vehicle is visible from a point 6 m behind the trailer whether it is loaded or not [6(5)]. A broken-down vehicle while being drawn does not require direction indicators [6(7)]. See also the 'General exemptions' section on page 167D.

All direction indicators, whether compulsory or optional, must comply with the following requirements [1796/89/18, 20, Sch. 7 and 2280/94].

(1) A motor vehicle with three or more wheels first used on or after 1 April 1986 must have, on each side, a single Category 1 front indicator, one or two (but not more than two) Category 2 rear indicators and, except for a vehicle with a maximum speed of 25mph, at least one Category 5 side repeater indicator. A trailer made on or after 1 October 1985 must have, on each side, one or two (but not more than two) Category 2 rear indicators. Additional indicators may be fitted to the side (excluding front and rear) of any such motor vehicle or trailer. Side repeater indicators must be not more than 2.6m

from the front of the vehicle and any indicator must be not more than 400mm from the side of the vehicle. The separation distance between indicators on opposite sides of the vehicle must be at least 500mm or, if the vehicle is less than 1.4m wide, 400mm. A front indicator fitted to a motor vehicle first used on or after 1 April 1995 must generally be at least 40mm away from any dipped-beam headlamp or front fog lamp. The minimum height above ground for an indicator is 350mm and, except for a motor vehicle with a maximum speed not over 25mph, the maximum height is 1.5m or, if the vehicle's structure makes this impractical, 2.3m. If two pairs of rear indicators are fitted there is no maximum height for one of the pairs. The angles of horizontal visibility of front, rear and side indicators are shown in the accompanying diagram. In the case of a motor vehicle with a maximum speed not over 25mph the inward angle for a front and rear indicator is 3° instead of 45° and where it is impractical to comply with the 5 degree blind angle of a side indicator this may be replaced by 10°. Indicators must also be visible through an angle of 15° above and below the horizontal, except that on a motor vehicle with a maximum speed not over 25mph the angles are 15° above and 10° below the horizontal if the lamp is less than 1.9m above ground and, on any vehicle where the lamp is less than 750mm above ground the angles are 15° above and 5° below the horizontal. Indicators must bear an approval mark and where two front or rear direction indicators are fitted they must be fitted to form a pair. If four rear indicators are fitted they must form two pairs.

(2) A motor vehicle first used on or after 1 April 1936 and before 1 April 1986 and a trailer made on or after 1 April 1936 and before 1 October 1985 must have, on each side, an arrangement of indicators which satisfy prescribed angles of visibility, but not more than one front and two rear indicators may be fitted at each side. Additional indicators may be fitted to the side (but not the front or rear) of a vehicle. The angles of visibility have to be such that at least one (but not necessarily the same) indicator on each side is plainly visible to the rear in the case of a trailer and to the front and rear in the case of any other vehicle. The minimum height above ground for an indicator fitted to a vehicle of this age is 350mm but no maximum height is specified.

(3) A motor vehicle first used before 1 January 1936 and a trailer made before that date must have an arrangement of indicators so as to make the intentions of the driver clear to other road users. The minimum height of any such indicator is 350mm.

All direction indicators must be amber in colour, except that in the case of a motor vehicle first used before 1 September 1965 and any trailer drawn thereby an indicator which shows only to the front may be white or amber, an indicator which shows only to the rear may be red or amber and an indicator which shows both to front and rear must be amber. A front or rear flashing indicator which does not have an approval mark must be of 15 to 36 watts and any indicator which does not have an approval mark must show a light visible from a reasonable distance. All indicators on one side of the vehicle and any trailer it draws must be operated by one switch and, if they are flashing indicators, they must flash in phase. At least one indicator on each side of the vehicle should be designed and fitted so that the driver, when in his seat, can readily be aware that it is in operation or the vehicle must be equipped with an operational tell-tale for front and rear indicators (including any rear indicators on the rearmost of any trailers drawn). (An operational tell-tale is an audible or visible warning device [3(2)]). Every indicator, except a semaphore arm, must flash between 60 and 120 times a minute and must perform efficiently regardless of the speed of the vehicle.

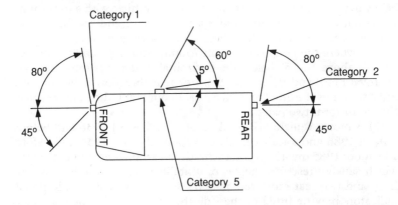

Categories of direction indicators showing their horizontal angles of visibility

Hazard warning

A hazard warning signal device is a device which is capable of operating simultaneously all the direction indicators with which a vehicle, or a combination of vehicles, is fitted [1796/89/3(2)].

Except where direction indicators are not fitted, a motor vehicle with three or more wheels and first used on or after 1 April 1986 must be fitted with a hazard warning signal device [18 and Sch. 1]. Such a device must be operated by one switch; cause all the direction indicators of the vehicle and any trailer drawn to flash in phase; have a closed-circuit tell-tale in the form of a flashing light which may operate in conjunction with the direction indicator tell-tale; and be able to function irrespective of the engine-start control [18 and Sch. 8].

A hazard warning light device which is fitted voluntarily to motor vehicles used before the above date must also comply with the above requirements [20 and Sch. 8].

A hazard warning device may be used only for (a) warning road users of a temporary obstruction when the vehicle is at rest, (b) in the case of a bus with more than 8 seats, for summoning assistance for the driver, conductor or inspector on the vehicle, (c) on a motorway or unrestricted dual-carriageway, to warn following drivers to slow down due to a temporary obstruction ahead or (d) in the case of a bus fitted with the prescribed children sign, when the vehicle is stationary and children under the age of 16 years are entering or leaving the vehicle, or about to enter or leave or have just left the vehicle [27 and 2280/94].

Reflective rear markings

Motor vehicles over 7,500kg plated design gross weight and trailers over 3,500kg plated design gross weight must be fitted with red and yellow rear markings [1796/89/18 and Sch. 1].

The following are exempt:

(a) a motor vehicle with a maximum speed of 25mph;
(b) a motor vehicle first used before 1 August 1982 not over 3,050kg unladen;
(c) a passenger vehicle other than an articulated bus;
(d) a tractive unit for an articulated vehicle;
(e) an incomplete vehicle going for completion, storage or display;
(f) a motor vehicle first used before 1 April 1986 being an agricultural vehicle, a works truck or engineering plant;
(g) a motor vehicle first used before 1 January 1940;
(h) armed forces vehicles;
(i) fire fighting and fire salvage vehicles;
(j) vehicles for servicing or controlling aircraft;
(k) vehicles for heating and dispensing tar or other material for use on roads;
(l) trailers being drying or mixing plant for asphalt or macadam;
(m) vehicles for carrying two or more vehicles, vehicle bodies or boats;
(n) a trailer drawn by a bus with more than 8 seats;
(o) a trailer made before 1 August 1982 not over 1,020kg unladen;
(p) a trailer which is an agricultural vehicle, works trailer or engineering plant

[18 and Sch. 1]

A rear marking is not required on a vehicle if another vehicle in a combination of which it forms part would obscure the marking [6(6)] and a rear marking is not required on a broken-down vehicle being drawn [6(7)].

See also the section 'General exemptions', page 167D.

A motor vehicle with a plated design gross weight over 7,500kg or an unladen weight over 3,000kg; a trailer with a plated design gross weight over 3,500kg or an unladen weight over 1,000kg; or a trailer being drawn by a vehicle which is required or permitted to be fitted with a rear marking, may be fitted with any number of rear markings (even if it is an exempt vehicle) as long as they comply with the requirements specified below [20 and Sch. 19].

A vehicle not mentioned above must not be fitted with rear markings [Sch. 19].

A motor vehicle first used before 1 April 1996 not over 13m long must be fitted with a rear marking complying with diagrams 1, 2 or 3 shown on page 165 or diagrams 1, 2, 3 or 4 on page 166. If over 13m long it must be fitted with a rear marking complying with diagrams 4 or 5 on the opposite page or diagrams 5, 6, 7 or 8 on page 167.

A trailer made before 1 October 1995

(a) forming part of a combination of vehicles not over 11m long must be fitted with a rear marking complying with diagrams 1, 2 or 3 shown on page 165 or diagrams 1, 2, 3 or 4 on page 166;

(b) forming part of a combination which is over 11m but not over 13m must be fitted with a rear marking complying with any of the diagrams on pages 165, 166 or 167;

(c) forming part of a combination of vehicles over 13m long must be fitted with a rear marking complying with diagrams 4 or 5 on page 165 or diagrams 5, 6, 7 or 8 on page 167.

A motor vehicle first used on or after 1 April 1996 not over 13m long must be fitted with a rear marking complying with diagrams 1, 2, 3 or 4 on page 166. If over 13m long it must be fitted with a rear marking complying with diagrams 5, 6, 7 or 8 on page 167.

A trailer made on or after 1 October 1995

(a) forming part of a combination of vehicles not over 11m long must be fitted with a rear marking complying with diagrams 1, 2, 3 or 4 on page 166;

(b) forming part of a combination which is over 11m but not over 13m must be fitted with a rear marking complying with any of the diagrams on pages 166 or 167;

(c) forming part of a combination of vehicles over 13m long must be fitted with a rear marking complying with diagrams 5, 6, 7 or 8 on page 167 [18, Sch.1 and 2280/94].

A rear marking must be at or near the rear of the vehicle; must not project beyond the side of the vehicle; the lower edge must not be

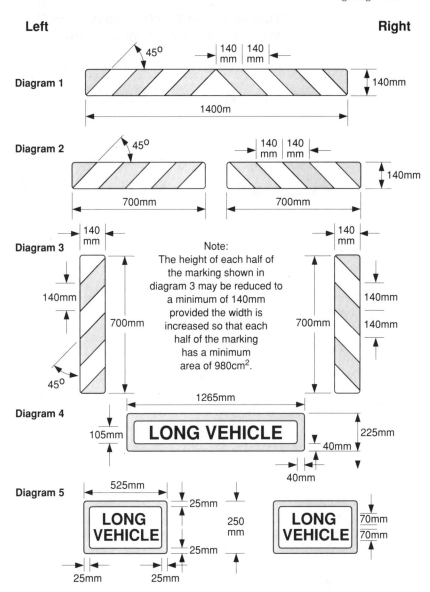

Size, colour and type of rear markings. The markings must consist of red fluorescent material in the shaded areas of the diagrams and yellow reflex reflecting material in the other areas. Letters must be black. The marking must be in the form of plates and marked with the specification number BA AU 152 [1796/89/Sch.19]

Rear markings prescribed for motor vehicles whenever first used and trailers whenever manufactured

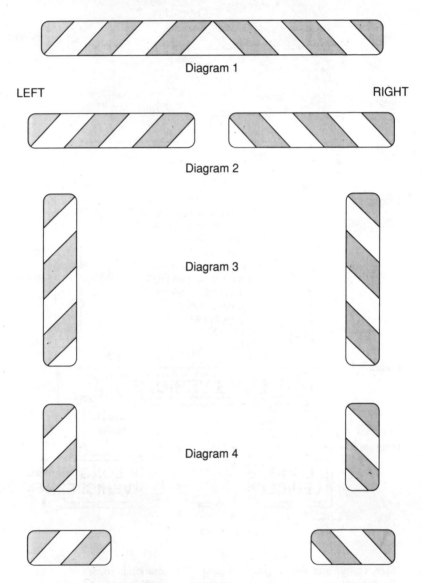

Diagram 1

LEFT   RIGHT

Diagram 2

Diagram 3

Diagram 4

The markings must consist of red fluorescent material in the shaded areas of the diagram and yellow retro reflective material in the other areas. No dimensions are specified in the regulations

Rear markings prescribed for motor vehicles first used and trailers whenever manufactured

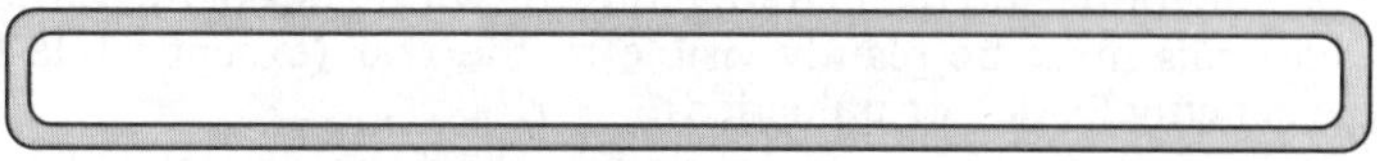

Diagram 5

LEFT   RIGHT

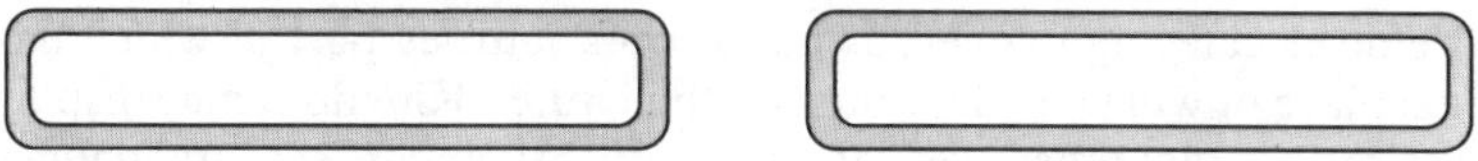

Diagram 6

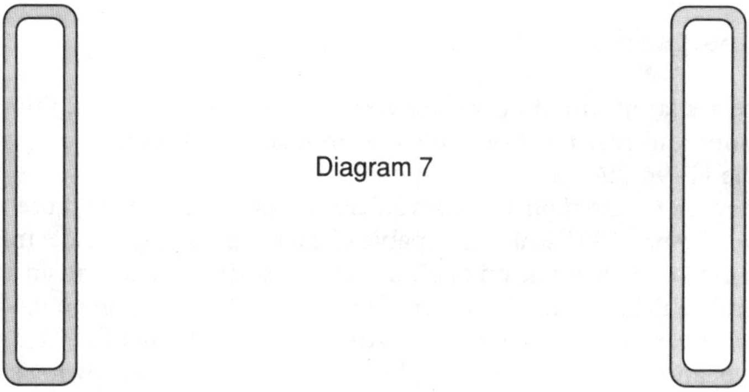

Diagram 7

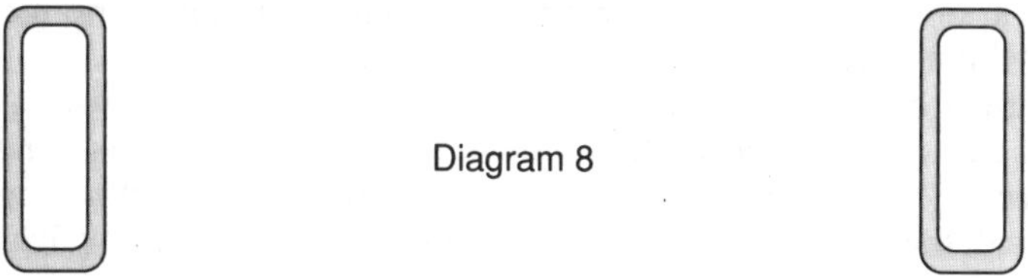

Diagram 8

The markings must consist of red fluorescent material in the shaded areas of the diagram and yellow retro reflective material in the other areas. No dimensions are specified in the regulations

higher than 1,700mm nor lower than 400mm above ground level; each part of the marking in diagram 2, 3 or 5 must be as near as practicable to the side of the vehicle; the centre of the marking in diagram 1 or 4 must be on the centre line of the vehicle; the lower edge of a marking must be horizontal and the marking must be within 20° of the vertical; and markings must be plainly visible to the rear (except while the vehicle is being loaded or unloaded).

The markings must be constructed in the form of plates, bear a British Standard mark and, in the case of those in diagrams 2, 3 and 5 they must be of equal size and shape and form a pair. Small tolerances are allowed on the specified dimensions [Sch. 19].

Vehicles carrying dangerous goods on a journey part of which has taken place or will take place outside the United Kingdom may display at the rear certain reflective plates indicating their contents and danger [2111/75].

End-outline marker lamps

These are lamps fitted near the outer edge of a vehicle, in addition to the front and rear position lamps, to indicate the presence of a wide vehicle [1796/89/3(2)].

They are required on a motor vehicle at least 2.1m wide first used on or after 1 April 1991 which is capable of exceeding 25mph and a trailer at least 2.1m wide made on or after 1 October 1990 other than an agricultural vehicle or a works trailer. They are not required on an incomplete vehicle going for completion, storage or sale [18 and Sch. 1].

Two lamps showing a white light to the front and two showing a red light to the rear, in each case forming a matched pair, must be fitted not more than 400mm of the side of the vehicle. The white and red lamp at one side of a vehicle may be combined into one lamp with a single light source.

At the front of a motor vehicle the top edge of the lamp must not be lower than the top edge of the windscreen. At the front of a trailer and at the rear of any vehicle they must be at the maximum height compatible with their lateral position, forming a pair and the use for which the vehicle is made. The light must be visible through an angle 80° outward from the side of the vehicle and 5° above and 20° below the horizontal. The lamps must bear an approval mark [18 and Sch. 13].

Any number of additional end-outline marker lamps may be fitted as long as they show white to the front and red to the rear [20 and Sch. 13].

A broken-down vehicle being drawn does not require end-outline marker lamps [6(7)] and such lamps must not be used to cause undue dazzle or discomfort to other persons using the road [27].

Switches and obscuration

Motor vehicles first used on or after 1 April 1991 must be made so that every position lamp, side marker lamp, end-outline marker lamp and rear registration plate lamp fitted to it is capable of being switched on and off by one switch only. But one or more position lamps can be capable of being switched on and off independently of the other lamps [1796/89/15].

At least part of the surface of any front and rear position lamp, front and rear direction indicator and rear retro reflector, required to be fitted to a vehicle, must be visible from directly in front of or behind the lamp or reflector when every door, tailgate, boot lid, engine cover, cab or other movable part of the vehicle is in a fixed open position [1796/89/19].

Reflective material, pairs of lamps, etc.

Material designed primarily to reflect light is, when reflecting light, to be regarded as showing a light and material capable of reflecting an image is not, when reflecting the image of a light, to be so treated [1796/89/3(3)].

A pair of lamps, reflectors or rear markings means one on each side of the vehicle, at the same height above ground and at the same distance from the outer edge of the vehicle [3(2)] and these provisions being complied with as far as practicable in the case of an asymmetric vehicle. A matched pair of lamps is a pair of lamps where both lamps emit light of substantially the same colour and intensity and both lamps are the same size and of such shape that they are symmetrical to each other [3(2)].

A work lamp—which is permitted to show a white light to the rear— is a lamp used to illuminate a working area or the scene of an accident, breakdown or roadworks in the vicinity of the vehicle to which it is fitted [3(2)]. A work lamp must not be used to cause undue dazzle or discomfort to the driver of any other vehicle or be lit for a purpose other than that given in the above definition [27].

The duty to maintain lamps and reflectors in good order is dealt with in the chapter on maintenance, page 187.

The power of enforcement bodies to inspect lighting equipment is dealt with in the chapter on powers of police, etc., page 263.

Signs on buses carrying children

A prescribed sign of yellow retro reflective material bearing the silhouette of two children (see below) can be fitted on the rear of a bus carrying children without contravening the restrictions on lamps and retro reflective material showing a light to the rear other than a red light [1796/89/11(2) and 2280/94].

A secondary sign of the same kind may be fitted to the rear of a bus, without contravening the above restrictions, if (a) its total retro-reflective area is no greater than that of the principal sign; (b) the sign contains no words or other markings apart from those which (i) indicate children are on board the bus when it is in motion, are likely to be on board or in the vicinity while it is stationary and (ii) are calculated to reduce the risk of road accidents involving those children. Asecondary sign fitted to a bus owned or hired by a local education authority or any person managing an education establishment attended by children under 16 years can also contain words or markings identifying that authority or establishment [1796/89/ 11(4)–(6) and 2280/94].

From 1 April, 1995 a bus carrying a child to or from his school must be fitted with the prescribed children's sign (page 167D) on the front and rear of the vehicle so that it is plainly visible to other road users [1796/89/17A and 2280/94]. This requirement does not apply where a bus is on a service available to the general public which qualifies for fuel duty grant [17A(2)].

A bus is a motor vehicle constructed or adapted to carry more than eight seated passengers (in addition to the driver) and a child is a child under the age of 16 years [3 and 17A(3)]. Carrying a child to or from his school means (a) carrying him to, or to a place in the vicinity of, his school on a day during term time before he has attended school that day or (b) carrying him from, or from a place in the vicinity of, his school on a day during term time after he has finished attending school on that day [17A(3)].

General exemptions

Nothing in the lighting regulations requires any lamp or reflector to be fitted between sunrise and sunset to a vehicle not fitted with any front or rear position lamp; an incomplete vehicle going to a works for completion; or a combat vehicle [1796/89/4(3)]. For this purpose a lamp is not treated as a lamp if it is painted or masked over so that it cannot readily be used or it is an electric lamp which is not, or cannot readily be, wired to an electrical source [4(4)].

The requirements relating to the fitting of lamps, reflectors, rear markings and devices do not apply to a vehicle having a base outside Great Britain from which it normally starts its journeys, provided a period of 12 months has not passed since the vehicle was last brought into Great Britain; a visiting vehicle for the purposes of the International Circulation Order; a combination of vehicles which includes a vehicle mentioned in the last two categories; a vehicle going to a port for export, as long as, in each of these cases, the vehicle complies with the requirements relating to lights and reflectors contained in the 1949 Geneva Convention on Road Traffic or the 1926 Paris Convention on Motor Traffic [5]. Details of these Conventions are given on pages 458 to 467.

Exemptions are made for military vehicles of home and visiting forces subject to specified conditions being complied with [7].

SIGN FOR BUS CARRYING CHILDREN

COLOUR
Shaded areas – yellow retro reflective material
Border and silhouette – black

DIMENSIONS
A
Front – not less than 250mm.
Rear – not less than 400mm.

B
Front – not more than 20mm.
Rear – not more than 30mm.

8 Livestock transport

Animal Health Act 1981
Transit of Animals (General) Order, **No. 1377/73**
Transit of Animals (Road and Rail) Order, **No. 1024/75**
Transit of Animals (Amendment) Order, **No. 815/88**
Welfare of Animals during Transport Order, **No. 3304/92**

Livestock transport

The transport of 'farm' animals in vehicles and containers by road is governed by the 1975 Order which is dealt with fully in this chapter.

The transport of domestic animals and poultry (including birds of any kind) is controlled by the 1973 Order which contains similar, but less detailed, requirements relating to the avoidance of injury or unnecessary suffering to animals; construction of vehicles and receptacles; feeding and watering; the carriage of unfit animals; and overcrowding. It does not require records to be kept.

For the purposes of the 1975 Order, animals are cattle, sheep, swine, goats and horses. Cattle are bulls, cows, steers, heifers and calves. Any reference to horses include ponies, asses, mules and hinnies [1024/75/2].

The Welfare of Animals during Transport Order, No. 3304/92 came into force on 1 January 1993 to implement EC Directive 628/91. It amended the 1973 and 1975 Orders in relation to the protection of animals during transport. In the 1992 Order references to animals include references to birds and it does not apply to the transport of pet animals unless done in the course of a trade or business.

CONSTRUCTION

A vehicle or receptacle must not be used to carry such animals unless it complies with specified construction requirements [3 and Sch. 1]. A vehicle is any kind of vehicle, including a trailer or detachable body, constructed or adapted for road use, whether drawn or propelled by animal or mechanical power. A receptacle is a crate, box or other rigid container which is not self-propelled and not part of a vehicle [2].

A road vehicle must be of substantial design and constructed and maintained to withstand the weather and the weight of animals thrown against it. Except where a vehicle is made and used only to carry horses facing the front and rear, the floor of a vehicle must have fittings attached to the body sides, not more than 1m apart, for securing partitions. A partition must be substantial and able to withstand the weight of animals thrown against it. Partitions and fittings must be such that any gap between the bottom of the partition and the vehicle floor will not cause damage or injury to an animal's limbs.

Each deck of a vehicle carrying animals must be equipped with barriers or, in the case of horses, straps made and maintained to prevent an animal falling out of the vehicle when the unloading ramp is lowered.

A vehicle floor must have suitable foot battens or other means of preventing animals from slipping during carriage. A vehicle's loading ramp (including a falling loading door) must have suitable battens or other means to give an animal using it a proper foothold and must not, when on the level, exceed a gradient of 4 in 7. The height of a step at the top of a ramp must not exceed 21cm and any gap between the top of the ramp and the vehicle must not exceed 6cm.

If a vehicle has two or more decks carrying animals each must have a suitable ramp or mechanical lifting gear (to be carried on the vehicle) to allow movement of animals between floors. Internal ramps must have suitable battens to give animals a proper foothold, railings or other means to prevent them falling when using the ramp and a gradient not exceeding 2 in 3 when the vehicle is on level ground.

A vehicle must be designed, constructed and maintained to ensure adequate and suitable ventilation for every animal on each deck and to enable the vehicle to be cleansed and disinfected in the prescribed manner.

Vehicles must have apertures and footholds to readily facilitate inspection, from outside, of the inside at each deck level. A door, other than one for loading, giving access to each deck will satisfy this requirement.

A vehicle used for carrying animals required to be secured must have sufficient tying points.

To prevent injury or unnecessary suffering to animals, wheel arches which protrude into a vehicle must be fully covered with permanent shields and the vehicle interior must be free from sharp edges or projections.

A vehicle used before 1975 to carry animals must have rigid sides and suitable overhead protection or be adapted to enable suitable covering to be fitted to the sides and top. A vehicle not used before 1975 to carry animals must have rigid sides and suitable overhead protection but the top floor may be removable or collapsible when not in use [1024/75/3 and Sch. 1, part I].

A receptacle must be of substantial design and be constructed and maintained to withstand the weather and the weight of animals thrown against it. It must be of sufficient size and height to ensure-

a. each animal can be carried without unnecessary suffering;
b. an animal can be fed and watered without being removed;
c. an animal can stand in its natural position;
d. there is adequate and suitable ventilation for each animal;
e. apertures are available for inspecting the interior;
f. easy access to the interior is available;
g. each animal is protected from the weather;
h. the interior has no sharp edges or projections likely to cause injury or unnecessary suffering; and
i. it can be adequately cleansed and disinfected in the specified manner.

A receptacle must be made to prevent leakage or escape of liquid, droppings, or waste feeding stuff and the floor must have battens or an anti-slip surface. The receptacle must be made and maintained to be capable of being properly and effectively secured to the carrying vehicle [1024/75/3 and Sch. 1, part III].

LOADING AND UNLOADING

Loading and unloading an animal into or out of a vehicle or receptacle must be done so that no injury or unnecessary suffering is caused by excessive use of anything used for driving the animal or it coming into contact with the vehicle, receptacle or any obstruction [4(1), (2)].

Except where the floor is 31cm or less above ground level, an animal must not be loaded or unloaded otherwise than by means of (a) the ramp carried on the vehicle, (b) a ramp not carried on the vehicle but of suitable height and design, (c) a loading bank of suitable height, (d) suitable mechanical lifting gear, whether carried on the vehicle or not, or (e) manual lifting or carrying [4(3), (5)]. When an animal has been loaded under (b) to (d) above, the vehicle must carry a ramp, of suitable height and design, for unloading it in case of emergency [4(4)].

When a ramp is used for loading or unloading a vehicle or receptacle it must have protection on each side to a height of at least 1.3m above the ramp, be of sufficient strength and length to prevent an animal on the ramp from falling and fitted so that any gap between the lower edge of the protection and the ramp will not cause damage or injury to an animal using the ramp. A ramp must be secured so that any gap between the side protection and the vehicle or receptacle will not result in injury or unnecessary suffering to an animal [4(6)]. But side protection is not needed for loading or unloading a horse from a vehicle specially made for horse transport and each horse is led on or off the vehicle [4(7)].

A receptacle containing animals must be kept upright when being loaded into or unloaded out of a vehicle [4(7A) and 815/88].

An animal must not be moved from one deck of a vehicle or receptacle to another except by means of a proper ramp, suitable mechanical lifting gear or manual lifting or carrying. The surface of a passageway within a vehicle or receptacle used for loading or unloading must be made, treated and maintained to prevent, as far as practicable, animals from slipping [5].

CARE IN TRANSIT

A carrier or other person in charge of an animal being carried must ensure it is carried to its destination as soon as possible and delays are minimised [6(1A) and 815/88].

When carried in a vehicle or receptacle, an animal must be protected against the weather; not be subjected to severe jolts or shaking; provided with adequate fresh air; prevented from escaping or falling out; and not caused injury or unnecessary suffering [6(2) and 815/88].

An animal must not be carried in a vehicle compartment or receptacle containing goods likely to prejudice its welfare [6(2A) and 815/88].

If two or more horses are carried loose in an undivided vehicle, receptacle or pen their hind feet must be unshod [6(4)].

A floor which is not anti-slip must be strewn with sufficient sand or other substance to give animals a proper foothold [6(5)].

An animal carried in a vehicle or receptacle must be accompanied by an attendant (who can be the driver) who is responsible for ensuring it is fed and watered [6(7)].

A vehicle or receptacle must have artificial lighting—fixed or portable—capable of adequately illuminating the interior [6(8)].

The floor of a vehicle or receptacle carrying calves or pigs must be covered with an adequate quantity of clean litter, unless the carriage is between the same points (except markets) on two or more consecutive occasions on the same day, when the same litter may be used [6(9)].

On a vehicle or receptacle with two or more decks there must be sufficient distance between each floor and roof to enable the animals to stand in their natural position; sufficient space above each animal for air circulation; and satisfactory access to each deck [6(10)]. When horses are carried the minimum floor to roof distance must be 1.98m [6(11)].

The carrier or person in charge of the animals being carried must ensure that the vehicle, receptacle or pen is not overcrowded so as to cause injury or unnecessary suffering to an animal [7].

A carrier or other person in charge of animals carried by road must ensure (a) that animal tethers will not break under normal conditions and are long enough to allow animals, if necessary, to lie down, eat and drink, and (b) cattle are not tethered by their horns [9A and 815/88].

Where animals are transported more than 50km the following rules must be complied with in addition to any of the foregoing legislation [3304/92/8]:

Animals in transport must be provided with sufficient room to lie down unless it would lead to risk of injury or harm. Solipeds must not be transported in vehicles with more than one deck and, except for unbroken foals or animals in individual boxes, must wear halters. Tethers must be of a kind which eliminate danger of strangulation or injury and animals must not be tied by a nose ring.

Animals of different species must be segregated in transport unless it would cause distress in a companion animal. Stallions must not be transported in the same vehicle as other stallions unless used to each other.

Animals must not be suspended by mechanical means nor dragged by the head, horns, legs, fleece or tail. The use of electric prods must be avoided as far as possible.

The vehicle floor must be covered with sufficient litter to absorb droppings unless droppings are regularly removed.

Livestock consignments must be accompanied by an attendant except (a) when transported in secure containers which are adequately ventilated and, where necessary, contain enough food and water in dispensers which cannot be tipped over, for a journey of double the anticipated time; or (b) when the consignor has appointed an agent to care for the animals at staging points.

Animals in milk must, where necessary, be milked and, in the case of cows, must be milked at intervals of about 12 hours and not more than 15 hours.

Loading may only be onto vehicles which have been thoroughly cleaned and, where appropriate, disinfected. Dead animals, litter and droppings must be removed as soon as possible.

A road vehicle in which animals are transported must be equipped with a weatherproof roof.

When animals are in a road vehicle on board a ship:

(a) the animal compartment must be properly fixed to the vehicle and the compartment and the vehicle must be equipped with adequate tying facilities for securing to the ship. On a covered deck of a ro-ro vessel sufficient ventilation must be maintained and, where possible, a vehicle must be placed near a fresh air inlet;

(b) the animal compartment must have sufficient vents or other means of ensuring it is adequately ventilated, bearing in mind the restricted air flow in the ship. There must be sufficient room inside the compartment and at each of its levels to ensure there is adequate ventilation above the animals in their normal standing position;

(c) direct access must be provided to each part of the compartment so that animals can, if necessary, be cared for, fed and watered during the voyage.

Accommodation for poultry and rabbits must be drained and kept in a sanitary condition.

[3304/92/Sch.1]

PARTITIONS

A partition to separate animals must be at least 1.27m high for horses and cattle (except calves) and 76cm in any other case [6(6)].

If the length of load space in a vehicle exceeds 3.1m when sheep, swine or goats are carried [8(2)(a)] or 3.7m when horses are carried [8(2)(b)], partitions must be used to form pens not exceeding those lengths. If the length of load space exceeds 3.7m when cattle (except calves) are carried, partitions must be fitted to form pens of a length which will ensure that they will not cause injury or unnecessary suffering by being thrown about by the vehicle's motion [8(3)]. If calves are carried and the length of load space exceeds 2.5m, partitions must be fitted to form pens not over 2.5m long [8(4)].

If the number of animals carried in a vehicle or receptacle is not enough to fill the available space, a partition must be placed to ensure they are not thrown about by the motion of the vehicle but not to cause overcrowding [8(5)].

If horses are in a vehicle so that

(a) each horse faces to the front or rear, each must be tied where necessary and each group separated from another group by a partition across the vehicle, or

(b) each horse stands across the vehicle,

each must be tied where necessary and adequately supported against the motion of the vehicle [8(6)].

USE OF CONTAINERS

When carried on a vehicle, a receptacle carrying animals must not be placed on top of another receptacle. It must be secured to (a) prevent moving by the motion of the vehicle or weather; (b) provide adequate ventilation for the animals; (c) provide unimpeded access to them; and (d) ensure it remains upright. It must bear a notice that it contains animals and state their species and carry a sign indicating the upright position. The receptacle must be escape proof, safe for the animals and easy to clean [8(7) and 815/88].

MIXING OF ANIMALS

An animal of the following description must not be carried in the same undivided vehicle, receptacle or pen as any other animal *of any species*:

a. a cow when suckling a calf or calves;
b. a bull over 10 months, which must be secured by the head or neck;
c. a sow with unweaned piglets;
d. a boar over 6 months;
e. a mare with a foal at foot; or
f. a stallion [9 and Sch. 2, para. 1, 2(1)].

The following animals may be carried in the same undivided vehicle, receptacle or pen but must be carried separately from any other species of animal:

i. horned cattle;
ii. cattle without horns;
iii. calves;
iv. ewes with unweaned lambs;
v. rams over 6 months;
vi. weaned lambs under 3 months;
vii. other sheep;
viii. weaned piglets under 3 months;
ix. other swine;
x. nanny goats with unweaned kids;
xi. billy goats over 6 months;
xii. weaned kids under 3 months;
xiii. other goats;
xiv. broken horses, other than asses, mules and hinnies;
xv. unbroken horses, other than asses, mules and hinnies;
xvi. asses;
xvii. mules and hinnies;
xviii.   any foal under 9 months old [9 and Sch.2, para.2(2)].

But a horse must not be carried in the same vehicle or receptacle as swine; a horse registered under the Rules of Racing may be accompanied in an undivided vehicle, receptacle or pen by a stable companion; horned and unhorned cattle can be carried together if they are all secured by the head or neck; and bulls over 10 months, reared together and for which an unlicensed bull permit is in force, may be carried in the same undivided vehicle, receptacle or pen without being secured [9 and Sch. 2, para. 4].

An unsecured animal must not be carried in the same undivided vehicle, receptacle or pen as a secured animal, except for unweaned young with a female animal suckling them or for a registered racehorse with a stable companion [9 and Sch. 2, para. 3].

FEEDING AND WATERING

A person in charge of an animal which is being transported on a vehicle must ensure that (a) according to its species, it has been provided with water and appropriate food before the start of any journey and (b) at suitable intervals during the journey it is provided with water, food and rest.

In relation to bovine, ovine, caprine, porcine or equine animals, the intervals must not exceed 15 hours. In relation to dogs and cats, the intervals between feeding must not exceed 24 hours and those between watering must not exceed 12 hours. None of these requirements apply to poultry or rabbits if their transport is completed within 12 hours (disregarding loading and unloading time) or to poultry chicks if their transport lasts not more than 24 hours and is completed within 72 hours of their hatching [3304/92/4].

UNFIT ANIMALS

An animal must not be transported in a way which causes or is likely to cause it injury or unnecessary suffering and an animal must not be transported if it is unfit by reason of it being newborn, diseased, infirm, ill, fatigued or having given birth within the preceding 48 hours or likely to give birth during the transport or for any other reason [3304/92/3(1),(2)].

However, a bovine, ovine, caprine, porcine or equine animal may be transported to the nearest place for veterinary treatment or slaughter if it is not likely to be subject to unnecessary suffering due to its unfitness, but it must not be dragged or pushed by any means or lifted by a mechanical device, unless it is done in the presence of and under the supervision of a veterinary surgeon who is arranging for it to be transported with all practicable speed to a place for treatment.

Exemption is also given to the transport of an animal for scientific research by a licensed person [3(3),(4)].

A deer in velvet must not be transported unless the journey is 50km or less and special precautions are taken to protect it from injury and unnecessary suffering [3(5)].

A carcase must not be carried in a vehicle or receptacle carrying a live animal unless it has died on the journey [1024/75/14(1)]. If an animal dies during a journey while carried in the same vehicle or receptacle as another animal, the person in charge of the dead animal must ensure the carcase does not remain with the other animal longer than necessary to take it to the nearest available disposal place [14(2)].

CLEANSING AND DISINFECTION

A vehicle and receptacle, its accessories and equipment used in connection with loading, unloading or carriage of an animal, must be cleansed and disinfected as soon as practicable after unloading and, in any case, before an animal, carcase or anything to be used with an animal is loaded into the vehicle or receptacle [15(2)]. But this does not apply to a vehicle or receptacle used only during a single day, for carrying animals between the same points (other than markets) but it must be cleansed and disinfected as soon as practicable after the last journey an animal was carried that day and, in any case, before it is used again to carry an animal [15(4)]. Neither does it apply to a vehicle or receptacle used only (a) by the owner for carrying his horse or (b) by the occupier of Jockey-Club licensed stables for carrying horses to and from race meetings or training. Here, the vehicle or receptacle, with its accessories and equipment, must be cleansed and disinfected before another animal is carried except in (a), a horse belonging to the vehicle owner or, in (b), a horse kept at those stables [15(5)].

A vehicle or receptacle used to carry a carcase or manure, along with its accessories and loading equipment, must be cleansed and disinfected, before an animal or anything to do with animals is loaded in the vehicle or receptacle [15(3)].

A vehicle or receptacle used to carry a diseases or suspected animal, or the carcase of such an animal, must, together with its loading equipment, be immediately cleansed and disinfected after unloading and, in any case, before it is used to carry an animal or anything to do with animals [15(7)].

Where a vehicle or receptacle is required to be cleansed and disinfected:

(a) the floor, sides and roof of the interior; the sides and ends of the exterior; and any other part the animal or its droppings has come into contact with must be

    (i) swept or otherwise cleansed and all sweepings, dung, etc removed, and

    (ii) washed and scrubbed with water and then treated with an approved disinfectant;

(b) sweepings, dung, etc must be destroyed or removed from contact with an animal; and

(c) all accessories must be cleansed and disinfected by spraying with, washing with or saturating in an approved disinfectant [15 and Sch. 3, para. 1].

If a vehicle or receptacle has been used to carry a diseased or suspected animal, or the carcase of one, it must be sprayed or saturated with an approved disinfectant before being swept out [15 and Sch. 3, para. 3].

If an inspector considers that cleansing and disinfection has not been properly carried out he can, by written notice, require the owner of the vehicle or receptacle, or person in charge or having use of it, to carry out the work within a time he specifies [16(1)].

RECORDS

Any person who controls an animal transport undertaking which transports animals in the course of a business or trade must:

1. ensure that during the journey the consignment is accompanied by a certificate signed by him or on his behalf stating the origin and ownership of the animals, their places of departure and destination, and the date and time of departure;

2. for journeys exceeding 24 hours, draw up a journey plan, which must accompany the consignment, showing (a) the arrangements for the animals to be rested, fed, watered and (if necessary) unloaded and given accommodation and (b) the arrangements for feeding and watering in the event that the planned journey is changed or disrupted;

3. ensure copies of the certificate and journey plan are kept for six months from the end of the journey and are produced when requested by an inspector;

4. ensure the animals are entrusted only to people with the knowledge needed to care for them;

5. ensure the consignee is prepared to receive animals which travel unaccompanied;

6. ensure the animals are transported without delay to their destination [3304/92/5].

EXEMPTIONS

Where bovine, ovine, caprine or porcine animals or domestic equines are transported
(a) for a distance of 50km or less to, from or within land used for agricultural purposes,
(b) in a vehicle owned by the owner or occupier of that land and
(c) the vehicle has an animal compartment not more than 3.1m long,
the following rules do not apply:
  (i)   Article 8(5) of the 1975 Order (page 173);
  (ii) in Schedule 1 of that Order, paragraphs 3 (barriers or straps to stop animals falling down a vehicle's loading ramp), 6 (internal ramps) and 11 (overhead protection) (page 170); and
  (iii) the above rules on consignment certificates and journey plans [3304/92/6(1)].
The rules on consignment certificates and journey plans do not apply to the transport of (a) equine animals kept for private recreation or private sporting purposes or (b) to poultry transported for 50km or less where the number of birds is less than 50 or the journey is within land occupied by the owner of the poultry [6(2)].
The rules on consignment certificates and journey plans do not apply to the transport for a distance of 50km or less of any animal not referred to in the two preceding paragraphs [6(3)].

Enforcement

All the foregoing requirements are made under the Animal Health Act 1981 and the police have the duty to enforce them [Act 1981/60(1)]. So too has a local authority [1024/75/21].
A constable can stop and detain a person committing or reasonably suspected of an offence. If the person's name and address are not known, or the constable is not satisfied with particulars given, he can arrest that person. A constable can also stop, detain and examine any animal or vehicle to which an offence relates and require it to be taken back to any place from which it was unlawfully removed. A person who obstructs, or assists in obstructing, a constable or other officer can be arrested [Act 1981/60].
A Ministry or local authority inspector appointed for the purposes of the Act has, in the area in which he acts, the same powers as a

constable under Section 60 [63(1)]. He also has power to enter land and buildings where he has reasonable grounds to believe there is a vehicle in relation to which an offence has been committed and to enter such a vehicle [63(2), (3)]. If required by the owner, occupier or person in charge of the land, building or vehicle he must state, in writing, his reasons for entering [63(4)].

FORM OF RECORD IN RESPECT OF THE CARRIAGE OF ANIMALS BY ROAD

Name and full address of owner or other
person having the management of vehicle ....

Description of vehicle ....

Registration number ....

Name of driver	Date and time of loading animals	Number and description of animals carried	(i) Premises from which moved person from whom delivery was taken (if known) (ii)	Time(s) and place(s) of feeding and watering (see Note 4)	Time of unloading animals	(i) Premises to which moved person taking delivery (if known) (ii)	Date when and premises where vehicle was cleansed and disinfected in accordance with the Order
(1)	(2)	(3)	(4)	(5)	(6)	(7)	(8)

NOTES

1. Entries relating to times of loading, feeding and watering, and unloading, to be made when loading, feeding and watering, and unloading, take place, and other entries as soon as possible after completion of the journey; and in any case within 18 hours.
2. Entries to be made in a permanent and legible form.
3. Record to be available at the office or usual place of business of the person having the management of the vehicle to which it relates; to be retained there for a period of 6 months from date of latest entry; and to be produced on demand.
4. Column (5) to be completed where a journey exceeds 12 hours.

9 Maintenance

Road Traffic Act 1988
Road Vehicles (Construction and Use) Regulations, No. 1078/86
Road Vehicles Lighting Regulations, No. 1796/89

Brakes

Every part of every braking system and its means of operation fitted
to a vehicle must be maintained in good and efficient working order
and be properly adjusted [1078/86/18(1)]. Each part of a braking
system must be maintained—*Kennet v BAA* [1975] RTR 164—and
all brakes, even if not required, must be maintained—*DPP v Young*
[1991] RTR 56.

Any fault in an anti-lock braking system is disregarded if the vehicle
is completing a journey on which the fault arose or is being driven to
a place for the ABS to be repaired and, in either case, the vehicle meets
its required braking efficiencies [18(1A), (1B)].

Except for an agricultural motor vehicle not driven at over 20mph,
a works truck and a pedestrian-controlled vehicle, a wheeled motor
vehicle must be maintained so that it has the service braking efficiency
and, in the case of a motor car first used on or after 1 January 1927
and a heavy motor car, the secondary braking efficiency shown in the
following table. A trailer referred to in the table is one required to be
fitted with brakes.

Class of vehicle	Efficiency—%	
	Service brake	Secondary brake
1. Vehicle first used on or after 1 April 1983 to which Reg. 15 applies (page 6) or which complies in all respects with that regulation or EC Directive 79/489, 85/647 or 88/194 or ECE Regulations 13.03, 13.04 or 13.05		
(a) when not drawing a trailer	50	25
(b) when drawing a trailer	45	25

Class of vehicle	Efficiency—%	
	Service brake	Secondary brake
2. Vehicle first used on or after 1 January 1968, not included above,		
(a) when not drawing a trailer	50	25
(b) when drawing a trailer made on or after 1 January 1968	50	25
(c) when drawing a trailer made before 1 January 1968	40	15
3. Goods vehicle over 1,525kg unladen first used on or after 15 August 1928 but before 1 January 1968		
(a) rigid vehicle with two axles not forming part of an artic		
(i) when not drawing a trailer	45	20
(ii) when drawing a trailer	40	15
(b) other vehicles, including those to form part of an artic, and whether or not drawing a trailer	40	15
4. Vehicle not included above (except a bus, artic, artic tractor and a heavy motor car goods vehicle used before 15 August 1928) having at least one means of operation applying to at least 4 wheels	50	25

[18(2), (3)]

A goods vehicle will be deemed not to comply with the above table unless it is capable of complying with those efficiencies both at its laden weight and at its design gross weight. Where the vehicle is drawing a trailer the efficiencies must be obtainable at the combined laden weight of vehicle and trailer and the vehicle's design train weight [18(4)].

The brakes of an agricultural motor vehicle first used on or after 1 June 1986 and not driven over 20mph, and of an agricultural trailer made on or after 1 December 1985, must be capable of achieving 25% efficiency when the weight of the vehicle is equal to the total maximum axle weights it is designed to have [18(5)].

A vehicle or combination of vehicles described below must be maintained so that its brakes are capable, without the assistance of stored energy, of holding it stationary on a gradient of the percentage specified:

Vehicle	% gradient
1. A vehicle in class 1 of the above table	
(a) when not drawing a trailer	16
(b) when drawing a trailer	12
2. A vehicle used before April 1983 and required to have a parking brake	16
3. A vehicle, not included in item 1, drawing a trailer made on or after 1 January 1968 and required to have brakes	16

[18(6)].

For these purposes the date of manufacture of a composite trailer will be that of the semi-trailer forming part of it [18(7)].

Tyres

A vehicle must not be used if a pneumatic tyre fitted to a wheel:

(a) is unsuitable to the use of the vehicle or to the other types of tyres fitted;
(b) is not correctly inflated;
(c) has a cut deep enough to reach the ply or cord and the length of the cut is 25mm or 10% of the width of the tyre, whichever is the longer;
(d) has any lump, bulge or tear caused by separation or partial failure of its structure;
(e) has any ply or cord exposed ('exposed' means exposed to view— *Renouf v Franklin* [1971] RTR 469);
(f) does not have the base of any groove which showed in the original tread pattern clearly visible;
(g) either
　(i) the grooves of the tread pattern do not have a depth of at least 1mm throughout a continuous band across at least three-quarters of the breadth of the tread and round the entire circumference of the tyre, or
　(ii) if the grooves of the original tread pattern did not extend beyond three-quarters of the breadth of tread, any groove in the original tread does not have a depth of at least 1mm;
(h) is not maintained as to be fit for the use to which the vehicle or trailer is put or has a defect which might damage the road or persons in the vehicle or using the road.

[1078/86/27(1)]

Paragraphs (f) and (g) above do not apply to passenger vehicles constructed to carry not more than 8 passengers (exclusive of driver); goods vehicles not over 3,500kg maximum gross weight; and trailers not over 3,500kg maximum gross weight. But the grooves of the tread pattern of every tyre fitted to the wheels of such vehicles must have a depth of at least 1.6mm throughout a continuous band comprising the central three-quarters of the breadth of tread and round its entire circumference [27(4) (d)-(f)].

Original tread pattern means, in the case of a re-treaded tyre, the tread pattern immediately after re-treading; on a wholly re-cut tyre, the manufacturer's re-cut tread pattern; on a partially re-cut tyre, the manufacturer's re-cut tread pattern on the part re-cut and, on the other part, the tread pattern of the tyre when new; in any other case, the tread pattern of the tyre when new [27(6)]. Breadth of tread is the breadth of the part of the tyre normally in contact with the road [27(6)].

The inflation of a tyre has to be fit for the vehicle's use at the time and not some possible future use—*Connor v Graham* [1981] RTR 291. In that case no offence was committed where a tyre pressure on an unladen truck was not at the pressure appropriate to the vehicle's design gross weight.

In *Coote v Parkin* [1977] RTR 61 it was held that the 'outer circumference of the tyre', in Regulation 27(1)(g), was the part of the tyre normally in contact with the road. The side walls and shoulders of the tyre were not to be included.

None of the above restrictions applies to an agricultural motor vehicle not driven at over 20mph, an agricultural trailer, or trailed appliance, or a broken-down vehicle or a vehicle going to a place for breaking up provided, in either case, it is not towed faster than 20mph. Paragraphs (f) and (g) above do not apply to a pedestrian-controlled works truck [27(4)].

A tyre which is deflated or not fully inflated and which has a defect described in paragraph (c), (d) or (e) above can be used if the tyre and wheel to which it is fitted are constructed to make the tyre fit for use in that condition and the outside walls of the tyre are marked to that effect [27(2)], and paragraph (a) does not apply to a passenger vehicle (not being a bus) by reason only of it being fitted with a temporary-use spare tyre unless it is driven over 50mph [27(3)]. A bus is a motor vehicle to carry 8 seated passengers in addition to the driver and a temporary-use spare tyre is a tyre designed for use only as a spare and at speeds lower than normal tyres [3(2)].

A recut pneumatic tyre must not be fitted to a wheel if the ply or cord has been cut or exposed by the recutting process or if it has been wholly or partially recut in a pattern other than the manufacturer's recut tread pattern [27(5)].

Pneumatic tyres of different types of structure must not be fitted to the same axle of a vehicle [26(1)].

A motor vehicle with two axles each of which is equipped with one or two single wheels must not be used on a road if (a) a diagonal-ply tyre or bias-belted tyre is fitted on the rear axle and a radial-ply tyre is on the front axle or (b) a diagonal-ply tyre is fitted on the rear axle and a bias-belted tyre is fitted on the front axle [26(2)]. This ban does not apply if an axle of the vehicle is fitted with wide tyres other than special wide tyres for engineering plant or to a vehicle which has a maximum speed not exceeding 30mph [26(3)]. Wide tyres are at least 300mm wide [3(2)].

Pneumatic tyres fitted to the steerable axles or driven axles of a vehicle must be the same type of structure [26(4)].

The restrictions in Regulation 26(1), (2) & (4) above do not prohibit the fitting of a temporary-use spare tyre on a passenger vehicle (other than a bus) unless it is driven over 50mph [26(5)].

The term 'axle', for these purposes, includes a pair of stub axles on opposite sides of the vehicle and a single stub axle which is not one of a pair. A 'stub axle' is defined as an axle on which only one wheel is mounted [26(6)].

Condition

It is an offence to use, or cause or permit to be used, a motor vehicle or trailer on a road when the condition of the vehicle, its accessories or equipment; the purpose for which it is used; the number of passengers carried and how they are carried; or the weight, position or distribution of its load or how it is secured, is such that the use of the vehicle involves a danger of injury to any person [Act 1988/40A and Act 1991]. The following High Court decisions were made in relation to this provision's predecessor, Regulation 100(1) of the Construction and Use Regulations. In *Leathley v Robson's Border Transport Ltd* [1976] RTR 503 it was held that the Regulation applied to a load on a vehicle and did not apply in a case when the load had fallen from the vehicle. In *Bindley v Willett* [1981] RTR 19 the High Court decided, for the purposes of the Regulation, that an insecure container was part of the vehicle and not a load. See also *Hawkins v Harold A. Russett Ltd* (page 28) where a demountable body was held to be part of the vehicle and not a load.

A load on a vehicle must be secured, if necessary by physical restraint other than its own weight, and be in such a position that neither danger nor nuisance is likely to be caused to any person or property by the load falling or being blown from the vehicle or by any movement on the vehicle [100(2)]. In *Cornish v Ferrymasters Ltd* [1975] RTR 292 using a vehicle with an insecure load contrary to this Regulation was held to be an absolute offence. Lack of knowledge that a pallet had inherent defects causing it to collapse and allow a drum to fall from the vehicle was no defence. In *St Albans Sand & Gravel Co Ltd v Minnis* [1981] RTR 231 defendants who used an unsheeted tipper lorry laden with dry sand were held to have been properly convicted under this Regulation even though there was no evidence of sand falling or being blown from the vehicle. In *R v Crossman* [1986] RTR 49 it was held that a driver had been properly convicted of causing death by reckless driving after an insecure load fell from his lorry and killed a pedestrian. In *Walker-Trowbridge Ltd v DPP* [1992] RTR 182 a load which collided with a bridge and was knocked from its carrying vehicle was held to have fallen from the vehicle. It was also said that in deciding whether a load was properly secured one had to consider the nature of the load, the way it was positioned, the way it was secured and the journey it was to be taken on.

A vehicle must not be used for a purpose for which it is so unsuitable that danger or nuisance is or is likely to be caused [100(3)]. In *BRS Ltd v Owen* [1971] 2 All ER 999 where a high load on a vehicle collided with a bridge, it was held that the vehicle had been used for an unsuitable purpose and the test of 'suitability' was not when it started the journey but when it approached the bridge. But where the jib of an excavator collided with a bridge it was held, in *Young v DPP* [1992] RTR 194, that the low-loader carrying it was suitable and the accident had occurred through improper loading.

A Code of Practice titled *Safety of Loads on Vehicles* has been published by the Department of the Environment and is available from HM Stationery Office.

Seat belts

In a vehicle which is required to be fitted with seat belts the seat belt, its anchorages, adjusting and fastening devices and retracting mechanisms have to be maintained as described below [1078/86/48(1)]. In the case of a seat with an integral seat belt, an anchorage point includes the means of securing the seat to the vehicle [48(2)]. Seat belt anchorage points must not be used for any other purpose [48(3)]. Load-bearing members or panelling within 30cm of an anchorage point must be in sound condition and free from serious corrosion, distortion or fracture; adjusting devices and retracting mechanisms must be maintained so that the belt can be readily adjusted; the seat belt and its anchorages, fastenings and adjusting device must be free from any obvious defect which would adversely affect performance in case of accident; the buckle or other fastener must be maintained so that the belt can be readily fastened or unfastened, be kept free from obstruction and be readily accessible to the seat occupant; webbing or other material of the seat belt must be free from cuts or other visible faults (e.g. extensive fraying) which would affect the belt under stress; the ends of a seat belt must be securely fastened to an anchorage point; and, in the case of a disabled person's seat belt, the ends of the belt must be securely fastened to the structure of the vehicle or the seat when the seat belt is in use [48(4)]. The requirements in Regulation 48(4) above do not apply to a vehicle where the defect arises on the journey or where steps have been taken to rectify the defect with reasonable expedition [48(5)].

Speedometer

A speedometer required to be fitted in a vehicle must be kept free from obstruction and at all material times be maintained in good working order. This requirement also applies to a tachograph used in place of a speedometer in a vehicle to which the tachograph rules do not apply. 'All material times' means all times when the vehicle is used on a road except (a) when on a journey during which the instrument became defective or (b) when steps have already been taken to have a defective instrument replaced or repaired with all reasonable expedition [1078/86/36].

Lights

When a vehicle is used on a road (a) every front position lamp, rear position lamp, headlamp, rear registration plate lamp, end-outline marker lamp, side marker lamp, rear fog lamp, retro reflector and rear marking with which it is required to be fitted, and (b) every stop lamp, direction indicator, running lamp, dim-dip device, headlamp levelling device and hazard warning signal device with which it is fitted (whether required or not), must be in good working order and, in the case of a lamp, clean [1796/89/23(1),(2)].

The above requirement does not apply to-

(a) a rear fog lamp on a vehicle which is part of a combination of vehicles any one of which is not required to be fitted with a rear fog lamp;
(b) a rear fog lamp on a motor vehicle drawing a trailer;
(c) a defective lamp, dim-dip device, headlamp levelling device or reflector, on a vehicle in use between sunrise and sunset, if the

defect arose during that journey or arrangements had been made
to have the defect remedied with all reasonable expedition; or
(d) a lamp, reflector, dim-dip device, headlamp levelling device or
rear marking, between sunrise and sunset, on a combat vehicle
[23(3)].

In *Payne v Harland* [1980] RTR 478 it was held that both side and
headlamps fitted to a vehicle had to be maintained and it was no
defence to a charge of failing to maintain side lamps to say that the
headlamps were in working order.

Windscreens, etc.

Glass and other transparent material fitted to motor vehicles must be
maintained so that it does not obscure the driver's vision
[1078/86/30(3)].
   Windscreen wipers and washers must be maintained in good and
efficient working order and be properly adjusted [34(6)].

Silencer

Every exhaust system and silencer must be maintained in good and
efficient working order and must not be altered so as to increase the
noise made by the escape of exhaust gases [1078/86/54(2)].

Smoke

An excess fuel device on a diesel engine must not be used to cause
excess fuel to be supplied to the engine while the vehicle is being driven
on a road [1078/86/61(5)(c)].
   The engine of certain petrol-engined vehicles first used on or after
1 January 1972 must be maintained so that crankcase vapours do not
escape into the atmosphere without first passing through the engine
combustion chamber [61(6)].
   A specified agricultural motor vehicle and a diesel-engined vehicle
which is required to have a type test certificate must not have its fuel
injection equipment, governor or other engine parts altered or
adjusted to increase smoke emission [61(5)(b)].
   A motor vehicle must not be used if any smoke, visible vapour, grit,
sparks, ashes, cinders, or oily substance is emitted which is likely to
cause damage or danger [61(5)(a)].
   Except for goods vehicles over 3,500kg maximum gross weight,

engineering plant, works trucks, or a vehicle being driven to a place for repair, a vehicle first used on or after 1 August 1975 and propelled by a four-stroke petrol engine must not be used on a road unless—
(a) the carbon monoxide content of the exhaust emissions does not exceed, in the case of a vehicle first used on or after 1 August 1983, 4.5 per cent, or, in any other case, 6 per cent, of the total volume of exhaust emissions; and
(b) the hydrocarbon content of the emissions does not exceed 0.12 per cent of the total volume of exhaust emissions [61(10A),(10B)].

Others

All steering gear fitted to a motor vehicle must be maintained in good and efficient working order and be properly adjusted [1078/86/29].

Any petrol tank fitted to a vehicle first used on or after 1 July 1973 must be maintained so that leakage of liquid or vapour from the tank, other than by a pressure relief valve, is adequately prevented [39(1)].

A rear under-run protective device required to be fitted to a vehicle must be maintained free from any obvious defect which would adversely affect its performance in the event of a rear impact [50].

A sideguard required to be fitted to a vehicle must be maintained free from any obvious defect which would be likely to adversely affect its effectiveness [52].

Every part of a spray containment device with which a vehicle is required to be fitted must be maintained free from any obvious defect which would be likely to adversely affect the effectiveness of the device [65].

Maintenance records

Section 74 of the Road Traffic Act 1988 enables the Secretary of State to make regulations requiring a goods vehicle operator to have his vehicle inspected and inspection records kept and preserved for up to 15 months. No regulations have yet been made. Licensing Authorities, however, are requiring such inspections to be made and records kept as a condition in granting operators' licences.

10 Motorways

Road Traffic Regulation Act 1984
Highways Act 1980
Motorways Traffic (Scotland) Regulations, **No. 1002/64**
Motorways Traffic (M63 Motorway Slip Road at the Princess Parkway Interchange, Manchester) (Bus Lane) Regulations, **No. 355/77**
Motorways Traffic (England and Wales) Regulations, **Nos. 1163/82**
Motorways Traffic (England and Wales) (Amendment) Regulations, **No. 374/83** and **1364/92**

Permitted traffic

For motorway law purposes traffic is divided into eleven classes but only vehicles of Classes I and II are normally allowed to use a motorway [Act 1984/17 and 1163/82]. Class I traffic is locomotives, motor tractors, heavy motor cars, motor cars, motor cycles over 50cc and trailers drawn by such vehicles provided the vehicles comply with Construction and Use Regulations and the following conditions: the vehicle is entirely on wheels, the wheels have pneumatic tyres, the vehicle is not pedestrian-controlled or licensed as an agricultural machine and, in the case of a motor vehicle, is capable of 25mph on the level under its own power when unladen and not drawing a trailer. Class II traffic is vehicles authorised under the Special Types Order including vehicles used for or in connection with the carriage of an abnormal indivisible load, vehicles constructed for defence purposes, vehicles for moving excavated material, vehicles going for export and engineering plant. The last three classes of vehicle must be capable of 25mph on the level under their own power when unladen and not drawing a trailer [Act 1980/Sch.4].

Restrictions

The restrictions listed in this chapter are contained in the Motorways Traffic (England and Wales) Regulations 1982 and relate to

190

motorways in England and Wales. In Scotland the same restrictions apply but they are contained in the Motorways Traffic (Scotland) Regulations 1964.

Drivers must comply with signs prohibiting entry to the carriageway (usually on slip roads), signs prohibiting left and right turns and must not make 'U' turns. The central reservation should be on the right-hand side of a driver [1163/82/6].

A vehicle must not be driven on a part of a motorway which is not a carriageway [5] except that when it is necessary for a vehicle to stop on the carriageway it must be moved on to the hard shoulder as soon as reasonably practicable [7(2)].

A vehicle must not stop on a carriageway but a vehicle may stop on a carriageway and may be driven on to and remain at rest on a hard shoulder for the following reasons only: (a) breakdown, mechanical defect, lack of fuel, oil or water, (b) accident, illness or other emergency, (c) for a person to move or recover anything which has fallen on to the motorway, or (d) to allow a person to give help in (a), (b) or (c). When a vehicle is on a hard shoulder in these circumstances it must not obstruct the carriageway and must not remain there longer than is necessary [7(2), (3) and 9]. In *Higgins v Bernard* [1972] 1 All ER 1037, [1972] 1 WLR 455 it was held not to be an emergency when a driver, feeling tired, stopped on the hard shoulder because there was evidence that he had felt drowsy before going on to the motorway.

A vehicle must not be reversed along a carriageway except to enable it to be driven forwards or to connect it to another vehicle [8]. A vehicle must not be driven on to the central reservation or verge [10]. A provisional licence holder who has not passed a test must not drive a vehicle on a motorway [11]. A pedestrian must not go on any part of a motorway other than a hard shoulder except to move anything which has fallen on to the motorway or to give assistance in the circumstances described in Regulation 7(2) [13]. An animal must not leave a vehicle on a motorway unless it escapes or unless it is necessary for it to leave a vehicle in which case it may only go on to the hard shoulder and must be on a lead [14].

Motor vehicles other than those in Classes I and II may use a motorway for specified maintenance purposes and, in cases of emergency, a chief officer of police may authorise the use of a motorway by excluded traffic [15]. The restrictions do not apply to emergency services working on a motorway or to specified maintenance purposes [16].

In *Trentham v Rowlands* [1974] RTR 164 the High Court held that a driver who overtook another vehicle on its near-side on a three-lane motorway had been rightly convicted of dangerous driving. But in *Dilks v Bowman-Shaw* [1981] RTR 4 a driver who had not inconvenienced other road users by overtaking on the inside was held, on the facts of that case, not to have driven without reasonable consideration.

Use of outside lane

(a) A goods vehicle with a maximum laden weight over 7.5 tonnes;
(b) a passenger vehicle over 12 metres long;
(c) a motor vehicle drawing a trailer; and
(d) a vehicle which is a motor tractor or locomotive,
must not be driven, moved, stop or remain at rest in the right hand or offside lane of a carriageway which has three or more traffic lanes and which are all open for the use of traffic travelling in the same direction [1163/82/12, 374/83 and 1364/92].

But this ban does not apply to a vehicle being driven in the offside lane in so far as it is necessary for it to pass another vehicle which is carrying or drawing a load of exceptional width [12(3)]. Nor does it require a vehicle to change lanes when it would not be reasonably practicable to do so without involving danger or inconvenience to traffic (e.g. when a vehicle is in the right hand lane of a two-lane motorway which becomes three- or four-laned) [12(4)]. Maximum laden weight is the vehicle's gross weight limit specified in the Construction and the Use Regulations or, if none is specified, the vehicle's design laden weight [12(5)].

A length of the M63 at Princess Parkway Interchange in Greater Manchester is reserved as a bus lane and, except with the permission of a uniformed policeman or traffic warden no person may cause or permit a vehicle other than a schedule express carriage, a stage carriage, a school bus or a works bus to enter the bus lane [355/77/3]. The ban does not apply to enable a vehicle (a) to remove an obstruction (b) to be used for police, fire or ambulance purposes (c) to avoid or prevent an accident or to give help in case of accident or other emergency or (d) to be used for maintaining the road or specified public services [4]. The general prohibition on heavy vehicles and vehicles drawing a trailer from the right-hand lane of a three-lane motorway does not apply to the length of road having the bus lane [5].

Speed limits on motorways are explained in the chapter on speed limits (page 352).

11 Operators' licensing

Transport Act 1968 as amended by Road Traffic Act 1974
Public Passenger Vehicles Act 1981
Transport Act 1982
Goods Vehicles (Operators' Licences, Qualifications and Fees) Regulations,
    No. 176/84
Goods Vehicles (Operators' Licences, Qualifications and Fees) (Amendment)
    Regulations, **Nos. 666/86, 841/87, 2128/88, 1849/90, 2319/92** and **1209/94**
Goods Vehicles (Operators' Licences, Qualifications and Fees) (Amendment)
    (No. 2) Regulations, **No. 1391/86, 2170/87, 2640/90** and **2239/91**
Transport Tribunal Rules, **No. 1547/86**
Traffic Areas (Reorganisation) Order, **No. 288/91**

When a licence is needed

An operator's licence is required by a person who uses, on a road, a
goods vehicle for the carriage of goods:

(a) for hire or reward, or
(b) in connection with any trade or business carried on by him
[Act 1968/60(1)].

Goods and goods vehicles

Goods includes goods or burden of any description. A goods vehicle
is a motor vehicle or trailer constructed or adapted for the carriage of
goods, which includes the haulage of goods [Act 1968/92].

In *Booth v DPP* [1993] RTR 379 it was held that an unladen semi-
trailer coupled to a tractor unit amounted to goods or burden on the
tractor unit and the tractor should have been authorised on an
operator's licence.

193

Exemptions

A small goods vehicle is exempt. It is:
  (i) a vehicle with a relevant plated weight not over 3.5 tonnes or, if not plated, with an unladen weight not over 1,525kg;
  (ii) a drawbar outfit, if the sum of the relevant plated weights of both drawing vehicle and trailer (disregarding a trailer not over 1,020kg unladen) is not over 3.5 tonnes or, if either vehicle is not plated, the sum of the unladen weights is not over 1,525kg; or
  (iii) an articulated vehicle, if the relevant plated weight of the trailer together with the unladen weight of the motor vehicle is not over 3.5 tonnes or, if the trailer is not plated, the sum of the unladen weights of both vehicles is not over 1,525kg [Act 1968/60(4)].

Relevant plated weight means the permitted gross weight shown on a Ministry plate or, if it does not have one, the maximum gross weight shown on a compulsory maker's plate [176/84/3(5)]

Many other vehicles are exempt because they are of a particular construction or use and not really operated for the commercial carriage of goods. They are as follows:

1. Any tractor defined in Schedule 3(2) of the Vehicles (Excise) Act 1971, i.e.
   (A) an agricultural tractor, or
   (B) a tractor (other than an agricultural tractor) which is
      (i) designed and constructed primarily for use otherwise than on roads, and
      (ii) incapable by reason of its construction of exceeding 25mph on the level under its own power;
   while being used for hauling:
   a. threshing appliances;
   b. farming implements;
   c. a living van for the accommodation of the tractor driver;
   d. water or fuel required for the tractor;
   e. articles for a farm required by the keeper, being either the occupier of the farm or a contractor employed to do agricultural work by the farm occupier;
   f. articles for a forestry estate required by the keeper, where the keeper is the occupier of the estate or employed to do forestry work on the estate by the occupier or a contractor employed to do forestry work on the estate by the occupier;
   g. within 15 miles of a farm or forestry estate occupied by the

keeper, agricultural or woodland produce of that farm or estate;

h. within 15 miles of a farm or forestry estate occupied by the keeper, material to be spread on roads to deal with frost, ice or snow;

i. a snow plough or similar for clearing snow;

j. where the keeper is a local authority, soil for landscaping or similar works or a mowing machine;

2. A dual purpose vehicle and any trailer it draws;

3. A vehicle used on a road only in passing between private premises belonging (except a vehicle on excavation or demolition work) to the same person if the road distance in a week does not exceed six miles;

4. A motor vehicle constructed primarily to carry passengers and their effects, and a trailer drawn by it, when so used;

5. A vehicle being used for funerals;

6. A vehicle being used for police, fire or ambulance purposes;

7. A vehicle being used for fire-fighting or rescue operations at mines;

8. A vehicle on which no permanent body has been constructed, which is carrying burden solely for test or trial, or articles which will form part of the completed vehicle when the body is constructed;

9. A vehicle being used under a trade licence;

10. A vehicle in the service of a visiting force or headquarters;

11. A vehicle being used by or under the control of H.M. United Kingdom forces;

12. A trailer not constructed primarily for the carriage of goods but is being used incidentally for that purpose in connection with the construction, maintenance or repair of roads;

13. A road roller and any trailer it draws;

14. A vehicle being used by H.M. Coastguard or of the Royal National Lifeboat Institution for the carriage of lifeboats, life-saving appliances or crew;

15. A vehicle fitted with a machine, appliance, apparatus or other contrivance which is a permanent or essentially permanent fixture, if the only goods carried on the vehicle are:

   (a) required for use in connection with the machine, appliance, apparatus, contrivance or the running of the vehicle;

   (b) to be mixed by the machine, appliance, apparatus or contrivance with other goods not carried on the vehicle on a road in order to thrash, grade, clean or chemically treat grain;

   (c) are to be mixed by the machine, appliance, apparatus or contrivance with other goods not carried on the vehicle to make fodder for animals; or

(d) mud or other matter swept up from the road by the vehicle;

In *North West Traffic Area Licensing Authority v Post Office* [1982] RTR 304 it was ruled that a vehicle used in connection with the erection of telegraph poles and which was fitted with an auger for boring holes in the ground did not come within this exemption because it carried telegraph poles which, though used in connection with the operations on which the machine was used, were not required in connection with the machine itself.

In *British Gypsum Ltd v. Corner* [1982] RTR 308 it was held that a water bowser which also carried pipes for a separate drilling rig did not come within this exemption. Neither did a trailer, in *DPP v. Scott Greenham Ltd* [1988] RTR 426, which carried counter weights for a separate crane vehicle.

But in *DPP v Howard* [1991] RTR 49 it was held that a vehicle fitted with a concrete mixer and which carried sand and cement for use in the mixer came within paragraph (a).

16. A vehicle being used by a local authority for the purposes of laws relating to weights and measures or the sale of food and drugs;

17. A vehicle being used by a local authority for civil defence;

18. A steam-propelled vehicle;

19. A tower wagon or trailer drawn by it, if the only goods carried on the trailer are required in connection with the tower wagon's ordinary work;

In *Anderson and Heeley Ltd v Paterson* [1975] 1 All ER 523 a platform truck fitted with a Hiab loader and used for carrying and installing street-lighting columns was held not to be a tower wagon.

20. A vehicle being used for the carriage of goods within an aerodrome;

21. An electrically propelled vehicle;

22. A showman's goods vehicle and any trailer it draws;

23. A vehicle first used before January 1, 1977, not over 1,525kg unladen weight and which has a maker's plated gross weight over 3.5 tonnes but not over 3.5 tons;

24. A vehicle being used by a highway authority for weighing vehicles or maintaining weighbridges;

25. A vehicle being held ready for emergency use by a water, electricity, gas or telephone service;

26. A recovery vehicle licensed and used as such.

27. A vehicle being used for snow clearing; for the distribution of grit, salt or other materials on frosted, ice-bound or snow-covered roads; for going to or from such operations; or any purpose directly connected with them.

28. A vehicle going to of from a testing station for examination as

long as the only load carried is one officially required for the purpose of the examination.
[176/84/Sch.5, 666/86, 841/87, 2170/87 & 2239/91].

Also exempt is

(a) the use of a goods vehicle for international carriage by a haulier established in a Member State, other than the UK, and not established in the UK;

(b) the use of a goods vehicle for international carriage by a haulier established in Northern Ireland and not established in the UK [Act 1968/60(2)(c)(d) and 3077/92/14]

'International carriage' means a journey between two Member States; between a Member State and a non-Member State; between non-Member States but transitting a Member State; or an unladen journey in connection with the above [3077/92/14 & EC 881/92]

Types of licence

A person who uses a goods vehicle to carry goods for hire or reward (i.e. a haulier) will require either:

(1) a standard international licence, which authorises goods vehicles to be used for the carriage of goods for hire or reward or in connection with the holder's trade or business on national and international operations; or

(2) a standard national licence, which authorises goods vehicles to be used for the carriage of goods for hire or reward on national operations only or in connection with the holder's trade or business on national and international operations.

A person who carries goods in connection with his trade or business (i.e. an own-account operator) but not for payment will require:

(3) a restricted licence, which authorises the carriage of goods for or in connection with the holder's trade or business on national and international operations.   [176/84/4(1),(3)].

The performance by a local or public authority of its functions constitutes the carrying on of a business [Act 1968/60(3)].

The transport of sludge and animal waste was not a hire and reward operation and could be done under a restricted licence—*Wessex Waste Disposal Ltd*, Appeal 1982/T19.

It is an offence for a person to use a vehicle under a restricted licence for carrying goods for hire or reward and for a person to use a vehicle on an international hire or reward operation under a standard national licence [176/84/33(2),(3)].

If a company carries goods for hire or reward for its subsidiary company, its holding company or another subsidiary of the same holding company it may hold a restricted licence instead of a standard licence [4(2)].

A company is a subsidiary of a holding company if the latter company:-

(a) holds a majority of the voting rights in the first company,
(b) is a member of the first company and has the right to appoint or remove a majority of its directors,
(c) is a member of the first company and controls alone, or by agreement with other members, a majority of the voting rights in it, or
(d) is itself a subsidiary of a company which is a holding company.

[Companies Acts 1985 & 1989].

The licence holder

The person using the vehicle must hold the licence. The user is deemed to be the driver, if the vehicle belongs to him or is in his possession under an agreement for hire, hire-purchase or loan, or, in any other case, the person whose servant or agent the driver is [Act 1968/92(2)].

As long as a licence holder can exercise sufficient control over a 'self-employed' driver he will be regarded as the licence holder's employee—*Gordon Wright Transport Ltd*, Appeal 1984/V14.

A holding company can take out a licence—standard or restricted— for vehicles belonging to, or in the possession of, a subsidiary company. In such a case the employees and activities of the subsidiary are deemed to be those of the holding company [176/84/32].

The Licensing Authority

The Licensing Authority (LA) is the Traffic Commissioner for a traffic area and he must act under the general directions of the Minister of Transport [Act 1968/59]. An LA is a creature of statute and his powers are limited to those contained in the Transport Act and statutory regulations—*L & P Traffic Services Ltd*, Appeal 1983/U10.

Great Britain is divided into eight traffic areas [288/91]. The counties they cover and their addresses are given at the end of this chapter [Act 1981/3 & 288/91].

The operating centre

An operating centre is the base or centre at which the vehicle is normally kept and references to a licence holder's operating centre are to any place which is the operating centre for vehicles authorised under the licence [Act 1968/92(1)].

An operating centre is the place where the vehicle normally stands when it is not being used and that use should not be confused with use for business operations—*Auto Industries Ltd,* Appeal 1984/V21 and *U.K. Corrugated Ltd,* Appeal 1984/V22.

Occasional use of another place to park a vehicle overnight, even on a regular basis, does not make that place the vehicle's operating centre if it is normally kept somewhere else—*J. Cryer & Sons Ltd,* Appeal 1985/W12.

A place in the area of the LA who granted an operator's must not be used as an operating centre for authorised vehicles unless it is specified in the operator's licence [69A(1)].

An applicant for a licence must give the LA whatever particulars he requires about each place in his area which will be an operating centre and, if required, particulars as to the proposed use, for authorised vehicles, of any such place [69A(2),(3)].

An LA should be careful about granting a licence for more vehicles than can be acceptably accommodated at an operating centre and imposing a condition limiting the number that can be there at any one time. He should be satisfied that the extra vehicles would be in use on a road or a suitable operating centre existed and could be used for that purpose—*W.H. Lodge, Appeal 1986/X11* and *West Lancashire D.C. v Ken Abram Ltd,* Appeal 1986/X10.

An operating centre does not have to be capable of accommodating all the vehicles authorised on the licence—*James Irlam & Sons Ltd,* Appeal 1991/C20.

A council-owned car and lorry park, open for public use, was held to be a suitable operating centre even though council policy was not to allow lorries to use it as an operating centre—*Epping Forest District Council v Freeman,* Appeal 1987/Y46. A council lorry park, which was the operating centre for 19 vehicles under 7 licences, was allowed to be used by another operator in *C.A. Ceasar,* Appeal 1988/Z22.

Applications

An application for a licence must be made to the Licensing Authority (LA) of the traffic area in which the vehicle operating centre is to be located [Act 1968/62(1)].

The application should be submitted to the LA at least nine weeks before the date it is to take effect, but the LA can deal with applications made at other times [176/84/12 & 14].

A person can hold separate licences for different traffic areas but, except for transitional provisions relating to the abolition of the Metropolitan traffic area, cannot hold more than one licence in the same traffic area [62(1)].

A separate application must be made in respect of each area in which an applicant has an operating centre but no licence. Only one application can be made in respect of all the operating centre in one traffic area [176/84/15].

An application must not be made to an LA if another application by the same person to the same LA has not been disposed of. This would not prevent an individual applying for a licence at the same time a company or partnership in which he was involved also applied for a licence [176/84/15(1)].

A person must not include in his application a vehicle
(a) specified in an existing licence unless the application is for a licence to replace the one in which it is specified or is for the vehicle to be deleted from one licence and added to another;
(b) specified in another application being considered by any LA unless the application is for the vehicle to be deleted from one licence and added to another;
(c) specified in a licence issued to him but suspended under Section 69; or
(d) which has ceased to be authorised under a licence issued to him due to it being curtailed under Section 69. This paragraph includes trailers whilst (a) to (c) refer only to motor vehicles [15(4)].

Further information and convictions.

The LA can require the applicant to give particulars of the motor vehicles he owns, hires or plans to acquire and use under the licence and state the number and type of trailers proposed to be used [Act 1968/62(2)].

An applicant must also give to the LA any further information he may reasonably require, in particular:

1. the purposes for which the vehicles will be used;
2. arrangements for ensuring drivers comply with the hours' and records' law and vehicles will not be overloaded;
3. maintenance facilities and arrangements;
4. details of any past activities in operating any kind of vehicles for trade purposes by
   (a) the applicant,

(b) any company of which the applicant is or has been a director,

(c) where the applicant is a company, any person who is a director,

(d) where the business is a partnership, any person who is a partner,

(e) any company of which a co-director or partner is or has been a director,

(f) any company of which the applicant is a subsidiary;

5. details of convictions during the five years preceding the application of any of the persons in 4. above for offences involving:

(a) plating and testing,

(b) maintenance of vehicles,

(c) speeding,

(d) overloading and the loading of goods vehicles,

(e) licensing of drivers,

(f) operator's licensing,

(g) forgery of, or making false statements to obtain, an operator's licence or fraudulent use of 'O' licence discs,

(h) drivers' hours or records, or conspiracy to contravene hours' and records' law,

(i) unlawfully using rebated fuel,

(j) the operator, or his servant or agent, in contravening Section 173 or 174 of the Road Traffic Act 1988, in relation to an international road haulage permit or of contravening a prohibition under the International Road Haulage Permits Act 1975 (conspiracy to contravene Section 173 is not within this paragraph—*Janet Murfitt*, Appeal 1982/T1),

(k) a restricted licence holder of carrying goods for hire or reward,

(l) a standard licence holder limited to national operations carrying goods on international operations;

(m) unlawful disposal of controlled waste or carrying controlled waste when not a registered carrier,

(n) contravention of waiting restrictions or prescribed lorry routes.

6. financial resources which are or are likely to be available to the applicant,

7. in the case of a company, the names of the directors and officers of the applicant company and of any company of which the applicant is a subsidiary and, in the case of a partnership, the names of the other partners. [Act 1968/62(4)].

Notifying other events

If any conviction of the kind listed in paragraph 5 of the previous section arises between the making of the application and it being disposed of by the LA, the applicant must notify the LA of it forthwith [Act 1968/62(4A)].

Where particulars of a transport manager have been given in an application, the applicant must notify the LA forthwith if, between the application being made and it being disposed of, any event occurs affecting the information given about the transport manager [176/84/5(5)].

Publication of applications and variations

An applicant for a licence must publish notice of his application in a local newspaper circulating in the locality affected by the application within the period beginning 21 days before the application is made and ending 21 days after it was made. If this is not done the LA must refuse the application without even considering its merits. The same rules apply to an application to vary a licence of which notice has been published by the LA in *Applications and Decisions*, [Act 1968/69E(1) & (2)].

A locality is to be taken as affected by the application if it contains a place which will be an operating centre of the applicant or, in the case of a variation, an existing operating centre of the applicant's and to which the application relates [69E(3)].

The newspaper notice must contain:

1. Name of applicant.
2. Trading name, if any.
3. Address for receipt of correspondence.
4. Whether the application is for a new licence or replacement or variation of an existing licence.
5. The places to be used as operating centre.
6. The number of vehicles and trailers to be kept at each operating centre.
7. The number of vehicles and trailers now kept, if different.
8. In the case of an existing licence, any proposed changes to, or removal of, environmental conditions.
    It must also contain the following wording:
Owners or occupiers of land (including buildings) in the vicinity of the operating centre or centres who believe the use or enjoyment of the land will be prejudicially affected, may make written representations to the Licensing Authority at (address of traffic area office) within the 21 days following the publication of this notice. Representors must, at the same time, send a copy of their representations to the applicant at the address given in this notice.
                    [176/84/13(2), Sch.3 & 666/86].

A newspaper notice which said an application was to replace a licence without change when it should have referred to an application for a new licence did not meet the above requirements and an LA's decision to grant the application was quashed—*Basingstoke & Deane Borough Council v Bayliss Transport*, Appeal 1993/E16.

The LA must publish, in *Applications and Decisions*, a summary which adequately specifies the subject matter of any application he receives for a licence or variation of a licence. But he need not publish information of a variation application which would reduce the number of specified vehicles, change the named transport manager, convert a restricted licence to a standard licence (or vice versa) or where the LA considers the application is so trivial that opportunity to object to it need not be given.

[Act 1968/63(1), 68(4) & 176/84/13(1)]. If a licence variation would result in no material change in the use of an operating centre it might come within the 'trivial nature' exception—*R. G. Bown*, Appeal 1985/W8.

Where a variation application is for a new place to be specified as an operating centre, for a specified operating centre to be removed from the licence or for an environmental condition to be varied or removed, the LA must, similarly, publish a summary of the subject matter, unless he considers the application so trivial that opportunity to object to it or make representations against it need not be given [Act 1968/69D(3) & 176/84/13(1)].

Access to applications

An LA who receives an application must, until the application has been determined, make available for inspection

(a) to a person authorised by a statutory objector, the whole or part of the application that person requests in writing to see, and

(b) to a person entitled to make a representation against the application, or a person authorised on his behalf, the part of the application which the LA considers relevant to the representation [176/84/16(1)].

The LA can meet these obligations by making the application or relevant part of it available at his offices or, on receipt of expenses, posting a copy to the person requesting the inspection [16(3)].

Interim licence

If an applicant for a new licence wants to commence operations as soon as possible he can request an interim licence. If the LA grants such a licence it will continue in force until the application is granted by the LA (or on appeal) or, if not granted, until it is refused [Act 1968/67(5)].

An interim licence is 'requested', not 'applied for'; its duration is unknown when granted; it is not open to objection or environmental representation; and the LA does not have to be satisfied on the matters listed in Section 64 which he has to be satisfied on before granting an application—*Kirk Bros. Ltd v Macclesfield B.C.*, Appeal 1986/X29. But he can issue the interim licence for fewer, more or different types of vehicles from those for which the interim licence is sought [67(5)].

It can only be granted if requested and cannot be granted for a fixed period—*Benbay Civil Engineering Group Ltd*, Appeal 1988/Z13.

A request for an interim licence is not to be treated as a licence application for the purposes of objection and refusal on environmental grounds, but the LA can specify in the licence such operating centres as he thinks fit [69B(7)].

Authorised vehicles

Vehicles authorised to be used under an operator's licence are:

(a) motor vehicles belonging to the licence holder or in his possession under an agreement for hire, hire-purchase or loan. They are specified on the licence by their registration number;

(b) trailers from time to time belonging to the holder of the licence or in his possession under an agreement for hire, hire-purchase or loan and not exceeding a maximum number specified in the licence. Trailers are not specified on the licence by any identification number;

(c) a maximum number of motor vehicles specified in the licence belonging to the licence holder or in his possession under an agreement for hire, hire-purchase or loan, but acquired by him, or coming into his possession under such an agreement, after the grant of the licence. Notice this paragraph does not include trailers.

When a motor vehicle is acquired by the licence holder, or it comes into his possession under an agreement, and becomes authorised under this paragraph, the authorisation ceases one month after the acquisition or possession unless, in that time, the licence holder has notified the LA that he has the vehicle. When the LA receives notice under this provision he must specify the vehicle on the licence [Act 1968/61(1),(3) & (4)].

In (b) and (c) above, different types of vehicles can be prescribed in the licence and a maximum number for each type can be specified [61(1)].

An operator's licence does not authorise the use of any vehicle unless its operating centre is in the area of the LA who granted the licence or, if it is outside that area, has not been the vehicle's operating centre for a period of more than three months. Two or more periods not separated from each other by an interval of at least three months are (excluding the time between them) added together to form a single period [61(2)].

A motor vehicle specified in an operator's licence is not capable of being effectively specified in another operator's licence [61(5)].

When an LA learns that a vehicle specified in a licence he granted has (a) ceased to be used under the licence (other than for business fluctuations or repair) or (b) is specified in another operator's licence, he can remove the vehicle from the licence [61(6)].

Hauliers' extra qualifications

An LA must refuse an application for a standard licence unless he is satisfied that requirements relating to good repute, professional competence and appropriate financial standing are satisfied [176/84/5(1)].

GOOD REPUTE

In deciding whether an individual (including a transport manager) is of good repute an LA shall have regard to any matter and in particular to:

(a) relevant convictions of the individual and his employees and agents, and
(b) other information the LA may have as to the individual's conduct which appears to relate to his fitness to hold a licence.

'Any matter' and 'other information ... as to conduct' include any convictions which are not spent and which have some bearing on the person's repute—*A.J.B. Motor Services*, Appeal 1988/Z4.

In deciding whether a company is of good repute an LA shall have regard to all material evidence and in particular to:

(a) relevant convictions of the company, its officers, employees and agents, and
(b) other information the LA may have as to previous conduct of:
  (i)   the company's officers, employees and agents appearing to relate to the company's fitness to hold a licence, and
  (ii) the company's directors, in whatever capacity, appearing to relate to that fitness.

Whilst the conduct of its directors is relevant to a company's repute, their repute is not and an LA should not make any finding they are not of good repute—*Ken Lane Transport Ltd*, Appeal 1988/Z24 and *O'Donovan (Waste Disposal) Ltd*, Appeal 1991/C3.

Where the applicant is a partnership, the LA has to be satisfied that every partner is of good repute.

A relevant conviction is any conviction listed on page 201 above or a corresponding conviction in Northern Ireland or a country outside the United Kingdom or is a below-described serious offence or a road transport offence and which, in any case, is not a spent conviction.

An LA must find that an individual is not of good repute if:

(a) he has been convicted of serious offences (a serious offence is a UK offence for which a sentence of more than three months imprisonment, a fine exceeding level 4 (now £2,500) or more than 60 hours community service was ordered, or a corresponding offence in another country for which a corresponding punishment was imposed), or
(b) he has been repeatedly convicted of road transport offences (a road transport offence is a UK offence relating to road transport, particularly drivers' hours and rest periods, weights and dimensions, road and vehicle safety, or a corresponding offence outside the UK),

but a spent conviction must be disregarded and an LA has discretion to disregard an offence if an "appropriate" time has elapsed since the conviction. An LA can decide a person is not of good repute for reasons other than the kind of convictions in (a) and (b).   [176/84/10A(1), Sch.6(1) & 1849/90]

The penalty for a serious offence relates to a single offence, not a total of offences; 'offences' is in the plural; and being convicted of different offences on the same occasion is not 'repeatedly convicted'—*R.F. Craven*, Appeal 1992/D33.

An LA should not decide that a person is not of good repute without first informing the person that his reputation is to be considered—*DFC International Ltd*, Appeal 1987/Y37.

Good repute is to be determined at the time of the public inquiry and not at the time of the conviction—*Beckside Haulage Ltd*, Appeal 1989/A5.

Failure to fulfil statements of intention or undertakings does not lose a person his good repute—*F.H. Howson*, Appeal 1988/Z16 (PSV).

By positive efforts a person may acquire a good reputation long before convictions become spent—*M & B Transport*, Appeal 1982/T11.

PROFESSIONAL COMPETENCE

Professional competence relates to an individual.

If an individual is not professionally competent, the competence requirement will be satisfied if, and so long as, he has a transport manager of his road transport undertaking who is of good repute and professionally competent.

A company satisfies the professional competence requirement if it has a transport manager or managers, or whatever number the LA may require, who is, or each of them is, of good repute and professionally competent.

A partnership satisfies the requirement if any of the partners managing the road transport business is professionally competent or any nominated transport manager employed is of good repute and professionally competent. The amount of time the competent partner spends on managing the business should be 'sufficient' rather than 'substantial'—*Baker Haulage*, Appeal 1983/U19,

Where a standard licence holder relies on a single transport manager and the manager

(a) dies or ceases, due to physical disability or mental disorder, to be capable of working as a transport manager,
(b) ceases to work for the business, or
(c) ceases to be of good repute,

the licence holder will not be treated as failing to satisfy the competence requirement for a period—not over 18 months—which the LA considers reasonable for the appointment of a new transport manager. This provision also applies to a firm where one of the partners or a single transport manager met the professional competence requirement.

Where a standard licence holder is a company with two or more transport managers and any of them ceases to be of good repute, the company will not be treated as failing to satisfy the competence requirement for a period the LA considers reasonable for his removal or the appointment of a new manager in his place. This provision also applies to a firm where two or more partners or two or more transport managers met the professional competence requirement.

An individual is regarded as professionally competent if:

(a) he has passed a written examination showing he possesses the requisite skills and holds a certificate to that effect,
(b) he is the holder of any other certificate of competence, diploma or other qualification recognised for this purpose by the Secretary of State.

[176/84/10A(3), Sch.6(2), 666/86, 1849/90 & 2640/90].

A transport manager is an individual who is, or is to be, in the employment of the licence holder and who, either alone or jointly, has continuous and effective responsibility for the management of the goods transport operations of the business [176/84/3(1)].

A transport manager did not have to reside in the same traffic area as the operating centres he was responsible for—*Scot Bowyers Ltd*, Appeal 1978/P13. In that case a transport manager based in Trowbridge, Wilts was responsible for six depots in South Wales. The Transport Tribunal also considered it proper to refer to the relevant EC Directive to assist in the interpretation of the UK regulations.

A cpc holder must be an active employee carrying out the functions of a transport manager in an adequate manner—*Veertran Ltd*, Appeal 1994/F5. In that case a company which nominated a cpc holder who did not carry out the duties of transport manager was found to have deceived the LA and, consequently, to have lost its good repute.

APPROPRIATE FINANCIAL STANDING

This means having available sufficient financial resources to ensure the establishment and proper administration of the road transport undertaking operated under the licence.

Except for a person who held a licence continuously before 11 October 1990 and up to the time a new licence is issued, the holder of a standard international licence (including a firm, in the case of a partnership) will not be considered to be of appropriate financial standing unless he has available capital and reserves equal to the lesser of:

(a) 3,000 European Currency Units per vehicle used under the licence, or

(b) 150 ECU per tonne of the total plated maximum gross weight of the vehicle(s).   [176/84/10A(3), Sch.6(3) & 1849/90].

The purpose of the Regulations is to ensure that operators' granted a licence have a far firmer financial base than operating on a shoestring—*Rosswood Ltd v RHA*, Appeal 1983/U9.

The 'continuous' holding of a licence refers to the holding of a licence in any traffic area, not solely the area in which the licence is applied for—*J.J. Adam (Haulage) Ltd*, Appeal 1992/D41.

An operator only has available financial resources or capital and reserves if he has money in the bank which is capable of being used (i.e. not already needed to pay debts), or an overdraft at his disposal (with a balance undrawn before the limit is reached), or he has debts which are obtainable because they are due and likely to be easy to collect, or he has assets from which money is easy to get in the sense that they can be readily sold without any adverse effect on the ability of the business to generate money, or he has some other way in which to come up with money at fairly short notice should it be needed— *J.J. Adam (Haulage) Ltd*, Appeal 1992/D41.

Objections to applications

An objection to an application can be lodged by a prescribed trade association or trade union, a chief officer of police, a local authority and a planning authority on the grounds that the requirements listed in paragraphs (a) to (d) in the next section are not satisfied by the applicant [Act 1968/63(3)].

The prescribed associations and unions are:
Road Haulage Association
Freight Transport Association
British Association of Removers
Transport and General Workers' Union
General and Municipal Workers' Union
National Union of Railwaymen
Union of Shop, Distributive and Allied Workers
United Road Transport Union [176/84/17]

A local authority, in England and Wales, is the council of a county, county borough, county district, London Borough or City of London and, in Scotland, a county or town council. A planning authority is any body, other than a local authority, which is theauthority for determining planning permission under the Town and Country Planning Act [Act 1968/63(6).

ENVIRONMENTAL

The environmental provisions, introduced by the Transport Act 1982 on June 1, 1984, give LAs control over the places which may be used as operating centres and the use to which they may be put for authorised vehicles, with a view to preventing or minimising any adverse effects on environmental conditions arising from the situation of a centre or its use for authorised vehicles [Act 1982/52(2)].

The statutory objectors referred to above can also object to the grant of an application on the grounds that any place to be used by the licence holder as an operating centre, if the licence is granted, is unsuitable on environmental grounds for that use [Act 1968/69B(1) & Act 1982/52 & Sch.4].

When considering objections under the above provision an LA is not confined to adverse environmental effects in the vicinity—as he is with representors—but should have regard, to such extent as he thinks relevant, to the adverse environmental effects of authorised vehicles going to or from the operating centre on access roads. How wide an area he takes into account is a matter for him to decide on the evidence before him along with consideration of adverse effects caused by other vehicles using the road—*Surrey C.C. v Express Hay and Straw Services*, Appeal 1986/X25. The noise of authorised vehicle using access roads can be taken into account when determining adverse effects—*W.R. Atkinson (Transport) Ltd*, Appeal 1986/X30.

In *Strathkelvin D.C. v Fife Forwarding Company Ltd*, Appeal 1985/W30, the Transport Tribunal gave a provisional view that road safety was not an environmental matter. It followed that view in *Middlesbrough Borough Council v T.P.M. McDonagh (Civil Engineering) Ltd*, Appeal 1989/A22, when it said road safety was not an environmental matter on which representors were permitted to make representations and road safety should not have been included as part of an objection or representations. But in *J.Simms*, Appeal 1990/B52 and *D.W. Sherwood*, Appeal 1991/C5, the Tribunal said that it was not constrained by its provisional view in *Strathkelvin* but said that matters to do with the condition and suitability of a particular road which, among other things, had significance for road safety could also have significance in a totally separate environmental context.

A person who is the owner or occupier of land in the vicinity of any place which would be used as an operating centre under a licence may make representations against the grant of the licence on the grounds that the place is unsuitable on environmental grounds for that use. But any adverse effects on environmental conditions arising from the use of the place as an operating centre have to be capable of prejudicially affecting the use or enjoyment of the land [69B(2)].

A person who makes a representation must first show that, on the balance of probability, the use of the operating centre will have an adverse effect on environmental conditions, before going on to show that use of the operating centre would be capable of prejudicially affecting the use or enjoyment of his own land—*A. Hetherington*, Appeal 1990/B12.

The term 'vicinity' is not defined but in *Express Hay and Straw Services* (above) the Transport Tribunal said that in determining what lies in the vicinity of an operating centre an LA should consider what was physically related or near to it. 'Physically related' meant adverse effects which could be transmitted physically, according to the laws of nature, such as vibration or noise—*Ings Transport Ltd*, Appeal 1988/Z37.

A residents' association which does not itself own or occupy land cannot make representations—*U.K. Corrugated Ltd*, Appeal 1984/V22. Whilst a parish council cannot make an objection itself it can be called as a witness by a valid objector provided its evidence is relevant to the environmental issue raised by the objector—*Mid Suffolk District Council v A. Dowell*, Appeal 1987/Y12.

The fact that lorries caused inconvenience in using the public highway (as opposed to noise, fumes and vibration which entered residents' property) is incapable of affecting the use or enjoyment of a person's land—*P.T. Chesney*, Appeal 1987/Y28.

Before an LA rules that a representor does not live within the vicinity of an operating centre he should give that person opportunity to be heard on the issue—*Ings Transport Ltd*, Appeal 1988/Z37.

The onus of proving any objection or representation lies on the person making it [63(5) & 69G(1)].

Notifying objections and representations

A general objection must state the grounds on which it is made and an environmental objection or representation must contain particulars of the matters alleged to be relevant to the LA's decision [Act 1989/63(4) & 69G(1)].

An objection or representation must be in writing and be signed (i) if made by an individual, by that person; (ii) if made by a partnership, by all the partners or by one of them authorised by the others; or (iii) if made by any other body of persons, by one or more individuals authorised for that purpose; or, in any case, a solicitor acting for the objector. The person making it must send a copy to the applicant at the same time as he sends it to the LA [176/84/18].

An objection which merely said 'on environmental grounds' did not make the applicant fully aware of the specific grounds of objection and was therefore not 'duly made'—*Surrey Heath Borough Council v NFT Distribution Ltd*, Appeal 1985/W17. In the same case it was said that statutory objectors must be assumed to have ready access to legal advice and an LA should set a severe standard in considering whether there were exceptional circumstances. An objection was not 'duly made' unless it complied with the Act and Regulations—*A. Hetherington*, Appeal 1990/B12.

In *Crewe & Nantwich B.C. v Yoxall*, Appeal 1992/D32, it was said:

a. an objection need not quote the relevant Section of the Act;
b. it is essential an objection is worded to make it clear whether it is made under Section 63(4)—in which case it must go on to identify which requirement of Section 64(2) cannot be met—or it is made under Section 69A;
c. an objection must set out sufficient details of what the objector proposes to say to enable the applicant to know the case he will have to meet;
d. an objection which contains more than one ground of objection should, as a better practice, set out each ground in a separate paragraph;
e. where different grounds of objection are advanced in different paragraphs, each paragraph should be treated as a separate objection. Valid objections should be allowed to stand while invalid ones are struck out;
f. an objection which is valid can be added to with 'further and better particulars' at a later date, subject to the applicant being given proper notice of the case he has to meet. The ability to add further particulars is not a licence to take the applicant by surprise at a very late stage;
g. it is not possible, after the time for objecting has expired, to amend or add anything to an invalid objection to make it valid.

An objection must be made so that it reaches the LA not later than 21 days from the date of publication of the application in *Applications and Decisions*. A representation must be received by the LA within 21 days of publication of notice of the application in a local newspaper [176/84/19]. The 21 days does not include the day of publication— *Borough of Haringey v Michli*, Appeal 1985/W9. A resident's letter received in the 21 days before publication of a newspaper notice was 'received too early to meet the requirements of Regulation 19'—*W.R. Atkinson (Transport) Ltd*, Appeal 1986/X30.

But the LA may, in circumstances which he considers exceptional, consider an objection or representation even though the above requirements have not been followed [20].

These rules must be strictly complied with by objectors and

representors. The fact that an applicant does not raise an objection to persons who have not followed the rules does not justify an LA in hearing, other than in exceptional circumstances, from persons who have not complied with the rules. The circumstances must be exceptional for an LA to waive the rules—*Auto Industries Ltd*, Appeal 1984/V21 and *U.K. Corrugated Ltd*, Appeal 1984/V22. In the case of statutory objectors, who must be assumed to have ready access to legal advice, an LA will rightly set a 'severe standard' in deciding whether there are exceptional circumstances—*Surrey Heath Borough Council v NFT Distribution Ltd*, Appeal 1985/W17.

In *UK Corrugated Ltd* it was also said that a petition, submitted in that case, could not amount to a representation. A petition which is not supported by any evidence from the petitioners should not be accepted in evidence—*J.E. Gray*, Appeal 1983/U2.

An LA is under no duty to bring supplementary information he obtains from an applicant to the notice of an objector. It is up to the objector to exercise his right to inspect the application at the LA's office—*Wellingborough B.C. v W. Brown*, Appeal 1986/X27.

LA's consideration of all applications

On every application for an operator's licence the LA must consider whether the following requirements are satisfied and, in doing so, must have regard to any objection properly made:

(a) that the applicant is a fit person to hold an operator's licence having regard to the information and convictions in paragraphs 4. and 5. in the 'further information and convictions' section above. This provision includes, in the case of a standard licence applicant, his good repute, financial standing and professional competence [176/84/36(1)];

(c) arrangements for ensuring drivers' hours and tachograph regulations will be observed and that vehicles will not be overloaded;

(d) there will be satisfactory facilities and arrangements for maintaining vehicles in a fit and serviceable condition and the vehicle's operating centre is suitable for that purpose; and

(e) that the applicant has sufficient financial resources to provide (d) above.   [Act 1968/64(1),(2)].

The fact that a person has been convicted of a criminal offence is not itself evidence that he is unfit to hold an operator's licence. It is necessary for the LA to consider the nature and number of the offences and the person's conduct between the date of the offence and the decision—*Peter Hooper*, Appeal 1984/V15.

In the absence of conduct amounting to fraudulent trading, a person's involvement in a liquidated company did not render him unfit to hold a licence—*Wilkinson Freight (UK) Ltd*, Appeal 1984/V7.

When deciding on the suitability of an operating centre, under this Section, an LA should not have regard to environmental matters. Whether premises were detrimental to the environment was a matter for planning law—*RHA v Cash & McCall*, Appeal 1975/M15. Difficulties in obtaining planning permission are no reason why a person should not have an operator's licence—*A.F. Mansfield v Leicester C.C.*, Appeal 1979/Q10. A person who wishes to operate a haulage business has two obstacles to overcome, one under the Transport Act and the other under planning law— failing to overcome the planning obstacle does not mean there must be a finding he has not overcome the Transport Act obstacle—*Cameron Shuttering Ltd*, Appeal 1982/T13. (But see subsequent environmental provisions below).

'Suitable' does not mean suitable in planning terms and an LA does not carry out his duties to assist planning authorities—*Basildon Council v Rees Haulage*, Appeal 1985/W21 and *C. Smith*, Appeal 1986/X1. The legislation has been drafted to keep planning considerations and transport considerations separate and the only circumstances in which planning considerations become relevant is in Regulation 22(1)(c) and that does not include the refusal or absence of planning permission or the absence of any planning application—*East Herts DC v Pallett*, Appeal 1989/B30 and *R.I. Johnston*, Appeal 1992/D3.

To be suitable an operating centre does not have to be capable of accommodating all the vehicles authorised on the licence—*James Irlam & Sons Ltd*, Appeal 1991/C20.

When considering the suitability of a place to be an operating centre, under (c) above, an LA should take into account the suitability of any private road or track linking that place to the public road, including the point where it joins the public road, and the considerations relevant to suitability might include road safety. The suitability of the public road beyond the point where the operating centre (or private road from it) debouched onto the public road was not included—*Scorpio International Ltd*, Appeal 1987/Y17 and *Monmouth District Council v Baldry*, Appeal 1988/Z11. An LA cannot take into account anything beyond the boundary of the proposed operating centre and its entrance to and from the public highway—*East Herts D.C. v Pallett*, Appeal 1989/B30.

A council-owned car and lorry park, open for public use, was held to be suitable even though council policy was not to allow lorries to use it as an operating centre—*Epping Forest District Council v Freeman*,

Appeal 1987/Y46. A council lorry park, which was the operating centre for 19 vehicles under 7 licences, was allowed to be used by another operator in *C.A. Ceasar*, Appeal 1988/Z22.

When an LA is in possession of documents or evidence which reflect adversely on the applicant, the LA must give the applicant opportunity to comment on them—*See You Transport Ltd*, Appeal 1985/W15. Where an LA proposes to refuse an application, the applicant has a right to be clearly informed of the grounds for that action and the evidence supporting those grounds. He also has a right to be heard, either at a public inquiry or by making written comments on the grounds and evidence—*L.C. Skips Ltd*, Appeal 1991/C8. See also *Jebb Transport*—page 228.

If an LA is not satisfied that the requirements as to good repute, appropriate financial standing and professional competence are met by an applicant for a standard licence he must refuse the licence [176/84/5]. In this connection, where the applicant is a partnership the LA has to be satisfied that every partner is of good repute and the partner who manages the road transport business is professionally competent or a professionally competent transport manager is employed [10A(1)].

An LA could not be satisfied that an applicant had sufficient financial resources (under (e) above) at the time of a licence grant if the situation was dependent on the occurrence of a future event—*RHA v John Dee Ltd*, Appeal 1992/D4.

LA's decision on all applications

If the LA is not satisfied on any of points (a) to (e) in the previous section, he must refuse the application. Otherwise—and subject to any action on environmental grounds—he must grant the application in the terms applied for or as modified [64(3)].

When granting a licence the LA can authorise motor vehicles other than those applied for, or reduce or increase the number of, or vary the type of, motor vehicles or trailers for which authority was applied for. He can also refuse authority on the licence for vehicles acquired after the licence grant [64(4)].

Section 64(4) does not empower an LA to grant a smaller number of vehicles than applied for as a punishment for, or disapproval of, past misconduct—*National Carriers Ltd*, Appeal 1975/M8.

The power to reduce vehicle numbers can be used for environmental purposes but should not be used if licence conditions would prevent or minimise adverse environmental effects—*Turbostar Ltd*, Appeal 1986/X15.

In considering point (e) the LA may be assisted by an assessor drawn from a panel appointed by the Minister for that purpose [64(5)].

An assessor's assistance is limited to point (e) but to provide that assistance an overall assessment of an applicant's finances may be necessary. If so, fairness dictates that it be set out in a report and the report is disclosed to the applicant so that he can comment on it—*J.J. Adam Haulage Ltd*, Appeal 1992/D41. The assessor is not to assist the LA on point (a)—*RHA v John Dee Ltd*, Appeal 1992/D4. The function of an assessor was described in *N.C.J. Pilbeam Transport*, Appeal 1992/D7 and *J.J. Adam Haulage Ltd*, Appeal 1992/D41.

Where an LA grants or refuses an application he must send a written statement, of his reasons to the applicant, every objector and, if he asks for one, a representor. But this does not apply where a licence is granted in the terms applied for and no objection or representation was made [176/84/24A & 2319/92].

When giving his decision an LA should state clearly his material findings of fact and make plain the basis in law for his decision—*Turbostar Ltd*, Appeal 1986/X15.

An LA must not refuse an application merely because he has refused an earlier, similar application from another operator but should give the applicant opportunity to say whether the circumstances are different—*R.G. Griggs*, Appeal 1988/Z12.

The LA must consider any objection or representation, made in the required manner, when considering whether or not to grant a licence [176/84/20].

An LA's decision on a licence application, other than an interim licence, must be published in *Applications and Decisions* [176/84/24].

LA's consideration and decision on environmental matters

If an application is opposed on environmental grounds, the LA must determine the suitability, on environmental grounds, of any place to be used as an operating centre [Act 1968/69G(3)]. In doing so he must have regard to the following considerations:

(a) the nature and use of any other land in the vicinity of the operating centre and any effect the operating centre would have on the environment in the vicinity;

(b) if the operating centre is, or previously has been an operating centre, the extent to which a grant of the application would result in any material change to that operating centre or its use which would adversely affect the environment in its vicinity;

Where a place is or has been used as an operating centre, an LA should determine 'What is that place being used for at present?' and then decide if a licence grant would result in a material change in use which would adversely affect the environment in the vicinity—*D.H. Wylie, trading as Sunnyside Removals*, Appeal 1986/X17. This was followed in *Kirk Brothers Ltd*, Appeal 1986/X29, where the Tribunal added that the fact that premises had an established use certificate for haulage and storage was immaterial.

(c) where the operating centre has not been previously used as such, any information he has about planning permission, or application for planning permission, relating to the operating centre or other land in its vicinity;

The fact that planning permission does not exist for an operating centre does not mean that a licence has to be refused— *Cameron Shuttering Ltd*, Appeal 1982/T13. The position under planning legislation (of an operating centre) is germane only to Regulation 22(1)(c)—*Wear Valley D.C. v Linsley*, Appeal 1988/Z32.

This paragraph permits an LA to take into account any information about any planning permission or application for planning permission relating to the land or any land in the vicinity. It does not permit him to take into account the absence of planning permission or a refusal of planning permission or the absence of any application for planning permission—*East Herts DC v Pallett*, Appeal 1989/B30 and *R.I. Johnston*, Appeal 1992/D4.

The use of land for a purpose for which planning permission has not been granted only becomes unlawful after enforcement action has been successfully taken. The planning authority has to surmount various hurdles on its way to successful enforcement action—*East Herts DC v Pallett*, Appeal 1989/B30.

(d) the number, type and size of authorised vehicles;

(e) the arrangements for parking authorised vehicles;

(f) the nature and times of use of the land for the purpose of an operating centre;

(g) the nature and times of use of equipment installed at the operating centre for its use as an operating centre;

(h) the means and frequency of vehicular ingress to and egress from the operating centre. [176/84/22].

When balancing the interests of an applicant with those of a representor an LA must not make an order more favourable to the representor than he would have made if the representor had a right of appeal—*R.A. Nightingale*, Appeal 1985/W4.

Where an objection or representation has been properly made on environmental grounds, the LA may refuse a licence application on the grounds that the parking of vehicles authorised under the licence at, or in the vicinity of, an operating centre would cause adverse effects on environmental conditions in its vicinity [69B(3)]. 'Parking of vehicles' referred to authorised vehicles which had been parked and not to parking manoeuvres—*D. & A. Transport Ltd v Lancashire C.C.*, Appeal 1985/W23.

Where such an objection or representation has been made, the LA may refuse the licence application on the grounds that any place which would be an operating centre under the licence is unsuitable on environmental grounds (other than parking), but
subject to safeguards for existing licence holders [69B(4)].

The safeguards are that a licence may not be refused if the applicant satisfies the LA that the grant would not result in any material change regarding:

(a) the place to be used as an operating centre under any previous licence or the licence applied for, or
(b) the use of a place already used as an operating centre under an existing licence [69B(5)].

'Or' at the end of paragraph (a) means 'and'—*J. Cryer & Sons Ltd*, Appeal 1986/W12.

An LA should take into account points (a) to (h) above before making a decision under the preceding paragraph. He should also have regard to all the uses—not solely as an operating centre—to which a place already in use as an operating centre is put when deciding whether the grant of the application will result in a material change. He should consider whether a grant would result in a material change of use when compared with lawful use being made of the place at the time of his decision—*D.H. Wylie, trading as Sunnyside Removals*, Appeal 1986/X17.

Under this provision, an LA is not concerned with the use of an operating centre in the past under a licence which has come to an end and use under an applicant's interim licence is not to be regarded as use under an existing licence—*Kirk Brothers Ltd*, Appeal 1986/X29.

A change of use which would not increase adverse effects on the environment, such as a reduction in the number of vehicles, was not a material change—*Turbostar Ltd*, Appeal 1986/X15. This was followed in *Middlesbrough B.C. v T.P.M. McDonagh (Civil Engineering) Ltd*, Appeal 1989/A22, when it was ruled that a change could not be material unless it was capable of prejudicially affecting the use or enjoyment of land.

Whether the alteration or removal of a movement condition amounts to a material change of use depends on the circumstances of the case—*L.R. Cobden*, Appeal 1992/D21.

Where an LA has power to refuse a licence on the above environmental grounds and the application includes a place to be used as an operating centre which is not unsuitable, the LA can, instead of refusing the application, issue a licence specifying only the place or places which are not unsuitable [69B(6)].

"Place" means the whole of the place and not a part of it—*Turbostar Ltd*, Appeal 1986/X15.

A place which is environmentally unsuitable cannot be authorised for a limited period—*Wear Valley DC v Linsley*, Appeal 1988/Z32.

When refusing an application an LA was right to disregard extra traffic which might have visited the operating centre from other depots of the applicant due to the refusal—*Duncan Lacey & Bros Ltd v Mid Sussex D.C.*, Appeal 1988/Z34. (In that case an industrial park was held to be environmentally unsuitable to keep 10 lorries).

Licence conditions

When granting a licence the LA may attach conditions requiring the licence holder to inform him of any change, of a kind specified in the condition, in the organisation, management or ownership of the business; in the case of a company, any specified changes in shareholders; or of any other kind of specified event affecting the licence holder [Act 1968/66].

Such a condition can also be attached to a licence when the LA has power to take disciplinary action against the licence [69(2)].

When granting a standard operator's licence the LA must attach a condition requiring the licence holder to inform him, within 28 days, of (a) any event which could affect the requirements as to good repute, financial standing or professional competence, and (b) any event which could affect the good repute or professional competence of a nominated transport manager. If the licence holder is a company, such a condition will not require notice of any change in the persons holding shares in the company unless it changes the control of the company [176/84/7]. A conviction is an event coming within (b) and a failure to notify it is a factor an LA can take into account when considering a person's fitness or good repute—*A.J.B. Motor Services*, Appeal 1988/Z4.

The legal effect of undertakings was queried by the Transport Tribunal, in *Mid Suffolk D.C. v Dowell*, Appeal 1987/Y12, when it said there might be some doubt as to whether undertakings, on matters which could not be included in a licence condition, were enforceable.

ENVIRONMENTAL

An LA may attach conditions to a licence which appear to him to be appropriate for preventing or minimising any adverse effects on the environment arising from the use, for authorised vehicles, of an operating centre [Act 1968/69C(1)].

The conditions apply only to vehicles authorised under the particular operator's licence and not to visiting vehicles—*C. Smith*, Appeal 1986/X1. An operator's intention to contract-out work to avoid the effect of a condition is no reason for not attaching a condition—*Eskett Quarries v Courtney*, Appeal 1987/Y3.

If no environmental objection (or representation) is made to an application, an environmental condition cannot be attached—*N. Daniels*, Appeal 1988/Z18. If an operating centre has no adverse effect on the environment, an environmental condition cannot be attached—*James Irlam & Sons Ltd*, Appeal 1991/C20.

The conditions are:

(a) the number, size and type of authorised vehicles which may at any one time be at an operating centre for the purpose of maintenance or parking;

(b) the parking arrangements to be provided for authorised vehicles at, or in the vicinity of, an operating centre;

(c) the times between which any maintenance or movement of authorised vehicles may be carried out at an operating centre and the times at which any equipment may be used for such maintenance or movement; and

(d) the means of ingress to and egress from an operating centre for authorised vehicles [176/84/21].

A condition under (a) above can apply only to the operating centre and not to the vicinity of the operating centre—*C. Smith*, Appeal 1986/X1.

Before an LA attaches a condition limiting the number of vehicles which may be parked at an operating centre to a number less than the number authorised on the licence, he should be satisfied that the extra vehicles would be in use on a road or a suitable operating centre existed and could be used for that purpose—*W.H. Lodge*, Appeal 1986/X11 and *West Lancashire D.C. v Ken Abram Ltd*, Appeal 1986/X10.

A condition which prohibits parking of authorised vehicles on the highway in the vicinity of an operating centre means those vehicles cannot be loaded and unloaded there—*London Borough of Havering v E. Hawkes (Ceramic Tiles) Ltd*, Appeal 1991/B49.

In *Monmouth District Council v Baldry*, Appeal 1988/Z11, paragraph (b) was used to control loading and unloading inside an operating centre and in *London Borough of Havering v E. Hawkes (Ceramic Tiles) Ltd*, Appeal 1991/B49, the Tribunal said the paragraph would regulate such arrangements outside the operating centre.

When attaching a parking condition, it is for the LA to decide on the arrangements and not leave it to the licence holder and local authority to reach agreement on them—*C. Smith*, Appeal 1986/X1.

A condition under (d) above can only relate to the points of ingress and egress from the operating centre and cannot be used to restrict the use of roads in the vicinity of the operating centre by authorised vehicles—*W.R. Atkinson (Transport) Ltd*, Appeal 1986/X30.

A condition which banned reversing into or out of an operating centre was not environmental but was aimed at road safety and an LA had no power to attach it—*SCC v Norman Marshall Ltd*, Appeal 1991/C9.

An environmental condition may be varied or removed by the LA at any time but it can be imposed only when the licence is granted or when the operator applies to add or remove an operating centre or vary or remove an environmental condition [69C(3),(4)].

Where an LA cannot refuse a licence on environmental grounds because there has been no material change to the operating centre or its use, he cannot attach an environmental condition to the licence without first giving the licence applicant opportunity to make representations about the condition's effect on his business. If such representations are made the LA must give them special consideration when deciding whether to attach the proposed condition to the licence [69C(5)]. For Section 69B(5) to operate there must first be findings of environmental unsuitability under Section 69B(4) and no material change under Section 69B(5) though it is prudent to give a licence applicant opportunity to make representations about proposed conditions in any event—*H.E. Baldry Ltd*, Appeal 1992/D34.

Any condition an LA proposes to attach to a licence under this provision should be put in writing to the operator who should then be given time to consider it and prepare his representation. The LA should then pay particular attention to those representations—*R.G. Bown*, Appeal 1985/W8 and *Thrapston Warehousing Co. Ltd*, Appeal 1985/W7. This ruling was followed in *M & G House*, Appeal 1985/W19, where the Tribunal also said that, in addition to inviting representations, the LA could have a hearing to hear submissions and, if necessary, evidence of the effect of the proposed conditions. But in *C. Smith*, Appeal 1986/X1, it said there was no legal requirement for representations to be supported by oral evidence.

When considering attaching, varying or removing a condition the LA must have regard to the specified environmental considerations (page 216), to information supplied by the applicant and any properly-made objections or representations [69G(3),(4)].

If a variation application is for an increase in fleet size, any environmental conditions apply to the whole of the fleet and not merely to the additional vehicles—*W.H. Martin Ltd*, Appeal 1988/Z39.

Licence variation

If a licence holder applies to the LA who granted it, for a variation of the licence, the LA can direct:

(a) additional motor vehicles be specified in the licence, that the maximum number of authorised vehicles be increased or a hiring margin be added;
(b) motor vehicles specified in the licence be removed or the maximum number of authorised vehicle be reduced;
(c) an alteration or addition to the nominated transport manager in a standard licence;
(d) an alteration to, or removal of, a licence condition of the kind mentioned in the preceding section;
(e) a restricted licence be converted into a standard licence or vice versa. [Act 1968/68(1)].

Except where the application is for a direction under (b), (c) or (e) above or the LA is satisfied the application is so trivial that opportunity to object to it should not be given, the LA must publish details of the application in *Applications and Decisions*.

Where a variation application is published by the LA he has to be satisfied on specified matters, in the same way as a licence application. [68(4)].

An application to vary a restricted licence by converting it to a standard licence is subject to the same requirements regarding haulier's qualifications and notification of convictions as a new application for a standard licence. If the holder of a standard national licence applies for it to be varied to cover international operations he must give details of the professional competence he relies on and, if not satisfied with them, the LA must refuse the variation [176/84/8].

Temporary replacement of motor vehicles unfit for service, to be overhauled or repaired, can be arranged with the LA without going through the full variation procedure [176/84/26].

ENVIRONMENTAL

On application of a licence holder, an LA may vary the licence by (i) adding or removing an operating centre or (ii) varying or removing an environmental condition on the licence [Act 1968/69D(1)].

Whilst no objection as to the suitability of the operating centre can be made under this provision, an LA should have regard to it in exercising the discretion given to him by the word 'may'—*Hi-Line Transport Ltd*, Appeal 1990/B24.

The 'no material change' protection for licence applications (see page 218) does not apply to variation applications—*D. &. A Transport Ltd v Lancashire C.C.* Appeal 1985/W23.

Objections to variations

If a variation application is published by the LA, it is open to objection by the statutory bodies in the same way as a licence application—see page 213 [Act 1968/68(4)].

ENVIRONMENTAL

A statutory body entitled to object to the grant of a licence may, if the LA has published notice of a variation application, object to the variation on the grounds that

(a) any place which will be used as an operating centre, if the application is granted, is unsuitable on environmental grounds, or
(b) the use of an operating centre in any manner which will be permitted, if the variation is granted, will have adverse effects on environmental conditions in the vicinity of the centre [69D(4)].

Because Section 69D(4)(b) refers to 'vicinity' the interpretation of Section 69B(1) given in Appeal 1986/X25 (*Express Hay & Straw*) does not apply to this provision—*Ings Transport Ltd*, Appeal 1988/Z37.

A person who is the owner or occupier of land in the vicinity of (i) any place which will be an operating centre if the variation is granted or (ii) any existing centre to which the application relates, may make representations against a variation application published by the LA on grounds (a) and (b) above, but only in relation to that place or operating centre. Any adverse environmental effects alleged by a representor must be capable of prejudicially affecting the use or enjoyment of his land [69D(5),(6)].

Where an objection or representation has been made, on environmental grounds, against a variation application, the LA may refuse the application on grounds (a) or (b) above [69D(7)].

Where an LA grants a published variation application he may direct that any environmental condition on the licence be varied or removed or that a condition be attached to the licence [69D(8)]. When attaching a condition on licence variation the LA does not have to give the operator opportunity to make representations about the effects of the condition on his business—*West Lancashire District Council v Ken Abram Ltd*, Appeal 1986/X10.

When deciding whether to refuse an application under (a) above or impose conditions, an LA has to consider the total use to be made of the premises as an operating centre—*British Road Services Ltd*, Appeal 1985/W16 and *D. & A. Transport Ltd v Lancashire C.C.* Appeal 1985/W23.

Interim variation direction

An applicant for a licence variation can request an interim direction pending the determination of the application. If he does so, the LA can give such a direction which continues in force until the application, or any appeal arising from it, is disposed of. A request for an interim direction is not treated as a variation application [Act 1968/84/68(5)].

An applicant for a variation to add or remove an operating centre or vary or remove an environmental condition on a licence can request an interim direction pending determination of the application. The LA can give a direction which continues in force until the application, or any appeal arising from it, is. disposed of and the direction is not treated as a variation application which is open to objections or representations [69D(9)].

Public inquiries

The LA can hold what inquiries he considers necessary for carrying out his work and, when considering whether to hold an inquiry, he must have regard to any objections or representations he has received [Act 1968/87(1) & 176/84/20].

The purpose of a disciplinary public inquiry is to give the licence holder opportunity of showing cause why the LA should not give the direction he has in mind—*Transport Holding Company*, Appeal 1966/C12.

The dates and places of inquiries must be published in Applications and Decisions [176/84/24].

NOTIFICATION

At least 21 days written notice of the time, date and place of an inquiry must be sent by the LA to every person entitled to appear at the inquiry. He may vary those details and, if he does so, must give 21 days written notice of the change to every person entitled to appear at the inquiry. The notice period may be reduced with the consent of every such person. If he varies the time or place but not the date the LA must give what notice he considers reasonable. An inquiry cannot be held before the date published in *Applications and Decisions* [176/84/23 & Sch.7, par 1 & 2319/92].

The above rules apply to an adjourned inquiry but if (a) the time, date and place of the resumed inquiry is announced before the adjournment no further notice is required, and (b) in any other case, the notice period is reduced from 21 days to 7 days [Sch.7, par 1].

A notice to a person under these provisions may be delivered to him or be sent to or left at his last known home or business address or place of employment. In the case of a company it may be sent to the company secretary and to the registered office; in the case of a partnership, to any of the partners; in the case of any other unincorporated association, be sent to any member of the governing body of the association and to its principal office in the UK. A person may notify a different address for the purpose of these notices [Sch.7, par 6]

If notice of an inquiry is not given in accordance with any of the above provisions, the LA may nevertheless proceed with the inquiry if satisfied no injustice or inconvenience would be caused [Sch.7, par 7].

The object of a 'call-up' letter to a public inquiry (under Section 69) should be to isolate the matters on the basis of which the LA is minded to exercise his powers. This means the letter should only set out those grounds which will be in issue at the hearing—*Mightyhire Ltd.*, Appeal 1990/B26.

A call-up letter to a disciplinary and licence-renewal inquiry should set out the grounds for the disciplinary action followed by the matters to be considered in the renewal along with reasons why the traffic commissioner will particularly need to be satisfied on any of those matters—*Amberline Taxis*, Appeal B40/1990.

The test of a good call-up letter should be to ask whether an unrepresented operator would be able to ascertain from the letter, coupled with a copy of the 1968 Act and/or the 1984 Regulations, the case which he would have to meet at the public inquiry. It should set out a full and fair summary of the facts and identify the precise statutory provisions—*R.B. & D. Smith Ltd*, Appeal 1993/E36.

ADMISSION

An inquiry must be held in public but an LA may direct that the whole or part of it be held in private if satisfied it is just and reasonable to do so due to

(a) the likelihood of intimate personal or financial circumstances being disclosed;
(b) the likelihood of commercially sensitive information or information obtained in confidence being disclosed; or
(c) other exceptional circumstances.

When a hearing is in private the LA may admit such persons as he considers appropriate. And, where the appropriate financial standing of a person is considered during an inquiry the LA may exclude such persons as he thinks fit from that part of the inquiry [Sch.7, par 2].

A provisional opinion has been given that an objector who had a right to appear at an inquiry could not be excluded—*Wilkinson Freight (UK) Ltd*, Appeal 1984/V7.

When attendance is restricted, information about a business must not be disclosed as long as that business continues, unless the person carrying on the business consents, it is necessary for the LA's work or for the purposes of any legal proceedings [Act 1968/87(5)].

APPEARANCES

At an inquiry in relation to an application, the persons entitled to appear are the applicant and a person who has duly made an objection to, or representation against, the application.

The licence holder is entitled to appear at an inquiry relating to action against the licence under Sections 69 or 69F.

A person who has requested an inquiry, under Section 69(9), is entitled to appear at it.

Where a transport manager has been given notice under Regulation 23A that an issue in the proceedings is whether or not he is of good repute or professionally competent, he has made a representation under that Regulation and the issue is to be considered at the inquiry, the transport manager is entitled to appear at the inquiry.

Any other person may appear at an inquiry at the discretion of the LA.

A person entitled or permitted to appear at an inquiry may do so on his own behalf or be represented by a barrister, solicitor or, at the discretion of the LA, any other person [Sch.7, par 3].

PROCEDURE

The procedure at an inquiry is determined by the LA. If no shorthand writer is available at a public inquiry, the LA is responsible for recording all that is or might be relevant and that task should not be delegated—*A.H. & M.J. Brown*, Appeal 1988/Z23.

A person entitled to appear at an inquiry is entitled to give evidence, call witnesses, cross-examine witnesses and address the LA on the evidence and the subject matter of the inquiry.

The giving of evidence, calling of witnesses, cross-examination of witnesses and making such addresses by other people at an inquiry is at the LA's discretion.

A person present at an inquiry may submit any written evidence or other matter in writing before the close of the inquiry.

The LA may refuse to permit evidence, cross-examination or presentation of other matter which he considers to be irrelevant, repetitious, frivolous or vexatious. The LA may require a person who is behaving in a disruptive manner to leave an inquiry and he may refuse to permit that person to return.

The LA may proceed with an inquiry in the absence of any person entitled to appear but, if he was required to give that person notice of the inquiry, he must not proceed unless satisfied the notice has been duly given or he decides to proceed on the basis that no injustice would be caused to the person as a result of the notice not having been duly given.

An LA must not take into account any written evidence or other matter in writing received by him before an inquiry opens or during an inquiry unless he discloses it at the inquiry [Sch.7, par 5].

Even though an applicant arrived at an inquiry after it had started, he should have been informed of the evidence he had missed and been given opportunity to deal with it—*A. Hetherington*, Appeal 1990/B12.

When representors attend an inquiry to oppose a licence grant they should give their evidence and be cross-examined before the licence applicant gives his evidence *R.G. Brimley*, Appeal 1985/W11. A council or other authority which proposes to object to an application should ensure its case is properly prepared before the public inquiry takes place—*C.T. Supplies*, Appeal 1992/D36

An LA can call a witness, even though he is not within Section 63, if he has material evidence to give bearing directly on the requirements in Section 64(2) or hauliers' repute, professional competence or financial standing. A licence applicant should be given early notification of such action together with the substance of the witness's evidence—*L. & P. Traffic Services Ltd*, Appeal 1983/U10.

Ministry examiners should not be encouraged to make comments about an operator but should confine themselves to statements of fact, including advice given and advice disregarded—*A.H. & M.J. Brown*, Appeal 1988/Z23. If an LA wants to rely on the evidence of a vehicle examiner it is desirable that the vehicle examiner with personal knowledge of the case is called to give evidence—*S. & P. Plant Contractors Ltd*, Appeal 1992/D31.

Letters from persons who were not statutory objectors (now

including representors) should not be taken into account by an LA and even letters from statutory objectors should not be taken into account unless the applicant agrees that their contents are true and could be used as evidence without live witnesses—*L. & P. Traffic Services Ltd*, Appeal 1983/U10.

When an operator is summoned to an inquiry he should be given full particulars of the case he has to meet—*L.G. Rogers*, Appeal 1980/R1. If adverse material information about an applicant comes to the attention of an LA's staff, he should be confronted with it in detail and asked to comment on it as part of the process leading to the LA's decision whether or not to call a public inquiry—*C.T. Transport Services*, Appeal 1992/D23.

If, at a public inquiry, an LA intends to investigate previous convictions, prohibitions or other information he has about an applicant, he should give the applicant detailed advance notice of those matters—*Jebb Transport*, Appeal 1990/B53. To do so prevents the applicant being confronted at the inquiry with things he should have applied his mind to beforehand but about which he might not be able to give an extempore account at the inquiry.

To give a person reasonable opportunity to present his case, he must be told the substance of the case against him or the substance of the case he has to meet. As long as the person knows in substance the case he has to meet there is no obligation to disclose the evidence by which it is believed the case will be proved. In order to comply with the 'right to prior notice' the LA must give the applicant or operator notice of the substance of the case in sufficient detail and in sufficient time to enable that person to prepare and present his case. An LA should give sympathetic consideration to an adjournment where detailed information available to him has taken the applicant or operator by surprise, even though the substance of it has been revealed—*Wilton Contracts (London) Ltd*, Appeal 1992/D37.

If an LA obtains additional information between the end of a public inquiry and his decision it is desirable that the parties to the application be given opportunity to comment on it—*C.A. Ceasar*, Appeal 1988/Z22. There was a breach of natural justice when an LA, after the close of a public inquiry, attached conditions to a licence based on evidence which the applicant and representors did not have opportunity to challenge—*L.R. Cobden*, Appeal 1992/D21. When a public inquiry has ended an LA should not see one of the parties in chambers in the absence of the other parties—justice must be seen to be done—*R.H.A. v John Dee Ltd*, Appeal 1992/D4.

At the end of a public inquiry 'a pause for thought and reflection will be very desirable' in the majority of cases where an LA is considering revocation of the licence—*R.F. Craven*, Appeal 1991/D33.

MULTIPLE ENQUIRIES

When an LA proposes to hold two or more inquiries under Sections 69 or 69F and he receives a request from two or more persons to hold a single inquiry he may do so in response to those requests [Act 1968/87(3)]. If an LA decides that two or more applications should be the subject of a single inquiry he may hold a single inquiry if it appears to him just and convenient to do so [176/84/23 & Sch.7, par 4].

Transport managers' protection

In any operators' licensing proceedings an LA must not decide that a transport manager is not of good repute or professionally competent unless satisfied the transport manager has been served with a notice:

(a) stating the matter is in issue in the proceedings;
(b) stating he is entitled to make representations within 28 days of receipt of the notice; and
(c) setting out the nature of the allegations against him.

Notice is deemed to have been served on the transport manager on the date it would normally have been delivered if sent by post at his last known address, regardless of it being returned as undelivered or not received by him for any other reason.

If the transport manager makes representations the LA must consider them when deciding whether to hold a public inquiry and when determining whether or not the transport manager is of good repute and professionally competent [176/84/23A & 2239/91].

Licence suspension, revocation, etc.

The LA who granted a licence can direct that it be suspended, curtailed, prematurely terminated or revoked on any of the following grounds:

(1) the licence holder has contravened a general condition or an environmental condition attached to the licence;
(2) during the five years preceding the date of the direction there has been:
    (a) a conviction of the licence holder, or a servant or agent of his, relating to:
        (i) plating and testing,
        (ii) maintenance,

    (iii) speeding,

    (iv) overloading and the loading of goods vehicles,

    (v) licensing of drivers,

    (vi) contravening Section 173 or 174 of the Road Traffic Act 1988, in relation to an international road haulage permit or of contravening a prohibition under the International Road Haulage Permits Act 1975,

    (vii) unlawful disposal of controlled waste or carrying controlled waste when not a registered carrier, or

  (b) a conviction of the licence holder relating to:

    (viii) operator's licensing,

    (ix) forgery of, or making false statements to obtain, an operator's licence or fraudulently using an 'O' licence identity disc,

    (x) drivers' hours or records, or conspiracy to contravene hours' and records' law,

    (xi) unlawfully using rebated fuel,

    (xii) conviction of a restricted licence holder of carrying goods for hire or reward,

    (xiii) conviction of a standard licence holder limited to national operations of carrying goods on international operations; or

  (c) there have been numerous convictions, relating to goods vehicles, of the licence holder, his servant or agent, of infringement of waiting restrictions or prescribed lorry routes; or

  (d) there has been a prohibition for using an unfit or overloaded vehicle which was owned by the licence holder at the time of the prohibition;

(3) the licence holder made a false statement to obtain the licence or variation or made a statement of intention or expectation which has not been fulfilled;

(4) the licence holder is bankrupt or in liquidation (except a voluntary liquidation for reconstruction purposes);

(5) since the licence or variation was granted there has been a material change in the licence holder's circumstances which is relevant to the grant;

(6) the licence is liable to such action because, contrary to a direction, a disqualified person is involved in the business;

(7) the licence holder has used as an operating centre a place not specified in the licence.   [Act 1968/69(1),(4) & 69F].

As long as convictions have occurred in the five-year period they can be considered even if they have already been considered in earlier proceedings—*George Allinson (Transport) Ltd,* Appeal 1990/B10. It is the cumulative effect of all the operator's shortcomings which have to be considered—*C.B. Delaney (Excavations) Ltd*, Appeal 1979/Q16.

If the holder of a restricted operator's licence is convicted on more than one occasion in a five-year period of using a vehicle for hire or reward the LA must revoke the licence [69(3A)].

In curtailing a licence the LA can direct that, for the duration of the licence or for a shorter period, vehicles be removed from the licence, the authorisation for trailers or after-acquired motor vehicles be reduced, the facility to after-acquire vehicles be removed and a place specified as an operating centre be removed from the licence [92(3)].

When suspending or curtailing a licence an LA can order that a vehicle specified in the licence cannot be used under any other operator's licence for up to six months or, if earlier, until the affected licence ceases to be in force [69(7A)].

A standard licence must be revoked by the LA who issued it if it appears to him that he holder no longer satisfies the requirements of good repute, appropriate financial standing and professional competence. Before doing so, the LA must give the licence holder written notice which states:

(a) he is considering revoking the licence;
(b) the grounds for that consideration; and
(c) that written representations can be made by the licence holder to the LA so as to be received within 21 days of the date of the notice;

and the LA must consider any representations made within that time [176/84/9]. If an LA does not comply with these conditions he cannot revoke the licence under this power—*Mightyhire Ltd*, Appeal 1990/B26.

These provisions apply to a partnership where any of the partners or any nominated transport manager ceases to be of good repute, no professionally competent partner remains with the firm or a sole nominated transport manager leaves the firm [10A(2)].

A licence revocation under Regulation 9 is treated as a revocation under Section 69 so that the following disqualification and suspension-of-decision provisions apply and

the direction can be appealed against [9(3),(4)].

An LA does not have power to direct that no further vehicles be added to a licence—*R.H. Kitchen Ltd*, Appeal 1986/X31.

An 'N' on a prohibition notice is not, in itself, evidence of the presence or absence of neglect or fault—*Shamrock Private Hire*, Appeal 1989/A41(PSV).

An LA must publish his decision to revoke, suspend, curtail or prematurely terminate a licence in *Applications and Decisions* [176/84/24].

Disqualification

When an LA directs that a licence be revoked, he can also disqualify the holder from obtaining another licence for any period he thinks fit. The disqualification can be limited to one or more traffic areas and, if it is, any licence held by the person in question in a different traffic area will not authorise the temporary use of vehicles from an operating centre in the banned area irrespective of the up-to-three-months temporary use rule [Act 1968/69(5)]. There can be no disqualification unless a licence is revoked—*DFC International Ltd*, Appeal 1987/Y37.

If a disqualification is ordered, the LA can also direct that if, during a specified period, the person in question:

(a)   is a director of, or holds a controlling interest in, a company which holds a licence or a holding company of a subsidiary which holds a licence or
(b)   operates goods vehicles in partnership with a person who holds an operator's licence,

the licence of that company or person will be liable to revocation, suspension, curtailment or premature termination [69(6)]. A controlling interest amounts to being the beneficial owner of more than half the company's equity share capital [69(11)].

The above powers to disqualify and make a direction can, where the licence holder was a company, be used against any director of that company and, where the licence holder was a partnership, against any of the partners [69(7)].

If an LA is contemplating giving a direction under these provisions he should state that very clearly in a letter to the licence holder—*I.C. Ireland*, Appeal 1984/V9. Followed in *Shamrock Private Hire*, Appeal 1989/A41(PSV), *N.C.J. Pilbeam Transport*, Appeal 1992/D7 and *G.A. Roedemer*, Appeal 1993/E41.

When imposing a disqualification an LA should give reasons for it— *R.B. & D. Smith Ltd*, Appeal 1993/E36 and *G.A. Roedemer*, Appeal 1993/E41.

Suspension of decision

When an LA takes action against a licence or person, he can postpone the effect of the direction or order until the end of the time allowed for making an appeal to the Transport Tribunal and, if an appeal is made, until it is disposed of. If the LA refuses to do so, the licence holder or person can apply to the Tribunal for such a postponement and its decision on that application must be given within 14 days [69(10)].

An application to the Transport Tribunal for a stay of a decision must be made by written notice with a copy being supplied to the LA. The notice must state the name and address of the applicant; the name and address of the LA; brief particulars of the decision in question; and the reasons for the application. Within 7 days of receiving the applicant's notice the LA must supply the Tribunal with a written statement of his reasons for the decision giving rise to the application and send a copy to the applicant. The Tribunal may give the applicant opportunity to be heard. The Tribunal's decision will be in writing and contain a summary of the reasons for the decision [1547/86/3-8].

Appeals

A person aggrieved at the following decisions of an LA can appeal to the Transport Tribunal against the decision if he is:

(a) an applicant for an operator's licence, or the variation of a licence, who is refused the application or aggrieved by terms or conditions of the licence or variation;

It is not the practice of the Transport Tribunal to allow appeals against conditions unless it was shown the LA misdirected himself on the law or evidence—*J. Cryer & Sons Ltd*, Appeal 1985/W12.

(b) the holder of a licence from which the LA has removed a specified vehicle on the grounds that it has ceased to be used under the licence or is specified on another licence;

(c) the holder of a licence which has been revoked, suspended, curtailed or prematurely terminated;

(d) a person against whom a disqualification order or ban on involvement with any other licence holder has been made;

(e) a licence holder against whom an order has been made banning motor vehicles removed from his licence being specified on another licence;

(f) an objector to an application or variation who is aggrieved by its grant. The 'grant' of a licence includes the terms on which the licence was granted—*London Borough of Havering v E. Hawkes (Ceramic Tiles) Ltd*, Appeal 1991/B49. [Act 1968/70(1)]

An appeal cannot be made on the grounds that a licence has been granted for longer or shorter than the normal five years if the grant was for administrative convenience [70(2)].

In relation to appeals against the exercise of an LA's discretion, the Transport Tribunal has repeatedly held that unless it is shown that the

LA has exercised his discretion in a way which no reasonable LA properly directing himself as to the law and the facts would have exercised it, appeals based on this ground are bound to fail. It is never for the Tribunal to substitute its own discretion for that of the LA, unless it is first established that the LA has behaved in a wholly unreasonable manner—*Veertran Ltd*, Appeal 1994/F5.

Transport Tribunal

Application procedure. When an LA takes action against a licence, or disqualifies a person, and refuses to suspend the effect of that decision while an appeal is made and heard, the licence holder or person can apply for such a suspension to the Transport Tribunal [Act 1968/69(10)].

The application must be by written notice and served on the Tribunal—which has High Court status—at its offices at 48/49 Chancery Lane, London WC2A 1JR. A copy must be sent to the LA [1547/86/4].

The applicant's notice must give his name and address, the name and address of the LA, brief particulars of the decision in question and reasons for the application [5].

Within seven days of receiving a copy of the applicant's notice, the LA must supply the Tribunal with a written statement of the reasons for his decision and send the applicant a copy [6].

The Tribunal can, at its discretion, give the applicant an opportunity to be heard. The Tribunal's decision will be in writing and contain a summary of the reasons for the decision. A copy will be sent to the LA and the applicant [7, 8]

Appeal procedure   An appeal against an LA's decision is made to the Tribunal by serving a written notice of appeal on the Tribunal at its offices. At the same time the appellant must serve a copy of the notice on the LA and, in the case of an appeal by a licence holder, on any objector and, in the case of an appeal by an objector, on the licence holder and any other objector [1547/86/10].

The object of a notice of appeal is to set out, with some precision, the points which the appellant will seek to make in argument. It is generally unhelpful to the Tribunal and unfair to the respondent if the notice states wide or general grounds under cover of which the appellant intends to advance very specific points. The specific points should themselves be spelt out—*J.J. Adam (Haulage) Ltd*, Appeal 1992/D41.

The notice must be served on the Tribunal not later than 28 days after the date of publication, in *Applications and Decisions*, of the decision. If the decision is not published within 21 days of it being notified to the appellant, the notice must be served on the Tribunal not later than 49 days after the notification. In special circumstances the Tribunal can accept a notice served outside these times [12].

The notice of appeal must give the name and address of the appellant and the LA; particulars of the appealed decision; reasons for the appeal; any reasons for appealing out of time; and the names and addresses of any persons to whom copies of the notice have been sent. The notice may be amended with the permission of the Tribunal [11].

When he receives a copy of the appeal notice, the LA must send to the Tribunal six copies each of (a) all documents produced in connection with the decision appealed against, (b) a verbatim record of any inquiry, and (c) a statement of his reasons for the decision. Parties to an appeal can request copies of these documents from the Tribunal office [13].

The LA must also send to the Tribunal a list of the names and addresses of any representors [13(2)]. The Tribunal office must notify each representor that an appeal has been made, give the name of the appellant, the reasons for the appeal and tell the representor he may, within 14 days of the notice, apply to become a party to the appeal [14].

Any person, other than the LA, to whom the appellant must supply a copy of his appeal notice, can supply the Tribunal with a written reply to the reasons for appeal. A copy of such a reply must be sent to every other party to the appeal. Except in special circumstances, such a reply must be supplied to the Tribunal within 28 days of receiving the notice of appeal. If a representor is given permission to be a party to the appeal, the time limit is 14 days after that permission was given. The Tribunal can require a party to supply whatever replies or other statements it considers necessary [17].

As soon as practicable after notice of appeal has been given, the Tribunal must fix a date, time and place for the hearing and its office must give all parties and the LA at least 14 days notice of the hearing [20].

Hearings must be in public unless it appears to the Tribunal that there are exceptional reasons why all or part of the hearing should be in private. Where the financial standing of a person is to be considered, the Tribunal can exclude any member of the public from that part of the hearing. A person whose conduct has disrupted, or is likely to disrupt, the progress of the hearing can be excluded [22].

If a party fails to appear at a hearing the Tribunal may, if the party is the appellant, dismiss the appeal or, in any case, hear and decide the appeal in the absence of that party [24].

The Tribunal must give each party to the appeal an opportunity to address it, amplify any oral or written replies or statements and make representations about the appeal generally. It may, if it thinks fit, allow a party to give evidence and to call witnesses [23] but it cannot take into consideration any circumstances which did not exist at the time of the decision appealed against [Act 1985/Sch.4/9(2)]. In *R.H. Kitchen*, Appeal 1986/X31, such evidence was allowed to be given because of the unusual nature of the case.

On an appeal the Tribunal has power to make such order as it thinks fit or to remit the matter to the Licensing Authority for a re-hearing and determination [Sch.4/9(1)].

The Tribunal may award costs against a person if he has been frivolous, vexatious, improper or unreasonable in making or resisting an appeal. Such an award was made in *R & G Transport*, Appeal 1986/X34 and *L.R. Houseman*, Appeal 1990/B2, because the appellants had been unreasonable in making an appeal which never had a reasonable prospect of success.

An appeal against the Tribunal's decision can be made, on a point of law only, to the Court of Appeal or, in Scotland, the Court of Session [Sch.4/14].

Duration of licence

A licence normally lasts for five years but the LA can direct a shorter period if he thinks it appropriate in the case of any applicant. For administrative purposes, the LA can direct a validity period longer or shorter than five years [Act 1968/67(2),(3)].

The power to limit the duration of a licence, under Section 67(3), is to be used only to secure that the requirements of Section 64(2) will be satisfied and not as a sanction in respect of past failures—*National Carriers Ltd*, Appeal 1975/M8. An LA's custom on not granting a licence for more than 12 months was wrong—*Mid-Suffolk D.C. v Dowell*, Appeal 1987/Y12.

If a licence expires after an application for renewal has been made the licence will continue in force until the application, or any appeal arising from it, have been disposed of. But this continuation provision does not prevent the LA from taking disciplinary action against the licence [67(4)]. An LA has no power to extend a licence beyond these times—*European Express Cargo Ltd*, Appeal 1993/E34.

The date it comes into force must be specified in the licence [67(1)]. This provision gives an LA a discretion to specify a future commencement date—*European Express Cargo Ltd*, Appeal 1993/E34.

A licence expires on the last day of the month before the fifth (or other specified) anniversary of its grant [67(2) & 176/84/31].

Death, bankruptcy, etc of licence holder

An operator's licence cannot be transferred or assigned to another person so that where the licence holder dies or is incapacitated the licence normally ceases to have effect. However, provisions exist to enable the business to be continued under the licence by another person [Act 1968/86, 176/84/32A & 2239/91]. The events covered by these provisions are where the licence holder:

(a) dies or becomes bankrupt;
(b) if a company, it goes into liquidation or an administration order is made;
(c) a receiver or manager is appointed to his trade or business; or
(d) he becomes a patient under the Mental Health Act or, in Scotland, becomes incapable of managing his own affairs.

After such an event, the LA may direct that a person carrying on the business of the licence holder shall himself be treated as the licence holder, for the purposes and extent specified in the direction, for 12 months following the event or, in special circumstances, 18 months, but the direction cannot extend the licence beyond its expiry date. Any vehicle which had belonged to, or been hired by, the previous licence holder will be treated as belonging to the new licence holder.

The direction can be made, in the case of a standard licence, whether or not the person carrying on the business is professionally competent and the LA does not have to revoke the licence because the professional competence requirement is not met [176/84/32A].

If a nominated transport manager dies or ceases, due to physical disability or mental disorder, to be capable of being transport manager, see section 'Professional competence' on page 207.

Licence fees

The fee for an operator's licence is (a) a basic fee of £185 plus (b) a fee of £8 for each motor vehicle specified on the licence for each three-month period [176/84/35(1A),(1D), 666/86 and 1209/94].

For a licence variation the fee is, if the variation results in an increase in number of the specified vehicles, £8 for each extra vehicle for each three-month period and, if notice of the application is required to be published in *Applications and Decisions*, an additional fixed sum of £185 [35(1B),(1D)]. But the extra £8 per vehicle per quarter does not have to be paid if the number of specified vehicles after the variation is no more than the highest number of vehicles specified on the licence between the time the licence was granted and the date of the variation [35(1C)].

The fee for an interim licence or interim variation is £10 for each vehicle authorised under the licence or variation [35(1E),(1F)].

Fees must be paid in the 7 days beginning on the date the licence or variation occurs [35(1D) & 2239/91].

If a licence is suspended, curtailed, revoked, prematurely terminated or surrendered, a refund of the £8 fees must be made but only for each complete 12-month period (a) for the time a licence is suspended, (b) for the time a licence would have continued in force but for its revocation, premature termination or surrender and (c) in the case of curtailment, for the number of vehicles taken off the licence. Periods of less than 12 months are disregarded [35(2)].

Licences and discs

An identity disc is issued for each motor vehicle specified on an operator's licence and it must show whether the licence is restricted, standard national or standard international. While a vehicle is specified on an operator's licence the identity disc must be displayed in a waterproof container adjacent to the place where the vehicle's excise licence is required to be displayed. The person in control of the vehicle must keep the disc readily legible and only the LA or a person he authorises may write on or make any alteration to the disc [176/84/25].

If a licence or disc is lost, destroyed or defaced, the licence holder must notify the LA who granted the licence and he may issue a copy. If the original licence or disc is found it must be returned to the LA [29].

If a licence holder changes his correspondence address he must notify the LA of the new address within 21 days [27].

Production and inspection of licences

The holder of an operator's licence must produce it if required by a police officer, goods vehicle examiner or person authorised by an LA and he may elect to produce it, within 14 days, at any operating centre covered by the licence, his head office within the traffic area or, if the requirement is made by police, at a police station chosen by the licence holder [176/84/28].

During the currency of a licence the LA must make a copy of it available for inspection by any person who appears to the LA to have reasonable grounds for making such an inspection. It can be made available at his office or, on payment, sent by post [16(2)].

Return of licences and discs

If the licence holder ceases to be the user of a specified vehicle he must, within 21 days, notify the LA, return the licence for variation and return the vehicle's identity discs [176/84/30(1)].

If a licence is varied the holder must, when required by the LA, return the licence and, if the number of vehicles has been reduced, return the identity discs of those vehicles [30(2)].

If a licence is revoked, suspended, curtailed, surrendered or a condition is to be attached to it, the holder must, on or before the date specified in a notice to that effect, return the licence and any discs which the LA may specify [30(3)].

Certificate of qualification

A person who wants to be a road haulage operator or transport manager of a road transport undertaking in an EC Member State (other than the UK) can apply to an LA or the Secretary of State for a certificate of qualification relating to his repute, professional competence and, where relevant, financial standing. The LA or SoS must issue the certificate if satisfied that he can properly do so and it appears to him to be of assistance to the applicant in meeting the law of another Member State. The fee is £20.

A person who holds a licence must make his application to the LA who issued the licence (or any of the LAs if he holds more than one licence) or, in any other case, to the Secretary of State [176/84/6].

Applications and Decisions

An LA must publish *Applications and Decisions* which contains notices of applications; dates and places he proposes to hold inquiries and the applications he proposes to consider there; dates and places of other inquiries; decisions to grant licences (other than interim licences); and directions to revoke, suspend, curtail or prematurely terminate a licence.

Publication of the date of an inquiry does not prevent the LA from adjourning, canceling or postponing the consideration of an application and any inquiry relating to it.

Copies of *Applications and Decisions* can be inspected at the offices of the LA or be bought from the LA's office [176/84/24].

TRAFFIC AREAS AND OFFICES

Area	Counties covered	Address
South Eastern and Metropolitan	Greater London, Kent, Surrey, Sussex	Ivy House, 3 Ivy Terrace, Eastbourne, BN10 4QT. Phone: 0323–721471 Fax: 0323–721057
Western	Avon, Berkshire, Cornwall, Devon, Dorset, Gloucestershire, Hampshire, Isle of Wight, Oxfordshire, Somerset, Wiltshire.	The Gaunt's House, Denmark Street, Bristol, BS1 5DR. Phone: 0272–755000 Fax: 0272–755055
South Wales	Dyfed, Gwent, Powys, South Glamorgan, Mid Glamorgan, West Glamorgan	Caradog House, 1, St Andrews Place, Cardiff, CF1 3PW Phone: 0222–394027 Fax: 0222–371675
West Midland	Hereford and Worcester, Shropshire, Staffordshire, Warwickshire, West Midlands	Cumberland House, 200 Broad Street, Birmingham, B15 1TD Phone: 021 631 3300 Fax: 021 631 3300
Eastern	Bedfordshire, Buckinghamshire, Cambridgeshire, Essex, Hertfordshire, Leicestershire, Lincolnshire, Norfolk, Northamptonshire, Suffolk	Terrington House, 13–15, Hills Road, Cambridge, CB2 1NP Phone: 0223-358922 Fax: 0223-532110
North Western	Cheshire, Clwyd, Cumbria, Derbyshire, Greater Manchester, Gwynedd, Lancashire, Merseyside	Portcullis House, Seymour Grove, Manchester, M16 0NE Phone: 061 886–4000 Fax: 061–886–4019
North Eastern	Cleveland, Durham, Humberside, North Yorkshire, Northumberland, Nottinghamshire, South Yorkshire, Tyne and Wear, West Yorkshire	Hillcrest House, 365 Harehills Lane, Leeds, LS9 6NF. Phone: 0532–833533 Fax: 0532–489607
Scottish	Scotland	83 Princes Street, Edinburgh, EH2 2ER Phone 031 225–5494 Fax: 031 225–5494

12 Plating and testing

Road Traffic Act 1988
Road Vehicles (Construction and Use) Regulations, **No. 1078/86**
Motor Vehicles (Tests) Regulations, **No. 1694/81**
Motor Vehicles (Tests) (Amendment) Regulations, **Nos. 1147/83, 401/84, 45/85, 253/91, 566/92, 3011/93** and **2136/94**
Motor Vehicles (Tests) (Amendment) (No. 2) Regulations, **Nos. 814/82, 1434/83, 834/85, 1694/89** and **628/90**
Motor Vehicles (Tests) (Amendment) (No. 3) Regulations, **Nos. 1477/82, 815/84, 1894/88, 1525/91** and **3160/92**
Motor Vehicles (Tests) (Amendment) (No. 4) Regulations, **Nos. 1715/82, 1126/84** and **2229/91**
Goods Vehicles (Plating and Testing) Regulations, **No. 1478/88**
Goods Vehicles (Plating and Testing) (Amendment) (No. 2) Regulations, **Nos. 1693/89, 2447/92** and **3013/93**
Goods Vehicles (Plating and Testing) (Amendment) Regulations, **Nos. 252/91, 564/92, 2048/93** and **328/94**

Most heavy goods vehicles and trailers are subject to a first examination at a Department of the Environment goods vehicle testing station 12 months after first registration or, in the case of trailers, 12 months after being supplied by retail. The first examination consists of a plating examination in which the vehicle's axle and gross weights are assessed and recorded on a plate, followed by a test of roadworthiness. The vehicles are then subject to a roadworthiness test every 12 months afterwards.

Motor vehicles constructed to carry more than eight passengers (excluding the driver), taxis and ambulances for medical or dental patients are subject to a roadworthiness test at an approved garage one year after first registration. Other passenger vehicles, dual-purpose vehicles and light goods vehicles are subject to that test three years after first registration. Thereafter all these vehicles are subject to an annual test [Act 1988/47]. (see page 252).

Additionally, public service vehicles require a certificate of initial fitness. This is dealt with in a following chapter (page 283).

Application

Plating and testing applies to the following goods vehicles:

(a) heavy motor cars and motor cars constructed or adapted to form part of an articulated vehicle,
(b) other heavy motor cars,
(c) other motor cars with a design gross weight over 3,500kg,
(d) semi-trailers,
(e) converter dollies of any unladen weight manufactured on or after 1 January 1979,
(f) other trailers over 1,020kg unladen.

[1478/88/4 and 252/91]

Exemptions

1. Dual-purpose vehicles not forming part of an articulated vehicle.
2. Mobile cranes subject to restricted use on public roads and not carrying or hauling any load.
3. Breakdown vehicles. A breakdown vehicle is defined as a motor vehicle which has permanently mounted apparatus for raising one disabled vehicle from the ground and for drawing that vehicle when so raised, and which is not equipped to carry any load other than articles required for that operation, the apparatus or repairing disabled vehicles.
4. Engineering plant or other plant being a motor vehicle or trailer specially designed and constructed for engineering operations.
   A goods vehicle modified for winching and lifting work was not engineering plant—*DPP v Ryan* [1992] RTR 13.
5. Trailers designed for the production of asphalt, tarmacadam, etc.
6. Tower wagons.
7. Road construction vehicles and road rollers.
8. Vehicles designed for fire-fighting and salvage purposes.
9. Works trucks, straddle carriers used only as works trucks, and works trailers.
10. Electrically propelled vehicles.
11. Vehicles used only for clearing frost, ice or snow from roads by means of a snow-plough or similar contrivance, whether forming part of the vehicle or not and/or spreading material on roads to deal with frost, ice or snow.
13. Motor vehicles used only for the haulage of lifeboats and carrying the necessary lifeboat gear.
14. Living vans not over 3,500kg design gross weight.
15. Vehicles equipped and used mainly for medical, dental,

veterinary, health, educational, clerical, experimental laboratory or display purposes and not used for direct sales or hire of goods nor for drain cleaning or collection of sewage or refuse.

16. Trailers which have only parking and overrun brakes.
17. Vehicles (and any trailer drawn) exempt from duty because they are used only on public roads to pass from one part to another part of land in the licensee's occupation and not travelling more than 6 miles in any week.
18. Agricultural motor vehicles and agricultural trailed appliances.
18A. Converter dollies used in agriculture, horticulture or forestry.
19. Agricultural trailers and agricultural trailed appliance conveyors drawn on roads only by an agricultural motor vehicle.
20. Licensed taxis and public service vehicles.
21. Vehicles used solely for funeral purposes.
22. Vehicles going to a port for export and those in use by a visiting force or of a headquarters.
23. Vehicles used by a vehicle manufacturer or importer for testing new or improved types of equipment.
24. Foreign-based motor vehicles brought temporarily into Great Britain within the last 12 months.
25. Motor vehicles currently licensed in Northern Ireland.
26. Vehicles based in the islands of Arran, Bute, Great Cumbrae, Islay, Mull, Tiree or North Uist.
27. Foreign-based trailers brought temporarily into Great Britain within the last 12 months.
28. Track-laying vehicles. 29. Steam-propelled vehicles.
30. Motor vehicles first used before 1960 used unladen and not drawing a laden trailer, and trailers made before 1960 and used unladen.
31. Street cleansing, refuse disposal or gully cleaning vehicles which are three-wheeled or incapable of exceeding 20mph or have an inside track less than 810mm.
32. Vehicles designed for servicing, controlling, loading or unloading aircraft on an aerodrome or, if and not laden or drawing a laden trailer, when on roads outside an aerodrome.
33. Aerodrome vehicles used for road cleansing, refuse disposal or gully cleaning.
34. Police vehicles maintained in workshops approved by the Secretary of State.
35. Articulated drawing units used only for drawing a trailer referred to in 14, 15 or 16 above or a trailer authorised under the Special Types Order.
36. Play buses

[1478/88/4, Sch. 2 and 252/91]

A vehicle is exempt from requiring a plating certificate and a test certificate in the following cases:

(a) submitting it by previous arrangement for, or bringing it away from, or during the course of, a first examination, a re-test, a periodical test, a notifiable-alteration examination or a re-examination following an appeal;
(b) where a test certificate is refused, (i) for delivering it by previous arrangement to, or bringing it away from, a place for repairing the failure defect or (ii) being towed to a place for breaking up;
(c) when unladen and used under a trade licence;
(d) in the case of an imported vehicle, while on the journey from the place of importation to the place it is to be kept;
(e) while used under the Special Types Order;
(f) while seized or detained by police;
(g) while removed, detained, seized, condemned or forfeited under the Customs and Excise Act;
(h) its removal under statutory powers.

[1478/88/44(1)]

Plating and test certificate requirements do not apply to any island or area mainly surrounded by water from which vehicles cannot be conveniently driven to any other part of Great Britain due to the absence of a bridge, tunnel, ford or other suitable way. This exemption does not apply though to the Isle of Wight or the islands of Lewis, Mainland (Orkney), Mainland (Shetland) or Skye [44(2)].

Temporary exemption

A certificate of temporary exemption from plating and testing can be issued by the person in charge of a testing station or the Goods Vehicle Centre, Swansea, when, by reason of exceptional circumstances, an examination cannot be completed by the prescribed date. The exceptional circumstances are defined as an accident, fire, epidemic, severe weather, failure in the supply of essential services or other unexpected happening (except a breakdown or mechanical defect in a vehicle or non-delivery of spare parts). A certificate can last for up to three months [1478/88/46].

Exemption from plated train weight

If a plating certificate issued for a goods vehicle does not specify a plated gross train weight it is an offence to use the vehicle to draw a trailer [Act 1988/63(2)] but motor vehicles not constructed or adapted to form part of an articulated vehicle are exempt from this restriction, unless made on or after 1 October, 1982 and first used on or after 1 April 1983 [1478/88/45].

General conditions

The purpose of a goods vehicle test is to ensure that prescribed construction and use requirements relating to a motor vehicle or trailer are complied with. The prescribed requirements are set out in Schedule 3 of the Regulations [1478/88/5]. Every examination must be carried out by or under the direction of a goods vehicle examiner [6] and he is authorised to drive the vehicle, whether on a road or not [7(2)]. The driver must, unless permitted otherwise, remain with the vehicle during its examination and drive it or operate its controls as directed [7(1)].

Examiners at testing stations can refuse to examine vehicles and trailers in the following cases:

a. If not submitted for examination at the appointed time;
b. Where the applicant, after being requested to do so, fails to produce the examination appointment notice (if any) and, in the case of motor vehicles, the registration book or other evidence as to the date of first registration and, for trailers, evidence of the date of manufacture;
c. If the examination fee has not been paid or offered in cash;
d. Where the particulars shown on the application form are found to be substantially incorrect;
e. Where a motor vehicle stated to be used to draw a trailer is not, if previously required, accompanied by a trailer;
f. Where a trailer is not accompanied by a motor vehicle suitable to draw it or operate its brakes;
g. If a vehicle is not marked in a conspicuous and readily accessible position with the chassis or serial number shown in the registration book or an identification mark allotted by the Ministry;
h. A motor vehicle or trailer in such a dangerous or dirty condition as to make it unreasonable for an examiner to carry out his work or the applicant does not produce a certificate requested in the appointment notice that a vehicle used to carry toxic, corrosive or inflammable loads has been properly cleaned or made safe;
i. If a motor vehicle is without sufficient fuel and oil for it to be driven or, where a trailer is to be examined, if it is not accompanied by a currently taxed motor vehicle with adequate fuel and oil supplies;
j. If a trailer examination cannot be completed on a road because its drawing vehicle is not taxed;

k. Where a motor vehicle or trailer is not loaded or unloaded as specified on the last examination appointment notice;
l. Where a motor vehicle or trailer examination cannot be completed due to the failure of any part which renders the vehicle or trailer incapable of being moved safely under the vehicle's own power;
m. Where the driver of a motor vehicle submitting a vehicle or trailer for a periodical test or re-test does not produce the last plating certificate (or a photo-copy of it) and the last goods vehicle test certificate (or photo-copy) issued for that vehicle or trailer;
n. Where a certificate of conformity or approval certificate has been issued for a vehicle and the driver does not produce it on first examination or a re-test following such examination;
o. In the case of a plated vehicle, if the Ministry plate is not fitted or contains particulars different from the vehicle;
p. The vehicle, or any motor vehicle with it, emits substantial quantities of avoidable smoke.

[1478/88/8, 252/91 and 2048/93].

First examination

A motor vehicle must be submitted for a first examination not later than the end of the month in which falls the first anniversary of its registration. A trailer must be submitted for first examination not later than the end of the month in which falls the first anniversary of the date on which it was supplied or sold by retail. [1478/88/9].

An application for a first examination must be made at least one month before the desired test date but not more than three months before the date by which it is required to be examined. Application should be made to the Goods Vehicle Centre, 91/92 The Strand, Swansea. If an application is not made at the correct time it can still be dealt with if there are reasonable grounds for the variation [13].

The required fee must accompany the application and the fees are £32.70 for a motor vehicle with 2 axles; £33.70, 3 axles; £34.70, 4 or more axles; and £16.70 for a trailer with 1 axle; £17.10, 2 axles; and £17.90 for 3 or more axles. For a Saturday examination these fees, which must be paid in advance, are increased by £19.50 for a motor vehicle and £12.20 for a trailer [12, 1693/89, 564/92 and 3013/93].

The applicant will be notified of the time, date and place of the examination and regard will be taken of his choice of time and place [14 and 42(3)].

A first examination consists of a plating examination and a goods vehicle test.

On the plating examination the vehicle is checked to see whether it is a make, model and type to which the Standard Lists apply; the construction particulars relating to it are substantially complied with; and the weights in the Standard Lists are applicable to the vehicle [1478/88/17]. The Standard Lists are published by the Goods Vehicle Centre and are available from HM Stationary Office.

A vehicle to which the plating and testing rules apply and for which a certificate of conformity or approval certificate has been issued under the Motor Vehicles (Type Approval for Goods Vehicles) (Great Britain) Regulations 1982 is subject to a different plating examination. On submission for examination the driver must produce the above certificate (or a substitute issued by the Secretary of State) which is treated as a plating certificate [18(2)]. The examiner checks that the particulars are appropriate to the vehicle and that no notifiable alteration has been made which has not been notified [18(3)]. If the examiner is satisfied that no such alteration has been made and the particulars are appropriate the certificate is deemed to have been issued under the Plating and Testing Regulations as well as the Type Approval Regulations [18(4)]. If the examiner is not so satisfied, the vehicle is subject to a normal plating examination, the re-examination fee for any unreported notifiable alteration must be paid and the certificate of conformity or approval certificate is of no effect [18(5)].

Except where Regulation 18(4) applies, if a vehicle is one to which the Standard Lists apply its plated gross and axle weights will be those shown in the Lists as the vehicle's design weights but, where necessary, reduced to ensure they do not contravene the limits in the Construction and Use Regulations. The plated gross train weight of a motor vehicle will be its design weight but, if necessary, this will be reduced to ensure that it does not exceed a C and U weight limit (ignoring weights for combined transport operations in Schedule 11A) [19(1)]. If a plated train weight determined under the above is less than the design weight in the Standard Lists and the vehicle is capable of being lawfully used on combined transport operations under Schedule 11A at a higher weight than that determined, a train weight applicable only to combined transport operations shall be determined [19(2) and 328/94].

If the vehicle is one to which the Standard Lists do not apply, the vehicle examiner determines the plated weights having regard to its construction and equipment; the stresses to which it is likely to be subject; any information about the original design weights; braking requirements and legal weight limits, including those relating to combined transport operations [20 and 328/94].

When the plated weight has been determined a plating certificate is issued unless the vehicle is within Regulation 18(4) or fails the goods vehicle test [21(1)]. The certificate contains its date of issue, plated weights, tyre sizes, etc [21(3)].

After plating or an examination under Regulation 18(3) the vehicle undergoes a goods vehicle examination to ascertain whether the Construction and Use requirements specified in Schedule 3 are complied with [22].

If the vehicle does not comply a notice of refusal is issued and this states the grounds for the refusal [23(1)]. If the vehicle passes the test a test certificate is issued [23(2)].

A test certificate issued following a first examination, or a re-test or appeal arising from such a test, is valid from the date of issue till the last day of the same month in the following year [11(1)].

Re-tests

A vehicle which does not pass the goods vehicle test can be submitted once or more for a re-test [1478/88/15] or an appeal can be made against the refusal of a test certificate or the determination of a plated weight to the Secretary of State [25]. Appeals are dealt with in a following section.

To submit a vehicle for a re-test a person must make arrangements with the Secretary of State as to the testing station and the time and date at which it is to be re-tested [15(2) and 2048/93].

Where a re-test is to be carried out within 14 days of a first examination or periodic test the re-test fee is £16.60 for a motor vehicle and £8.80 for a trailer [16(1), 2048/93 and 3013/93]. The fee for a re-test outside that 14-day period is the fee payable on first examination (page 246 above) except where a re-test is carried out with 14 days of a re-test for which the first-examination fee was paid, in which case the second re-test fee is £16.60 for a motor vehicle and £8.80 for a trailer. The fee for a re-test within 14 days carried out on a Saturday at the applicant's request is increased by £9.80 for a motor vehicle and £6.10 for a trailer [16(2)-(5) and 3013/93]. No fee is payable where the re-test is made either on the same day as the first examination or periodical test or on the next day the station is open and the failure was due to minor, specified defects [16(6)]. Fees must be paid on submission of the vehicle for the re-test [16(7)].

If a re-test follows a first examination where no plating certificate was issued the examiner must first determine the vehicle's plated weights [24(1)]. If the re-test is under Regulation 15(2) or (3) the examiner is obliged only to examine the items specified in the last notice of refusal [24(2)]. If the vehicle complies with the requirements a plating certificate and test certificate are issued [24(3)]. If the vehicle fails the test a notice of refusal is issued [24(4)].

In the case of a re-test under Regulation 15(4) the vehicle undergoes the full goods vehicle test. Again, either certificates or a notice of refusal is issued following the test [24(5)].

Periodical tests

In each year following the issue of a first goods vehicle test certificate a vehicle must be submitted for a periodical test either (a) not later than each anniversary of the date by which the vehicle was required to have its first examination or (b) if a test certificate in force has an expiry date different from that anniversary, by that expiry date [1478/88/10(1)]. The method and timing of a periodical test and the fees payable are the same as for a first examination [12,13,14].

On a periodical test a vehicle is examined to see if it complies with the prescribed Construction and Use requirements. Either a test certificate or a refusal notice is issued following the examination [26].

If a vehicle fails the test it can be submitted for a re-test, following the same procedure for first-examination re-tests described above (page 218) except that there is no plating examination, or, an appeal can be made to the Secretary of State [27, 29 and 2048/93].

A test certificate issued following a periodical test, or a re-test or appeal arising from such a test, is valid from the day of issue till the date in (a), (b), (c) or (d) as follows:

Where a vehicle is submitted for its periodical test:

(a) more than 2 months before the expiry date of the current test certificate, the last day of the same month in the following year;
(b) two months or less before the expiry date of the current test certificate, the last day of the month in which falls the anniversary of that expiry date;
(c) after the expiry date of the last test certificate, the last day of the month in which falls the anniversary of that date, unless it would result in a validity of 2 months or less, when it will be the last day of the month of the second anniversary of that expiry date;
(d) after the expiry date of the last test certificate and the last vehicle licence has expired or been surrendered, the last day of the same month in the following year [11(2)].

Notifiable alterations

If alterations to a vehicle or its equipment come within the definition of 'notifiable alterations', an operator must declare details of the alterations on an approved form to the Goods Vehicle Centre at Swansea before the vehicle can legally be used on a road. The sender can ask for the plating certificate to be amended [1478/88/30].

Notifiable alterations are defined as: alterations made to the vehicle or its fixed equipment which varies the carrying or towing capacity;

alterations affecting the braking or steering system; or alterations made to the vehicle or its fixed equipment which would render the vehicle unsafe to operate at its plated weights [3].

If a request is made for the plated weights to be amended, the Centre will notify the operator as to the time and place where a re-examination will take place [33]. The re-examination fee is £13.50 (£21.90 on a Saturday at the applicant's request) [34, 1693/89 and 3013/93]. Re-examination may be required if no such request has been made but, if this is done, no fee is payable [33(2)].

Where any particular on a plate becomes no longer applicable to the vehicle, otherwise than by a notifiable alteration, the operator can apply for that particular to be amended. The application to the Centre must be accompanied by a fee of £13.50 (£21.90 on a Saturday at the applicant's request) and the operator will be notified of a re-examination in the usual manner [32, 34, 1693/89 and 3013/93].

Vehicles submitted for re-examination must be in the prescribed condition (page 245) and the plating certificate must be produced if required [35]. Examination will be confined to the plating aspect. On completion, the examiner will notify the operator in writing that the alterations have not changed the plated rating, or amend the certificate to show new weights, or issue a new certificate [36].

Any person aggrieved by the result of the re-examination can appeal to the Secretary of State [37 and 2048/93].

Appeals

An appeal can be made to the Secretary of State by a person aggrieved by the result of the first examination; the refusal of a test certificate on either the first examination periodical test or a re-test.

The appeal must be lodged on an approved form at the office of the traffic area concerned not later than 10 days after the examination was made, and it must be accompanied by a fee of £25. The appeal officer will then send the appellant a notice stating when and where the re-examination will take place. It may be at a testing station or any other place he considers convenient. If required, the plating certificate or refusal notice, whichever is in dispute, must be produced. Information can also be sought about any alterations, repairs, accident or anything else which may have affected the vehicle since the date of the test appealed against. The list of conditions applicable to the first examination—embodying the production of documents and the state of the vehicle—apply equally to examinations on appeal [25 and 2048/93].

Payment of fees

The fee for a first examination, periodical test, re-test or re-examination is payable even if the vehicle is not presented for test at the appointed time or was not carried out for the reasons in Regulation 8 (page 243). But, if (a) the applicant gives the testing station concerned at least 7 days' notice before the appointment that he does not propose to keep the appointment or (b) that due to exceptional circumstances (defined on page 242) occurring not more than 7 days before the appointment (and of which the Secretary of State is notified within 3 days) he cannot or could not keep the appointment then, within 28 days of the notice, the applicant can (1) request that the fee be used for another examination or (2) state that no other examination is required, in which case the fee will be repaid, less £1.50 [1478/82/39].

Appeal fees can be repaid to the operator, either wholly or partly, at the discretion of the Secretary of State where it appears to him that there were substantial grounds for appealing [40(1)].

If a vehicle to be re-examined following an appeal is not submitted for examination, the fee is lost. But if at least 2 days before the examination the operator notifies the office where the appeal was lodged that the vehicle will not be submitted for re-examination the fee will be repaid unless another time is arranged for the re-examination [40(2)].

In calculating the number of days' notice to be given in the various parts of the Regulations, no account has to be taken of Saturdays, Sundays and public holidays [42].

Replacing lost plates

If a plate, plating certificate (including a certificate of conformity or approval certificate), test certificate or Ministry test date disc is lost or damaged a replacement can be obtained from the Secretary of State. They cost £9.50 each [1478/88/41(1), 2447/92 and 2048/93].

In such a case the Secretary of State can require the vehicle to be re-examined and, if he does, the examination will be carried out as though it was a first examination and that test fee must be paid [41(2),(3)].

Test date disc

When a test certificate is issued for a trailer a test date disc is issued with it. The disc contains the trailer's identification mark, the date of expiry of the certificate and the number of the testing station issuing the certificate. The disc must be carried in a readily accessible position so that it is clearly visible from the near-side of the road. It must not be displayed after the test certificate to which it relates has expired or after the date a new certificate is issued [1078/86/73].

Display of plate

A goods vehicle to which the plating and testing regulations apply must be fitted with a Ministry plate in a conspicuous and readily accessible place, in the cab of the vehicle if it has one, (a) in the case of a vehicle to which the Motor Vehicles (Type Approval for Goods Vehicles) Regulations apply, from 14 days after the plate is issued or (b), in the case of any other vehicle, from the date by which it has to be plated [1078/86/70]. The alternative forms of plate are shown on pages 259 to 262.

Enforcement of weights

The weights shown in column 2 of a plating certificate (which gives the same weights as the plate) must not be exceeded when the vehicle is on a road [1078/86/80(1)(b)]. If two or more axles are fitted with a compensating arrangement the sum of their plated weights must not be exceeded [80(2)]. See also page 436.

Tests for large passenger vehicles, light goods vehicles and cars

Subject to specified exceptions, motor vehicles constructed for more than 8 persons (excluding driver), taxis and ambulances in each case registered for over one year and all other motor vehicles registered for more than three years must, at any time when used on a road, have in force a test certificate issued during the preceding 12 months [Act 1988/47]. If a vehicle is used on roads, whether in Great Britain or elsewhere, before being registered the three years counts from the time of first use but any use of the vehicle before being sold or supplied by retail is disregarded [47(2), (4)].

Vehicles which are exempt are:

(a) locomotives and motor tractors,
(b) tracked vehicles,

(c) goods vehicles with a design gross weight over 3,500kg (excluding dual-purpose vehicles and motor caravans),

(d) an articulated vehicle not being an articulated bus,

(e) works trucks,

(f) pedestrian-controlled vehicles,

(g) certain invalid carriages,

(h) licensed Metropolitan taxis,

(i) vehicles going to a port for export and, vehicles of visiting forces,

(j) vehicles temporarily in Great Britain,

(k) vehicles licensed in Northern Ireland or which have a Northern Ireland test certificate,

(l) vehicles exempt from duty due to travelling less than 6 miles a week on public roads,

(m) certain taxis tested on behalf of local authorities,

(n) certain hire cars tested on behalf of local authorities,

(o) police vehicles maintained in approved workshops,

(p) imported military vehicles,

(q) electrically propelled goods vehicles not over 3,500kg design gross weight,

(r) agricultural motor vehicles,

(s) a street cleansing, refuse or gully vehicle which is (i) a three-wheeled vehicle or (ii) any other vehicle incapable of exceeding 20mph or with an inside track not over 810mm.

[1694/81/6(1) and 253/91]

A test certificate is not required for a vehicle being taken to a test previously arranged, being brought away from a test or during a test; a vehicle authorised under the Special Types Order; an imported vehicle while on the journey from the point of importation to the residence of the owner or driver; a vehicle being removed under a statutory power of removal; a vehicle detained or seized by police; a vehicle detained or seized under the Customs and Excise Act; or a vehicle being tested by a motor trader during or after repairs to the vehicle [6(2)]. A test certificate is not required for the use of a vehicle in any island or area mainly surrounded by water, except for vehicles in Classes I to VI the Isle of Wight, Arran, Bute, Great Cumbrae, Islay, Lewis, Mainland (Orkney), Mainland (Shetland), Mull, North Uist, and Skye and, for vehicles in Class VII, the Isle of Wight, the islands of Lewis, Mainland (Orkney), Mainland (Shetland) and Skye [6(3) and 253/91].

A public service vehicle does not require a test certificate where a certificate of temporary exemption has been issued, by a person authorised by the Secretary of State, in a case of accident, fire, epidemic, severe weather, failure in the supply of essential services or other unexpected happening (excluding a breakdown or mechanical defect in the vehicle or non-delivery of spare parts). A certificate is not valid for more than 3 months [1694/82/28 and 1715/82].

For the purposes of this kind of test motor vehicles are divided into the following six classes:

Class I: light motor bicycles,
Class II: motor bicycles,
Class III: light motor vehicles (i.e. motor vehicles with 3 or more wheels and not over 450kg unladen),
Class IV: heavy motor cars and motor cars (not in Class III, V, VI or VII),
Class V: large passenger-carrying vehicles (i.e. for more than 12 persons excluding driver), play buses; public service vehicles which are of a type mentioned in the next paragraph and are constructed to carry more than 12 seated passengers,
Class VI: public service vehicles other than those specified for Class V.
Class VII: goods vehicles with a design gross weight over 3,000kg but not over 3,500kg.
             [1694/81/5, 814/82, 1477/82, 1126/84 and 253/91].

The psvs specified for Class V are those which can be used without a certificate of initial fitness as community buses under Section 23 of the Transport Act 1985; local authority school buses under Section 46 of the Public Passenger Vehicles Act 1981 or small buses used under a permit under Section 19 of the Transport Act 1985 [5(3) and 1894/88].

An application for an authorisation to carry out tests may be made to the Secretary of State by an individual, a partnership or a company [7]. The applicant may then be authorised to carry out examinations of vehicles of a particular class or classes [8].

Examiners have to comply with specified conditions. These include exhibiting in the test station in a conspicuous place the testing station authorisation and a list of names of persons authorised to carry out or supervise examinations and to sign test certificates. A prescribed sign must be fastened to a wall outside the testing station [9].

An applicant for a Class VI vehicle test must apply in writing to the PSV Centre, 91/92 The Strand, Swansea. An application for re-examination of a Class VI vehicle need not be in writing if made within 28 days of the last examination [1694/82/12(1), (1A) and 1694/89].

A person who wishes to have a vehicle of any other class examined can apply by telephone, in person, or in writing to an authorised examiner or a designated council at the vehicle testing station concerned for a test appointment. He can also submit the vehicle for examination at the testing station of an examiner or a designated council without a prior appointment. An application can also be made to the Secretary of State [12(2)].

Authorised examiners and councils must ensure that:

(a) where a test appointment is requested an appointment is offered at the earliest time which is reasonably practicable for the examination to be carried out;

(b) where a vehicle is submitted without prior appointment, the applicant is informed that the test can be carried out forthwith or, if not, of the earliest time which is reasonably practicable to carry out the test;

(c) except in circumstances beyond the control of the examiner or council, examinations are carried out in accordance with the appointment or at another time agreed between the parties [12(3)].

The time and date of an appointment or arranged time for the test and the name of the person who asked for it must (except where no appointment is made) be recorded by the authorised examiner or designated council [12(4)]. Whilst an examination may be carried out even though the conditions in Regulation 12 are not complied with [12(5)] nothing in the Regulation is to be taken as entitling an examiner to test vehicles of a class not specified in his authorisation [12(6)].

An examiner is not obliged to carry out an examination:

i. where on submission of the vehicle for test the applicant does not, on request, produce the vehicle's registration document or other evidence of its date of first registration or manufacture;

ii. where the vehicle or any part is in such a dirty condition as to make examination unreasonably difficult;

iii. where the test cannot be carried out without the vehicle being driven and it does not have enough fuel and oil;

iv. where goods on the vehicle are required by the examiner to be removed or secured and they are not removed or secured;

v. where the examiner is not satisfied that a fee payable in advance has been paid;

vi. a Class VI vehicle is not submitted at the time arranged or the driver is requested to remain with the vehicle, drive it, operate its controls, remove or refit panels, open or close doors, and he declines to do so [13 and 2229/91].

Methods to be used and apparatus required for testing brakes, steering, lighting equipment, seat belts, tyres, wipers and washers, exhausts and bodywork are specified [4(4) and Sch. 3].

Where a vehicle is submitted for examination the examiner, designated council or Secretary of State, as the case may be, has responsibility for loss of or damage to the vehicle and loss of or damage to any other property or personal injury arising in connection with the examination as if a contract, with no provision as to liability, existed between the parties [14(1)]. A person submitting a vehicle for test must not be requested or required by an examiner, a designated council or the Secretary of State to accept responsibility for, or to give any release or indemnity in respect of, any loss, damage or injury for which the examining body is responsible under Regulation 14(1) [14(2)]. These provisions do not prevent a person being requested or required to accept responsibility for (a) loss of or damage to the vehicle while still in possession of the examiner but after the time it should have been removed from the premises under Regulation 17(1) (explained below) or (b) loss, damage or injury arising while repairs are carried out at the request of the person submitting the vehicle for test [14(3)].

Vehicles in Classes I to V are examined to ascertain that they comply with prescribed Construction and Use requirements. Class VI vehicles have also to meet those requirements, additional Construction and Use provisions and specified requirements of the PSV (Conditions of Fitness, Equipment, Use and Certification) Regulations, 1981 [1694/82/4 and Sch. 2].

If the vehicle condition conforms to statutory requirements a test certificate, in the prescribed form, is issued. If the requirements are not met, a notification of the refusal of a test certificate is issued with reasons for its refusal. Test certificates and notifications of refusal should be issued on the same date as the examination. Where this is not practicable, they must be issued not later than the next day (not a Sunday or a public holiday) provided that, in the case of a test certificate, between the issue and when the vehicle examination is completed, the vehicle has remained in an unaltered condition at the testing station [15].

When, during an examination, it is found that the construction or condition of a vehicle or its equipment or accessories is so defective that a brake test would be likely to cause danger or damage the examiner can refuse to carry out the braking test but must continue with the rest of the examination. In such circumstances a test certificate will be refused [16].

Fees payable on application for examination are £26.10 for a Class IV vehicle; £33.04 for Class V; £40.30 for a Class VI vehicle with more than 12 seats and £28.20 in any other case; and £28.84 for a Class VII vehicle. The Class VI fees are increased by £27.50 and £20 respectively if the test is on a Saturday at the applicant's request [20, 1694/89, 1525/91, 566/92, 3011/93 and 2136/94].

Except for Class VI vehicles, where the statutory requirements are not complied with or where a brake test cannot be carried out then if the vehicle is left at the same testing station for repair no further test fee is payable on completion of those repairs [20(3)]. No fee is payable for re-examination of a vehicle, other than in Class VI, if it is re-examined at the same testing station before the end of the next day on which examinations are accepted and the examination relates only to specified minor items [20(3A), 1525/91 and 3160/92].

Where the statutory requirements are not complied with in the case of a Class VI vehicle or its brake test cannot be carried out the fee payable for a further examination within 14 days is £19.80 (£33.55 on a Saturday) or, if not within 14 days, £40.30 (£67.80) in the case of a vehicle made for more than 12 passengers. For a Class VI vehicle for 12 or less passengers the fee for re-examination within 14 days is £14.10 (£24.10) or, outside 14 days, £28.20 (£48.20) [20(4), 1694/89 and 3011/93]. But the fee is not payable if the vehicle is re-examined before the end of the next day following the earlier examination, the examiner is on the premises and the re-examination relates only to specified, minor defects [20(7), 1525/91 and 2229/91].

Test fees are payable even though the vehicle is not submitted for an examination which has been arranged but, in the case of a vehicle not in Class VI, if at least one day's notice is given by the test applicant that the vehicle is not to be submitted for examination then the fee must be re-paid unless another time is arranged for carrying out the examination. In the case of a Class VI vehicle, if the test applicant gives the Secretary at least 7 days' notice that the vehicle is not to be submitted for examination or satisfies the Secretary of State that the vehicle could not be submitted due to exceptional circumstances occurring not more than 7 days before the test date and of which notice is given within 3 days of the occurrence, then the applicant can make arrangements for another test for which the fee will be used or can ask for a refund of the fee less £1.50 [1694/81/20(5), (5A), (5B) and 1126/84]. Exceptional circumstances means an accident, fire, epidemic, severe weather, failure of essential services or other unexpected happening (including breakdown, mechanical defect or non-delivery of parts for the vehicle [20(8)].

An appeal by any person aggrieved by the refusal or the grounds for refusal of a test certificate can be made to the Secretary of State and must be lodged with an area traffic office not later than 14 days after receiving the notification of refusal [18]. The fee for an appeal, which must accompany the notice, is the same as for the vehicle's test. All or part of such fee can be refunded where the Secretary of State finds there were substantial grounds for contesting the whole or part of the decision appealed against [21].

A person who submits a vehicle for test must remove it from the custody of the examiner, designated council or Secretary of State:

(a) where an appointment was made for carrying out the test on a particular day and it has been completed on or before that day, before the end of the second day after the appointed day, or
(b) in any other case, before the end of the second day after the day on which he receives notice (written or verbal) (i) that the test has been carried out or (ii) that the test has not been carried out for reasons under Regulation 13 and he is to remove the vehicle [17].

Duplicate certificates to replace lost or defaced originals can be obtained on application to the authorised station or authority issuing the originals for a fee equal to half of the test fee. In the case of a Class VI vehicle an application for a duplicate certificate must be made to the PSV Centre at Swansea or any goods vehicle testing station and the fee is £9.30 [23, 1525/91, 2229/91 and 566/92].

MINISTRY PLATE – SCHEDULE 10

DEPARTMENT OF TRANSPORT

Road Traffic Act 1972, Sections 40 and 47
Examination of Goods Vehicles

			Serial No.
PLATE			DTp REF. NO.

REGISTRATION/IDENTIFICATION MARK	YEAR OF ORIGINAL REGISTRATION	YEAR OF MANUFACTURE	FUNCTION	MAKE AND MODEL
CHASSIS/SERIAL No.		UNLADEN WEIGHT		

(1) DESCRIPTION OF WEIGHTS APPLICABLE TO VEHICLE		(2) WEIGHTS NOT TO BE EXCEEDED IN GREAT BRITAIN	(3) DESIGN WEIGHTS (if higher than shown in col (2))	DATE OF ISSUE
		KILOGRAMS	KILOGRAMS	
AXLE WEIGHT (Axles numbered from front to rear)	AXLE 1			
	AXLE 2			
	AXLE 3			
	AXLE 4			
GROSS WEIGHT (see warning opposite)				
TRAIN WEIGHT (see warning opposite)				

WARNING

1. A reduced gross weight may apply in certain cases to a vehicle towing or being towed by another.
2. A reduced train weight may apply depending on the type of trailer drawn.
3. All weights shown are subject to fitting of correct tyres.

Notes:
1. A Ministry plate may contain the words "MINISTRY OF TRANSPORT" or "DEPARTMENT OF THE ENVIRONMENT" instead of the words "DEPARTMENT OF TRANSPORT", and may contain the words "Road Safety Act 1967, Sections 8 and 9" or of the words "Road Traffic Act 1972, Sections 40 and 45". (In a case where the Type Approval For Goods Vehicles Regulations do not apply). It may also contain additional columns in Columns (2) and (3) showing the weights in tons.
2. Entries in respect of train weight are required in the case of (a) a motor vehicle constructed or adapted to form part of an articulated vehicle; and (b) a rigid vehicle which is constructed or adapted to draw a trailer and is first used on or after 1st April 1983.
3. A Ministry plate shows the unlade weight and function of the vehicle in a case where the Type Approval for Goods Vehicles Regulations apply.
4. A Ministry plate may have separate spaces for the 'make' and 'model' of the vehicle.
5. A Ministry plate may have no 'Reference Number' or may refer to the "Department of the Environment Reference No."

MINISTRY PLATE – SCHEDULE 10A

PLATE VTG 6A	DEPARTMENT OF TRANSPORT Road Traffic Act 1972. Sections 40, 45 and 47 Examination of Goods Vehicles	SERIAL NUMBER	
		UNLADEN WEIGHT	DTp REF No

5. VEHICLE DIMENSIONS

REGISTRATION/ IDENTIFICATION MARK	YEAR OF ORIGINAL REG	YEAR OF MANUFACTURE	FUNCTION	LENGTH (L)		
				WIDTH (W)		

MANUFACTURER/MODEL		a. (See Note 1) COUPLING CENTRE TO VEHICLE FOREMOST PART	MAXIMUM	MINIMUM
TYPE APPROVAL/ VARIANT No				
VEHICLE IDENTIFICATION No				

(1) DESCRIPTION OF WEIGHTS APPLICABLE TO VEHICLE	(2) WEIGHT NOT TO BE EXCEEDED IN Gt. BRITAIN	(3) EEC MAXIMUM PERMITTED WEIGHTS (See Note 4)	(4) DESIGN WEIGHTS (if higher) than shown in column 2)	b. (See Note 2) COUPLING CENTRE TO VEHICLE REARMOST PART	MAXIMUM	MINIMUM
GROSS WEIGHT (See warning below)						
TRAIN WEIGHT (See warning below)						
MAXIMUM TRAIN WEIGHT (See Note 3)	✕		✕			
AXLE WEIGHTS (Axle numbered from front to rear) Axle 1						
Axles 2						
Axle 3						
Axle 4						
MAXIMUM KINGPIN LOAD (Semi-trailers only)	✕			DATE OF ISSUE		

N.B. ALL WEIGHTS IN KILOGRAMS/ALL DIMENSIONS IN MILLIMETRES.

WARNING

a. A reduced gross weight may apply in certain cases to a vehicle towing or being towed by another.
b. A reduced train weight may apply depending on the type of trailer drawn.
c. All weights shown are subject to the fitting of correct tyres.

NOTES

1. This dimension only applies to drawing vehicles of trailers and semi-trailers.
2. This dimension only applies to trailers and semi-trailers.
3. This weight only applies to a 3 axle tractor with a 2 or 3 axle semi-trailer carrying a 40 foot ISO container as a combined transport operation.
4. Where there is no weight shown in the EEC maximum permitted weights column this is because there is no EEC standard relating to that weight.

NOTES

1. Entries in respect of train weight are required in the case of – (a) a motor vehicle constructed or adapted to form an articulated vehicle; and (b) a rigid vehicle which is constructed or adapted to draw a trailer and is first used on or after 1st April 1983.
2. A Ministry plate shows the unladen weight and function of the vehicle in a case where the Type Approval for Goods Vehicles Regulations apply.
3. A Ministry plate may have no 'Reference Number'.

MINISTRY PLATE – SCHEDULE 10B

Department of Transport		
ROAD TRAFFIC ACT 1988 SECTIONS 41, 49, 57 & 58 *EXAMINATION OF GOODS VEHICLES*	Serial No.	**V**
Plate VTG 6T Rev. 92	DTp Ref. No.	

Reg./Ident. Mark	Vehicle Identification No.	Type Approval No./Variant

Manufacturer/ Model	Speed Limiter Exempt

Function *(See note 3 below)*	Year of Original Registration	Year of Manufacture

(1) Description of Weights applicable to vehicle	(2) Weights not to be exceeded in Gt. Britain	(3) Design Weights *(If higher than* *shown in* *column 2)*	
Gross Weight *(See notes 1 & 4 below)*			
Train Weight *(See note 2 below)*			
Max. Train Weight *(See note 5 below)*			Date of Issue
Axle Weights *(Axles* *numbered* *from front* *to rear)* *(See note* *1 overleaf)*	Axle 1		
	Axle 2		
	Axle 3		
	Axle 4		

NOTES

1. A reduced gross weight and/or axle weight may apply in certain cases to a vehicle towing or being towed by another.
2. The MAXIMUM permissible train weight can vary depending on the type of suspension and trailer drawn.
3. If the last letter in the function box is 'R' road friendly suspension is fitted.
4. All weights shown are subject to the fitting of correct tyres.
5. This weight applies to combined transport operations.

Tyre use conditions
applicable to vehicle

N.B. All Weights in Kilograms

Note: A weight is not required in the box for Maximum Train Weight unless the vehicle is capable of being lawfully used on a road in Great Britain, having regard to Schedule 11A, at a greater train weight than the train weight at which it could lawfully be used ignoring that Schedule.".

MINISTRY PLATE – SCHEDULE 10C

Department of Transport		
ROAD TRAFFIC ACT 1988 SECTIONS 41, 49, 57 & 58 *EXAMINATION OF GOODS VEHICLES* This is issued as proof of compliance with the Weights and Dimensions Directive 85/3/EEC	Serial No.	**B**
	DTp Ref. No.	

Plate VTG 6A

Reg./Ident. Mark	Vehicle Identification No.	Type Approval No./Variant

Manufacturer/ Model	Speed Limiter Exempt

Function *(See note 3 below)*	Year of Original Registration	Year of Manufacture

(1) Description of Weights applicable to vehicle	(2) Weights not to be exceeded in Gt. Britain	(3) Maximum permitted weights *(See note 8 below)*	(4) Design Weights *(If higher than shown in column 2)*	Length		Width
Gross Weight *(See notes 1 & 4 below)*				a. Coupling cen.re to vehicle foremost part *(See note 6 below)*	Max Min	
Train Weight *(See note 2 below)*				b. coupling centre to vehicle rearmost part *(See note 7 below)*	Max Min	
Max. Train Weight *(See note 5 below)*		////////		Date of Issue		
Axle Weights *(Axles numbered from front to rear) (See note 1 overleaf)* Axle 1						
Axle 2						
Axle 3						
Axle 4				Tyre use conditions applicable to vehicle		
Maximum Kingpin Load *(Semi-Trailers only)*	////////					

NOTES

1. A reduced gross weight and/or axle weight may apply in certain cases to a vehicle towing or being towed by another.
2. The maximum permissible train weight can vary depending on the type of suspension and trailer drawn.
3. If the last letter in the function box is 'R' road friendly suspension is fitted.
4. All weights shown are subject to the fitting of correct tyres.

NOTES *(Cont'd)*

5. This weight applies to combined transport operations.
6. This dimension only applies to drawing vehicles of trailers and semi-trailers.
7. This dimension only applies to trailers and semi-trailers.
8. Where there is no weight shown in the EEC maximum permitted weights column this is because there is no EEC standard relating to that weight.

N.B. All Weights in Kilograms. All Dimensions in Millimetres

Note: A weight is not required in the box for Maximum Train Weight unless the vehicle is capable of being lawfully used on a road in Great Britain, having regard to Schedule 11A, at a greater train weight than the train weight at which it could lawfully be used ignoring that Schedule.".

13 Powers of police, examiners, etc.

Road Traffic (Foreign Vehicles) Act 1972
Refuse Disposal (Amenity) Act 1978
Public Passenger Vehicles Act 1981
Road Traffic Regulations Act 1984
Road Traffic Act 1988
Road Traffic Offenders Act 1988
Road Traffic Act 1991
Weights and Measures Act 1985
Functions of Traffic Wardens Order, **No. 1958/70**
Functions of Traffic Wardens (Scotland) Order, **No. 374/71**
Road Vehicles (Registration and Licensing) Regulations, **No. 450/71**
Weighing of Motor Vehicles (Use of Dynamic Axle Weighing Machines)
     Regulations, **No. 1180/78**
Goods Vehicles (Operators' Licences, Qualifications and Fees) Regulations,
     No. 176/84
Removal and Disposal of Vehicles Regulations, **No. 183/86**
Removal and Disposal of Vehicles (Loading Areas) Regulations, **No. 184/86**
Road Vehicles (Construction and Use) Regulations, **No. 1078/86**
Functions of Traffic Wardens (Amendment) Order, **No. 1328/86**
PSV (Operator's Licences) Regulations, **No. 1668/86**
PSV (London Local Service Licences) Regulations, **No. 1691/86**
Motor Vehicles (Driving Licences) Regulations, **No. 1378/87**
Removal, Storage and Disposal of Vehicles (Prescribed Sums and Charges,
     etc.) Regulations, **Nos. 744/89, 366/91, 550/93** and **1415/93**
Road Vehicles Lighting Regulations, **No. 1796/89**
Driving Licences (Community Driving Licence) Regulations, **No. 144/90**
Weighing Equipment (Non-automatic Weighing Machines) Regulations,
     Nos. 876/88 and **3037/92**
Road Vehicles (Prohibitions) Regulations, **No. 1285/92**
Removal and Disposal of Vehicles (Amendment) Regulations, **Nos. 278/93**
     and **1708/93**
Functions of Traffic Wardens (Amendment) Order, **No. 1334/93**

Inspection of vehicles

An authorised examiner can test any motor vehicle or trailer on a road
to check that the construction and use requirements are complied with

263

and the condition of the vehicle is not such that its use on a road would involve danger. For this purpose he may drive the vehicle and may require the driver to comply with his reasonable instructions [Act 1988/67(1), (2)].

Authorised examiners are Ministry examiners, London taxi examiners, authorised police officers and persons appointed by a police chief for the purposes of this Section [67(4)]. When an examiner wishes to test a vehicle under this section the driver can elect for a deferred test unless an accident has occurred due to the vehicle's presence or if it appears to a constable that the vehicle is so defective it ought not to proceed [67(6)]. In electing for a deferred test the vehicle owner should specify a period of 7 days in the next 30 days (disregarding any day the vehicle is outside Great Britain) when the test can be made and the premises where it can be done. The examiner must then give at least 48 hours' notice of the time he proposes to test the vehicle. The place and time of the test can be varied by agreement between the examiner and owner [Schedule 2]. It is an offence to obstruct an examiner or fail to comply with a requirement of the Section [67(9)].

A Ministry vehicle examiner, London taxi examiner, police officer in uniform or person appointed under Section 67 of the 1988 Act may, subject to conditions, test and inspect the brakes, silencer, steering gear or tyres of any vehicle on any premises where it is located. The conditions are that the person carrying out the test produces his authorisation if required; he does not enter the premises without first obtaining the consent of their owner; and he does not test a vehicle unless (i) the vehicle owner consents, (ii) notice of the test has been given to the vehicle owner personally or left at his address at least 48 hours before the test (72 hours if sent by recorded delivery post); or the test is made within 48 hours of a notifiable accident. The owner of a vehicle is its registered keeper or, if used under a trade licence, the holder of that licence, or, in the case of a temporarily imported vehicle, the foreign resident who brought the vehicle into Great Britain [1078/86/74].

A Ministry vehicle examiner may at any time, on production of his authority if required, inspect any goods vehicle, public service vehicle or other passenger vehicle constructed to carry more than 8 passengers and can detain the vehicle during the time required for inspection [Act 1988/68(1) and Act 1991]. He may at any reasonable time enter premises he has reason to believe a goods vehicle or public service vehicle (other than one used only under a Section 19 or 22 permit) is kept [68(1), (6)]. It is an offence to intentionally obstruct an examiner acting under these provisions [68(3)]. An examiner or police officer in uniform can require the driver of a stationary goods vehicle on a road to take the vehicle to a place for inspection up to 5 miles away [68(4)].

An authorised examiner can, at any reasonable time, enter premises where used vehicles are sold, supplied or offered for sale or supply, exposed or kept for sale to ascertain whether they are in an unroadworthy condition. To test a vehicle he may drive it on a road. Authorised examiners are the same persons referred to in Section 67, above, and it is an offence to obstruct an examiner [Act 1988/77].

The examiner may enter at any reasonable hour premises where vehicles or vehicle parts of a class to be prescribed for type-approval purposes are sold, supplied, offered for sale or supply, exposed or kept for sale or supply. He can test the vehicle or part and to test a vehicle or trailer may drive it on a road [77]

Weighing

Persons authorised by a highway authority and police officers authorised by their chief constable can, on production of their authority, require the person in charge of any vehicle to take it to a weighbridge and allow it to be weighed. Failure to comply or to obstruct an authorised person is an offence [Act 1988/78(1), (3)]. Traffic examiners and certifying officers have the same powers in respect of goods vehicles [79(2)]. The requirement can apply to vehicles on harbour premises [78(8)]. It is unlawful for such a person to require or allow the vehicle to be unloaded for it to be weighed unladen [78(4) proviso]. Regulations may be made as to how a vehicle is to be weighed and the limits within which, unless the contrary is proved, a weight is to be presumed accurate [78(5)]. An authorised person can require the driver of a vehicle to drive it or do any other thing in relation to the vehicle or load for the purpose of weighing it in accordance with those regulations [78(2)].

If the vehicle is more than 5 miles from the weighbridge when the requirement is made and the vehicle is found not to be overloaded the operator can claim for any loss he sustains [78(6)]. When a vehicle is weighed under these provisions the driver must be given a certificate of weight (whether the vehicle is overloaded or not) and this exempts the vehicle from being weighed again on the same journey with the same load [79(1)].

A prescribed form of certificate issued by an authorised person stating the weight of a vehicle weighed under Section 78 is evidence of the matters it states [79(4)]. If, in connection with weighing a vehicle under Section 78 an authorised person (a) drives or does anything in relation to the vehicle or its load or (b) requires the driver to drive in a particular way, to a particular place or do anything in relation to the vehicle or load neither he nor the driver shall be liable in respect of any damage or loss to the vehicle or load unless it is shown he acted without reasonable care [79(5)].

Where a vehicle is weighed on a dynamic axle weighing machine the weighing shall be made by causing the vehicle to be driven across the weighing platform in accordance with the instructions of an authorised person in a manner and at a steady speed to ensure that (a) the machine can show successively each axle weight and (b) if the machine does not print a record of each weight, so that the authorised person can record the weights [1180/78/3]. Unless the contrary is proved, the weights determined by a dynamic axle weigher will be presumed accurate to within plus or minus 150 kilograms for each axle [4]. A certificate of weight is prescribed for the purposes of Section 79(4) of the 1988 Act, above [5].

When, under the Weights and Measures Act 1985, the whole of a vehicle's load is being carried for sale to, or delivery after sale to, the same person and a conveyance note has to be carried on a vehicle and the quantity of goods is stated, an inspector of weights and measures can require the vehicle to be taken to a weighbridge and weighed, require the driver to have it check-weighed (both gross and tare) and/or require goods to be unloaded [Act 1985/40] but these powers may be exercised only if reasonably necessary to enforce the Act.

A non-automatic weighbridge used for trade must not be used for multiple weighing [876/88/4(7)]. Use for trade includes the use of weighing machines available for public use [Act 1985/7(4)] but the ban on multiple weighing on a public weighbridge does not apply if the machine is used only for check-weighing and it bears a conspicuous notice to that effect [876/88/3(2)]. A non-automatic weighing machine must be erected and used in such a way that, during a weighing operation, the load is stationary and supported only by the load receptor [26 and 3037/92].

The Secretary of State can, on giving 7 days' notice in writing, require an owner to produce a goods vehicle (including any alternative or additional body and any alternative parts which are required to be included in its unladen weight) at any given time at a specified weighbridge for the purpose of weighing the vehicle in the presence of an officer of the council [450/71/45].

Prohibitions

MECHANICAL

If, on inspecting a vehicle under his statutory powers, it appears to a vehicle examiner that, owing to any defects, the vehicle is, or is likely to become, unfit for service he can prohibit the driving of the vehicle on a road absolutely, for specified purposes or except for specified purposes [Act 1988/69(1) and Act 1991]. 'Driving a vehicle', in the case of a trailer, means driving the vehicle by which it is drawn [73(3)].

If, on inspecting a vehicle under his statutory powers, it appears to an authorised police constable that, owing to defects in the vehicle driving it would involve a danger of injury to any person, he may prohibit the driving of it absolutely, for specified purposes or except for specified purposes [69(2)].

A person imposing a prohibition must give written notice of it forthwith to the person in charge of the vehicle and the notice must specify the defects and the effect of the prohibition. Written exemption can be granted for the use of the vehicle in specified circumstances and it can be varied or suspended [69(6)-(8)].

A prohibition comes into force immediately written notice has been given if (a) it is imposed by a vehicle examiner and in his opinion the defects are such that driving it would involve a danger of injury to any person or (b) it is imposed by an authorised constable [69(3)]. Apart from where danger is involved, a vehicle examiner can delay the effect of a prohibition he imposes for up to 10 days [69(4)].

A person imposing a prohibition on a public service vehicle or a passenger vehicle adapted to carry more than 8 passengers can make it irremovable until the vehicle has been inspected at an official PSV testing station [69A(1)]. A prohibition on a goods vehicle subject to plating and testing can be made irremovable until the vehicle has been inspected at an hgv testing station [69A(2)]. A prohibition on a vehicle subject to an MoT test, or which would be if it had been registered for over 3 years, can be made irremovable until the vehicle has undergone an MoT test and a test certificate obtained [69A(3)]. In any other case the prohibition can be made irremovable until the vehicle has been inspected [69A(4)].

OVERLOADING

Where a goods vehicle or passenger vehicle adapted to carry more than 8 passengers has been weighed under Section 78 (above) and it appears to a vehicle examiner or authorised person that (a) a weight limit applicable to the vehicle has been exceeded or (b) by reason of excessive weight driving the vehicle would involve danger to any person, he can prohibit the driving of the vehicle on a road until the weight has been reduced to the limit or is no longer excessive and official notification has been given that the vehicle can proceed [Act 1988/70(1), (2) and Act 1991].

The examiner or authorised person can give the person in charge of the vehicle a written direction to remove it (and any trailer drawn) to a place specified in the direction [70(3)].

Official notification that a vehicle can proceed must be in writing and may be withheld till the vehicle has been re-weighed [70(4)].

ENFORCEMENT

It is an offence to drive, or cause or permit to be driven, a vehicle in contravention of a prohibition or to fail to comply within a reasonable time with a direction to move an overweight vehicle [Act 1988/71 and Act 1991]. If, in any proceedings for contravening an overloading prohibition, a question arises as to whether the weight had been reduced to the legal limit or it has ceased to be excessive, the burden of proving it rests on the defendant [Road Traffic Offenders Act 1988/17(3)].

A vehicle is exempt from the prohibition when driven on a road:

(a) for submitting it, by previous arrangement, for inspection by an examiner or authorised policeman with a view to removal of the prohibition;
(b) for submitting it, by previous arrangement, for inspection by an examiner with a view to removal of the prohibition and issue of a test certificate;
(c) during an inspection for removal of a prohibition;
(d) within three miles of where it is or has been repaired solely for test or trial with a view to removal of a prohibition [1285/92/3(1)].

If a prohibition has been imposed with a direction that the vehicle undergo an MoT test, the prohibition does not apply to driving the vehicle to or from a previously arranged test or, when a certificate has been issued, driving it to a police station for the prohibition to be removed [1285/92/3(2), (3)].

REMOVAL

A prohibition may be removed by a vehicle examiner or authorised constable if he is satisfied the vehicle is fit for service [72(1)]. But if it has been made irremovable under Section 69A(1) or (2) (psv or hgv) it may not be removed unless the vehicle has been inspected as directed [72(2)].

A prohibition under Section 69A(3) (requirement for MoT test) may be removed by

(a) a vehicle examiner who issues the test certificate or a person authorised by the Secretary of State for that purpose and to whom the certificate is produced or

(b) a person authorised by a chief police officer and to whom a test certificate is produced at a police station [72(3) and 1285/92/4].

A prohibition under Section 69A(4) (non-testable vehicle) may not be removed unless the vehicle has been inspected by a vehicle examiner or authorised constable [72(4) and 1285/92/5].

The fee for inspection of a vehicle leading to removing a prohibition on a goods vehicle subject to the Plating and Testing Regulations is the same as the fee for a periodical examination under those regulations, including re-test reductions and increases for Saturday inspections. In relation to any other vehicle, it is the MoT test fee, including re-test reductions and increases for Saturday inspections of Part VI vehicles [1285/92/7,8].

If an examiner or authorised constable refuses to remove a prohibition the aggrieved person can appeal to the Secretary of State [72(5)]. The appeal must be in writing, state the grounds of appeal and be made within 14 days of the refusal. The appeal fee for goods vehicles is £25 and for other vehicles it is its MoT test fee [1285/92/6].

NOTIFICATION

If a prohibited vehicle is authorised under a goods vehicle operator's licence or used under a PSV operator's licence the person imposing it must, as soon as practicable, notify (a) the traffic commissioner who issued the licence and (b) the holder of the licence (if he was not in charge of the vehicle at the time). In any other case he must notify the owner of the vehicle (if he was not in charge of it at the time) [Act 1988/73(1)-(1B) and Act 1991].

A person removing a prohibition must notify the owner of the vehicle and, where relevant, the licence holder and traffic commissioner [72(7) and 73(1C)].

MISCELLANEOUS

Under the Road Traffic (Foreign Vehicles) Act 1972 (as amended by the Transport Act 1978) police and traffic examiners have additional powers in relation to foreign goods and public service vehicles. They are described on page 454.

A traffic examiner has power under the International Road Haulage Permits Act 1975 to prohibit a vehicle from leaving the United Kingdom if a prescribed document is not carried on the vehicle—see page 380.

The Radioactive Material (Road Transport) Act 1991 gives a goods vehicle examiner and appointed inspector power to prohibit the driving of a vehicle used to transport radioactive packages if the operation contravenes regulations made under that Act; the vehicle or any package has been involved in an accident; or a package has been lost or stolen from the vehicle. An examiner and inspector also have power to enter a vehicle and an inspector can enter premises.

Production of licences, etc

A constable or vehicle examiner can require the following to produce a driving licence:

(a) a person driving a motor vehicle on a road;
(b) a person believed to have been the driver when an accident occurred or when a traffic offence was committed; or
(c) a person who supervises a provisional licence holder in (a) or (b).

A constable can also require such a person to give his date of birth if :

(1) he fails to produce his licence forthwith or
(2) produces a licence
    (i) granted by a local authority;
    (ii) which the constable suspects was not granted to him, was granted in error or is altered with intent to deceive;
    (iii) in which the driver number has been altered, removed or defaced; or
    (iv) if he supervises a provisional licence holder and he suspects he is under 21 years of age [Act 1988/164(1) and 1378/87/26].

Instead, a person can produce at the time, or within 7 days at a police station he specifies, a licence receipt issued under the fixed penalty system and, if required, produce the licence immediately on its return at a police station specified at the time [164(7)]. If a person does not produce his driving licence it is a defence for him to show that:

(a) within seven days after production was required he produced it at a police station he specified; or
(b) he produced it there as soon as was reasonably practicable; or
(c) it was not reasonably practicable for him to produce it there before proceedings were commenced for not producing it [164(8)].

If a licence has been revoked or obtained by a false statement a constable or vehicle examiner can require its production [164(3), (4)]. If a person required to produce his driving licence by a court fails to do so, he can be required by a police officer to produce it and, on its production, the officer can seize it and deliver it to the court [164(5)]. References here to a licence include,where it comes into force on or after 1 June 1990, its counterpart[144/90/2].

A person authorised by a traffic commissioner has, in relation to goods vehicles and passenger-carrying vehicles, the same powers as police to require the production of a driving licence [166 and Act 1991]. For traffic wardens see page 276.

A constable or vehicle examiner can require a person driving a motor vehicle on a road, or a person believed to have been driving at the time of an accident or traffic offence, to give his and the owner's name and address and to produce a certificate of insurance or security, a test certificate (where compulsory) and, in the case of a goods vehicle, a plating certificate or goods vehicle test certificate [165(1), (2)]. A person will not be convicted of failing to produce such a certificate if he shows that:

(a) within seven days after production was required it was produced at a police station he specified; or
(b) it was produced there as soon as was reasonably practicable; or
(c) it was not reasonably practicable for it to be produced there before the proceedings were commenced for not producing it [165(4)].

A person who supervises a provisional licence holder in the above circumstances can be required by a constable or vehicle examiner to give his own and the vehicle owner's name and address [165(5)]. A person authorised by a traffic commissioner is given the same power in respect of goods vehicles and passenger-carrying vehicles [166].

A chief officer of police can require the owner of a vehicle to give third-party insurance details in any case where the driver fails to produce a certificate or if a certificate is not produced following an accident involving injury [Act 1988/171]. He can also require a vehicle keeper to state who the driver was when a specified traffic offence was committed. But it is a defence for the owner to show that he did not know and could not with reasonable diligence have discovered the driver's identity [172].

The production of psv, lgv and pcv licences is dealt with on page 104.

A psv operator's licence or operator's disc must be produced within 14 days by the holder if required by a constable, certifying officer, psv examiner or any person authorised by the Traffic Commissioners to inspect the licence or disc. The licence or disc may be produced at the holder's operating centre or principal place of business within the traffic area issuing the licence [1668/86/14].

A London local service licence must be produced within 7 days by the holder if required by a constable, certifying officer, psv examiner or other person authorised by the Metropolitan traffic commissioner. The holder may elect to produce it within the Metropolitan Traffic Area at his operating centre or principal place of business [1691/86/18].

The holder of a goods vehicle operator's licence must produce it when required by a constable, goods vehicle examiner or person authorised by the Licensing Authority, and the holder may elect to do so, within 14 days, at any operating centre covered by the licence, his head office or principal place of business within the traffic area, or, if the requirement is made by a constable, at a police station chosen by the licence holder [176/84/28].

Record sheets and tachographs

The powers to require production and inspection of record books, registers, tachograph sheets and other documents in connection with the drivers' hours law are described on page 132.

Removal and disposal of vehicles

In specified circumstances a police officer can require the owner, driver or other person in control or in charge of a vehicle to move or cause the vehicle to be moved from a road. The requirement may include a direction, that the vehicle is not to be moved to any road or place on a road which he may specify [183/86/3(2)].

The specified circumstances are where a vehicle (a) has broken down or been left on a road in such position, condition or circumstances as to cause obstruction or be likely to cause danger to other road users or (b) has been left on a road in contravention of a waiting prohibition or restriction made under listed legislation [3(1)]. The legislation is listed in Schedule 1 of the Regulations and names the statutory powers under which are made the various waiting restrictions on ordinary roads and motorways.

Where a vehicle:

(a) comes within the above described circumstances;
(b) having broken down on a road or on land appears to a police officer to have been abandoned without lawful authority; or
(c) has been left on a road or on land in such position, condition or

circumstances as to appear to a police officer to have been abandoned without lawful authority,

a police officer may remove or arrange for the removal of the vehicle [4].

A traffic warden may, in the above specified circumstances, remove or arrange for the removal of the vehicle to a place which is not on a road or to another position on that or another road but only in relation to a vehicle which is on a road and only in England or Wales [4A and 278/93].

A local authority has power to remove a vehicle which appears to them to have been abandoned without lawful authority in circumstances (ii) and (iii) above except where the authority is under a duty to remove a motor vehicle under the Refuse Disposal (Amenity) Act 1978 [5].

A parking attendant, acting on behalf of a local authority, may, where a vehicle is parked on a road in England or Wales in contravention of specified statutory prohibitions, remove or arrange for the removal of the vehicle to a place which is not on a road or to another position on that or another road. In some cases 15 minutes must elapse from the end of a period for which a parking charge has been made before this power can be exercised [5A and 1708/93].

A vehicle may be removed by driving, towing or any other manner and a person may take such measures in relation to the vehicle to enable him to move it [6].

Before an authority removes a vehicle from land it must give written notice of its intention to the occupier of the land [Act 1984/99(3) and 183/86/8]. The occupier, may, within 15 days of receiving the notice, object to the removal of the vehicle [9].

Where an authority proposes to remove a vehicle which appears to have been abandoned and in their opinion is in such condition that it ought to be destroyed they must, seven days before moving it, fix a notice to it of their intention to remove it for destruction [Act 1984/99(4) and 183/86/10].

A chief officer of police or local authority may dispose of a vehicle which appears to have been abandoned and which has been or could be removed under the above provisions:

(a) in the case of a vehicle which in their opinion is in such a condition that it ought to be destroyed and on which no current excise licence is displayed, at any time after its removal;

(b) in the case of a vehicle as in (a) but on which a current licence was displayed, at any time after the licence expires;

(c) in any other case, at any time after steps have been taken to find the vehicle's owner and either (i) the owner has not been found or (ii) the owner has failed to comply with a notice requiring him to remove the vehicle from their custody;but not earlier than the expiration of any excise licence which appears to be in force for the vehicle [Act 1984/101(3)].

The steps which have to be taken to find the vehicle owner, the manner of serving notices on the owner to remove the vehicle and the period during which its owner can remove the vehicle are prescribed [183/86/12 to 16].

If within one year of the date a vehicle is disposed of by sale a person satisfies the authority concerned that he is the owner of the vehicle the authority must pay him the proceeds of sale less the prescribed charges for removal, storage and disposal [Act 1984/101(5)].

Prescribed charges for removing, storing and disposing of vehicles can be made by the appropriate authority and recovered as a civil debt from the vehicle owner (unless he had no knowledge of the matter) or the driver [Act 1984/102(2)]. The 'appropriate authority' is the local authority or, where the vehicle is moved by a police officer or a person assisting the police, the chief officer of police [102(8)].

This means that where the police engage a garage to move a vehicle it is the police—not the garage—who can recover the statutory charge. The practice in some areas of the garage demanding payment for the removal and detaining the vehicle till it is paid is without any legal foundation. Where the police engage a garage to move a vehicle it is they who must pay for its services.

The prescribed charge for removing a vehicle is £105. For storing a vehicle a charge of £12 can be made for each 24-hour period commencing at noon on the day following the removal and the charge for disposing of a vehicle is £50 [744/89, 336/91, 550/93 and 1415/93].

Section 3 of the Refuse Disposal (Amenity) Act 1978 places a duty on a local authority to remove a motor vehicle from land if it appears to the authority to have been abandoned without lawful authority. The procedure to be taken before disposing of the vehicle and the charges which can be made are the same as those described above.

Under Section 61 of the Road Traffic Regulation Act 1984 a local authority may designate certain areas of land as loading areas in which vehicles may be loaded or unloaded for such trades or businesses as may be specified in its order. An authorised officer of the local authority may require the driver, owner or other person in charge of a vehicle illegally parked in any loading area to move or cause it to be moved [184/86/3]. If (i) a person fails to comply with such requirement or (ii) no person is present or in the vicinity who is in charge of and capable of moving the vehicle, the officer may move or arrange for the removal of the vehicle [4].

A vehicle removed from a loading area may be disposed of by the local authority but subject to the procedure laid down in the Regulations referred to above [4]. The charge for removing a vehicle from a loading area is £105. Storing a vehicle is chargeable at £12 for each 24-hour period commencing at noon on the day following the removal. A charge of £50 can be made for disposing of a vehicle [744/89, 336/91 and 550/93].

Eyesight test

If a constable suspects that a person is driving a vehicle when he cannot perform the driving test eyesight requirement—reading a number plate having 79.4mm high figures at 20.5m—can require that person to take such an eyesight test [Act 1988/96].

Arrest

A constable may arrest a person who is in charge of, driving or attempting to drive a motor vehicle on a road or other public place if he is unfit to drive through drink or drugs [Act 1988/4]. A constable may arrest a person who takes a breath test and the device used indicates that the person's proportion of alcohol in the blood exceeds the prescribed limit. He may also arrest a person who fails to take a breath test but who he believes to have alcohol in his body [6(5)]. A person who has been arrested under these provisions and required to provide a specimen of blood or urine may be detained at a police station till he is fit to drive but he may not be detained if there is no likelihood of his driving or attempting to drive while unfit [10].

In Scotland, a constable can arrest the driver of a motor vehicle who, within his view, commits an offence of reckless, careless or inconsiderate driving unless the driver either gives his name and address or produces his ordinary driving licence for examination [Act 1988/167]. A constable in uniform can arrest any person driving or attempting to drive a motor vehicle on a road and whom he suspects is a disqualified driver [103(3)].

A constable can arrest a person he has reasonable cause to suspect has contravened the PSV Conduct regulations if he refuses to give his name and address or does not satisfactorily answer questions to verify a name and address given [Act 1981/25(2)].

Traffic wardens

A police authority may appoint traffic wardens [Act 1984/95] and they may be employed in enforcing the law with respect to an offence of (a) parking without lights or reflectors, (b) a vehicle obstructing a road or waiting, parking, loading, or unloading on a road or other public place, (c) contravening the Vehicles (Excise) Act, (d) parking charges or (e) causing a vehicle to stop on a pedestrian crossing in contravention of regulations. They may also give out fixed penalty notices (except where the offence appears to involve obligatory endorsement, unless the vehicle is stationary); be employed as attendants at street parking places, at car-pounds and as school crossing patrols; and may be employed in making inquiries about the identity of a driver and in regulating traffic (but not from a moving vehicle) [1958/70/Schedule, 1328/86, 1334/93 and RTO Act 1988/86].

In carrying out the above functions traffic wardens are given the same powers as a constable in preventing obstruction in the Metropolitan and City of London areas; in giving directions to drivers and pedestrians when engaged in the regulation of traffic; to require a pedestrian who ignores a traffic direction to give his name and address; the disposal of abandoned vehicles removed under statutory powers; and the immobilisation of vehicles illegally parked [3(2) and 1334/93].

A traffic warden can require a driver, or person believed to have been a driver, to give his name and address if he has reasonable cause to believe that an offence has been committed (a) of parking without lights or reflectors, (b) by a vehicle obstructing, waiting, parking, loading, or unloading, (c) of failing to comply with a traffic sign or direction when engaged on traffic regulation, (d) against the Vehicles (Excise) Act, or (e) in relation to parking meter charges [3(3)].

The above powers are also conferred on traffic wardens in Scotland [374/71].

The production of a driving licence can be required by a traffic warden (1) if he has reasonable cause to believe an offence has been committed by a vehicle being stopped on a pedestrian crossing or by a vehicle being left on a road in a dangerous position or (2) where he is employed at a car-pound and he has reasonable cause to believe that an offence has been committed by the vehicle obstructing, waiting, being parked, loaded or unloaded in a road [1958/70/3(4) and 1334/93].

A traffic warden has no power to require production of insurance or test certificates.

14 PSV conduct, etc.

London Transport (Lost Property) Regulations, **No. 2125/71**
PSV (Lost Property) Regulations, **No. 1684/78**
London Transport (Lost Property) (Amendment) Regulations, **No. 1791/78**
PSV (Lost Property) (Amendment) Regulations, **No. 1623/81**
PSV (Carrying Capacity) Regulations, **No. 1406/84**
PSV (Conduct of Drivers, Inspectors, Conductors and Passengers)
Regulations, **No. 1020/90**

Conduct of drivers, conductors and inspectors

The rules apply to any vehicle used as a public service vehicle other than a vehicle used under a Section 19 permit [1020/1990/3(1).

When any vehicle is in motion the driver must not hold a microphone, or any attachment to one, except in an emergency or on grounds of safety [4(1)].

He must not speak to any person either directly or by means of a microphone except (a) when obliged to do so in emergency or on grounds of safety; (b) when speaking to the operator or his employee about the operation of the vehicle as long as he can do so without being distracted from driving; or (c) when making short statements, except on excursions tours or sight-seeing trips, about the vehicle's location or operation as long as it does not distract him from driving [4(2)–(4)].

A driver and conductor must take all reasonable precautions to ensure the safety of passengers on, entering or leaving the vehicle [5(1)]. A driver, conductor or inspector must, if required by police or a person having reasonable cause, give his name, that of his employer and, in the case of a driver, particulars of his psv or pcv licence. A driver, conductor or inspector must not smoke on a vehicle except (a) where the vehicle is not available for carrying passengers and the person is in a part of the vehicle where smoking is allowed or (b) the vehicle is on hire and the person has the permission of the operator and hirer [5(3), (4)].

When picking up or setting down passengers a driver must stop the vehicle as close as reasonably practicable to the nearside of the road [5(5)]. While a vehicle is in motion the conductor must not, without reasonable excuse, distract the driver's attention or obstruct his vision [5(6)].

A driver, conductor and inspector must take reasonable steps to ensure the rules regarding conduct of passengers are complied with [5(2)].

Conduct of passengers

A passenger on a vehicle must not:

a. use a door designated for a particular purpose for any other purpose unless directed or authorised by a driver, conductor or inspector;
b. put at risk, unreasonably impede or cause discomfort to a person on, leaving or entering the vehicle or to the vehicle's staff;
c. throw or trail any article from the vehicle;
d. smoke, carry lighted tobacco or light a match or cigarette lighter in a part of the vehicle where, by notice, smoking is banned, unless the vehicle is on hire and the operator and hirer have given permission;
e. distribute any paper or other article for giving or seeking information without permission of the operator;
f. sell or offer for sale any article without permission of the operator;
g. speak to the driver except in emergency, on grounds of safety or to give directions as to the stopping of the vehicle;
h. without reasonable cause, distract the driver's attention, obstruct his vision or give any signal which he might reasonably interpret as a signal to stop in emergency or start the vehicle;
i. travel on part of the vehicle not intended to carry passengers;
j. remain on the vehicle when told to leave by the driver, conductor or inspector because the vehicle exceeds its marked seating or standing capacity, he is causing a nuisance, his condition is likely to cause offence or his clothing would soil the fittings of the vehicle or clothing of other passengers;
k. play or operate a musical instrument or sound reproducing equipment to the annoyance or likely annoyance of any person on the vehicle; or
l. intentionally interfere with any of the vehicle's equipment [6(1)]

A passenger who has with him any bulky or cumbersome article, any article or substance which (a) causes or is likely to cause annoyance to a person on the vehicle or (b) could constitute a risk of injury or damage to persons or property on the vehicle or to the vehicle, must put it where directed on the vehicle or remove it from the vehicle if requested by the driver, conductor or inspector [6(2), (4)].

A passenger who has with him any animal must put it where directed on the vehicle or remove it from the vehicle if requested by the driver, conductor or inspector. But a guide-dog accompanying a person who has a card issued by the Guide Dogs for the Blind Association may not, under this provision, be removed from (a) a double-decked vehicle or (b) a single-decked vehicle over 8.5m long if, in either case, there is not more than 1 dog already on it or (c) from a single-decked vehicle not over 8.5m long if there is no dog already on it [6(2), (3)].

A passenger on a vehicle being used to carry passengers at separate fares must not use a ticket which has been altered or defaced; use another person's non-transferable ticket; or use an expired ticket [7(1)].

A passenger on such a vehicle must (a) if requested by a driver, conductor or inspector, declare his journey; (b) on a one-man-operated vehicle, pay his fare immediately on boarding the vehicle or as otherwise directed; (c) on a vehicle with a conductor, pay the fare for the journey immediately when requested to do so; (d) accept and retain for the rest of the journey any ticket provided; (e) produce a ticket when required by a driver, conductor or inspector; and (f) when he has completed the journey for which he has a ticket, leave the vehicle or pay a further fare [7(2)]. A passenger must not leave the vehicle without having paid the fare, except by agreement with the driver, conductor or inspector [7(4)]. A passenger who has with him a ticket he is not entitled to retain must surrender it to the driver, conductor or inspector when required to do so [7(5)].

A passenger on a vehicle who is reasonably suspected of contravening these regulations must give his name and address to the driver, conductor or inspector (and, in Scotland, to a police constable) on demand [8(1)]. A passenger who contravenes these regulations may be removed from the vehicle by the driver, conductor or inspector or, on request by such person, by a police constable [8(2)].

Lost property

Separate Regulations are in force which deal with lost property found on public service vehicles generally and that which is found on London Transport vehicles.

In the general regulations it is laid down that a person who finds property in a public service vehicle must immediately hand it to the conductor or, if not practicable, to the vehicle operator's lost property office [1684/78/5]. At the beginning or end of each journey the conductor must search the vehicle for lost property [6(1)]. In the case of a one-man-operated bus any reference in the regulations to a conductor means a reference to the driver [3(2)]. A conductor who finds property on the vehicle or has property handed to him must deliver it to the vehicle operator as soon as possible and in any case within 24 hours unless he first returns it to its owner [6(2)]. When a person satisfies the conductor that property belongs to him it must be returned to him forthwith without charge on that person giving his name and address to the conductor. The conductor must then report the matter to the operator [6(3)].

Operators must keep records of found property and keep the property in safe custody. Official books and documents must be returned to their issuing authority. If the owner's name and address is readily ascertainable from the property he must be notified by the operator that it is in his possession. Records of property must be kept for 12 months after an item is disposed of and they can be inspected by police or a person authorised by the Traffic Commissioners [7].

Property which is in the possession of the operator must be returned to the owner if the operator is satisfied that the claimant is the owner. The operator can charge prescribed fees which range from 50p to £20 [8 and Sch. 2].

If any property in the custody of an operator is not claimed within a period of (a) one month, in the case of property (except certain documents) worth 50p or less; (b) three months, in the case of official documents; or (c) three months, in the case of any other property, by a claimant proving he owns it and who pays the prescribed charge, the property vests in the operator [9(1) and 1623/81]. An operator entitled to such property and charges paid under Regulation 8 can dispose of them as he thinks fit [9(2)].

Perishable goods not claimed or returned to the owner within 48 hours may be disposed of by the operator. Any property which becomes 'objectionable' may be disposed of at any time by the operator [10]. Post and packing costs incurred in returning property to the owner must be paid in advance to the operator [11]. The operator may open and examine property to trace the owner or ascertain its nature and value [12].

None of the above provisions apply to property found on vehicles belonging to and under the control of the London Transport Executive [4(2)].

Provisions of the London Transport Regulations are similar to the general Regulations. The main differences relate to the amount of fees charged for property claimed. If a person claims property before it is delivered to a Lost Property Office of the London Transport Executive he must pay a fee related to the nature of the property. The fees are set out in a schedule to the Regulations and range from 25p for small items such as hats, umbrellas, etc., to £20. If property is claimed from the Lost Property Office the charges are doubled [2125/71/8 and 1791/78].

Seating and standing capacity

The maximum seating capacity of a public service vehicle is (a) where, on or after 1 April 1981, there has been issued a certificate of initial fitness or certificate of conformity for the vehicle, the seating capacity specified on that certificate, or (b) where no such certificate has been issued on or after 1 April 1981, the seating capacity as calculated in Regulation 42 of the Road Vehicles (Registration and Licensing) Regulations 1971. In either case a greater or lesser capacity can be authorised by a certifying officer. Maximum seating capacity does not include the seat of the driver or a crew member [1406/84/4]. The 1971 Regulations state that seating capacity is calculated at the rate of one person per seat or, in the case of continuous seating, one person for each 16 in of seat.

A person must not drive, or cause or permit to be driven, a psv if the number of seated passengers exceeds the number of seats available [5(1)]. But a child under five years who is not occupying a seat does not count as a passenger and three children under 14 years of age count as two passengers. For the purposes of this latter concession, a child is deemed to be 14 years of age until the last of August next following his fourteenth birthday [5(2), (3)].

The maximum standing capacity of a psv is (a) where, on or after 1 April 1981 there has been issued a certificate of initial fitness or certificate of conformity for the vehicle, the standing capacity specified in the certificate, or (b) where no such certificate has been issued on or after 1 April 1981, one third of the number of passengers for which the vehicle, or the lower deck of a double-deck vehicle, has seating capacity, or eight, whichever is the less. In any case a certifying officer can authorise a greater or lesser number of standing passengers [6(1)]. The standing capacity of a psv with a seating capacity for less than 13 passengers; a vehicle with a gangway any part of which is less than 1.77m high; and a half-decked vehicle, is nil [6(2)].

A vehicle must not be driven on a road if the number of standing passengers exceeds the specified capacity [7(1)]. Standing is prohibited on (a) the upper deck and steps leading to the upper deck of a double-decker, (b) any part of the gangway forward of the rearmost part of the driver's seat, and (c) any part of the vehicle the operator has, by notice, indicated that no standing is allowed [7(2)].

The operator of a vehicle must mark on the inside or outside of the vehicle, in letters not less than 25mm high and in a contrasting colour, (a) the legal seating capacity or, if it is less and the operator so wishes, the number of passenger seats fitted on the vehicle, and (b) the legal standing capacity (whether nil or otherwise) or, if it less, the number of standing passengers the operator is willing to have on the vehicle [8].

A person who increases the seating or standing capacity of a vehicle which is being used under a psv operator's licence must, when the increase occurs, notify the traffic commissioners and the vehicle must not be used as a psv until the notification has been made and a certificate issued as a result [9].

None of the above restrictions applies to a psv registered in a county outside the United Kingdom [11].

15 PSV fitness, equipment and use

Public Passenger Vehicles Act 1981
Minibus (Conditions of Fitness, Equipment and Use) Regulations, **No. 2103/77**
Minibus (Conditions of Fitness, Equipment and Use) (Amendment) Regulations, **No. 142/80**
PSV (Conditions of Fitness, Equipment, Use and Certification) Regulations, **No. 257/81**
Minibus (Conditions of Fitness, Equipment and Use) (Amendment) Regulations, **Nos. 1599/81, 1484/82 and 1813/86**
PSV (Conditions of Fitness, Equipment, Use and Certification) (Amendment) Regulations, **No. 20/82**
PSV (Conditions of Fitness, Equipment, Use and Certification) (Amendment) (No. 2) Regulations, **No. 1058/82**
PSV (Conditions of Fitness, Equipment, Use and Certification) (Amendment) Regulations, **Nos. 1763/84, 340/88, 2359/89 and 3012/93**
PSV (Conditions of Fitness, Equipment, Use and Certification) (Amendment) (No. 2) Regulations, **No. 1812/86**
Public Passenger Vehicles (Exemptions, and Appeals against Refusals to issue Certificates or Remove Prohibitions) Regulations, **No. 1150/87**

Certification of fitness

A psv adapted to carry more than 8 passengers must not be used on a road unless:

(a) a certifying officer has issued a certificate of initial fitness to the effect that prescribed conditions of fitness are fulfilled on the vehicle, or
(b) a type-vehicle certificate has been issued for the vehicle, or
(c) a type approval certificate or certificate of conformity has been issued for the vehicle [Act 1981/6(1)].

A certificate of fitness issued under Section 129 of the Road Traffic

283

Act 1960 and in force on 1 April 1981 has effect as a certificate of initial fitness [Sch. 6(3)].

The conditions of fitness for Section 6(1) are prescribed in Part II of the PSV (Conditions of Fitness, Equipment, Use and Certification) Regulations 1981 and are described in the 'Fitness' section of this chapter. They do not apply in their entirety to articulated buses or vehicles having a designated ECE approval mark. Such vehicles have to conform to paragraph 5 of ECE Regulation 36 and to Regulations 6 to 12; 14 to 18; 23; 24; paragraphs 1(a) and (h) of 28; and 29 to 34 of the 'Fitness' Regulations [257/81/5 and Sch. 3].

An application for a certificate of initial fitness must be made to the Secretary of State, PSV Centre, Welcombe House, 91-92 The Strand, Swansea. On first application the fee for a certificate is £129 and on any subsequent application it is £129 if the testing involved includes a stability test and £15.40 in any other case [257/81/46, 1763/84 and 3012/93].

Applications for a type approval certificate must be made to the Minister of Transport. If the applicant says that the vehicle, its chassis or body, conforms to a vehicle, chassis or body which has already been type approved he can refer to that type approval [257/81/48(2)]. Similar reference may be made where a vehicle has a chassis or body which have formed parts of different vehicles already type approved [48(3)]. Applications must be accompanied by two sets of such drawings, specifications or calculations as the Minister may require and facilities must be given for the inspection and testing of the vehicle [48(4)].

The fee for type approval under Regulation 48(2) is £744.70 but if the Minister is satisfied that the vehicle conforms, except in unimportant details, to an already approved vehicle it is £69.90. The fee for approval under Regulation 48(3) is £368.60 and, in any other case, £1592.30 [50, 1763/84 and 3012/93].

An application for a certificate of conformity must be accompanied by a declaration, by the vehicle's manufacturer or his authorised person, that the vehicle conforms in design, construction and equipment to a type approved vehicle [257/81/52]. A certificate of conformity costs £14.50 [53 and 340/88].

If a certificate of fitness or conformity is issued before a vehicle is registered, the person who applies for registration must notify the Minister of the assigned registration mark and return the certificate for noting [55].

If a certificate of conformity or initial fitness is lost or destroyed the vehicle owner must notify the Minister who may issue a duplicate. If the original is found it must be returned to the Minister. A defaced or illegible certificate must be returned to the Minister so that a duplicate, costing £8.80, can be issued [57, 340/88 and 3012/93].

If a certifying officer refuses a certificate of initial fitness or a type approval certificate under Section 10 of the 1981 Act, the applicant can appeal to the Secretary of State [Act 1981/51(1)]. The appeal must be made in writing within 28 days of the refusal and state the grounds for the appeal [1150/87/5].

Conditions of fitness for minibuses authorised under the Minibus Act 1977 are given at the end of this chapter (page 290).

Of the following fitness, equipment and use requirements, those specified in Regulations 6 to 33, 35 to 44 and in 45A do not apply to a minibus first used on or after 1 April 1988 which fulfills or is exempt from the requirements of Regulations 41 to 43 of the Road Vehicles (Construction and Use) Regulations 1986—see page 24. A minibus for this purpose is a motor vehicle constructed or adapted to carry more than 8 but not more than 16 seated passengers in addition to the driver [1812/86].

Fitness

STABILITY

Every public service vehicle must pass a stability test.

For a double-decker this consists of tilting to an angle of 28 degrees without overturning. When undergoing the test, the vehicle must be complete and fully equipped for service and loaded with weights (at the rate of 63.5kg per person) to represent a full complement of passengers on the top deck only, plus the driver and conductor, if carried.

Single-deckers and half-deckers must be tilted to 35 degrees without overturning. This test must be made when the vehicle is complete and fully equipped for service with weights representing driver, a full complement of passengers, any crew for whom a crew seat is provided and conductor, if carried.

Any wheel stop used when carrying out these tests may not be higher than two-thirds of the height of the appropriate wheel rim above ground level [257/81/6 and 1058/82].

GUARD RAILS

If there is a space of more than 610mm between any two wheels on either side of a vehicle there must be an effective guard to within 230mm of the front wheel, 155mm of the rear wheel and 310mm of the ground (when unladen and on level ground) [257/81/8].

FUEL TANK

On single-deckers with 13 or more seats, half-deckers, and the lower deck of double-deckers, no fuel tank may be placed under any part of any gangway or, on vehicles first registered on or after 1 April 1959, any passage leading to an emergency exit which, in either case, is within 2ft of any entrance or exit [257/81/3]. It is not illegal, however, to fit a fuel tank under a passage leading to a secondary emergency exit.

On single-deckers with 12 or fewer seats registered before 28 October 1964, no fuel tank may be placed under any entrance or exit and no tank filling point may be under or immediately adjacent to any entrance or exist [13(1)(b) and Sch. 2(3)].

On similar vehicles first registered on or after 28 October 1964, no fuel tank may be placed under or within 12in of any entrance or exit and no filling point may be situated at the rear of the vehicle [13(1)(b)].

No part of any fuel tank or fuel supply apparatus may be placed in any compartments or spaces provided for the driver or passengers on vehicles first registered on or after 1 April 1959 [13(1)(c)].

Every tank and 'all apparatus supplying fuel to the engine' must be so placed or shielded that no leaking fuel can fall on to any part of the vehicle where it can be readily ignited or into any receptacle where it can accumulate [13(2)].

All filling points must be outside the body, with caps that can be securely fixed. The vent hole, if any, must be of the non-splash variety, and protected from danger of penetration by fire [13(3)].

A device must be provided which can readily cut off the supply of petrol or diesel to the engine. The means of operation must be accessible from outside the vehicle and, except for a diesel-engined vehicle, must be visible from outside the vehicle. Where it is visible the 'off' position must be marked and where it is not visible its position must be marked together with the means of operation. This requirement does not apply to a diesel-engined vehicle registered before 1 April 1959, or to a petrol-engined vehicle registered before this date if it has a cock to cut off the supply of petrol to the carburettor and its 'off' position is marked on the outside of the vehicle [13(1)(d)].

EXHAUST PIPE

The exhaust pipe must be kept clear of any inflammable material on the vehicle and placed or shielded so that no such material can be thrown on to it from any other part of the vehicle. The outlet of the pipe has to be at the rear or on the off-side of the vehicle and far enough to the rear to prevent, as far as practicable, fumes from entering the vehicle [257/81/14].

LIGHTING

In public service vehicles adequate artificial illumination must be provided for each deck with a permanent top and at least one lamp as near as is practicable to the top of every staircase leading to an upper deck without a permanent top.

On vehicles first registered on or after 1 April 1959, entrance or exit steps or platforms (other than emergency exits) must be adequately lighted. On vehicles first registered on or after 28 October 1964, circuits must be so arranged that an electrical failure in any sub-circuit cannot extinguish all lights on any deck [257/81/16].

All electric leads must be adequately insulated [17(1)].

In every electrical circuit (other than high-tension) of over 100V there must be an isolating switch in each pole of the main circuit and readily accessible to the driver or conductor but this does not apply to a vehicle registered before 19 June 1968, if a 100V circuit has been installed in the vehicle after that date. The isolating switch must not be capable of disconnecting the vehicle's obligatory front and rear lamps [17(2)].

BODY

The body of a vehicle must be securely fixed to the chassis, trap-doors must be secure against vibration and their lifting devices must not project above the level of the floor [257/81/18].

General construction requirements, which are usually incorporated when a vehicle is built, are also specified. These include requirements as to the height of the body sides [19]; steps, platforms and stairs [20 and 2359/89]; entrances and exits [21, 22]; doors [23 and 2359/89]; emergency exits [24]; access to exits [25]; gangways [26, 27]; seats [28 and 2359/89]; driver's accommodation [31] and crew seats [28A and 1058/82].

WINDSCREEN AND WINDOWS

Unless the driver's windscreen can be opened to give him a clear view of the road ahead it must be fitted with an adequate demisting and defrosting device [257/81/32]. All transverse windows not made of safety glass must be guarded against breakage by passengers being thrown against them [29(1)]. An emergency exit or ventilating panel (other than a window) in the roof of a vehicle made on or after 1 October 1981 must be constructed of metal, specified safety glass or safety glazing [29(2)].

MISCELLANEOUS

Adequate ventilation must be provided for the passengers and driver without the need to open any main window or windscreen [257/81/30]. Except for vehicles adapted for less than 13 passengers, there must be means to enable passengers to signal to the driver [33]. Luggage racks must be designed and constructed so that if any article falls from them it is not likely to fall on the driver or interfere with his control of the vehicle [15]. A vehicle must comply in all respects with the Road Vehicles (Construction and Use) Regulations and its bodywork, upholstery and fittings must be soundly and properly constructed of suitable materials, well finished and in good and serviceable condition [34(1)]. The vehicle must be capable of being fitted with a lighting system which complies with legal requirements [34(2)].

Equipment

This section does not apply to a local authority vehicle used for providing free school transport whether used wholly or partly for providing such transport or a local bus service [257/81/4 and 20/82].

FIRE-EXTINGUISHER

A suitable and efficient fire-extinguisher of a specified type must be readily available for use on a public service vehicle [257/81/35]. The types specified should comply with a British Standards Institution specification BS 5423:77, BS 5423/80 or BS 5423/87 and (a) have a minimum test rating of 8A or 21B and (b) contain water, foam, halon 1211 or halon 1301. Extinguishers containing halon must be marked accordingly [35, Sch. 4 and 2359/89].

FIRST AID

On an express carriage or contract carriage there must be a receptacle containing specified first aid dressings. The receptacle must be prominently marked and be readily available for use.

The first aid equipment must include (a) ten antiseptic wipes, foil packed; (b) one conforming disposable bandage (not less than 7.5cm wide); (c) two triangular bandages; (d) a packet of 24 assorted adhesive dressings; (e) three large sterile unmedicated ambulance dressings (not less than 15cm by 20cm; (f) two sterile eye pads with attachments; (g) twelve assorted safety pins; and (h) a pair of rustless blunt-ended scissors [257/81/36 and Sch. 5].

Use

This section does not apply to a vehicle in the public service of the Crown or in the service of a visiting force or headquarters or to a local authority vehicle providing free school transport or a local bus service [257/81/4 and 20/82].

While passengers are being carried no person must cause or permit any unnecessary obstruction of an entrance, exit or gangway [257/81/37]. No person shall cause or permit any obstruction of the driver [38]. The body of a vehicle, windows, fittings and passengers' seats must be maintained in good and clean condition while passengers are being carried [39]. During the hours of darkness gangways leading to exits and exits must be adequately lit by interior lighting, except the upper deck of a double-decker if a barrier across the stairs prevents access to that deck [40]. Controls for power-operated doors can be used only by authorised persons except in cases of emergency [41]. While a vehicle engine is running a petrol filler cap must not be removed and petrol must not be put into the tank [42]. Except for local authority free school transport vehicles, on a stage carriage with seating capacity for more than 20 a conductor must be carried except (a) if the vehicle seats not more than 32, the emergency exit and entrance are at the front in the driver's view and the driver can become aware if a person is trapped in a door or (b) if a certifying officer has stated in writing that a conductor is not required [43 and 20/82]. Restrictions are also placed on the carriage of inflammable or dangerous substances [44].

In a conspicuous place on the near-side of the vehicle, in letters not less than 25mm tall and in colours which contrast with their background there must be marked the owner's name and principal place of business [45].

Passengers and crew must not be permitted to use seats which do not comply with the fitness requirements of Regulations 28 and 28A [45A and 1058/82]

If radio, television, video or recorded music equipment is installed in a motor coach a licence must be obtained from the Performing Rights Society, 29-33, Berners Street, London, W1 (phone 071-580 5544). The licence is renewable on 6 July each year and for video equipment the fee is £78.03 per player and it can be moved from one coach to another. For radio, television and recorded music the fee is £69.37 per coach or, if the coach has been registered for more than three years before commencing date of the licence, £17.34. The minimum charge payable is £173.39 per coach operator but, where any of his coaches were registered more than three years before the commencement of the licence, the minimum charge is £52.02. The fee for a vehicle with not more than 20 seats, irrespective of age, is £86.71. The fees are revised in January each year.

MINIBUS CONDITIONS OF FITNESS

Minibuses authorised under Section 42 of the Public Passenger Vehicles Act 1981 have to comply with Regulations governing their fitness, equipment and use [2103/77]. If a contravention of these Regulations arises the minibus ceases to be treated, under Section 42, as not being a public service vehicle [Act 1981/44(3)].

In this section any reference to a minibus is to a minibus within Section 42 of the 1981 Act. The given requirements do not apply to a minibus authorised under a psv licence or to a minibus which does not carry passengers for hire or reward.

The following requirements do not apply to a minibus first used on or after 1 April 1988 which fulfills or is exempt from the minibus construction requirements of Regulations 41 to 43 of the Road Vehicles (Construction and Use) Regulations 1986—see page 24 [1813/86].

Fitness

STABILITY

With weights of 63.5kg placed in positions to represent the driver and passengers the minibus must not overturn when tilted 35 degrees from the horizontal on either side [5]. An efficient suspension system must be fitted so that there is no excessive body sway and a failure of a spring, torsion bar or other resilient component is not likely to cause the driver to lose control [6]. Brakes must act on the wheels and not through the transmission but a mechanical handbrake can act through the transmission as long as there is no universal joint between the brake and the wheel [7]. The steering mechanism must be such that no overlock is possible and the wheels must not foul any part of the vehicle [8].

FUEL TANK, PUMP AND PIPES

No fuel tank, pump or pipes must be placed in the driver's or passengers' compartments. They must be placed or shielded so that no overflowing or leaking fuel can fall or accumulate on any woodwork or other part of the vehicle where it might readily ignite or accumulate in a receptacle. Fuel tank filling points should be accessible only from outside the minibus. A fuel cut-off device must be provided on a minibus so that (a) in the case of a vehicle fitted with a fuel injection system, the position and means of operation are clearly marked on the outside of the vehicle and the means of operation is readily accessible from outside the vehicle and is clearly indicated and (b) in any other case, the device is readily visible and accessible from outside the vehicle and the 'off' position is marked [9].

EXHAUST PIPE

A minibus exhaust pipe must be fitted or shielded so that inflammable material cannot fall or be thrown on to it from the vehicle; so that it is not likely to cause fire by being near inflammable material; and its outlet is either at the rear or on the off-side and so far to the rear as to prevent fumes from entering the vehicle [10].

LOCKING OF NUTS

Moving parts and all parts subject to severe vibration and which are connected by bolts or studs and nuts must be fastened by lock nuts; nuts and spring or lock nut washers; castellated nuts and split pins; or some other efficient device to prevent their working loose [11].

ELECTRICAL APPARATUS

Electrical apparatus and circuits must be constructed and installed to guard against the risk of electric shock or fire. Electrical circuits which carry over 100V must be provided with an isolating switch inside the vehicle and in a place readily accessible to the driver [12].

ENTRANCES AND EXITS

The positioning of entrances and exits on a minibus depends on the location of the fuel tank. Where the fuel tank is behind the rear wheels the vehicle must have (a) an exit on the near-side and (b) an emergency exit on either the off-side or rear face of the minibus. Where the fuel tank is not behind the rear wheels the minibus must have (a) an exit on the near-side and an emergency exit on the off-side or rear face or (b) an exit and entrance on the rear face of the vehicle [13(1), (2)]. Such an exit may be a tail lift to assist disabled persons but it must not be fitted on the offside of the vehicle and it must comply with normal exit measurements [13(2A) and 1599/81]. An exit must be at least 1.17m high and 530mm wide [13(3)]. No entrance, other than the driver's entrance, may be on the off-side of the vehicle [13(4)]. Grab handles must be fitted to every entrance and exit (other than an emergency exit) [13(5)].

Except for the driver's seat and any seat alongside his seat, there has to be unobstructed access from every seat in the minibus to every exit [14]. Special provisions are made for exits which are tail lifts [14(3) and 1599/81].

Doors must not obstruct clear access to any entrance or exit from inside or outside the vehicle. Means must be provided for keeping doors closed or open. Two devices must be provided for operating the means for securing each door in the closed position and one of these must be on the outside of the vehicle. The devices must be easily accessible to a person of normal height; if the device is not on the door it must be so placed as to be readily associated with the door; and a single movement of the device must open the door. The method of operation of a device and its position, if not on the door, must be indicated [15]. Tail-lift opening doors must comply with some of these requirements [15(4A) and 1599/81].

Emergency exits must be clearly marked on both the inside and outside of the vehicle (except for rear end tail-lift exits); their doors must open outwards, be readily accessible to passengers and not be power-operated [16 and 1599/81].

SEATING

A length of 400mm measured across the front of each seat is to be allowed for each seated passenger. If a seat is so placed that its occupant is liable to be thrown through any entrance or exit or down any steps an effective screen or guard must be provided to prevent that event occurring. No seat may be fitted to a door and all seat supports must be securely fixed in position [17 and 1484/82].

DRIVER'S SEAT OR COMPARTMENT

A minibus must be so constructed that the seated driver has adequate room and can readily reach and operate the controls. Means must be provided, if necessary, of preventing the vehicle's interior lighting inconveniencing the driver. When access to the driver's seat is on the off-side of the vehicle the opening must be at least 455mm wide (discounting any wheel arch) and if its lower edge is more than 690mm above ground level a convenient step must be provided. When a separate and enclosed compartment is provided for the driver and access is obtained from the off-side of the vehicle an emergency exit at least 530mm by 455mm must be provided for him otherwise than on the off-side [18].

MISCELLANEOUS

Luggage racks fitted in a minibus must be so designed that anything dislodged from them is unlikely to fall on the driver or interfere with his driving [19].

Internal lighting adequate to illuminate the exits and adequate ventilation must be provided [20, 21].

Transverse windows which are not made of safety glass, safety glazing or specified safety glass must be protected against being broken by passengers thrown against them [22].

Every minibus must be a single-deck vehicle and its length must not exceed 7m [24, 23].

A minibus must conform to the Construction and Use Regulations as regards construction, weight and equipment. Its bodywork and fittings must be soundly and properly constructed of suitable materials and be in good and serviceable condition. It must be designed to be capable of withstanding loads and stresses likely to be met with in the normal operation of the vehicle [25].

Equipment

SEATING CAPACITY

The seating capacity must be painted in characters not less than 25mm high either (a) on the inside of the vehicle so as to be readily visible from the outside or (b) on the rear or near-side of the outside of the vehicle [26].

FIRE-EXTINGUISHER

A minibus must carry suitable and efficient apparatus for extinguishing fire which complies with BS 5423:1977 or BS 5423:1980 and, in either case, contains water, foam, halon 1211 or halon 1301 and, if containing halon, must be marked accordingly. The extinguisher must be readily available for use, marked with the BS number and maintained in good and efficient working order [27, 142/80 and 1484/82]. First aid equipment of a specified kind (same as psv) must be carried in a prominently marked receptacle and be readily available for use [28 and 142/80].

Use

While passengers are carried no person must cause or permit any unnecessary obstruction of any entrance, exit or gangway [29]. No passenger shall unnecessarily obstruct the driver or divert his attention from controlling the vehicle [30]. While carrying passengers the windows of a minibus must be kept clean and in good condition [31]. While the engine is running no person must remove the petrol tank filler cap or put petrol into the tank [32]. No highly inflammable or otherwise dangerous substance may be carried unless carried in containers and so packed that damage or injury is unlikely [33]. A trailer may not be drawn unless all passengers have access to an exit on the near-side of the vehicle [34].

16 PSV operators' licensing and permits

Public Passenger Vehicles Act 1981
Transport Act 1985
Road Traffic (Driver Licensing and Information Systems) Act 1989
Community Bus Regulations, **No. 1313/78**
Minibus (Designated Bodies) Order, **No. 1356/80**
PSV (Traffic Regulation Conditions) Regulations, **No. 1030/86**
Community Bus Regulations, **No. 1245/86**
Operation of PSV (Partnership) Regulations, **No. 1628/86**
PSV (Traffic Commissioners: Publication and Inquiries) Regulations, **No. 1629/86**
PSV (Operators' Licences) Regulations, **No. 1668/86**
PSV (London Local Service Licences) Regulations, **No. 1691/86**
Minibus and other Section 19 Permit Buses Regulations, **No. 1230/87**
Operation of PSV (Partnership) (Amendment) Regulations **No. 1850/90**
PSV Operators (Qualifications) Regulations, **No. 1851/90**
PSV (Operators' Licences) (Amendment) Regulations, **No. 1852/90**
PSV Operators (Qualifications) (Amendment) Regulations, **No. 2641/90**
Traffic Areas (Reorganisation) Order, **No. 288/1991**
PSV (Traffic Commissioners: Publication and Inquiries) Regulations, **No. 2754/93**

PSV operators' licensing

TRAFFIC COMMISSIONERS AND TRAFFIC AREAS

The Traffic Commissioner for a traffic area is responsible for issuing operators' licences [Act 1981/4(1)].

A TC is appointed by the Secretary of State for each traffic area. He must act under the general directions of the Secretary of State and retire at the age of 65 or, if permitted, 66. Before appointing a TC the Secretary of State must ask him to declare whether or not he has any financial interest in any goods or passenger transport business in Britain. The terms of service of a TC and his deputies are prescribed in Schedule 2 to the Act [4].

Great Britain is divided into eight traffic areas [Act 1981/3(3) and 288/91]. They are defined according to local government areas in the Schedule to the 1991 Order and are listed on page 240.

WHEN A LICENCE IS NEEDED

A person who uses a public service vehicle on a road for carrying passengers for hire or reward requires a PSV operator's licence [Act 1981/12(1)].

An operator's licence cannot be granted to an unincorporated body or to more than one person jointly, except in the case of persons in partnership [Act 1981/58, 1626/86 & 1850/90].

It is a defence for a person charged with operating a psv without a licence to prove he took all reasonable precautions and exercised all due diligence to avoid the commission of the offence [68(3)].

EXEMPTIONS

A school bus used by a local education authority to provide free school transport or a local service (see page 320) [Act 1981/46(1)].

A bus used by educational and other bodies under a permit and subject to specified restrictions (see page 316) [Act 1985/18(1)].

A bus used for social and welfare needs under a community bus permit (see page 318) [Act 1865/18(1)].

PUBLIC SERVICE VEHICLE

A public service vehicle is a motor vehicle (other than a tramcar) which:

a. if adapted to carry more than 8 passengers is used for carrying passengers for hire or reward (In *Westacott v Centaur Overland Travel Ltd* [1981] RTR 182 the High Court would not disagree with a magistrates' finding that an 11-seat minibus with four seats blanked off was, at that time, not adapted to carry eight or more passengers); or

b. if adapted to carry 8 or less passengers is used for carrying passengers for hire or reward at separate fares in the course of a business of carrying passengers   [Act 1981/1(1].

A vehicle is being used for a. or b. above if it is being used as described in a. or b. or it has been so used and that use has not been permanently discontinued [1(2)].

A journey on which one or more passengers are carried at separate fares is not treated as made in the course of a passenger-carrying business if (i) the total fares do not exceed the vehicle's running costs for the journey and (ii) the payment of fares was arranged before the journey began. Running costs will be taken to include an appropriate amount for depreciation and general wear [1(4)]. This provision has the effect of taking a cost-shared vehicle with 8 or less seats out of Section 1(1)(b).

For the above purposes and Schedule 1 (described below):

a. a vehicle is treated as carrying passengers for hire or reward if payment is made for, or for matters which include, the carrying of passengers, irrespective of the person to whom the payment is made and, in the case of a transaction made by or on behalf of a member of any association of persons (whether incorporated or not) on the one hand and the association or another member thereof, notwithstanding any rules of law as to such transactions;

b. a payment made for carrying a passenger shall be treated as a fare even though it is made in consideration of other matters in addition to the journey and irrespective of the person by or to whom it is made;

c. a payment shall be treated as made for the carrying of a passenger if made in consideration of a person being given a right to be carried, whether for one or more journeys and whether or not the right is exercised [1(5)].

A minibus adapted to carry more than 8 passengers used to carry children to and from school by a parent who did not ask for but received ad hoc payments from other parents was held to be a public service vehicle in *DPP v Sikondar* [1993] RTR 90. The High Court ruled that Section 1(5)(c) above was not to be taken as defining the only circumstances in which a vehicle could be used for hire or reward and, following the decision in *Albert v Motor Insurers' Bureau* [1972] RTR 230, it was not necessary for the prosecution to establish a legally enforceable agreement. In this latter case the House of Lords ruled that a vehicle in which passengers were carried for hire or reward meant a vehicle used for the systematic carrying of passengers for reward, not necessarily on a contractual basis, going beyond the bounds of mere social kindness and amounting to a business activity.

In *Rout v Swallow Hotels Ltd* [1993] RTR 80 the hotel provided two courtesy coaches which carried hotel patrons and their friends. The hotel manager had a discretion as to whether to run the coaches, their destinations and who was carried. No payment was made and no one had a right to be carried. The High Court ruled that the payment made by hotel guests for rooms and meals included an element which included the provision of amenities by the hotel, one of which was the provision of the coaches. It held that the coaches were public service vehicles.

An air fare is not treated as paid in consideration of the carriage of a passenger by road if, in the case of mechanical failure, bad weather or other circumstance outside the operator's control, part of the journey may be made by road [1(6)].

A fare includes the price of a contract or season ticket [82].

SCHEDULE 1 MINIBUS CONCESSIONS

A vehicle not adapted to carry more than 8 passengers and which is carrying passengers at separate fares in the course of a passenger-carrying business but in the circumstances set out in Part I or III of Schedule 1 to the Act is not regarded as a public service vehicle [Act 1981/1(3)].

Part I—sharing of taxis and hire-cars

1. The making of the agreement for the payment of separate fares must not have been initiated by the driver or owner of the vehicle, by any person who has made the vehicle available under any arrangement or by any person who receives any remuneration in respect of the arrangements for the journey.

2. The journey must be made without previous advertisement to the public of facilities for its being made by passengers to be carried at separate fares, except where the local authorities concerned have approved the arrangements under which the journey is made as designed to meet the social and welfare needs of one of more communities, and their approvals remain in force.

   In relation to a journey, the local authorities concerned for the purpose of this paragraph are those in whose area any part of the journey is to be made. 'Local authority' means:
   (a) in England and Wales, the council of a county, metropolitan district or London borough and the Common Council of the City of London;
   (b) in Scotland, a regional or islands council.

Part III—alternative conditions

5. Arrangements for the bringing together of all the passengers for the purpose of making the journey must have been made otherwise than by, or a person on behalf of:
   (a) the holder of the operator's licence under which the vehicle is to be used, if such a licence is in force;
   (b) the driver or the owner of the vehicle or any person who has

made the vehicle available under any arrangement, if no such licence is in force;

and otherwise than by any person who receives any remuneration in respect of the arrangements.

6. The journey must be made without previous advertisement to the public of the arrangements therefor.
7. All the passengers must, in the case of a journey to a particular destination, be carried to, or to the vicinity of that destination or, in the case of a tour, be carried for the greater part of the journey.
8. No differentiation of fares for the journey on the basis of distance or time must be made.

Part V—supplementary

9. For the purposes of paragraphs 2. and 6. no account shall be taken of any of the following advertisements:
   (a) a notice displayed or announcement made:
      (i) at or in any place of worship for the information of persons attending that place of worship;
      (ii) at or in any place of work for the information of persons who work there;
      (iii) by any club or other voluntary association at or in any premises occupied or used by the club or association;
   (b) a notice or announcement contained in any periodical published for the information of, and circulating wholly or mainly among:
      (i) persons who attend or might reasonable be expected to attend a particular place of worship in a particular place;
      (ii) persons who work at a particular place of work or at any of two or more particular places of work; or
      (iii) the members of a club or other voluntary association.

APPLICATIONS

A licence is granted by the TC of the traffic area in which there will be one or more operating centres of vehicles used under the licence [Act 1981/12(2)].

An operating centre is the place where a vehicle is normally kept [82(1)].

A person can hold two or more licences each granted in a different traffic area but cannot, at one time, hold more than one licence granted in the same traffic area [12(3)]. But a person in partnership is treated as a person separate from that person as an individual or in any other partnership [1628/86].

An application must be in the form required by the TC and an applicant must give the TC such information as he may reasonably require for the purpose of disposing of the application [12(4)].

A TC who receives an application must, until it is determined, make it or part of it available for inspection by any person authorised by a chief officer of police or a local authority and who makes such a request in writing [1668/86/4].

GIVING FURTHER INFORMATION

A person who has applied for an operator's licence must notify the TC forthwith if, in the interval between making the application and its being disposed of, a relevant conviction occurs of the applicant, an employee or agent of his, or any person proposed to be a transport manager [Act 1981/19(1)]. Where the applicant is a partnership, the duty to notify relates to convictions of each of the partners and the employees or agents of the firm [1628/86].

The holder of a licence must notify the TC in writing of any relevant conviction of his and of any relevant conviction of any officer, employee or agent of his committed in the course of the licence holder's passenger transport business. In the case of his own or transport manager's convictions the licence holder must give the notice within 28 days of the conviction and, in relation to any other person, within 28 days of the conviction coming to his notice [Act 1981/19(2)]. Where the holder of a licence is a partnership, the duty to notify relates to convictions of each partner and to officers, employees and agents of the firm [1628/86].

The holder of a licence must give the TC written notice within 28 days of (a) his bankruptcy or liquidation, sequestration of his estate or the appointment of a receiver, manager or trustee of his passenger transport business and (ii) any change in the identity of his transport manager [Act 1981/19(3)]. In the case of a partnership this duty to notify arises if the firm is dissolved [1628/86].

The TC, on granting or varying an operator's licence, can require the holder to inform him forthwith or within a specified time of any material change he specifies in any of the licence holder's circumstances which were relevant to the grant or variation [19(4)].

The holder of a psv licence must notify the Secretary of State as soon as reasonably practicable of any failure or damage on a psv owned by him which affects the safety of occupants or other road users [20(1)]. Except for the replacement of parts, any alteration to the structure or equipment of a psv which he owns must be notified by the licence holder to the Secretary of State [20(2)].

A TC can require a licence holder to supply information about psvs owned by him and kept at an operating centre within the traffic area.

Similar demands can be made of the former holder of a licence [20(3)].

A person who does not comply with the above requirements commits an offence but it is a defence to prove that there was a reasonable excuse for the act or omission charged [19(5), 20(4) & 68(1)].

A person who, under Section 20(3), supplies information which is false or which he does not believe to be true commits an offence [20(5)].

TYPES OF LICENCE

A licence can be either a standard licence or a restricted licence [Act 1981/13(1)].

A standard licence authorises the use of any psv and may authorise either

(a) national and international operations, or

(b) national operations only [13(2)].

An international operation is one starting or ending in the United Kingdom and involving an international journey by the vehicle, whether or not any driver leaves or enters the UK with that vehicle [82(1)].

A restricted licence authorises the use (whether on national or international operations) of:

(a) psvs not adapted to carry more than 8 passengers;

(b) psvs not adapted to carry more than 16 passengers when used

    (i) otherwise than in the course of a business of carrying passengers (a local authority vehicle is not so regarded unless used by the authority's own psv undertaking), or

    (ii) by a person whose main occupation is not the operation of psvs adapted to carry more than 8 passengers [13(3),(4)].

THE LICENCE HOLDER

The person using the vehicle must hold the operator's licence.

Except for hired vehicles dealt with in the following paragraph, the operator of a vehicle is defined as (a) the driver, if he owns the vehicle; and (b) in any other case, the person for whom the driver works (whether under a contract of employment or any other description of contract personally to do work) [Act 1981/81(1)].

Where a vehicle is made available from one psv licence holder to another under a hiring arrangement, the operator of the vehicle is to be regarded as the person from whom it is hired where:

a. the licence holder to whom it is hired is not, under the hiring agreement, entitled to keep it for more than 14 days;

b. there have been at least 14 days between the start of the hire and the end of a previous hire of the vehicle from the same person;

c. when the vehicle is used for carrying passengers for hire or reward during the hire period a licence disc issued to the person from whom the vehicle is hired is fixed to the vehicle;

d. if hired by the holder of a restricted licence the vehicle is not adapted to carry more than 16 passengers; and

e. the vehicle is not a licensed taxi under a special licence [1668/86/18].

LICENCE HOLDER'S REQUIREMENTS

An application for a standard or restricted licence will not be granted unless the TC is satisfied:

a. there will be adequate facilities and arrangements for maintaining the vehicles proposed to be used under the licence in a fit and serviceable condition;

b. there will be adequate arrangements for ensuring compliance with legal requirements relating to the driving and operation of those vehicles [Act 1981/14(3)].

An application for a standard licence will not be granted unless the TC is satisfied the applicant is of good repute, has appropriate financial standing and is professionally competent [14(1)].

An application for a restricted licence will not be granted unless the TC is satisfied the applicant is of good repute and has appropriate financial standing [14(1)].

For Transport Tribunal rulings on these matters see pages 205 to 209.

Good repute

In deciding whether an individual (including a transport manager) is of good repute the TC shall have regard to all the relevant evidence and in particular to:

(a) relevant convictions of the individual and his employees and agents, and

(b) other information the TC may have as to his previous conduct, in whatever capacity, in relation to the operation of any kind of vehicle in the course of a business.

[Act 1981/Sch.3/1(1)].

In deciding whether a company is of good repute a TC shall have regard to all the relevant evidence and in particular to:

(a) relevant convictions of the company, its officers, employees and agents, and

(b) other information the TC may have as to previous conduct of

(i) the company's officers, employees and agents in relation to the operation of any vehicles in the course of a business carried on by the company, and

(ii) the company's directors, in whatever capacity, in relation to the operation of any vehicles in the course of any other business. [Sch.3/1(2)].

A TC must find that an individual is not of good repute if:

(a) he has been convicted of serious offences (a serious offence is a UK offence for which a sentence of more than three months imprisonment, a fine exceeding level 4 (now £2,500) or more than 60 hours community service was ordered, or a corresponding offence in another country for which a corresponding punishment was imposed), or

(b) he has been repeatedly convicted of road transport offences (a road transport offence is a UK offence relating to road transport, particularly drivers' hours and rest periods, weights and dimensions, road and vehicle safety, or a corresponding offence outside the UK),

but a spent conviction must be disregarded and a TC has discretion to disregard an offence if an 'appropriate' time has elapsed since the conviction. An LA can decide a person is not of good repute for reasons other than the kind of convictions in (a) and (b). [Sch.3/1(3)-(5),(8),(9) & 1851/90].

Where the applicant is a partnership, the TC has to be satisfied that every partner is of good repute [1628/86].

Relevant convictions are a conviction of:

1. the holder of, or applicant for, a psv operator's licence;
2. any partner where the licence holder or applicant is a partnership
3. any transport manager employed or proposed to be employed by the licence holder or applicant;
4. any officer, employee or agent of the licence holder or applicant in relation to any business of the holder or applicant;

of any of the following in relation to a public service vehicle or its operation:

a. an offence under the 1981 Act;
b. an offence under Parts I and II and Section 101 of the 1985 Act;
c. an offence specified in Parts I,II,III or IV of the 1972 Act;
d. offences against specified sections of the 1972 Act dealing with production of licences, test and insurance certificates; giving of names and addresses; forgery and false statements;
e. any speeding offence;
f. any offence relating to new bus grants, fuel duty grants or vehicle excise licensing;
g. any contravention of traffic regulation orders or motorway traffic regulations;

h. any contravention of drivers' hours and records requirements under the Transport Act 1968;
i. specified liquor licensing offences;
j. a serious offence or serious road transport offence as described above   [1668/86/17 & Sch & 1852/90].

Appropriate financial standing

This means having available sufficient financial resources to ensure the establishment and proper administration of the business [Act 1981/Sch.3/2(1)].

Except for a person who held a licence continuously before 11 October 1990 and up to the time a new licence is issued, an applicant for, or the holder of, a licence authorising international operations (including a firm, in the case of a partnership) will not be considered to be of appropriate financial standing unless he has available capital and reserves equal to the lesser of:

(a) 3,000 European Currency Units per vehicle used under the licence, or
(b) 150 ECU for each passenger seat in that number of vehicles
                              [Sch.3/2(2), 1851/90 & 1850/90].

In considering any financial question which appears to him to arise a TC may be assisted by an assessor [17A & Act 1985].

Professional competence

Professional competence relates to an individual and a company satisfies the professional competence requirement if it has a transport manager or managers of its road transport business who is, or each of whom are, of good repute and professionally competent [Act 1981/Sch.3/3].

A partnership satisfies the requirement if any of the partners managing the road transport business is professionally competent or any transport manager(s) employed is of good repute and professionally competent [1628/86 & 1850/90].

If an individual is not professionally competent, the competence requirement will be satisfied if, and so long as, he has a transport manager of his road passenger transport business who is of good repute and professionally competent [Sch.3/4].

Where a licence holder relies on a single transport manager and the manager

(a) dies or ceases, due to physical disability or mental disorder, to be capable of working as a transport manager,
(b) ceases to work for the business, or
(c) ceases to be of good repute,

the licence holder will not be treated as failing to satisfy the competence requirement for a period which the TC considers reasonable for the appointment of a new transport manager. This provision also applies to a firm where one of the partners or a single transport manager met the professional competence requirement [Sch.3/5(1), 1628/86, 1850/90 & 1851/90].

Where a licence holder is a company with two or more transport managers and any of them ceases to be of good repute, the company will not be treated as failing to satisfy the competence requirement for a period the TC considers reasonable for his removal or the appointment of a new manager in his place. This provision also applies to a firm where two or more partners or two or more transport managers met the professional competence requirement [Sch.3/5(2), 1628/86, 1850/90 & 1851/90].

An individual is regarded as professionally competent if:
(a) he has passed a written examination showing he possesses the requisite skills and holds a certificate to that effect,
(b) he is the holder of any other certificate of competence, diploma or other qualification recognised for this purpose by the Secretary of State [Sch.3/6 & 2641/90].

A transport manager is an individual who either alone or jointly, has continuous and effective responsibility for the management of the road passenger transport operations of the business [Act 1981/82(1)].

'Grandfather' rights

The provisions in the following two paragraphs apply in relation to the holder of, or an applicant for, a standard licence, where an individual or company was authorised to be a road passenger transport operator at the time in question. For this purpose a person was authorised to be a road transport operator if:
(i) he was the holder or joint holder of a psv licence for vehicles adapted to carry more than 8 passengers;
(ii) by virtue of a permit he was deemed to be the holder of such a licence;
(iii) he was so authorised under the law of another Member State; or
(iv) he was the transport manager of a person within (i) to (iii) [Act 1981/Sch.3/8].

An individual or company authorised to be a road transport operator at any time before 1 January 1978 is deemed, until the contrary is proved, to satisfy the requirement to be of good repute and appropriate financial standing and, if authorised before 1 January 1975, to be professionally competent [Sch.3/9(1)]. An applicant for, or the variation of, a standard licence is not obliged to supply the TC, in connection with his application, information about matters deemed to be satisfied unless it appears to the TC that there are grounds for thinking they are not satisfied [9(2)].

An individual who was authorised to be a road transport operator before 1 January 1978 and was authorised (a) for a total of two years between 1 January 1975 and 31 December 1979, or (b) for any period between 1 January 1970 and 31 December 1974, is regarded as professionally competent [Sch.3/10].

If the TC determines all the above requirements are satisfied he must, subject to provisions relating to the duration and conditions on the licence, grant the licence as applied for [14(4)].

OBJECTIONS

A chief officer of police or a local authority may object to the grant of an operator's licence on the grounds that the requirements of good repute, financial standing, professional competence, maintenance arrangements or measures to ensure compliance with the law relating to driving and operating the vehicles are not satisfied [Act 1981/14A(1)]. This provision does not apply to an application for a special licence (i.e. taxis on local services) under Section 12 of the Transport Act 1985 [14A(5)].

An objection must be made within the prescribed period, in the prescribed manner and contain particulars of the ground on which it is made [14A(2)].

Notice of objection must be made so as to be received by the TC within 21 days (excluding bank holidays) of the application being published in *Notices and Proceedings* and a copy must be sent, at the same time, to the applicant. In exceptional circumstances a TC can consider an objection which does not meet these requirements [1668/86/5 & 22].

The onus of proof of the existence of the ground on which an objection is made lies on the objector [14A(3)].

CONDITIONS

On granting a psv operator's licence a TC must attach one or more conditions specifying the maximum number of vehicles which the licence holder may use at any time [Act 1981/16(1)]. In the case of a restricted licence the maximum specified must not exceed two [16(1A)] but this limit does not apply to a licence held by the Post Office [1668/86/23]. Different maximum numbers may be specified for different descriptions of vehicles [16(2)].

When granting a licence or at any time thereafter, a TC may attach prescribed conditions to it for restricting or regulating the use of vehicles under the licence [16(3)]. Designated sporting events, under the Sporting Events (Control of Alcohol) Act 1985, have been prescribed for this purpose and conditions may be imposed as to (a) the times of departure and arrival of outward and return journeys, and (b) the lengths and places of any breaks on such journeys [1668/86/7].

A TC may vary a licence by altering or removing a condition [16(5)] and the licence holder can apply for such action to be taken. Where an application is made the licence holder must give the TC such information as he may reasonably require in relation to the application [16(6)].

Before (a) attaching a condition under Section 16(3) (other than when granting the licence); (b) altering a condition attached under Section 16(3) (except a local service condition under Section 26 of the 1985 Act); or (c) removing a condition attached under Section 16(3) (including a local service condition under Section 26 of the 1985 Act), the TC must notify the licence holder of his proposal and consider any representations he receives from the operator within 14 days of the notice [1668/86/8].

Compliance with a licence condition can be temporarily dispensed with by the TC if satisfied that compliance would be unduly onerous due to unforseen circumstances [16(8)].

A condition attached to a licence in one traffic area does not affect the use by the licence holder of a vehicle used (a) under an operator's licence granted to him in another traffic area or (b) in circumstances where another person is treated as the user of the vehicle (such as a Regulation 18 hiring arrangement) [16(9)].

A licence holder can be fined for contravening a licence condition [16(7)] but it is a defence for him to prove that he took all reasonable precautions and exercised all due diligence to avoid the commission of the offence [68(3)].

LOCAL SERVICE CONDITIONS

If it appears to a TC in relation to an operator to whom he has granted, or is proposing to grant, an operator's licence that—

a. the operator has failed to operate a local service registered under Section 6 of the 1985 Act;
b. the operator has operated a local service in contravention of that Section;
c. the arrangements for maintaining vehicles used under the licence in a fit and serviceable condition are not adequate in relation to the local service in question;
d. the operator, or any employee or agent of his, has:

(i)   intentionally interfered with the operation of a local service provided by another operator;

(ii) operated a local service in a manner dangerous to the public; or

(iii) been guilty of any other serious misconduct (whether or not amounting to a criminal offence) in relation to the operation of a local service; or

e. a traffic regulation condition in relation to a local service has been contravened;

he may, when granting the licence or at any later time, attach to the licence a condition prohibiting the operator from using vehicles under the licence to provide any local service of a description specified in the condition or one prohibiting him from so using vehicles to provide local services of any description [Act 1985/26(1)].

A condition may be attached under a. or b. above only if it appears to the TC that the operator did not have a reasonable excuse for his conduct or that it is appropriate to attach the condition in view of (1) the danger to the public involved in the operator's conduct or (2) the frequency of conduct of the kind in question on the part of the operator [26(2)].

Where the effect of a condition is that the operator of a registered local service is prohibited from using vehicles under the licence to provide that service, the TC may cancel the registration or, where the service is registered with another TC, direct that it be cancelled [26(3)].

Where it appears to a TC that

a. vehicles used under the licence (or any previous licence held by the operator) have not been maintained in a fit and serviceable condition; or

b. the operator has been involved in arrangements with another operator for the use of each other's vehicles with a view to hindering enforcement of any legal requirement relating to the operation of those vehicles;

he may, on granting the licence or at a later time, attach a condition restricting the vehicles which the operator may use under the licence to vehicles specified in the condition [26(5)]. Such a condition will apply only to vehicles which have an operating centre within the TC's area and be in addition to, and not prejudicial to, any conditions attached under Section 16 of the 1981 Act relating to the maximum number of vehicles which may be used under the licence [26(6)].

Before attaching any condition under Section 26, a TC must hold an inquiry if he has, within the prescribed time (given in the next paragraph), received a request for one from the licence holder or applicant [Act 1985/27(1)]. This requirement does not apply if the

TC is satisfied the condition should be attached without delay [27(2)] but if he attaches a condition before holding an inquiry he must hold one as soon as is reasonably practicable if the licence holder, within 14 days of notice that the condition has been attached, asks him to do so [27(3) and 1668/86/9(4) & 22].

Except on granting the licence or where Section 27(2) applies, before attaching or varying any condition under Section 26, the TC must give notice to the licence holder—

a. that he is considering such action;
b. the grounds on which that consideration is based;
c. that within 14 days of the notice the licence holder may make representations about the action considered;
d. that those representations must be in writing; and
e. either—

    i. he proposes to hold an inquiry in relation to the action being considered and the date of it (not being less than 14 days from the notice); or

    ii. he does not propose to hold an inquiry in relation to that action unless the licence holder, within 14 days of the notice, requests him in writing to do so [1668/86/9(1)].

The TC must take into account any representations he receives under c. above before deciding whether or not to take the action he was considering [9(2)]. The TC can take into account representations he receives, other than in accordance with the above paragraph, including any advanced, in writing or orally, at any inquiry held [9(3)].

A bank holiday is excluded when calculating any of the above 14-day periods [1668/86/22].

LICENCE REVOCATION, SUSPENSION, ETC

A TC must revoke a standard licence if it appears that the holder no longer satisfies the requirements of good repute, appropriate financial standing or professional competence [Act 1981/17(1)]. In the case of a partnership, this power applies if one or more of the partners ceases to be of good repute, if the firm ceases to be of appropriate financial standing or the transport manager ceases to be of good repute or ceases to be employed by the firm [1628/86].

The TC who granted a licence may revoke it; suspend it; curtail its duration; or vary or impose a condition on the licence as to the number of authorised vehicles. This action may be taken on the grounds that—

a. the licence holder made, or procured to be made, in an application a statement which (whether to his knowledge or not) was false or a statement of intention or expectation which has not been fulfilled;
b. there has been a contravention of a licence condition;

c. a prohibition has been imposed on a vehicle owned or operated by the licence holder or he has been convicted or contravening a prohibition;
d. in the case of a restricted licence, that the holder is no longer of goods repute or appropriate financial standing;
e. since the licence was granted or varied there has been a material change in the licence holder's circumstances which were relevant to the grant or variation;
f. the licence is affected by a disqualification order made under Section 28 of the Transport Act 1985 [17(2),(3)].

In considering any financial question which appears to him to arise a TC may be assisted by an assessor [17A & Act 1985].

Action against a psv operator's licence must not be taken without first holding an inquiry if the licence holder asks for one [17(4)].

A TC may delay the time a licence revocation takes effect to enable the business to be transferred to a person licensed to carry it on [17(5)].

When a TC revokes a psv operator's licence he may also disqualify the holder from holding or obtaining such a licence either indefinitely or for a period he thinks fit [Act 1985/28(1)]. A licence granted to a person during a period of disqualification is of no effect [28(2)]. The ban may be confined to one or more traffic areas [28(3)].

Where a TC makes a disqualification order he may also direct that if that person at any time during a period specified is (a) a director of, or holds a controlling interest in, a company which holds a licence or a holding company of such a company, or (b) operates a psv in partnership with another person who holds a licence, the licence of that company or partnership is liable to revocation, suspension, etc [28(4)].

A disqualification order must not be made unless notice of such action has been given to the person concerned—*Shamrock Private Hire*, Appeal 1989/A41 *and Target Travel (Coaches) Ltd*, Appeal 1991/C2.

If the revoked licence were held by a company or a partnership, the powers to disqualify and make a direction can also be exercised against any officer of that company or any of the partners [28(5)].

A disqualification order or direction must not be made without first holding an inquiry if the person affected requests one [28(6)].

Before taking any action against a licence under Section 17 or making an order under Section 28 the TC must give notice to the licence holder—
a. that he is considering such action;
b. the grounds on which that consideration is based;
c. that within 14 days of the notice the licence holder may make representations about the action considered;
d. that those representations must be in writing; and

e. either—
   i. he proposes to hold an inquiry in relation to the action being considered and the date of it (not being less than 14 days from the notice); or
  ii. he does not propose to hold an inquiry in relation to that action unless the licence holder, within 14 days of the notice, requests him in writing to do so [1668/86/9(1)].

The TC must take into account any representations he receives under c. above before deciding whether or not to take the action he was considering [9(2)]. The TC can take into account representations he receives, other than in accordance with the above paragraph, including any advanced, in writing or orally, at any inquiry held [9(3)].

A bank holiday is excluded when calculating any of the above 14-day periods [1668/86/22].

INQUIRIES

A TC must not refuse an application or grant it other than as requested without giving the applicant opportunity to state his case at an inquiry, except where the application or the applicant's conduct is frivolous or unreasonable [1668/86/6].

A TC may, at places which appear to him convenient, hold inquiries in connection with his functions [Act 1981/54(1) & Act 1985/4].

An inquiry must be in public, except that a TC can restrict attendance where it relates to the financial position of any person [54(3) & 1629/86/7]. Information given at an inquiry while admission is restricted must not be disclosed as long as the trade or business is carried on, except (a) with the consent of the person carrying it on, (b) for the purpose of discharge of functions under operators' licensing or (c) with a view to instituting, or for the purposes of, any legal proceedings arising from operators' licensing [54(8),(9)].

If a TC receives a request from two or more people he may hold a single inquiry in response to those requests [54(2)].

A TC must publish a notice of the date and place of an inquiry in *Notices and Proceedings* but publication does not prevent the TC from postponing or adjourning consideration of any matter to an inquiry at a later date [54(4) & 1629/86/6].

If a party to an inquiry has been responsible for frivolous, vexatious, improper or unreasonable conduct in relation to an inquiry an order can be made against him by the TC for payment of costs incurred by him or the Secretary of State in connection with holding the inquiry. The maximum payment which can be ordered is £125 a day or part of a day the inquiry is held or would have been held. A TC must not make a costs' order against a person without first giving him opportunity to make representations against it [(54(5) & 1629/86/8].

NOTIFICATION OF DECISION

A TC must notify a licence applicant of his decision on the application and must inform the applicant and any objector of the reasons for his decision when he refuses an application, grants an application other than as requested or grants an application despite objections [1668/86/15].

APPEALS

A person who has applied for a psv operator's licence may appeal to the Transport Tribunal against a decision of a TC to refuse to grant the licence as applied for and to attach any condition otherwise than in accordance with the application [Act 1981/50(1)].

If a licence is in force at the time the holder applies for its renewal it will continue in force till the appeal is disposed of, but without prejudice to a TC's powers to suspend or revoke the licence [50(2)].

A person who has made an objection, under Section 14A, to the grant of a psv operator's licence may appeal to the Transport Tribunal if he is aggrieved by the grant of the licence [50(3)].

The holder of a licence can appeal to the Transport Tribunal against a TC's decision

(a) to refuse an application by the holder for a condition attached to the licence to be varied or removed;

(b) to vary or add any condition otherwise than on application by the holder; or

(c) to revoke or suspend the licence or curtail its period of validity [50(4)].

A psv licence holder or other person against whom a disqualification order or other direction has been made under Section 28 of the 1985 Act may appeal to the Transport Tribunal [50(5)].

When a TC makes a decision in (b) or (c) above or disqualifies or makes a direction under Section 28 of the 1985 Act, the person concerned can ask the TC for a direction that it does not take effect till the appeal period expires or the appeal is disposed of [50(6) but such a direction can be withdrawn at any time [50(7)]. If the request for a stay is refused or a stay is withdrawn the person can apply to the Transport Tribunal for a stay and the Transport Tribunal must give its decision on the application within 14 days [50(8)].

The above provisions do not apply to traffic regulation conditions attached to a licence under Section 8 of the 1985 Act [50(9)]. Appeals against such conditions are made to the Secretary of State under Section 9 of that Act—see page 326.

The manner in which an appeal must be lodged and the time within which it must be made are laid down in the Transport Tribunal Rules—see page 234.

A person should not seek an order of certiorari to quash the TC's decision without first following the statutory appeal procedure. In *R v Traffic Commissioners for the North Western Traffic Area, ex p British Rail* an application for certiorari was refused where an objector had not had an appeal to the Minister disposed of.

In *R v Secretary of State for Transport, ex p Cumbria County Council* [1983] RTR 88 it was ruled that in disposing of an appeal the Minister was entitled to depart from the conclusions reached by his inspector on findings of fact.

LICENCE DURATION

In a psv operator's licence there must be specified the date it comes into operation and expires. The expiry date will be that which the TC considers appropriate in the circumstances but the duration of the licence will not exceed five years [Act 1981/15(1)]. The TC can also direct that the duration will be a period, not exceeding five years, which he considers desirable to arrange a reasonably convenient programme of work [15(2)].

If an application to renew a licence is before a TC on the expiration date the licence will continue in force until the application is disposed of, unless it is revoked or suspended [15(3)].

If a licence is not renewed by a TC he may direct that the expiring licence continues in force for a period he considers reasonable to enable the business to be transferred to a licensed person [15(4)].

DEATH, ETC OF LICENCE HOLDER

A licence held by an individual terminates on his death; if he is adjudged bankrupt or, in Scotland, his estate is sequestrated; or he becomes a mental patient or, in Scotland, incapable of managing his own affairs [Act 1981/57(2)].

In the case of a partnership the licence will terminate if the partnership is dissolved; if a partner becomes a mental patient or, in Scotland, incapable of managing his own affairs with the result that only one other partner remains in the firm; or a person who alone fulfilled the firm's professional competence requirement ceases to be a partner or becomes a mental patient or incapable [1626/86].

A licence held by a company terminates on the making of a winding-up order; or the passing of a resolution for voluntary winding up [Act 1981/57(3) & 1668/86/21].

A TC can direct that termination be deferred for up to 12 months or, in special circumstances, up to 18 months and may authorise the business to be carried on under the licence, but subject to any conditions he may impose, by some other person during the deferment [57(4)].

Apart from the above circumstances a psv operator's licence is not assignable or transmissible on death or in any other way [57(1)].

DISCS

On granting an operator's licence the TC supplies discs equal to the maximum number of vehicles which may be used under the licence [Act 1981/18(2)].

A disc showing particulars of the operator and licence must be fixed and exhibited on a vehicle being used under a psv operator's licence [18(1)]. The disc must be fixed to the vehicle in a weatherproof container or on the inside of the vehicle and be in a position adjacent to the vehicle excise licence, so that the driver's view is not unduly impaired and it can be easily read in daylight from outside the vehicle [1668/86/10]. The disc must contain the name of the licence holder who operates the vehicle, the licence number and expiry date [11(1)]. A disc for a standard international licence is green; a standard national licence blue; and a restricted licence orange; and the type of licence must be marked below the expiry date [11(2)].

RETURN OF LICENCES AND DISCS

If a licence is surrendered, suspended or revoked the licence holder must, within 14 days of being notified of such action, return the licence to the TC together with any discs relating to the licence [1668/86/12(1)]. A suspended licence and discs will be returned, if still valid, after the suspension [12(2)]. If a licence is curtailed the licence holder must, within 14 days of being notified of such action, send or deliver the licence to the TC who will amend and return it. The licence and discs must be returned on their revised expiry [12(3)].

If a TC attaches, removes or alters a condition on a licence the holder must, within 14 days of being notified, return the licence for amendment [12(4)]. Where the variation of a condition reduces the number of authorised vehicles the licence holder must return any discs above the new authorised number [12(5)].

If a licence or disc is lost or destroyed the holder must notify the TC and be issued with a duplicate [13(1)]. If the original licence or disc is subsequently recovered by the licence holder he must forthwith return it to the TC [13(2)] If a licence or disc becomes defaced or illegible the licence holder must return it and be issued with a duplicate [13(3)].

NOTICES AND PROCEEDINGS

Every TC must publish *Notices and Proceedings* at least once a fortnight. He must send a copy to every chief officer of police, Passenger Transport Executive and local authority whose area falls wholly or partly within his traffic area and, if all or part of his area falls within London, to London Regional Transport. He must also make a copy available, by post if required and on payment of a fee, to anyone who asks for one [Act 1981/5].

Notices and Proceedings must include particulars relating to the registration of local services; variation or cancellation of local services; applications for psv operator's licences; revocation, etc of psv operators' licences; disqualification of psv operators; conditions attached to licences; unregistered or unreliable local services in relation to fuel duty grants; and notices of public inquiries [1629/86/3].

Copies of *Notices and Proceedings* may be inspected, free of charge, at the office of the TC issuing them or be purchased for £3.50 each [4 & 2754/93].

TC'S RECORDS AND INSPECTIONS

A TC must keep a duplicate copy of any licence he grants, a record of any condition he attaches to a licence, a record of all traffic regulation conditions he determines and a record of all particulars registered for local services along with variations and cancellations of such registrations. He must allow such records to be inspected at all reasonable times by members of the public [Act 1981/56 & 1629/86/5].

FEES

The fee for a licence is £4.50 for each month, or part of a month, it is expressed to have effect and it must be paid before the licence is granted. The fee for the second and each subsequent disc issued is £4.50 for each month, or part of a month, during which it may be used and it must be paid before the disc is issued. The fee for a special licence is £40 which must be paid when the application is made [1668/86/19 & 2753/93].

A refund of the fee for each unexpired complete month will be made where licence (other than a special licence) or discs are returned [20].

CERTIFICATE OF QUALIFICATION

A person who wishes to carry on a road passenger transport business, or be a transport manager of such a business, in another Member State or Northern Ireland can apply to a TC for a certificate as to his repute and professional competence and, where relevant, his financial standing [Act 1981/21].

Permits for buses used by educational and other bodies

A psv operator's licence is not required for the use of a bus adapted to carry more than 8 passengers if:
a. it is used under a permit granted under Section 19 of the Transport Act 1985;
b. it is not used to carry members of the general public, nor with a view to profit nor incidentally to an activity carried on with a view to profit;
c. it is used in accordance with any permit conditions; and
d. it is not used in contravention of regulations made for these purposes [Act 1985/18, 19(2)].

A permit for the use of a small bus (i.e. adapted for more than 8 but not more than 16 passengers) may be granted (i) by a body designated by the Secretary of State either to itself or any other body to which it is permitted to grant a permit, and (ii) by a TC to any body appearing to him to be carrying on an activity concerned with education, religion, social welfare, recreation or other activities of benefit to the community [19(3),(4)].

A permit for a large bus (i.e. more than 16 passengers) may be granted by a TC to any body which assists and co-ordinates the activities of bodies which appear to him to be concerned with education, religion, social welfare or other activities of benefit to the community [19(5)]. A permit for a large bus must not be granted unless the TC is satisfied there will be adequate facilities and arrangements for maintaining the buses in a fit and serviceable condition [19(6)]

The TC or other body granting a permit may attach conditions (a) limiting the passengers in a bus used under the permit to persons of specified classes, and (b) relating to other matters which may be prescribed [20(4)]. A permit may be varied or revoked by the TC or body who granted it and, in the case of a permit granted by a designated body, by the TC for the area in which any bus has been used under the permit [20(5)]. A permit may not be varied to substitute another body for the body to whom it was granted [20(6)]. A permit remains in force until it is revoked or the designated body which granted it ceases to be designated [20(7)].

The driver of a bus used under a permit must either (a) hold a psv driver's licence, or (b) hold a full ordinary driving licence for the class of vehicle and be at least 21 years of age [1230/87/3]. However, a later Act states that a person may drive a vehicle used under a Section 19 permit even if his British driving licence does not authorise him to drive vehicles of the class to which the vehicle belongs [18 and Act 1989/Sch.3/4(c)].

The fee for a permit granted by a TC is £14 for a large bus and £7 for a small bus [1230/85/4]. The permit must describe conditions to be complied with and these will include the above driving licence requirements, the duty to display a disc, the conditions of fitness to be complied with and any other condition which may be attached under Section 20(4) of the 1985 Act [5].

When a permit is granted, a disc is issued with it and, when the vehicle is the vehicle used under the permit, the holder must cause the disc to be fixed inside the vehicle so that it can be easily read from outside and so that it does not interfere unduly with the driver's view [6].

If a permit or disc is lost or destroyed the holder must notify the issuing authority forthwith and he will be issued with a duplicate. If the original is recovered the holder must return it to the issuing authority. If a permit or disc becomes defaced or illegible the holder must return it forthwith to the issuing authority and he will be issued with a duplicate [7].

When a permit terminates due to revocation or because the issuing body has ceased to be designated, the permit and disc must be returned to the TC or body who revoked the permit or, where it was issued by a body ceasing to be designated, to the TC of the area in which a vehicle was last used [8].

The fitness requirements a small bus first used before 1 April 1988 and used under a permit must comply with are either (a) Regulations 5 to 28 of the Minibus (Conditions of Fitness, Equipment and Use) Regulations 1977 (see page 285), or (b) Regulations 41 to 43 of the Road Vehicle (Construction and Use) Regulations 1986 (see page 24). In the case of a small bus first used on or after 1 April 1988 the requirement in (b) above must be complied with [9].

A permit granted under Section 42 of the 1981 Act is deemed to have been granted under Section 19 of the 1985 Act. A permit granted by a council for a large bus is deemed to have been granted by a TC. A permit granted for a small bus by a body designated under Section 42 of the 1981 Act which is not designated under Section 19 of the 1985 Act is deemed to have been issued by a body which has ceased to be designated [10].

The bodies appearing to the Secretary of State to be concerned with education, religion, social welfare or other activities for the benefit of the community have been designated and the classes of bodies to whom they may issue permits specified. They include the councils of counties; non-metropolitan counties; metropolitan districts; inner and outer London boroughs; the City of London; the Scottish regions and districts; the Orkney, Shetland and Western islands; the Inner London Education Authority; and 65 charitable bodies. All these bodies can grant permits in respect of small passenger-carrying vehicles but only the councils (except Scottish district councils and the ILEA) can grant permits for large passenger-carrying vehicles [1356/80/3, 4].

After granting a permit a designated body must send a copy of it to the TC of the area and give notice of every grant, variation or revocation within one month [1356/80/5(1)]. In January each year TCs must send a return to the Secretary of State giving details of permits granted, varied or revoked in the preceding calendar year by themselves and designated bodies [6].

Community bus permits

A certificate of initial fitness or psv operator's licence is not required for a vehicle used under a community bus permit [Act 1985/18 & 23(7)].

A community bus permit relates to the use of public service vehicle in providing (a) a community bus service, or (b) a community bus service and carrying passengers for payment (other than on a local service) where their carriage will directly assist the provision of the community bus service by providing financial support for it [22(1)]. A community bus service is a local service provided by a body concerned for the social and welfare needs of one or more communities, without a view to profit and by means of a vehicle adapted to carry more than 8 but not more than 16 passengers [22(1)].

A community bus permit may be granted by the TC for the area in which will be the operating centre of a vehicle [22(2)] but only if he is satisfied there will be adequate facilities and arrangements for maintaining the vehicles in a fit and serviceable condition [22(3)].

A body may hold more than one permit but can use only one vehicle at any one time under a permit [22[4]].

It is a condition of every community bus permit:

(a) that the driver of the vehicle does not receive payment for driving, apart from reimbursement of reasonable expenses and lost earnings;

(b) the driver must either (i) hold a pcv driver's licence, or (ii) be at least 21 years of age, hold a full ordinary driving licence for the class of vehicle. However, a later Act states that a person may drive a Community bus even if his British driving licence does not authorise him to drive vehicles of the class to which the vehicle belongs [18 and Act 1989/Sch. 3/4(c)]. The driver must comply with the PSV (Conduct of Drivers, Inspectors, Conductors and Passengers) Regulations 1990 (see page 277); and

(c) the vehicle complies either with the construction requirements of Regulations 41 to 43 of the Road Vehicles (Construction and Use) Regulations 1986 (see page 24) or, in the case of a vehicle first used before 1 April 1988, complies with Regulations 5 to 28 of the Community Bus Regulations 1978 (these conditions of fitness are the same as those prescribed for minibuses—given on pages 290 to 294—except that there is no restriction on a community bus drawing a trailer but there is a further requirement that exit lamps be kept lit at night while passengers are carried) [23(1)(2) & 1245/86].

The holder of a permit must, within 14 days of being required by TC, produce or send the permit to the area traffic office for traffic regulation conditions to be attached to it [1245/86/5].

The holder of the permit commits an offence if a licence condition is contravened but it is a defence to prove that he took all reasonable precautions and exercised all due diligence to avoid the commission of the offence [Act 1985/23(5)].

A TC can revoke a permit on the grounds that he is no longer satisfied about maintenance facilities, a permit condition has been contravened or a defects' prohibition has been placed on a vehicle used under the permit [23(6)].

The fee for a permit is £37. With each permit a disc is issued which must be fixed inside the vehicle so that it can be easily read from outside the vehicle and it does not interfere unduly with the driver's view. If a permit or disc is lost, destroyed or defaced the holder must notify the TC who will issue a duplicate. If a lost or destroyed permit or disc comes into the possession of the holder it must be returned to the TC. If a permit is revoked or the holder ceases to operate local services the holder must forthwith surrender the permit and disc [1245/86/4].

School buses

A local education authority may (a) use a school bus, when it is being used to provide free school transport, to carry fare-paying passengers and (b) use a school bus which belongs to the authority to provide a local service when it is not being used to provide free school transport [Act 1981/46(1)]. A school bus belonging to a local education authority and used under these provisions is not subject to psv initial fitness requirements or psv operator licensing [46(1)].

A school bus is a motor vehicle used by a local education authority for providing free school transport under Section 55(1) of the Education Act 1944 to get pupils to school [46(3)].

17 PSV services

Public Passenger Vehicles Act 1981
Transport Act 1985
EC Regulation **684/92**
PSV (Traffic Regulation Conditions) Regulations, **No. 1030/86**
PSV (Registration of Local Services) Regulations, **No. 1671/86**
PSV (London Local Service Licences) Regulations, **No. 1691/86**
PSV (London Local Service Licences) (Amendment) Regulations, **No. 408/88**
PSV (Registration of Local Services) (Amendment) Regulations, **Nos. 1879/88, 1064/89 and 2752/93**

Local services

A local service is a service, using one or more public service vehicles, for the carriage of passengers at separate fares, except:
(a) a service on which every passenger is set down at a place more than 15 miles from the place where he was taken up or some point on the route is 15 miles or more from either of those places,
(b) a service operated under a Section 19 permit (see page 316), or
(c) a private trip complying with Part III of Schedule 1 to the 1981 Act (see page 298) [Act 1985/2].
In determining what a fare is, Section 1(5)(b) & (c) and 1(6) of the 1981 Act apply (given on page 297) [2(5)].
A local service must not be provided in a traffic area in which it has a stopping place unless particulars have been registered by the service operator with the Traffic Commissioner (TC) for that area, the period of notice (see below) relating to the registration has expired and the service is operated in accordance with the registered particulars [6(2)]. This requirement does not apply to an excursion or tour unless it is operated at least once a week for at least 6 consecutive weeks [1671/86/10]. An excursion or tour is a service for the carriage of passengers at separate fares on which they travel together on a journey from one or more places to one or more other places and back [Act 1985/137].

321

REGISTRATION

An application for registration will only be accepted from a person who holds a psv operator's licence (without a condition banning local services) or a community bus permit or is using, or planning to use, a school bus under Section 46 of the 1981 Act (see page 320) [6(4)].

The prescribed particulars which have to be registered are:

1. the name of the operator and the number of his psv licence or community bus permit;
2. the principal starting and finishing points of the service;
3. whether the service includes excursions or tours;
4. a description of the route sufficient to identify the roads and a map showing those roads;
5. details of stopping arrangements;
6. details of stops where vehicles will stand for longer than is needed to pick up or set down passengers;
7. details of any reversing manoeuvres or ways of turning the vehicle round;
8. the date the service is to start;
9. a service timetable including the frequency of service and the days of the year it will be operated;
10. in the case of an excursion or tour, instead of items 4, 6 and 9, an outline of the route including any picking up points, the period in the year the service will be operated and the maximum number of vehicle departures a day;
11. apart from an excursion or tour and, due to the nature of the service items 2, 4 or 9 cannot be completed, such further particulars which might be required to provide a complete description of the service [1671/86/4, Sch. and 1879/88].

An application for registration of a service having stopping places in more than one traffic area must be made to the area in which the service starts [1671/86/3(1)]. A service which has stopping places in London and outside London must be made to the Metropolitan TC [3(2)]. A registration application will not be accepted unless the applicant gives the TC information as he may reasonably require about it [3(3)]. A copy of the application must be sent to any Passenger Transport Executive or county, regional or highland council within whose area there will be a stopping place, no later than the date application is made to the TC [3(4)]. The TC must notify the applicant and any relevant PTE or council of the date he accepts the registration [3(5)].

PERIOD OF NOTICE

The period of notice is 42 days from the date the TC accepts the application or, if longer, the period beginning with the registration and ending with the notified date for starting the service [Act 1985/6(3) & 1671/86/5(1)].

The period of notice is changed to 'such period as the TC may determine' where the application is to register a service, or vary or cancel a registration, and there will be only minor effects on the public or where, due to circumstances the operator could not have foreseen, he failed to make application in time for the full notice period to operate [1671/86/7, 8].

VARIATION

The registration of a local service can be varied or cancelled on application by the service operator [Act 1985/6(7)]. The variation or cancellation takes effect 42 days (or other period determined under the preceding paragraph) after the date the TC accepts the application or, if later, the date given by the operator as the effective date for variation or cancellation [6(8) & 1671/86/5(1)].

A registered service may be varied without the variation being registered where
(a) in England and Wales, the variations relate to journeys on 24 December, Christmas Day, Good Friday or a bank holiday,
(aa) in Scotland, the variations relate to a journey in any week which includes Christmas Day, 26 December, New Year's Day, any bank holiday or local holiday in a district or island council's area through which the service operates,
(b) a registered excursion or tour is withdrawn,
(c) the timetable is varied to change registered timings by not more than 5 minutes,
(d) the route is temporarily varied due to traffic restrictions or police directions,
(e) the route number or name registered under transitional provisions is abandoned or altered,
(f) a local education authority school's service not available to the general public is varied temporarily and
(g) additional vehicles are provided to operate over part of the service route and as closely as possible to the registered timetable. An operator must notify relevant authorities and the TC of an intended variation under (a) or (aa) at least 21 days before it takes effect [1671/86/9 and 1879/88].

CANCELLATION

If a TC is satisfied a service is no longer being provided by the person who registered it he must cancel the registration. But this action may not be taken without the TC first sending the operator written notice of his intention to cancel and 28 days elapsing from the date of the notice, except where the operator has died or ceased to hold an unconditional psv operator's licence or where a company or partnership has been dissolved. The TC must notify relevant authorities of any cancellation [1671/86/9A and 1879/88].

FEES

The fee to register or vary a non-subsidised community bus service is £10. For any other service it is £38. No fee is payable for a service which has a stopping place in London or where the variation is made to comply with statutory traffic regulation or restrictions. Fees must be paid when the application is made [1671/86/12, 1064/89 & 2752/93].

FARE TABLE

While a vehicle is being used to provide a service, other than a under a special licence or an excursion or tour, the operator must cause (a) a fare table and timetable to be displayed inside the vehicle or be available on request, and (b) a notice, clearly legible from outside the vehicle, indicating the vehicle's destination and route [1671/86/13].

FUEL GRANT DETERMINATION

If a TC is satisfied that the operator of a local service has, without reasonable excuse, failed to operate a service registered under Section 6 or, to a significant extent, operated a local service in contravention of Section 6, he may make a determination to that effect [Act 1985/111(1)].

Where a TC makes such a determination he must notify the Secretary of State and the operator in writing forthwith [111(2)]. When a determination has been made a sum equal to 25 per cent of bus fuel grant paid to the operator in respect of all services operated during the three months ending with the date of the determination is payable to the Secretary of State [111(3)]. The operator can appeal to the Transport Tribunal [111(4)].

A finding that a service has not been operated under Section 6 does not mean that a determination has also to be made under Section 111. Before making a determination the TC should inquire about the amount of money involved and give reasons for the determination— *Clayton Jones*, Appeal 1987/Y9.

In *Evans Coaches Ltd*, Appeal 1990/B33, the Transport Tribunal said a TC should have assessed the extent of failures to provide services in the light of the number of services properly operated and should have had information about the money payable before making a determination.

TRAFFIC REGULATION CONDITIONS

A traffic authority can ask the TC to determine traffic regulation conditions which must be met by a person providing a local service in the area affected by the conditions [Act 1985/7(1)]. A traffic authority is, in England and Wales, the council of a metropolitan district or non-metropolitan county, and, in Scotland, the council of any region or islands area [7(15)].

A TC must not determine traffic regulation conditions unless he is satisfied that, after considering traffic in the area, conditions are required in order to prevent danger to road users or to reduce severe traffic congestion [7(4)]. The TC must have regard in particular to the interests of operators who have registered services to operate in the area, users of such services and the elderly or disabled [7(5)]. The purposes for which traffic regulation conditions may be determined are the regulation of service routes, stopping places, the times vehicles can stop and for how long, the roads to be used and manoeuvres to be performed when turning a vehicle [7(6) & 1030/86/3].

Traffic regulation conditions must apply to all services operated in the area they apply to or to a class of services specified in the conditions [Act 1985/7(7)].

Before determining a traffic regulation condition, a TC must hold a public inquiry if asked to do so (within 28 days of publication in *Notices and Proceedings* of the request for a determination) by the traffic authority which asked for the condition, any other traffic authority which asked for the condition, any other traffic authority likely to be affected by the condition or an operator who has registered a local service in the area affected. An inquiry need not be held first if the TC is satisfied the condition should be determined without delay but an inquiry must be held as soon as reasonably practicable if one of the above bodies requests an inquiry (within 28 days of the determination being published in *Notices and Proceedings*) [7(9) to (11) & 1030/86/5].

Before asking a TC to determine a condition in relation to a trunk road, the traffic authority must first obtain leave from the Secretary of State, but the giving of such leave does not indicate the Secretary of State's approval of any conditions determined [Act 1985/7(12)].

A TC may vary or revoke a traffic regulation condition when

requested by a traffic authority or the operator of any service affected by the condition [7(13)].

Where a traffic regulation condition has been determined, the TC must attach it to any psv operator's licence or community bus permit if a local service operated by the holder is affected by the condition [Act 1985/8(1), (2)]. If such a condition is varied or revoked it is the duty of the TC to secure that it is varied on or removed from the licence [8(4)]. A traffic regulation condition is of no effect if it is incompatible with a legal provision prohibiting or restricting the use of a road [8(5)].

If an operator is unable to operate both a local service in accordance with the registered particulars and comply with traffic regulation conditions or provisions prohibiting or restricting use of roads, any failure to operate the service in accordance with his registered particulars during the 28 days beginning with the commencement of the condition or provision will be disregarded to the extent attributable to compliance with the condition or provision [8(6) & 1671/86/11.

APPEALS

An appeal may be made to the Secretary of State against (a) the determination, variation or revocation of traffic regulation conditions, by an operator of a local service affected by the conditions or any traffic authority aggrieved at the decision, and (b) the refusal of a TC to comply with a request to determine, vary or revoke a condition, by the person who made the request [Act 1985/9(1), (2)]. The appeal must state the grounds on which it is made and quote the condition or request reference number. It must be received by the Secretary of State within 28 days of (i) the date notice of the determination, variation or revocation was published in *Notices and Proceedings*, or (ii) the date notice of the request refusal was sent. A copy must be sent to the TC, traffic authority likely to be affected by the conditions and, if an inquiry were held, any person who made representations at the inquiry. If a condition were determined by a TC without first holding an inquiry (under Section 7(10) of the 1985 Act) the Secretary of State must not decide an appeal until either an inquiry has been held or the time for requesting an inquiry has expired without an inquiry being requested. On deciding an appeal the Secretary of State must give notice of his decision and the reasons for it to the appellant [1030/86/6].

For local service conditions see page 307.

London local services

A London local service is a local service with one or more stopping places in London [Act 1985/34(1)]. A local service is defined on page 321 and London is defined as the administrative area of Greater London [137].

If a service is provided both inside and outside London, any part of the service outside London is treated as a separate service if there is a stopping place in the part of the service outside London [34(1)]. The application to register the part of the service outside London must be made to the Metropolitan TC [1671/86/3(2)]—see 'Local services' above for registration formalities.

A licence granted by the Metropolitan TC is required for a London local service, except for a service provided for the Railways Board due to interruption of a rail service [Act 1985/35(1) to (3)]. A licence is not required for a service (excluding an excursion or tour) provided by London Regional Transport or any of its subsidiaries or any other person under an agreement with LRT [36(1)].

Except where a licence is held by a local education authority, a licence is of no effect unless the holder also holds a psv operator's licence (which is not suspended) or a community bus permit [35(4), (5)].

If a London local service is provided without a licence the operator commits an offence, but it is a defence to prove that he took all reasonable precautions and exercised all due diligence to avoid committing the offence [35(6)].

The provisions of the 1981 Act which state that a psv licence cannot be granted to an unincorporated body other than a partnership (see page 296) also apply to London Local service licences [Act 1985/44].

APPLICATIONS

An application for a London local service licence must be in the form required by the Metropolitan TC and the applicant must give information required to dispose of the application [Act 1985/37(1)]. In the case of a service other than an excursion or tour, the application must give details of its starting and finishing points and its route; any route number or name; the period in the year it will operate; and the frequency of service. In the case of an excursion or tour, details must be given of its starting and finishing points and any other points where passengers are to be taken up or set down; a description of the route; the period of the year it will operate; and the maximum number of vehicle departures to be made on any one day [1691/86/4]. A copy of any application must be made available for inspection by the TC at his offices [5(1)]. If an applicant intends to produce documents at any inquiry he must, if required by the TC, supply at his own expense a reasonable number of copies of the document for use there [5(2)].

The TC must grant the application unless satisfied that to do so would be against the public interest and, if he grants the licence, must do so in accordance with the application except to the extent he is satisfied would be against the public interest [Act 1985/37(2)].

In considering the public interest the TC must have regard to:

(a) the transport needs of London as a whole and of particular communities;

(b) any transport policies made and drawn to his attention by a London Borough or the City of London; and

(c) any objections or representations he considers relevant [37(3)].

An objection or representation must state the specific grounds on which it is based, specify conditions which the maker considers should be attached to the licence and be received by the TC within 28 days of the date notice of the application appeared in *Notices and Proceedings*, but the TC has discretion to hear and consider objections not so made [1691/86/8(1), (3)]. A person making an objection or representation must send a copy to the applicant at the same time it is sent to the TC [8(2)].

CONDITIONS

On granting a licence the TC may attach conditions he thinks fit having regard to the public interest, in particular paragraphs (a) to (c) above, and for securing that suitable routes are used, that passengers are taken up and set down only at specified points and generally for the safety and convenience of the public, including the elderly or disabled. No condition as to fares may be made [Act 1985/38(1) to (3)]. The TC may, having regard to the public interest, vary a licence by altering, removing or attaching a condition or additional condition as he thinks fit [38(4)]. When the holder of a licence applies for a condition to be altered or removed the TC must do so except to the extent he is satisfied would be against the public interest [38(5)]. The TC may temporarily dispense with compliance with a condition if he is satisfied that to do so would be unduly onerous due to circumstances not foreseen when the condition was attached or altered and the dispensation would not be against the public interest [38(6)].

If a condition attached to a London local licence is contravened the licence holder commits an offence, but it is a defence to prove that he took all reasonable precautions and exercised all due diligence to avoid committing the offence [38(7)].

Before altering or removing a condition the TC must (a) where the licence holder applies to vary the licence, notify other persons likely to be affected or publish notice of the application in *Notices and Proceedings*, or (b) where the TC proposes to vary a condition, notify the licence holder and other persons likely to be affected or publish notices of it in *Notices and Proceedings* and notify the licence holder. A licence holder or other person who desires to object to or make representations about a variation, application or proposal must do so within 28 days of the date of the notice, but the TC has discretion to hear and consider objections and representations not made within that time including any made at an inquiry [1691/87/9]. If a licence is granted for 6 months or less the notification and publication requirements do not apply unless the TC otherwise decides [10].

EXCURSIONS AND TOURS

Where the TC is satisfied that an application for a licence relates to an excursion or tour which would not compete directly with a licensed or LRT bus service or that it would operate only to enable passengers to attend special events, the provisions of Sections 35, 37 and 38 are modified [Act 1985/39(1) to (3)].

REVOCATION

A London local service licence may be suspended or revoked by the TC on the grounds that there has been a contravention of a condition attached to it, but that action must not be taken unless contraventions are frequent, committed intentionally or are a danger to the public [Act 1985/40].

Before suspending or revoking a licence the TC must notify the holder that he is considering such action, specify the grounds on which it is based, that within 14 days the holder and any person affected may make representations about it, that an inquiry is or is not to be held (unless the holder requests one) and notice of the matter is published in *Notices and Proceedings*. Before reaching a decision the TC must take into account any representations he receives including any made at an inquiry [1691/85/11].

APPEALS

An applicant for a licence may appeal to the Secretary of State against the refusal of a licence or the attachment of any condition [Act 1985/42(1)]. The appeal must be received by the Secretary of State within 42 days of the date the decision is published in *Notices and Proceedings* [1691/86/19].

A licence holder may appeal against the TC's refusal to vary or remove any condition from a licence; to vary or attach a condition otherwise than on the licence holder's request; or to suspend or revoke the licence [Act 1985/42(3)]. The appeal must be received within 28 days of the date the decision is published in *Notices and Proceedings* [1691/86/19].

The TC may direct that his decision to revoke or suspend a licence, or to vary or add new conditions, does not take effect until the end of the appeal period and, if an appeal is made, until the appeal is disposed of. If he refuses to do so the licence holder can apply to the Secretary of State for such a direction and he must give his decision within 14 days [Act 1985/42(4), (5)].

If the TC fails to come to decision within a reasonable time on an application for a licence, or the variation or removal of a condition, the applicant can appeal to the Secretary of State as if the application had been refused [42(6)].

An appeal to the Secretary of State against the TC's decision to grant, suspend or revoke a licence, or to attach, remove or vary a licence condition, can be made by a local authority affected and, except in the case of an excursion or tour, a person who provides transport facilities along or near the route of the service provided under the licence, and who, in either case, has made objections or representations to the TC during the proceedings resulting in his decision [42(7) to (9)]. Such an appeal must be made within 28 days of the date the decision is published in *Notices and Proceedings* [1691/86/19].

Every appeal must state the application or licence reference number and state the grounds of the appeal. At the time the appeal is made a copy must be sent (a) to the TC, (b) if made by the operator, to any person who has made an objection or representation, or (c) if made by any other person, to the operator and any objector or representor. A person applying to the Secretary of State for a direction under Section 42(5) must give details of the decision, the grounds for his application and send a copy to the TC [19].

An appeal against a decision of the Secretary of State on a point of law may be made to the High Court [43].

DURATION AND FEES

A licence lasts for 5 years or if, for special reasons, the TC determines a shorter period. A licence can be granted for particular periods or occasions. If an application has been made to renew a licence, the existing one continues in force until the application is disposed of, but without prejudice to the TC's power to suspend or revoke it [Act 1985/41].

The provisions of the 1981 Act regarding termination of a psv licence on death, etc (see page 313) also apply to a London local service licence [Act 1985/44]. A licence held by a company terminates on the making of a winding-up order or the passing of a resolution for voluntary winding-up [1691/86/16].

The fee for an application for a licence is £100 and it must be paid at the time of application. The fee for the licence itself is £20 per year or part of a year, but where a licence is granted for 6 months or less the fee is £10. A licence fee must be paid before the licence is granted [1691/86/12 and 408/88].

FARE TABLES

Except for an excursion or tour, while a vehicle is used to provide a service under a licence the holder must cause to be displayed, or be available to passengers, a fare table and a timetable (but if the service frequency is 10 minutes or less a statement of that fact may be given). A notice legible from outside the vehicle must be displayed indicating the destination and route of the service [1691/86/13].

RETURN OF LICENCES

If the holder of a licence ceases to operate the licensed service he must notify the TC and surrender the licence [1691/86/14].

If a licence is suspended or revoked the holder must, within 14 days of receiving notice of that fact, produce the licence to the TC at an address he specifies and, if sent by post, it will not be treated as being produced until it is actually received. On the removal of a suspension an unexpired licence will be returned to the operator [15].

If a licence is lost or destroyed the holder must forthwith notify the TC who will issue a duplicate. If the original licence is recovered it must be returned to the TC. Where a licence becomes defaced or illegible the holder must return it to the TC who will issue a duplicate [17].

London Regional Transport

A London local service licence is not required for a London local service (excluding excursions or tours) provided by London Regional Transport, any subsidiary of LRT or any person acting under an agreement with LRT made under Section 3(2) of the London Regional Transport Act 1984 [Act 1985/36(1)].

If any of the above bodies proposes to provide a new London bus service or to vary an existing service, LRT must, before reaching a decision, consult with the police commissioner, local authorities affected, the Passengers Committee (set up under the 1984 Act) and any other person it thinks fit [36(2)].

Where LRT or a subsidiary proposes to discontinue a service or not to renew a Section 3(2) agreement, LRT must, before reaching a decision, consult with local authorities affected, the Passenger Committee and any other person it thinks fit [36(4)].

Where a Section 3(2) agreement relates to a service only part of which is in London, any provision in the agreement relating to passengers other than those both taken up and set down in London, shall be of no effect if it is inconsistent with traffic regulation conditions attached to the operator's psv licence or community bus permit [36(5)].

EC inter-state services

Common rules for the carriage of passengers by bus or coach, contained in EC Regulation 684/92, apply to all international road passenger transport operations which begin and end in a Member State and on which vehicles with a capacity for more than eight passengers (exclusive of the driver) are used. Such operations are divided into regular services, shuttle services and occasional services.

REGULAR SERVICES

Regular services are services which provide for the carriage of passengers at specified intervals on specified routes, passengers being picked up and set down at predetermined stopping points. Regular services for special categories of passengers, such as workers or schoolchildren, are included and known as special regular services. The fact that a service may be varied according to needs does not affect its classification as a regular service [EC 684/92/2(1)].

SHUTTLE SERVICES

Shuttle services are services consisting of repeated outward and return journeys on which groups of people, assembled in advance, are carried from a single area of departure to a single area of destination with groups carried on an outward journey being carried back to the place of departure on a subsequent journey. The area of departure or destination means the place where the journey begins and ends including its surrounding locality within a 50km radius. A group is assembled in advance when the person responsible for it has contracted and paid for the service or received all reservations and payments before departure.

Groups may be picked up and set down at up to three different places outside the departure and destination areas.

A shuttle service with accommodation includes accommodation for at least 80 per cent of the passengers at the place of destination and, where necessary during the journey. Passengers must stay at the destination for at least two nights. Such services may be provided by groups of carriers acting for the same contractor and passengers may make the return journey with a different carrier of the same group or, while in an EC country, catch a connection en route with a different carrier of the same group [2(2)].

OCCASIONAL SERVICES

Occasional services are those which are neither regular services nor shuttle services.

They include:

a. tours on which the same vehicle is used to carry one or more previously assembled groups and each group is brought back to its place of departure;
b. services on which previously assembled groups are not brought back to the place of departure in the course of the same journey and which, where there is a stay at the destination, cover accommodation or other tourist services not ancillary to carriage or accommodation;
c. services for special events, such as cultural, sporting or conferences.
d. closed-door tours where the same vehicle is used to carry the same group throughout the journey and bring it back to the place of departure;
e. services which carry passengers on an outward journey and return empty;
f. services preceded by an empty journey from one EC country to another provided
   (i) the travellers' transport has been arranged before they arrived in the country of pick-up,
   (ii) they have previously been brought to that country as in e. above, or
   (iii) the passengers are a group formed solely for the journey in question and have been invited to another EC country by a person paying for the transport; and
g. any other service (referred to as a residual service).

A group is assembled in advance when the person responsible for it has contracted and paid for the service or received all reservations and payments before departure and it consists of at least 12 people or at least 40 per cent of the vehicle's capacity.

Such services may be provided by a group of carriers acting for the same contractor and travellers may, in an EC country, catch a connection en route with a different carrier of the same group[2(3)].

OWN-ACCOUNT OPERATIONS

Own-account operations are those carried out by an undertaking for its own employees or by a non-profit-making body for transport of its members in connection with its social objectives provided the transport is only an ancillary activity and the vehicle belongs to the undertaking or body and is driven by a member of its staff [2(4)].

FREEDOM TO PROVIDE SERVICES

A hire and reward carrier can undertake regular, shuttle or occasional services without discrimination as to nationality or place of establishment if he:

a. is authorised in his country of establishment to undertake such services;
b. satisfies the conditions for admission to the occupation of road passenger transport operator in national and international operations, i.e. good repute, financial standing and professional competence; and
c. meets road safety requirements on the standards of drivers and vehicles [3(1)].

An own-account carrier can carry out his transport services without the above discrimination if he:

a. is authorised in his country of establishment to undertake carriage by bus and coach; and
b. meets road safety requirements on the standards of drivers and vehicles [3(2)].

ACCESS TO THE MARKET

An EC authorisation is not required for:

1. shuttle services with accommodation and occasional services (except residual services);
2. special regular services if they are covered by a contract between the organiser and the carrier;
3. journeys by empty vehicles in connection with the above services.

An EC authorisation is required for regular services, shuttle services without accommodation and residual services [4].

AUTHORISATIONS

Authorisations are issued by a competent authority of the EC country containing the place of departure which, for regular services, can be either termini. An authorisation entitles the holder to operate regular services and shuttle services without accommodation in all EC countries [6]. In Great Britain authorisation are issued by the International Road Freight Office, Newcastle upon Tyne.

Authorisations are issued in the name of the transport undertaking and cannot be transferred to third parties. But an undertaking can, with the consent of the authority, operate the service through a sub-contractor whose name must appear on the authorisation along with a note that he is a sub-contractor [5(1)].

For regular services an authorisation is valid for five years and for shuttle services without accommodation, two years [5(2)].

An authorisation must specify the type of service; places of departure and destination; the route; period of validity; and, for regular services, the stops and timetable [5(3)].

Authorisations must be issued in agreement with the competent authorities of the EC countries in whose territories passengers are picked up or set down. The authorising authority must forward to those other authorities—and those of any transit EC country—a copy of the application, relevant documents and its assessment [7(1)].

The authorities whose agreement has been requested must notify their decision within two months of receipt of the documents. If no reply has been received within that time the authorities consulted will be deemed to have given their agreement. The authorities in transit countries may notify the authorising authority of their comments within the two-month period [7(2)].

An authority must take a decision on an application within three months of its submission. But if EC countries do not agree the matter may be referred to the Commission within the three-month period. Then, after consulting the EC countries concerned, the Commission must, within six weeks, take a decision which will take effect within 30 days of its notification to the countries concerned. That decision will continue to apply until the countries reach agreement [7(3), (6), (7) & (8)].

An application may be rejected:
a. if the operator is unable to provide the service with equipment directly available to him;
b. if he has failed to comply with road transport legislation, particularly

in relation to authorisations, or has committed serious offences against safety legislation, particularly rules applicable to vehicles and drivers' hours;

c. in the case of a renewal, authorisation conditions have not been complied with;

d. the service would compromise an existing authorised regular service, except where it is carried out by a single carrier or group of carriers;

e. if the service would seriously affect the viability of a comparable rail service;

f. if it appears the service is aimed only at the most lucrative of services existing on the links concerned.

The fact that an operator offers lower prices than other road or rail operators or that the link in question is already operated by other carriers may not in itself constitute justification for rejecting the application [7(4)].

When the above procedures have been completed the authority must grant the authorisation or formally refuse it and give the reasons for refusal. Undertakings must be given opportunity to make representations if their application is refused [8].

Except for force majeure, the operator of a regular service must operate the service as authorised. A carrier must display the service route, bus stops, timetable, fares and conditions of carriage so that it is readily available to users [10].

CONTROL DOCUMENTS

Shuttle services with accommodation and occasional services exempt authorisation must be carried out under a control document which consists of a journey form and a set of translations of the form. The journey form must be completed before each journey and specify the type of service; main itinerary; carrier; and, on a shuttle service with accommodation, the duration, dates of departure and return, areas of departure and destination, and the taking-up and setting-down points [11].

LOCAL EXCURSIONS

As part of an international shuttle service with accommodation or an international occasional service an operator may carry out local excursions in an EC country other than that in which he is established. The services are for non-resident passengers previously carried by the same carrier on one of the above services and on the same vehicle or on another vehicle from the same group of carriers [12].

OWN-ACCOUNT CERTIFICATES

Own-account operations are exempt from any system of authorisation but are subject to a system of certificates. A certificate is issued by the competent authority of the vehicle's country of registration and is valid for the entire journey [13].

TICKETS

Passengers using a regular service (except a special regular service) or a shuttle service must, throughout the journey, be in possession of tickets, either individual or collective, which indicate the points of departure and destination, period of validity and price. A ticket must be produced at the request of an authorised inspector [14].

ENFORCEMENT

An authorisation or control document must be carried in the vehicle and be produced at the request of an authorised inspecting officer. On a special regular service, the contract or a certified true copy of it will serve as a control document.

Carriers operating international passenger transport must allow all inspections to ensure operations are being conducted correctly, particularly drivers' hours. Authorised officers must be empowered to check books and other documents; make copies of them; have access to the undertaking's vehicles, sites and premises; and require production of any information in books, documents and databases.

An authorising authority must withdraw an authorisation if the holder no longer fulfils the conditions under which it was granted. An authority must prohibit a carrier from operating a service under this Regulation if he repeatedly commits serious breaches of road safety rules, in particular those applying to vehicles and drivers' hours [15, 16].

18 Special types vehicles

Highways Act 1980
Motor Vehicles (Authorisation of Special Types) General Order, **No. 1198/79**
Motor Vehicles (Authorisation of Special Types) (Amendment) Order,
Nos. 1664/81, 1810/84, 745/85, 313/86, 1327/87, 2161/87 and **1662/89**

Motor vehicles and trailers which do not comply in all respects with
the Road Vehicles (Construction and Use) Regulations 1986 can be
used on a road if they come within a class of vehicle specified in the
Motor Vehicles (Authorisation of Special Types) General Order 1979.
If a vehicle can be authorised under the Order the operator must
comply with conditions which may be attached to the movement by
the Order. The Order is of a permissive nature in that failure to comply
with conditions of movement is not an offence in itself but such a
failure removes the protection given by the Order and the operator will
become liable for any contraventions of the Construction and Use
Regulations which arise—see *Siddle C. Cook v Arlidge* [1962] 1 WLR
203n.

Abnormal indivisible loads

Heavy motor cars and trailers specially designed and constructed for
the carriage of abnormal indivisible loads and locomotives and motor
tractors specially designed and constructed to draw such trailers and
which do not comply in all respects with the Construction and Use
Regulations can be used on a road provided they comply with specified
C and U requirements and with other specified conditions
[1198/79/18].

An abnormal indivisible load is defined as a load which cannot
without undue expense or risk of damage be divided into two or more
loads for the purpose of carriage on roads, and cannot, owing to its
size, be carried by a heavy motor car or trailer or a combination of both
complying with all the requirements of the Construction and Use

Regulations, or which, owing to its weight, cannot be carried by a heavy motor car or trailer or a combination of both with a total laden weight of under 38,000kg and complying with all the C and U requirements [3]. A vehicle carrying 12 beams each 51ft 6in long could not be authorised under the Order because the load was divisible into 12 separate beams—*Smith v North Western Traffic Area Licensing Authority* [1974] RTR 236—but see Article 18(2)(l), page 342.

Vehicles used for moving abnormal indivisible loads are placed into three categories:

Category 1   A vehicle or combination of vehicles where the total weight of the vehicle or vehicles carrying the load is not over 46,000kg.

Category 2   As above, but not over 80,000kg.

Category 3   As above, but not over 150,000kg

[18(1A) & 1327/87].

Where the use of a vehicle made before October 1989 is authorised under the Order the following Construction and Use Regulations do not apply to it:

Vehicle	*Regulations*
Heavy motor car	8, 16 (in part), 15, 18(2) to (8), 22, 24, 25, 45, 63, 75 to 80, 82 and 83(1).
Locomotive or motor tractor	8, 22, 25, 45, 75(3) and 76.
Trailer	7, 8, 16 (in part), 15, 18(2) to (8), 21, 22, 24, 25, 63, 64, 75 to 80, 82 and 83(1)

[18(2)(p), 1327/87 & 2161/87].

Where the use of a Category 2 or 3 vehicle made on or after 1 October 1989 or a Category 1 vehicle whenever made is authorised under the Order the following Construction and Use Regulations do not apply:

Category	*Regulations*
1	7, 8, 80 and 82
2 & 3	7, 8, 15, 16, 18(2) to (8), 25, 45, 64, 65, 75 (except locomotive gross weights), 76 to 80, 82 and 83(1)

[18(2)(q), 1327/87 & 2161/87].

Construction and Use length limits do not apply (a) to any articulated vehicle or drawbar combination if the trailer is a low-loader and the height or stability of the load requires the use of such a trailer, or (b) to a vehicle or combination in Category 2 and 3 unable to meet the length limits due to the axle spread required, in paragraph (2) (k), for a particular weight [18(2)(u) & 1327/87].

The main conditions of movement are as follows:

The overall width of a heavy motor car or trailer must not exceed 2.9m unless a load can be carried safely only on a wider vehicle [18(2)(c)]. The width of a locomotive or motor tractor must not exceed 2.9m unless drawing a trailer which exceeds that width, as above [18(2)(d)]. But the overall width of any vehicle or load must not exceed 6.1m [18(2)(f), (g)].

The overall length of a vehicle must not exceed 27.4m and the length of a load, including the vehicles on which it rests, must not exceed 27.4m, except that when a load is carried by a motor vehicle and trailer the length of the motor vehicle is disregarded [18(2)(h)].

A vehicle must be wheeled and its tyres must be pneumatic or made of soft or elastic material [18(2)(i),(j)].

The following weight restrictions apply:

Category 1 vehicles. Regulations 75, 76 and 78 of the Construction and Use Regulations apply; Regulation 79 applies to two and three closely-spaced axle; on a semi-trailer with four axles with a maximum outer spread of 3.25m and a minimum of 0.87m between any adjacent axles, the weight on any axle must not exceed 6,000kg; and, for an articulated vehicle, Regulation 77 applies, except that an artic with five or more axles with the axle spacing given in the following table may be used at the total weight indicated.

Distance from rearmost tractor axle to rearmost trailer axle—metres	Weight kg.
at least 6.5	40,000
at least 7.0	42,000
at least 7.5	44,000
at least 8.0	46,000

Category 2 vehicles. The total weight must be transmitted to the road through at least 5 axles; the weight on an axle must not exceed 12,500kg or, on one wheel, 6,250kg; if the distance between two adjacent axles is 1.1m to 1.35m the weight on those axles must not exceed 12,000kg or, on one wheel, 6,000kg; the distance between two adjacent axles must not be less than 1.1m; where the axles are in two or more groups so that adjacent axles in each group are less than 2m apart and adjacent axles in different groups are more than 2m apart, the total weight of any one group of axles must not exceed 50,000kg; and where the distance between the foremost and rearmost axles of the vehicle or vehicles carrying the load is at least that given in the following table the total weight of the vehicle or combination of vehicles must not exceed the weight indicated.

Distance from rearmost tractor axle to rearmost trailer axle—metres	Weight kg.
5.07	38,000
5.33	40,000
6.0	45,000
6.67	50,000
7.33	55,000
8.0	60,000
8.67	65,000
9.33	70,000
10.0	75,000
10.67	80,000

Category 3 vehicles. The total weight must be transmitted to the road through at least 6 axles; the weight on an axle must not exceed 16,500kg or, on one wheel, 8,250kg; if the distance between two adjacent axles is 1.1 to 1.35m the weight on those axles must not exceed 15,000kg or, on one wheel, 7,500kg; the distance between two adjacent axles must not be less than 1.1m; where the axles are in two or more groups so that adjacent axles in each group are less than 1.5m apart and adjacent axles in different groups are more than 1.5m apart, the total weight of any one group of axles must not exceed 100,000kg (or 90,000kg for a group where any two adjacent axles of that group are less than 1.35m apart); and where the distance between the foremost and rearmost axles of the vehicle or vehicles carrying the load is at least that given in the following table the total weight of the vehicle or combination of vehicles must not exceed the weight indicated.

Distance from rearmost tractor axle to rearmost trailer axle—metres	Weight kg.
5.77	80,000
6.23	85,000
6.68	90,000
7.14	95,000
7.59	100,000
8.05	105,000
8.50	110,000
8.95	115,000

Distance from rearmost tractor axle to rearmost trailer axle—metres	Weight kg.
9.41	120,000
9.68	125,000
10.32	130,000
10.77	135,000
11.23	140,000
11.68	145,000
12.14	150,000

For the purposes of the weight restrictions in this paragraph, an axle is any number of wheels in a transverse line and any lines of wheels up to 1.02m apart are treated as one axle [18(2)(k), 1327/87 and 1662/89].

A vehicle or combination of vehicles cannot carry more than one abnormal indivisible load at any one time except (a) as long as the vehicle's Construction and Use weight limits are not exceeded more than one such load of the same character can be carried or (b) more than one load can be carried if the vehicles are in Category 1 or 2, the carriage of more than one load does not cause the vehicle's overall length to exceed 18.3m or the overall width to exceed 2.9m (but any of the loads can be up to 27.4m long and up to 6.1m wide) and the loads carried are loaded at the same place and carried to the same destination [18(2)(l)].

If a load consists of engineering plant from which parts have been detached the load and parts can be carried on the same vehicle provided (i) the detached parts do not protrude further than the load; (ii) the load and parts are loaded at the same place and have the same destination; and (iii) the vehicles are in Category 1 or 2 [18(2)(m)].

The braking standard for pre-1968 trailers, in Regulation 16 of the Construction and Use Regulations, applies to all trailers [18(2)(n)]. Category 2 or 3 vehicles made on or after 1 October 1989 must comply with specified EC braking standards [18(2)(r) & 1662/89].

A Category 2 or 3 vehicle made after 1 October 1988 must have a plate complying with the Road Vehicles (Marking of Special Weights) Regulations 1983 (see page 23) (but no weight need be given in relation to speeds not over 12mph); the plate must be marked with the words 'Special Types Use'; if the vehicle is made up of modules each may have a plate; and a vehicle with this plate must not be used at a weight in excess of that specified on the plate in relation to its speed. A Category 1 vehicle must not be used at a weight higher than its maker's plated design weights [18(2)(s) and 1327/87].

Regardless of the rule that a heavy motor or trailer be used only in connection with the carriage of an abnormal indivisible load [18(2)(a)], a vehicle consisting of two or more modules may, when being used in connection with the carriage but not at the time carrying such a load, be disassembled and arranged so that one part carries the others [18(2)(v) & 1327/87].

The vehicle or, in a combination of vehicles, the drawing vehicle must be fitted with a prescribed sign indicating its Category. The sign, shown below, must be at the front of the vehicle facing forwards and, as near vertical as possible, have white lettering on a black background and be kept clean and unobscured. The given dimensions may vary by 5% [18(2)(t) & 1327/87].

Special Types Category Sign

400mm

250mm

105mm

70mm

Note: the category number 3 is shown as an example; the number could be 1, 2 or 3 depending upon the category of the vehicle or combination of vehicles.

SPEED

Category 1 vehicles are subject to normal speed limits (page 354). Category 2 vehicles are limited to 40mph on motorways, 35mph on other dual-carriageways and 30mph on other roads. Category 3 vehicles are limited to 30mph on motorways, 25mph on other dual-carriageways and 20mph on other roads [21(1) and 1327/87].

ATTENDANT

If the overall width of the vehicle, including the load, exceeds 3.5m; the overall length of a vehicle, including the load, but excluding a load-bearing drawing unit, exceeds 18.3m; the overall length of a combination of vehicles, including the load, exceeds 25.9m; the length of a forward projection of the load exceeds 1.83m or the length of a rearward projection of the load exceeds 3.05m then one person, in addition to the driver, must be employed to attend to the vehicle and load and warn the driver and any other road user of any danger likely to be caused by the vehicle's presence [22(1), (2)]. The driver of an assisting vehicle cannot be classed as an attendant. If three or more such vehicles are travelling in convoy the requirement applies to the foremost and rearmost ones [22(3)].

MARKERS

If the load projects more than 1.83m to the front or rear, marker boards must be fitted to it in the manner set out in the C and U Regulations (see page 371) and if a load projects to the rear more than 1.07m but not over 1.83m it must be made visible to other road users [23]. An end marker board is not required if the load is fitted with reflective rear markings [23(5)].

EXTRA WIDTH

If the overall width of vehicle together with its load exceeds 5m the prior approval of the Secretary of State, on Form VR 1, must be obtained [24]. The VR 1 must be carried on the vehicle while on the authorised journey [24(2)(b)].

NOTICE

If a vehicle, including the load, has an overall width over 2.9m or an overall length over 18.3m (excluding a load-bearing drawing unit); or a combination of vehicles has an overall length over 25.9m; a forward or rearward projection of the load is over 3.05m; or a vehicle combination's total weight exceeds 80,000kg then two days' notice of the movement of the load must be given to the chief officer of each police area through which the vehicle passes. Saturdays, Sundays and bank holidays are not counted as days for this purpose [3(1)]. The police can vary the time, date or route of the vehicle, and, while on a journey, cause it to halt in the interests of road safety or to avoid traffic congestion [25]. The form the notice must take is set out at the end of this chapter.

A highway and bridge authority must be given 5 days' notice of the movement of a vehicle which exceeds 80,000kg gross weight and two days' notice in any other case when a C and U axle or gross weight is exceeded. An indemnity must also be given to highway and bridge authorities before using such a vehicle on a road [26]. Where a London borough or metropolitan district council delegates its road and bridge functions to another such council or has an agreement with another person for them to be carried out, the notice and indemnity can be served on that other council or person [26(2A) & 313/86]. The authority may agree to take a shorter period of notice but may not dispense with a notice entirely—*George Cohen 600 Group Ltd v Hird* [1970] 2 All ER 650, [1970] 1 WLR 1226. The form the notice and indemnity must take are set out on pages 350 and 351.

BRIDGE RESTRICTIONS

A vehicle carrying an abnormal indivisible load must not be driven on to a bridge at the same time as another such vehicle is known by him to be on it and must not be parked on a bridge except in circumstances beyond the driver's control [27]. If a vehicle exceeding 38,000kg (laden or unladen) stops on a bridge it must be moved off it as soon as practicable and if it is necessary to jack-up the vehicle on a bridge the advice of the bridge authority or other person responsible for its maintenance and repair must be sought as to the use of spreader plates [28, 313/86 and 1327/87].

Load over 4.3m wide on normal vehicle

A load over 4.3m wide can be carried on a vehicle which otherwise complies in all respects with the Construction and Use Regulations provided specified conditions are complied with [20]. These conditions are that the vehicle's speed does not exceed 30mph on a motorway, 25mph on other dual-carriageways and 20mph on other roads [21]; an attendant is employed [22]; if the width exceeds 5m, the approval of the Secretary of State has been obtained on form VR 1 which is carried on the vehicle [24]; and police notice is given [25(1)(g)].

Engineering plant

Engineering plant is defined as movable plant or equipment being a motor vehicle or trailer specially designed and constructed for engineering operations and which cannot comply with certain requirements of the Construction and Use Regulations or the Track-Laying Regulations and which is not constructed primarily to carry a load other than a load being excavated material raised from the ground by apparatus on the motor vehicle or trailer, or materials which the vehicle or trailer is specially designed to treat while carried thereon, or a mobile crane which does not comply with certain of the requirements of the same two sets of Regulations [1198/79/3 and 1664/81].

Such vehicles can be used on a road subject to conditions contained in Article 19, other relevant Articles and specified C and U Regulations being complied with.

Engineering plant may be used only for test or demonstration; delivery on sale; going to or from repairs or maintenance; or going to or from engineering operations or while engaged in such operations. Engineering plant may carry its own necessary gear and equipment but no other load except (a) when on road works, materials to be treated on the vehicle or which have been excavated by the vehicle, and (b) when engaged on engineering operations a mobile crane may lift or transport a load [19(4)(a) & 1327/87].

A motor vehicle over 7.93m long must not draw a trailer other than a broken-down vehicle [19(n)]. A mobile crane must not draw a trailer and engineering plant must not draw a trailer other than engineering plant, a living van or office used in connection with road works [19(c), (d)]. A mobile crane which comprised a motor vehicle with a jib carried horizontally and supported by the motor vehicle at one end and a four-axled bogie at the other was held to be a single vehicle and not a vehicle and trailer—*DPP v Evans* [1988] RTR 409.

The total laden weight of the vehicle must not exceed 152,400kg and except for heavy motor cars first registered or trailers constructed before 1 January 1952, the weight transmitted to a road by any wheel must not exceed 11,430kg. For this purpose any two wheels are counted as one if the distance between the centres of the areas of contact between such wheels and the road surface is less than 610mm.

In the case of wheels not fitted with pneumatic tyres, the total weight on any wheels in line across the vehicle must not average more than 765kg per 25mm width of tyre in contact with the road.

Limits are also placed on the weight bearing on a strip of road at right angles to the vehicle. A weight of 45,720kg is allowed on a strip of road surface up to 610mm wide; thereafter up to a width of 2.13m weight is allowed at the rate of 30,000kg per metre and thereafter at the rate of 10,000kg per metre [19(k)(o)(r)].

Engineering plant (other than gritting machines) which is not fitted with pneumatic or soft or elastic tyres must have smooth tyres with the edges rounded to a radius of from 12 to 25mm. Gritting machines can have some or all types consisting of equal-sized diagonal cross-bars, not less than 1in wide, with spaces not greater than the width of the bars [19(j)].

Except in the case of a steamer with a reversible engine every motor vehicle must be equipped with an efficient brake. On motor vehicles registered on or after 1 January 1952 this brake must be capable of acting also as a parking brake unless another brake is available for that purpose [19(l)].

A trailer must have an efficient brake or suitable scotches or other similar devices [19(m)].

A vehicle must not exceed 27.4m overall length or 6.1m overall width [19(p),(q)].

A vehicle authorised under Article 19 must not exceed 12mph [21(2)]. But, if a vehicle or combination of vehicles, regardless of its date of manufacture, complies with Article 18(2)(k),(q),(r),(s) and (t) (which relate to abnormal indivisible loads) it is allowed the same speed limits as if it were authorised under Article 18 [19(2A) & 1327/87].

An attendant, police notice, highway and bridge authority notice and indemnity are required in the same circumstances as apply to the carriage of abnormal indivisible loads [22, 25, 26].

If a special appliance or apparatus fitted to the vehicle projects over 1.83m forward or rearward it must be fitted with marker boards. If it projects over 1.07m rearwards but not over 1.83m steps must be taken to make it visible to other road users [23].

If engineering plant weighing over 38,000kg is caused to stop on a bridge it must be moved off it as soon as practicable and the advice of the bridge authority must be sought as to the use of spreader plates before jacking-up the vehicle on a bridge [28].

If a vehicle exceeds 5m wide special approval for the movement must be obtained from the Secretary of State on Form VR 1 and this form must be carried on the vehicle on the journey [24].

Outsize dumpers

Subject to certain conditions, heavy motor cars or trailers or articulated vehicles constructed for use in private premises primarily for moving excavated material and fitted with a tipping body or movable platform and which do not conform to certain requirements of the Construction and Use Regulations can be used on roads only to go to and from the private premises, or between private premises and a port or vice versa. No load other than the vehicle's 'necessary gear or equipment' must be carried.

Requirements are laid down as to axle and gross weights, length, speed, attendants needed and notice to police and highway authorities [1198/79/15].

Agricultural vehicles

Only if the width of the vehicle cannot, without undue expense or risk of damage, be reduced, (a) an agricultural motor vehicle, (b) an agricultural trailer designed for functions, other than carrying goods, which necessitate on overall width over 2.5m, or (c) an agricultural trailed appliance, can be used on a road even though its width exceeds 2.5m as long as conditions specified in Schedule 4 (given below) are complied with [1198/79/13(1) and 1810/84]. These agricultural vehicles have the same definition as in the Construction and Use Regulations, (page 3).

An agricultural motor vehicle towing an offset agricultural trailer or agricultural trailed appliance where the overall width of the combination exceeds 2.5m can be used if the conditions in Schedule 4 are complied with [13A].

For the above purposes, an agricultural implement rigidly mounted on one of the above vehicles is to be treated as part of that vehicle whether or not (a) the implement is permanently attached, and (b) part of its weight is transmitted to the road otherwise than by the carrying vehicle [13B].

The conditions of movement are that if the overall width of a vehicle, or combination of vehicles, exceeds 2.5m it must not be driven at a speed over 20mph and, if it exceeds 3.5m, not over 12mph. If the overall width of a vehicle, or offset combination of vehicles, exceeds 3m and the journey is to be made on a road subject to a speed limit of 40mph or less or is to exceed 5 miles, the operator of the vehicle must (1) before using the vehicle on a road, give at least 24 hours notice of the intended use to the police including the time, date and route of the journey and information about the vehicle and its width, and (2) use the vehicle in accordance with the notified particulars unless the police vary the time, date and route. Police may dispense with the requirement as to length of notice and information about the vehicle. Where the overall width of a vehicle, or an offset combination, exceeds 3m the vehicle or combination must not draw any trailer, or other trailer, except (i) a two-wheeled trailer used solely for carrying equipment for the drawing vehicle, (ii) an agricultural trailed appliance, or (iii) an unladen trailer specially designed for use with the drawing vehicle when harvesting. If the overall width of an agricultural motor vehicle, an agricultural trailer on which an implement is mounted, an agricultural trailed appliance or an off-set combination of vehicles exceeds 3.5m (a) at least one person must be employed, in addition to the driver, to warn road users of any danger likely to be caused and (b) the extremities of the vehicle must be clearly visible at a reasonable distance to other road users and, during the hours of darkness or in seriously reduced visibility, this condition shall be satisfied by the use of lights required under the Lighting Regulations. The overall width of a vehicle, or off-set combination of vehicles, must not exceed 4.3m [1198/79/Sch. 4].

An agricultural motor vehicle, an agricultural trailer and an agricultural trailed appliance which, in each case, has an agricultural implement rigidly mounted on it which has forward or rearward projection over 1m may be used if conditions specified in Schedule 5 are complied with [1198/79/13C].

The conditions are that if the implement projects more than 1m beyond the foremost or rearmost point of the vehicle on which it is mounted the end of the projection must be clearly visible to other road users and, during the hours of darkness or seriously reduced visibility, this condition shall be satisfied by the use of lights required under the Lighting Regulations. If the projection exceeds 2m it must be fitted with an end marker board and side marker boards which must, during the hours of darkness or in seriously reduce visibility, be kept lit. If the projection exceeds 4m it must have marker boards and police must be given 24 hours notice of the movement (as in Schedule 4 above). If the projection exceeds 6m it must be fitted with marker boards, there must be police notice of the movement and an additional person to warn other road users of the likely danger [1198/79/Sch. 5].

Other vehicles

The Order also authorises the use of many specialised vehicles subject to conditions laid down for each type of vehicle. The types of vehicle include track-laying vehicles [1198/79/5]; military vehicles [6]; grass-cutting machines and hedge trimmers [7, 9]; pedestrian-controlled road maintenance vehicles [10]; vehicles on trial [11]; straddle carriers [12]; vehicles for export or on test [16]; and vehicles fitted with movable platforms [17].

Liability for damage

If a highway authority is obliged to incur extraordinary expense in repairing a road as the result of the passage of excessive weight or other extraordinary traffic, the additional expense as compared with normal repair costs may be recovered from the person responsible. The operator and highway authority, may, however, agree in advance on

THE MOTOR VEHICLES (AUTHORISATION OF SPECIAL TYPES)
GENERAL ORDER, 1979

(Subject to the prior agreement of each of the authorities to which this notice is sent, it may be used to give notice of additional journeys, different vehicles, routes and destinations.)

List of all Police Forces, Highway and Bridge Authorities to which this form is sent.

Operator..	Telephone No. ....
Address	Telex No. ....
....	Operator's Licence No. ....
....	Operator's Reference No. ....

In pursuance of Article(s)   of the above mentioned Order, I/we being the operator of the undermentioned vehicle(s) to which the Order applies, hereby give notice that it is my/our intention to use the said vehicle(s) on the roads specified below. The route and Department of Transport Classification numbers proposed to be used are:

PARTICULARS OF JOURNEY

FROM (full address)	TIME AND DATE	via ....

TO (full address)	TIME AND DATE

PARTICULARS OF LOAD

LOAD PROFILE (rough sketch showing outline of laden vehicle from front or rear. This to be omitted if sent by telex).

PARTICULARS OF VEHICLE

Registration No. of vehicle (or substitute)	Type of vehicle	DESCRIPTION OF LOAD

Overall length of vehicle		Projection —front		Projection —rear		Total length	

Overall width		Maximum height		Gross weight or Gross train weight	

No. of wheels per axle								
Axle weight								
Axle spacing								

the payment of a sum by way of composition of such liability, and in this event no proceedings for the recovery of damages can be taken. Proceedings must, in any case, be begun within 12 months of the damage or not later than 6 months after the completion of the work occasioning the damage [Act 1980/59].

FORM OF INDEMNITY

I/We hereby agree to indemnify you and each and every highway or bridge authority or other person responsible for the maintenance and repair of any road or bridge on the journey to which the above notice relates in respect of any damage which may be caused to any such road or bridge:
    (a) by (any of) the above-mentioned vehicle(s)—
        (i) by reason of the construction of or weight transmitted to the road surface by (any of) the said vehicle(s); or
        (ii) by reason of the dimensions, distribution or adjustment of the load carried by (any of) the said vehicle(s); or
    (b) by any other vehicle by reason of the use of (any of) the above-mentioned vehicle(s) on the road or, as the case may be, the bridge, except to the extent that the damage was caused or contributed to by the negligence of the driver of the other vehicle
provided that any claim in respect of damage so caused by any vehicle shall be made in writing within twelve months from the date on which the vehicle is last used on the journey to which the above notice relates, stating the occasion and place of the damage.
Date   Signed

Note—Paragraph (a)(ii) above only applies where vehicles are carrying an abnormal indivisible load and in other cases should be omitted.

19   Speed limits

Road Traffic Regulation Act 1984
Road Traffic Offenders Act 1988
Motor Vehicles (Variation of Speed Limits) Regulations, **No.** 2192/47
Motorways Traffic (Speed Limit) Regulations, **No.** 502/74
Port Talbot By-Pass (Speed Limit) Regulations, **No.** 1855/74
70mph, 60mph and 50mph (Temporary Speed Limit) Order 1977
70mph, 60mph and 50mph (Temporary Speed Limit) (Continuation) Order,
   No. 1548/78
Motorways Traffic (M621 Motorway) (Speed Limit) Regulations,
   No. 1280/83
Restricted Roads (Classification or Type) (Scotland) Regulations,
   No. 1888/85
Motor Vehicles (Variation of Speed Limits) Regulations, **No.** 1175/86
Road Traffic Offenders (Prescribed Devices) Orders, **Nos.** 1209/92 and
   1698/93

General limits

On restricted roads the normal maximum speed limit is 30mph [Act 1984/81(1)]; lower or higher speeds may be permitted by Order [81(2)]. On unrestricted roads in England, Scotland and Wales, the limit is 70mph on dual carriageways and 60mph on other roads but many such roads have lower limits applied to them [1977 Order and 1548/78. On motorways the general limit is 70mph [502/74].

A restricted road is defined as a road on which street lamps are placed not more than 200 yards apart [Act 1984/82(1)] but sections of restricted roads, furnished with the frequency of lamps mentioned, can be specified as unrestricted roads and, likewise, sections of unrestricted roads can be specified as restricted roads [82(2)]. In Scotland a road is restricted if it has lamps not more than 185m apart and the road is a Class C or unclassified road [1888/85].

There is a speed limit exemption covering fire-brigade, ambulance and police vehicles whenever the observance of this limit would hinder the execution of their duties [Act 1984/87].

On roads, other than restricted roads, speed limits may be ordered by the Secretary of State, in the case of trunk roads, and by a local authority in the case of other roads [84]. It is their duty to erect signs to indicate the presence of a speed limit [85(1)]. Where a road is not a restricted road but it is subject to a speed limit, a person will not be convicted of exceeding that limit unless the limit is indicated by means of signs [84(4)]. In proceedings for exceeding the speed limit on a restricted road (i.e. street lamps not more than 200 yards apart), evidence of the absence of signs to indicate that the road is not a restricted road shall be evidence that the road is a restricted road [85(5)].

A person prosecuted for speeding will not be convicted solely on the evidence of one witness to the effect that, in the opinion of the witness, the person prosecuted was exceeding a speed limit [89(2)]. But in *Nicholas v Penny* [1950] 2 KB 466 it was held that evidence of a policeman who had consulted a speedometer was sufficient since the speedometer reading was evidence of fact, not of opinion. And in *Crossland v DPP* [1988] RTR 417 it was held that evidence of speed based on calculations made from accident damage and skid marks was not solely evidence of opinion and Section 89(2) could not be invoked.

In a speeding prosecution evidence of a fact may be given by the production of a record produced by a prescribed device and a certificate as to the circumstances in which the record was produced [Act 1988/20]. A record produced or measurement taken by a prescribed device is not admissible unless the device is of a type approved by the Secretary of State and conditions relating to the approval are satisfied [20(4)]. A document is not admissible in evidence under these provisions unless, at least seven days before the hearing or trial, the defendant has been served with a copy of the document; and nothing in the document other than matters shown on a record produced by the prescribed device is admissible if the defendant serves a notice, not less than three days before the hearing or trial, on the prosecutor requiring the attendance of the person who signed the document [20(8)]. The devices prescribed by the Secretary of State are (a) a device for measuring the speed of motor vehicles by radar and (b) devices for recording a measurement of speed activated by sensors or cables on or near the surface of the highway or activated by light beams [1209/92 and 1698/93].

If an employer issues a time-table or schedule, or gives any directions that a journey is to be completed in a specified time, and it is not practicable to complete the journey in the time laid down without exceeding a speed limit the time-table, schedule or directions shall be evidence that the employer procured or incited the employee to commit the offence [Act 1984/89(4)].

Where road works are being carried out a highway authority can make an order temporarily restricting the speed of vehicles [Act

1984/14(1)]. The offence carries a fine but not disqualification or licence endorsement [RTO Act 1988/Sch. 2]. In *Platten v Gowing* [1983] RTR 352 it was held that temporary speed restrictions were not speed 'limits' for which a higher standard of proof was required.

On a specified section of the M4 motorway and on four of its slip roads in London; the Heathrow Airport spur; the Mancunian Way A57(M) in Manchester; part of the M1 at Hendon; parts of the Acton Expressway and Gravelly Hill interchange, Birmingham; parts of the Leeds South East Urban Motorway; Glasgow Inner Ring Road; Port Talbot By-Pass and the M621 at Leeds there is a limit of 50mph for all vehicles. On the southern motorway approaches to Blackwall Tunnel, London, there is a limit of 60mph [502/74, 1855/74, 1280/83 and 2129/94].

Limits for specified vehicle classes

For particular classes of vehicle and vehicles drawing a trailer speed limits are prescribed in Schedule 6 of the Road Traffic Regulation Act 1984 according to the type of road on which the vehicle is used [Act 1984/86 and 1175/86]. They are as follows:

Class of vehicle	MAXIMUM SPEED—MPH		
	Motorway	*Other dual carriageway*	*Other road*
Passenger vehicle, motor caravan or dual-purpose vehicle not drawing a trailer but being over 3,050kg unladen or adapted to carry more than 8 passengers:			
(a) if not over 12m long	70	60	50
(b) if over 12m long	60	60	50
Passenger vehicle, motor caravan, car-derived van or dual-purpose vehicle drawing one trailer	60	60	50
Goods vehicle with a permitted laden weight not over 7.5 tonnes and which is not an articulated vehicle, a car-derived van or drawing a trailer	70	60	50
Goods vehicle which is (i) an articulated vehicle with a permitted laden weight not over 7.5 tonnes, or (ii) a motor vehicle (other than a			

Class of vehicle	MAXIMUM SPEED—MPH		
	Motorway	*Other dual carriageway*	*Other road*
car-derived van) drawing one trailer where the total permitted laden weight of both vehicles does not exceed 7.5 tonnes.	60	60	50
Goods vehicle which is (i) an articulated vehicle with a permitted laden weight over 7.5 tonnes; (ii) a motor vehicle with a permitted laden weight over 7.5 tonnes and not drawing a trailer; or (iii) a motor vehicle drawing one trailer where the total permitted laden weight of both vehicles exceeds 7.5 tonnes.	60	50	40
Motor tractor (other than an industrial tractor) and a locomotive (a) which complies with requirements as to springs and wings and is either (a) not drawing a trailer or (b) is drawing one trailer which complies with those requirements	40	30	30
(b) in any other case	20	20	20
Works truck	18	18	18
Industrial tractor	—	18	18
Motor vehicle or trailer which has resilient tyres or a mixture of resilient and pneumatic tyres	20	20	20
Motor vehicle or trailer any wheel of which is not fitted with a resilient or pneumatic tyre	5	5	5
Agricultural motor vehicle	40	40	40

For the above purposes a car-derived van is defined as a goods vehicle which is constructed or adapted as a derivative of a passenger vehicle and which has a maximum laden weight not over 2 tonnes [Sch. 6/Part IV/2].

A vehicle falling within two or more classes in the Schedule is to be treated as falling in the class for which the lowest limit is specified [Sch. 6/Part IV/4].

Naval, military and air force vehicles are subject to the speed limits on restricted roads and other roads where there is a speed limit order in force. But such vehicles which are combat vehicles, personnel carriers, gun tractors or carriers, mobile cranes for raising aircraft, fire tenders or ambulances are not subject to the limits in Schedule 6 above [Act 1984/130 and 2192/47].

20 Use of vehicles

International Road Haulage Permits Act 1975
Highways Act 1980
Public Passenger Vehicles Act 1981
Roads (Scotland) Act 1984
Road Traffic Regulation Act 1984
Weights and Measures Act 1985
Road Traffic Act 1988
Road Traffic Offenders Act 1988
Road Traffic Act 1991
EC Regulation 881/92
Agriculture (Avoidance of Accidents to Children) Regulations, **No. 366/58**
London Traffic (Misc. Prohibitions and Restrictions) Regulations, **No. 659/58**
Various Trunk Roads (Prohibition of Waiting) (Clearways) Order, **No. 1172/63**
Vehicles (Conditions of Use on Footpaths) Regulations, **No. 2126/63**
Quarry Vehicles Regulations, **No. 168/70**
Functions of Traffic Wardens Order, **No. 1958/70**
'Zebra' Pedestrian Crossing Regulations, **No. 1524/71**
Motor Vehicles (Third Party Risks) Regulations, **No. 1217/72**
Goods Vehicles (International Road Haulage Permits) Regulations, **No. 2234/75**
Cubic Measures (Ballast and Agricultural Materials) Regulations, **No. 1962/78**
Motor Vehicles (Wearing of Seat Belts by Children) Regulations, **No. 1342/82**
Road Vehicles (Marking of Special Weights) Regulations, **No. 910/83**
Goods Vehicles (Authorisation of International Journeys) (Fees) Regulations, **No. 1831/83**
Freight Containers (Safety Convention) Regulations, **No. 1890/84**
Builders' Skips (Markings) Regulations, **No. 1933/84**
Traffic Signs (Temporary Obstructions) Regulations, **No. 463/85**
Weights and Measures (Liquid Fuel carried by Road Tankers) Order, **No. 778/85**
Builders' Skips (Markings) (Scotland) Regulations, **No. 642/86**
Road Vehicles (Construction and Use) Regulations, **No. 1078/86**
Immobilisation of Vehicles Illegally Parked (London Boroughs of Camden, Kensington and Chelsea, Westminster and the City of London) Order, **No. 1225/86**
'Pelican' Pedestrian Crossings Regulations and General Directions, **No. 16/87**

Goods Vehicles (Authorisation of International Journeys) (Fees) (Amendment) Regulations, **Nos. 2012/87, 2058/89** and **2646/91**

Cubic Measures (Ballast and Agricultural Materials) (Amendment) Regulations, **No. 765/88**

Weighing Equipment (Non-automatic Weighing Machines) Regulations, **No. 876/88**

Merchant Shipping (Weighing of Goods Vehicles and other Cargo) Regulations, **No. 1275/88**

Merchant Shipping (Weighing of Goods Vehicles and other Cargo) (Amendment) Regulations, **No. 270/89**

Merchant Shipping (Weighing of Goods Vehicles and other Cargo) (Application to non-UK Ships) Regulations, **No. 568/89**

Immobilisation of Vehicles Illegally Parked (London Borough of Hammersmith and Fulham) Order, **No. 1746/89**

Driving Licences (Community Driving Licence) Regulations, **No. 144/90**

Fixed Penalty Offences Order, **Nos. 335/90** and **345/92**

Fixed Penalty Offences (Scotland) Order, **No. 466/90**

Fixed Penalty (Increase) Order, **No. 346/92**

Vehicles (Charges for Release from Immobilisation Devices) Regulations, **No. 386/92**

Fixed Penalty (Increase) (Scotland) Order, **No. 435/92**

Road Traffic Offenders (Prescribed Devices) (No. 2) Order, **No. 2843/92**

Motor Vehicles (Compulsory Insurance) Regulations, **No. 3036/92**

Goods Vehicles (Community Authorisations) Regulations, **No. 3077/92**

Road Traffic Act 1988 (Amendment) Regulations, **No. 3105/92**

Motor Vehicles (Wearing of Seat Belts by Children in Front Seats) Regulations, **No. 31/93**

Motor Vehicles (Wearing of Seat Belts) Regulations, **No. 176/93**

Road Traffic (Parking Adjudicators) (London) Regulations, **No. 1202/93**

Traffic Signs Regulations and General Directions, **No. 1519/94**

Accidents

If an accident occurs owing to the presence of a vehicle on a road and personal injury is caused to any person other than the driver of that vehicle, or damage is caused to any vehicle other than that vehicle or its trailer, or damage is caused to any animal other than one carried in that vehicle or trailer, or to any property forming part of the land on which the road runs or adjacent land, the driver of that vehicle must stop. A policeman or any person having reasonable grounds may demand the driver's name and address and also the name and address of the owner and the registration number of the vehicle [Act 1988/170(1),(2)]. Section 170(2) creates only one offence even though it imposes two requirements—*DPP v Bennett* [1993] RTR 175.

'Animal' means any horse, cattle, ass, mule, sheep, pig, goat or dog [170(8)]. A driver who collides with a stationary, unoccupied vehicle is under no duty to inquire as to the whereabouts of the vehicle's owner—*Mutton v Bates* [1984] RTR 256—but he must stay at the scene long enough for a person to obtain information from him—*Lee v Knapp* [1966] 3 All ER 961.

If in the event of any such accident the driver, for any reason, does not give his name and address to any such person, then he must report the accident at a police station or to a police constable as soon as reasonably practicable but in any case not later than 24 hours after the accident [170(3), (6)]. If a driver does not report the accident as soon as reasonably practicable though it is inside the maximum 24 hours allowed he commits an offence—*Bulman v Bennett* [1974] RTR 1 and *Bulman v Lakin* [1981] RTR 1. The report must be made in person and not by telephone—*Wisdom v Macdonald* [1983] RTR 186.

Similarly, accidents involving personal injury to a third party must be reported within 24 hours unless the relevant certificate of insurance was produced at the time of the accident to a police constable or to some person who, having reasonable grounds, required its production then [170(6)].

In *Harding v Price* [1948] 1 KB 695, [1948] 1 All ER 283 it was held that a driver who was unaware that his vehicle had been involved in an accident could not be convicted of failing to stop and report. But in *DPP v Drury* [1989] RTR 165 it was ruled that a driver, not aware of an accident at the time it occurred, but who became aware of it within 24 hours of its occurrence, had to report it within that 24 hours. The burden of proving he was unaware of an accident rests on the defendant—*Selby v Chief Constable of Avon and Somerset* [1988] RTR 216.

Any failure in or damage to a public service vehicle of a nature calculated to affect the safety of passengers or other persons using the road must be reported without delay to the Secretary of State [PPV Act 1981/20(1)].

Any contract for the conveyance of a passenger in a public service vehicle is declared to be void so far as it purports to avoid any liability for injury to or death of a passenger while being carried in, entering, or alighting from the vehicle [PPV Act 1981/29].

In *Wilkie v London Passenger Transport Board* [1947] 1 All ER 258 it was held that a free pass issued to an employee was a licence to travel and was not a contract so that conditions attached to it excluding liability were valid. But in *Gore v Van der Lann* [1967] 2 QB 31, [1967] 1 All ER 361 a free pass granted to a pensioner was held to be a contract since she had to apply for it and all the elements of a contract were present. In that case conditions excluding liability were invalid.

Breakdown sign

A sign consisting of a traffic cone, traffic pyramid, traffic triangle or warning lamp may be placed on a road to warn of a temporary obstruction other than road works [463/85/8]. Traffic cones and pyramids must have red and white surfaces and the white surface must be reflectorised [Schs. 1 and 2]. Two types of traffic triangle are specified and they must have red reflectorised and red fluorescent surfaces [Schs. 3 and 4]. A warning lamp must show a flashing amber light and be placed that it is not more than 1.2m above ground level [7].

If traffic cones or pyramids are used there must be at least four of them and they must be placed upright and so as to guide traffic past the obstruction [9 and 11]. A traffic triangle must be placed upright at least 45m away from the obstruction and to warn traffic approaching on the same side of the road as the obstruction [10].

A warning lamp may be used only in conjunction with traffic cones, pyramids and a triangle and it must be placed so that it does not obscure them from approaching traffic. Not more than one warning lamp may be used with each triangle, cone or pyramid [9].

Bridging plate

A person must not use a motor vehicle or trailer constructed to carry other vehicles if any part of the weight of any vehicle which is being carried rests on a bridging plate fitted to the trailer. A bridging plate is designed for enabling vehicles to be moved from the trailer onto the motor vehicle while loading and vice versa when unloading. The restriction does not apply while the vehicle is being loaded or unloaded or if the plate is folded or withdrawn so that it does not bridge the gap between vehicle and trailer [1078/86/88].

Causing danger

A person commits an offence if, intentionally and without lawful or reasonable excuse, he causes anything to be on or over a road; interferes with a motor vehicle or trailer; or interferes with traffic equipment, where it would be obvious to a reasonable person that to do so would be dangerous [Act 1988/22A and Act 1991].

Children on farm vehicles

Children who have not attained the age of 13 years may not ride on any of the following vehicles while they are being used in agricultural operations or while they are going to or from the place of such operations: tractors; self-propelled agricultural machines; trailers; conveyor trailers; machines mounted on tractors or vehicles or towed or propelled by them; and binders or mowers drawn by animals [366/58/3(1)]. But a child may ride in a trailer if he rides (a) on the floor or (b) on a load provided the trailer has 4 sides each higher than the load [3(2)]. A child must not drive a tractor, self-propelled vehicle or machine while it is being used for agricultural operations or is going to or from the place of such operations [4]. A child must not ride on implements mounted wholly or partly on tractors or vehicles or implements towed or propelled by vehicles or on animal-drawn rollers [5].The expression 'trailer' does not include horse-drawn vehicles [2].

Dangerous and careless driving

A person who causes the death of another person by driving a mechanically-propelled vehicle dangerously on a road or other public place commits an offence [Act 1988/1 and Act 1991]. A person who drives a mechanically propelled vehicle dangerously on a road or other public place commits an offence [2].

A person will be regarded as driving dangerously if the way he drives falls below what would be expected of a competent and careful driver and it would be obvious to such a driver that driving in that way would · be dangerous [2A(1)].

A person will also be regarded as driving dangerously if it would be obvious to a competent and careful driver that driving a vehicle in its current state would be dangerous. Here dangerous refers to danger either by injury to any person or serious damage to property. In deciding what would be expected of, or obvious to, a competent and careful driver regard must be had not only to the circumstances he could be expected to be aware of, but to any shown to have been within the accused's knowledge [2A(2), (3)].

In determining the state of a vehicle regard may be had to anything attached to or carried on it and to the manner in which it is attached or carried [2A(4)].

A person who drives a mechanically propelled vehicle on a road or other public place without due care and attention or reasonable consideration for other persons using the road or place commits an offence [3].

Drawing a trailer

An articulated bus may not draw a trailer. A bus, other than an articulated bus or a minibus, may draw a broken-down bus if only the driver is carried on each vehicle and it may draw a trailer [1078/86/83(1)].

A locomotive may not draw more than three trailers; a motor tractor, one, or if unladen, two trailers; and a motor car or heavy motor car, one trailer. A broken-down articulated vehicle is classed as one trailer when being drawn following the breakdown but only if it is unladen. A water trailer drawn by a steam-propelled vehicle does not count as a trailer under these provisions [83(4)]. In *DPP v Yates* [1989] RTR 134 it was held that a recovery vehicle drawing a lorry and trailer by suspended tow was a locomotive, not a heavy motor car.

An agricultural motor vehicle may draw (a) two unladen agricultural trailers; (b) one agricultural trailer, whether laden or not, and one agricultural trailed appliance; (c) two agricultural trailed appliances; or (d) the number of non-agricultural trailers according to its classification as a locomotive, motor tractor, heavy motor car or motor car [83(1)].

A composite trailer comprising a dolly convertor and semi-trailer is treated as one trailer for the purpose of Regulation 83[3(11)].

A motor car or heavy motor car may draw two trailers if one of them is a towing implement and the other is a vehicle which rests on or is suspended from the towing implement [83(1)]. A towing implement is described as a device on wheels to enable a motor vehicle to draw another vehicle with that other vehicle resting on or suspended from the device so that some but not all of the wheels on which the other vehicle runs are raised from the ground [3(2)]. A towing implement which is attached only to the vehicle drawing it is exempt from most construction requirements provided specified conditions are met [4(4)].

An agricultural motor vehicle must not draw one or more trailers if the weight ratio between the drawing vehicle and the trailer(s) is greater than 1 to 4, unless the brakes fitted to the trailer are operated directly by the service brake of the drawing vehicle [85(1)].

A motor vehicle must not tow an agricultural trailer if (a) more than 35% of its weight is borne by the drawing vehicle, or (b) it is over 14,230kg gross weight, unless fitted with brakes as mentioned in the last paragraph [85(2)].

An agricultural trailer made on or after 1 December 1985 which is drawn by a motor vehicle made on or after that date and first used on or after 1 June 1986 must have either (a) brakes fitted in accordance with Regulation 15 which can be applied progressively by a means of operation on the drawing vehicle by the driver from his normal driving position and while keeping control of that vehicle, or (b) overrun brakes [85(3)].

A trailer must not be used to carry passengers for payment, except a trailer which is, or is carrying, a broken-down vehicle drawn at not over 30mph and which, if the trailer is a bus, is attached by a rigid drawbar. A living van trailer with two wheels or four close-coupled wheels must not carry a passenger, except when tested by its maker or by a repairer, distributor or dealer [90].

When a trailer is drawn by means of a rope or chain the distance between vehicles must not exceed 4.5m and if the distance between vehicles exceeds 1.5m steps must be taken to render the rope or chain clearly visible to other road users [86(1)].

Except in the case of a trailer fitted with overrun brakes and a trailer which is a broken-down vehicle which cannot be steered, the brakes of a trailer must be capable of being applied by the driver of the drawing vehicle unless another person is in a position to apply them [19]. When a trailer is detached from the drawing vehicle and parked at least one of its wheels must be prevented from moving by setting a brake or using a chain, chock or other device [89].

The laden weight of an unbraked trailer must not exceed its maximum design weight. An unbraked trailer must not be drawn on a road if the kerbside weight of the drawing vehicle is less than double the weight of the laden trailer. But these restrictions do not apply to (a) an agricultural trailer or (b) a trailer of a kind listed in Regulation 16(3) as being exempt brakes (see page 13) [87].

Fixed penalties

If a police constable in uniform finds a person he believes is committing or has committed a fixed penalty offence on that occasion he may issue him with a fixed penalty notice [RTO Act 1988/54(1), (2)]. A notice may not be given for an offence which appears to involve obligatory licence endorsement unless (a) the person produces his driving licence, (b) the constable is satisfied the person would not be liable to disqualification (under the 12 penalty points rule) if he were convicted of the offence, and (c) the person surrenders his driving licence to the constable [54(3)].

In the case of a stationary vehicle, if a constable believes that a fixed penalty offence is being or has been committed he may attach a fixed penalty notice to the vehicle unless it appears that the offence involves obligatory licence endorsement [62(1)]. A notice attached to a vehicle must not be removed or interfered with except by or under the authority of the driver or person in charge of the vehicle or liable for the offence [62(2)].

Fixed penalty offences are listed in Schedule 3 of the Act [51(1)]. Failing to give precedence at a pedestrian crossing is also a fixed penalty offence [335/90 and 466/90]. So too is driving a vehicle while a child under 14 years is not wearing a seat belt in a rear seat [345/92].

Causing or permitting another person's offence is not to be treated as a fixed penalty offence [51(2)].

If a constable in uniform finds a person he believes is committing or has committed a fixed penalty offence which appears to involve obligatory endorsement and the person does not produce his driving licence for inspection, the constable may give him a notice that if, within 7 days, he produces his licence with the notice at a police station the person specifies, he will be given a fixed penalty notice for the offence at the police station [54(4)]. If the person produces his licence and the notice, in person, to a constable at the specified police station within the 7 days and (a) the constable is satisfied that the person would not be disqualified (under the penalty points rule) on conviction for the offence, and (b) the person surrenders his licence, the constable must give him a fixed penalty notice for the offence in question [54(5)]. This provision does not apply to offences committed in Scotland and a person given a notice under Section 54(4) cannot specify a police station in Scotland [54(8)]. References here to a licence include, where it comes into force on or after 1 June 1990, its counterpart [144/90/2].

The fixed penalty is £40 for offences involving obligatory endorsement and £20 in other cases except that, in London, it is £40 for a parking offence on a red route and £30 on any other route [53, 346/92 and 435/92].

For power of traffic wardens to issue certain fixed penalty notices see page 276.

No proceedings may be brought against a person for the fixed penalty offence until the end of 21 days following the date of the notice or a longer period, if any, specified in the notice. This is referred to in the Act as the 'suspended enforcement period' [52(3), 78].

Where a person has been handed a fixed penalty notice no proceedings may be brought against him for the offence unless, before the end of the suspended enforcement period, he requests a court hearing. If he does not request a hearing and the penalty has not been paid, a sum equal to the penalty plus one half may be registered against him as a fine [55].

Where a fixed penalty notice has been attached to a vehicle and, within the suspended enforcement period, the penalty has not been paid and the driver has not requested a hearing, a notice to owner may be served by police on the owner of the vehicle [63(2)]. The owner is the person by whom the vehicle is kept and it will be presumed that the registered keeper was the owner at the time of the offence, but it is open to both prosecution and defence to prove otherwise [68(1), (2)].

The notice to owner gives particulars of the offence and penalty, the time allowed for paying it, and, if it is not paid, a request that a statutory statement of ownership be supplied to police before the end of the same period [63(4)].

On the statement of ownership the person completing it must say whether or not he was the owner of the vehicle at the time of the offence and, if he was not, whether (a) he was never the owner, or (b) he ceased to be the owner before, or became the owner after, the offence. In the latter case he must give details of the previous or new owner if he knows them. Accompanying that form will be a statutory statement of facts on which can be given the name and address of the driver at the time of the offence. If the driver completes the form it acts as a request for a court hearing [Sch. 4].

Where a notice to owner has been served within six months of the day the ticket was fixed to the vehicle and the fixed penalty has not been paid before the end of the time allowed for replying to the notice, the fixed penalty plus half that amount may be registered against the notice recipient as a fine unless a summons for the offence has been served on the driver in the 2 months following the period allowed for responding to the notice [64(2)]. Proceedings for the offence may be brought against the person on whom the notice was served [64(3)]. But a person will not be liable if he were not the owner of the vehicle at the time and he has supplied a statutory statement of ownership to that effect [64(4)]. In proceedings it will be conclusively presumed that the person (even if not an individual) was the driver of the vehicle at the time of the offence, unless it is proved that the driver was in possession of the vehicle without the consent of the owner [64(5), (6)]. The time allowed for responding to the notice to owner is 21 days or a longer period, if any, specified on the notice [63(5)].

Court proceedings for the offence cannot be brought against the vehicle owner unless he has, within the time allowed, asked for a hearing [65(2)].

Once an increased fixed penalty has been registered against the vehicle owner as a fine no proceedings can be brought against any other person for the offence [65(4)]. If the fixed penalty is paid before the end of the suspended enforcement period proceedings may not be brought against anyone for the offence [78(2)].

Where a driving licence is surrendered, the licence may be endorsed without a court order unless a court hearing is requested in the suspended enforcement period and the fixed penalty has not been paid [57(1)(2)].

When a person surrenders his licence to a constable he must be issued with a receipt for it [56]. If the driver is subsequently required by police to produce his driving licence while it is surrendered he can produce the receipt instead and, if required, the licence when it is returned to him [Act 1988/164(7)].

In the case of hired vehicles, the hirer is made liable, instead of the vehicle owner, where (a) the notice to owner has been served on a vehicle-hire firm, (b) the vehicle was let under a hiring agreement at the time of the offence, and (c) within the period allowed for responding to the notice, the firm supplies the police with a statement that the vehicle was hired, a copy of the hiring agreement and a copy of a statement by the hirer that he would be liable for any fixed penalty notice [66]. These provisions only apply where the hire is for a fixed period of less than six months and they do not apply to hire purchase agreements [66(7)(8)].

Freight containers

Britain's responsibilities under the International Convention for Safe Containers signed at Geneva in 1972 and ratified by the United Kingdom in 1978 are implemented by the Freight Containers (Safety Convention) Regulations 1984.

A container for these purposes is defined as an article of transport equipment which is-

(a) of a permanent character and strong enough for repeated use;
(b) designed to facilitate the transport of goods by one or more modes of transport without intermediate re-loading;
(c) designed to be secured or readily handled or both, having corner fittings for these purposes; and
(d) the area enclosed by the outer bottom corners is either-
    (i) at least 7 square metres if the container has top corner fittings, or
    (ii) at least 14 square metres in any other case   [1809/84/3].

The owner or lessee of a container must not use or permit it to be used unless-
1. it has a valid approval;
2. it has a valid safety approval plate fixed to it;
3. it is properly maintained;
4. specified examination requirements are met; and
5. any gross weight marking on the container is consistent with that on the plate, except that if construction of the container commenced before 1 January 1984 this requirement does not apply until 1 January 1989 [4(1)].

Any other person using or permitting the use of a container has to ensure, as far as reasonably practicable, that 2 and 5 above are complied with [4(2)]. If there is an express term in a bailment (i.e. a contract for hire, loan or use) that the bailee is responsible for ensuring the container is maintained and examined, the bailee is, in addition to any responsibility under Regulation 4(2) specifically responsible for 3 and 4 above [4(3)].

A container approval is valid only if issued by the Health and Safety Executive, a person or body appointed by the HSE or issued by or under the authority of a government which is bound by the Convention [5(1)]. The safety approval plate has to be fitted to the container in a position where it is readily visible, adjacent to any other official plate on the container and where it is not likely to be easily damaged. The construction, size and information to be given on the plate are prescribed [1890/84/Schedule].

It is a defence to a charge of using a container without the specified type of approval to show that it has been approved by a body authorised for that purpose by the HSE before these Regulations came into operation (1 January 1985) and the approval has not been withdrawn [4(4)]. It is a defence to a charge of using or permitting use of a container which has not been properly maintained or examined to show that at the time a bailment or lease was in force and it was someone else's duty to ensure the container was maintained and examined [4(5)].

Fuel deliveries

Where a road tanker carries any liquid fuel for delivery to a buyer, the person in charge of the tanker must, before the journey begins, be provided with a document showing the quantity of each type of fuel, including the quantity of each grade of petrol, carried on the vehicle [778/85/3(2)]. He must also be provided with a delivery document for the buyer of each load on the vehicle, which gives particulars of the buyer and seller; the date of delivery; and the quantity of each type of fuel and grade of petrol to be delivered to the buyer [3(2)].

If liquid fuel is carried in a road tanker in other circumstances (e.g. not for a buyer) the person in charge of the vehicle must, before the journey begins, be provided with a document giving details of the consignor, the delivery point, the date of delivery and either a statement that Article 3 does not apply to the load or details of the quantity of any fuel carried, including each grade of petrol [4].

After delivering fuel to a buyer the person in charge of the tanker must give the delivery document to the buyer having, if necessary, amended it to show the quantity of fuel delivered. Any separate meter ticket must be attached to the document [6]. Liquid fuel does not include liquefied gas, fuel other than at ambient temperature or fuel for use by the armed forces or visiting forces. A road tanker is a vehicle or trailer which carries fuel in a tank forming part of the vehicle (other than for propelling the vehicle) and includes any tank with a capacity of over 3 cubic metres carried on a vehicle [1].

Gas propulsion and equipment

A gas propulsion system of a vehicle must not be used on a road unless the whole of the system is in a safe condition [1078/86/94(1)]. The only gas which may be used for propelling a vehicle is liquefied petroleum gas (i.e. butane, propane or a mixture of both) [94(2)]. A gas-propelled vehicle must not be used on a road unless its gas is stored in a container on the motor vehicle, and not any trailer, and in the case of an articulated vehicle it is on that part of the vehicle to which the engine is fitted [94(3)].

A gas-fired appliance must not be used in a vehicle unless the whole of the appliance and the gas system fitted to it is in an efficient and safe condition [95(1)]. A gas-fired appliance is defined as a device carried on a motor vehicle or trailer which consumes gas, other than a motor vehicle engine, a Gas Board gas-detecting device or an acetylene lamp [3]. No fuel other than liquefied petroleum gas may be used in a gas-fired appliance in a vehicle on a road [95(2)]. A gas-fired appliance must not be used unless the vehicle is ventilated to that the appliance has an ample supply of air; the use of the appliance does not adversely affect the health or comfort of persons using the vehicle; and any unburnt gas is safely disposed of to the outside of the vehicle [95(3)]. When a gas-fired appliance is not in use its gas supply has to be shut off when the vehicle is on a road [95(4)].

A gas-fired appliance in a vehicle must not be used while the vehicle is in motion on a road, except (a) an appliance fitted to engineering plant while it is being used for engineering operations; (b) an appliance permanently fitted to a bus, provided that an appliance for heating or cooling the interior does not expose a naked flame on the outside of the appliance; or (c) in any other vehicle, a refrigerator or any other appliance which does not expose a naked flame on the outside and which is permanently attached to the vehicle for heating the interior [96(3)]. Vehicles coming within the above exceptions have to comply with specified construction requirements and be fitted with a stop valve if the appliance fails to work and causes gas to be emitted [96(4)]. The requirements of Regulations 96(3) and (4) do not apply to temperature-controlled goods vehicles [96(2)].

Height notice

If the overall travelling height of a specified vehicle exceeds 3.66m there must be carried in the vehicle a notice which shows, in figures at least 40mm high, the overall travelling height. This requirement applies to:

(a) a motor vehicle constructed to lift and carry a skip;
(b) a motor vehicle which is carrying a container or is drawing a trailer carrying a container;
(c) a motor vehicle which is engineering plant, which is carrying engineering equipment or which is drawing a trailer carrying engineering equipment.

The notice must be attached to the vehicle so that it can be read by the driver when in the driving position. For these purposes a container is a piece of equipment, other than a vehicle, which has a volume of at least 8 cubic metres, is made wholly or mainly of metal and intended for repeated use in carrying goods. Overall travelling height is the distance from the ground to the highest part of the load or equipment on the vehicle or trailer plus 25mm [1078/86/10].

Insurance

A person must not use, or cause or permit another person to use, a motor vehicle on a road unless the use of the vehicle is covered by a policy of insurance or security in respect of third-party risks specified in the Act [Act 1988/143(1)]. It is a defence for an employee-driver charged with using a vehicle without insurance to prove that the vehicle did not belong to him and that he did not know or have reason to believe that the use of the vehicle was not insured[143(3)].

Third-party insurance is not compulsory in the case of vehicles owned by county and local authorities; vehicles owned or used under the direction of the police; salvage vehicles used under the Merchant Shipping Act 1894; vehicles used under the directions of the armed forces; certain vehicles made available under the National Health Service; or to vehicles owned and controlled by a person who has deposited £500,000 with the Supreme Court [144].

The policy must be issued by authorised insurers who are members of the Motor Insurers' Bureau and must insure persons specified in the policy in respect of

(a) any liability which may be incurred by him in respect of death or injury to any person, or damage to property, due to the use of the vehicle on a road,
(b) liabilities required to be covered by compulsory insurance when in other member states of the Community, and
(c) any liability for the payment of emergency treatment.
 The policy is not required to cover

   (i)   death or injury to an employee of the policyholder being carried
         in the course of his employment,
  (ii)   property damage exceeding £250,000 in one accident,
 (iii)   damage to the insured vehicle,
  (iv)   goods carried for hire or reward,
   (v)   damage to property under the control of a person, or
  (vi)   any contractual liability [145].

But the exemption in paragraph (i) is not available unless cover is
in fact provided under the Employers Liability (Compulsory
Insurance) Act 1969 [3036/92/2].

A policy of insurance is of no effect for these purposes until the
insurers deliver a certificate of insurance to the insured [147(1)]. A
certificate of insurance must be issued by the insurers not later than 4
days after the date of issue or renewal of the policy [1217/72/6]. If a
policy is cancelled the certificate must be returned to the insurers not
later than 7 days after the cancellation [Act 1988/147(4)].

Long, wide or projecting loads

A load over 4.3m wide cannot be moved under the Construction and
Use Regulations [1078/86/82(1)] but can be moved under the Special
Types Order by a vehicle which complies with the Construction and
Use Regulations or by a vehicle constructed to carry abnormal
indivisible loads (pages 338 to 345).

Apart from loose agricultural produce, a load which projects over
the side of a vehicle more than 305mm or the overall width of which
exceeds 2.9m cannot be carried unless-
(a) the load is indivisible,
(b) it is not reasonably practicable to comply with the measurements
     above,
(c) the police are given two clear days' notice of movement of the load
     and marker boards are fitted, and
(d) if the load exceeds 3.5m wide, an attendant is employed [82(2)].

The marker boards required in (c) above must be fitted within
50mm of the outermost part of a load which projects beyond a side of
a vehicle, be visible from the front and rear of the vehicle, be kept clean
and, between sunset and sunrise, be lit by indirect light [Sch. 5].

A load cannot be carried on a vehicle or vehicles if the overall length
of the vehicle(s) including the distance between them, together with
any forward or rearward projection of the load exceeds 27.4m (the
length of a load-carrying drawing unit is excluded) [82(3)].

A load cannot be carried on a vehicle or vehicles if the overall length
of the vehicle(s), including the distance between them, together with
any forward or rearward projection of the load exceeds 18.65m unless

the police are notified of movement and an attendant is employed. The length of a load-carrying drawing unit is excluded [82(4)(a)].

A load cannot be carried on a trailer or trailers drawn by a motor vehicle where the overall length of the combination of vehicles, including distances between vehicles and projections of the load, exceeds 25.9m unless police notice is given and an attendant is employed [82(4)(b)].

A trailer with an overall length over 18.65m must not be used on a road unless police have been given two days' notice of the movement of the vehicle and an attendant is employed [7(9)].

If a vehicle has a special appliance of apparatus, or carries a load, which has:

(a) a rearward projection over 1m but not over 2m, steps must be taken to make the projection visible to other road users;
(b) a rearward projection over 2m but not over 3.05m, an end marker board must be fitted to the projection and, if it is over 3m, side marker-boards must be fitted;
(c) a forward projection over 2m but not over 3.05m, an attendant must be employed and end and side marker boards fitted; or
(d) a forward or rearward projection over 3.05m, police notice must be given, end and side marker boards fitted and an attendant employed [82(7)].

An end marker board is not required on a load which projects to the rear if it carries a rear marking in accordance with the Lighting Regulations [Sch. 12(3)].

Special provisions are made for a projecting load consisting of a racing row-boat and a load carried by a straddle carrier [82(7)(8)].

If the weight of a load is borne by more than one vehicle (such as an artic) a projection is to be measured from the front of the foremost vehicle and the rear of the rearmost vehicle [81(d)(ii)]. Where a load carried on a vehicle projects over (but is not borne by) a pulling or pushing vehicle the projection, for marker-board purposes only, is to be measured from the front or rear of the pulling or pushing vehicle, as the case may be [82(9)].

None of these requirements applies to vehicles used for fire, ambulance, police or defence purposes or to a vehicle used for moving a traffic obstruction if compliance with them would hinder their use [82(10)].

An agricultural, horticultural or forestry implement rigidly, but not permanently, mounted on an agricultural motor vehicle, agricultural trailer or agricultural trailed appliance, whether or not part of its weight is on its own wheels, must not be used if (a) the overall width of the vehicle together with any projection of the implement exceeds

2.5m, or (b) the implement projects more than 1m forwards or rearwards of the vehicle except where part of the implement's weight is supported by one or more of its own wheels and most of the implement will articulate in relation to the rear part of the vehicle [82[11)].

When police notice is required in any of the foregoing circumstances it must be given to the chief officer of each police area in which the vehicle travels at least two clear days (excluding Sundays and bank holidays) before the movement takes place. The form of notice is not prescribed but it must contain the time, date and route together with details of length, width and projections, as appropriate. Unless the journey is varied by the chief police officer, and apart from delays caused by the vehicle being stopped by a constable to avoid congestion or in the interests of road safety, the vehicle must be used only in accordance with the notified particulars [1078/86/Sch. 12(1)]. The police can accept shorter notice and fewer particulars and will generally do so by telephone provided written confirmation is sent.

When an attendant is required he must be additional to the driver. His duties are to warn the driver of the vehicle and any other person of any danger likely to arise from the use of the vehicle. If three or more vehicles requiring an attendant travel in convoy it is sufficient if only the foremost and rearmost vehicles have an attendant [Sch. 12(2)].

Marker boards must conform to the shape, dimensions and colour shown in the accompanying diagram. An end marker board must not be fitted more than 500mm from the end of the projection, not more than 2.5m above ground level and must face squarely to the front or rear, as the case may be. On projections over 3m to the rear or 2m to the front a side marker board must be fitted to each side of the projection not more than 1m away from the end marker board (or reflective rear marking), not more than 2.5m above ground level and must face squarely to the side. If a forward projection exceeds 4.5m or a rearward projection exceeds 5m additional side marker boards must be fitted so that the distance between the end of the vehicle and a side marker or between side markers does not exceed 2.5m on a forward projection or 3.5m on a rearward projection. Marker boards must be lit by indirect light between sunset and sunrise [Sch. 12(3)].

The movement of abnormal indivisible loads is dealt with in the chapter on special types vehicles, pages 338 to 345.

In London the use of all roads within a 3-mile radius of Charing Cross and of many other roads beyond that area is subject to special daytime restrictions. Except under a written permit issued by the police, the following prohibitions apply to the scheduled roads between 10am and 7pm on any weekday:

No load may exceed 8ft 6in in width or 36ft in length or project more than 8ft 6in beyond the rearmost part of the vehicle (excluding

DIAGRAM OF END MARKER SURFACE

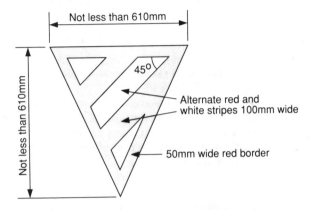

Not less than 610mm

Not less than 610mm

45°

Alternate red and
white stripes 100mm wide

50mm wide red border

DIAGRAM OF SIDE MARKER SURFACE

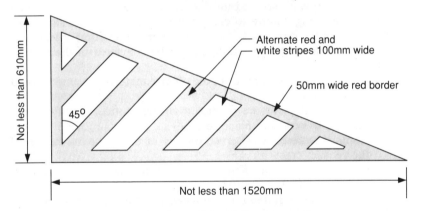

Not less than 610mm

Alternate red and
white stripes 100mm wide

50mm wide red border

45°

Not less than 1520mm

tailboard), whilst a *motor* vehicle may not carry a load longer than one
and three-quarter times its own length (excluding tailboard).

Fire-brigade vehicles are exempt from these provisions [659/58/15,
16].

Mascots

A motor vehicle first used on or after 1 October 1937, must not carry
a mascot in a position likely to strike a person with whom the vehicle
collides unless the mascot has no projections likely to cause injury
[1078/86/53(1)].

Instead of complying with this requirement a vehicle may comply with Community Directives 74/483 or 79/488 or ECE Regulation 26.01 [53(2)].

Noise

Causing noise by failing to exercise reasonable care is an offence on the part of the driver [1078/86/97].

The action of any machinery attached to or forming part of a vehicle must be stopped for the prevention of noise when a vehicle is stationary, other than in a traffic stop, for testing purposes or when machinery attached to or forming part of the vehicle has to be worked for some ancillary purpose [98].

Notice of prosecution

A person who is prosecuted for dangerous, careless or inconsiderate driving; speeding; failure to comply with specified traffic signs (see page 392) or the directions of a constable on traffic duty; or leaving a vehicle in a dangerous position; cannot be convicted of the offence unless:

(a) he was warned at the time of the offence that a prosecution would be considered, or

(b) within 14 days of the offence a written notice, specifying the offence, its time and place and indicating that a prosecution was being considered, was served on him or the registered keeper of the vehicle, or

(c) within 14 days of the offence a summons for the offence was served on him [RTO Act 1988/1].

A notice is not required for an offence if at the time or immediately thereafter an accident occurs owing to the presence of the offending vehicle [2]. But if the defendant is unaware of the accident a notice must be given as required by Section 1—*Bentley v Dickinson* (1983) LS Gaz 16 March.

The place of the offence must be sufficiently specified in the notice—*Young v Day* (1959) 123 JP 317. An oral warning which is not heard or understood by the recipient is not effective—*Gibson v Dalton* [1980] RTR 410.

A written notice is deemed to be served if sent by registered post or recorded delivery to the accused's last known address, even if it is returned or not received by him [1(2)]. In *Nicholson v Tapp* [1972] 3 All ER 245, [1972] 1 WLR 1044 it was held that the requirement had not been complied with when a notice was sent by recorded delivery on the 14th day after the offence and consequently could not be received by the accused within the stipulated 14 days. The requirement to give notice is deemed to have been complied with unless the contrary is proved [1(3)] and failure to give notice in 14 days will not prevent conviction if failure was due to the accused's or registered keeper's identity not being known or was due to the conduct of the accused [2(3)].

Parking

A person must not cause or permit a vehicle to remain at rest on a road in a position, condition or circumstances as to involve a danger of injury to any other person [Act 1988/22]. A person in charge of a vehicle must not cause or permit it to stand on a road so as to cause unnecessary obstruction [1078/86/103]. Leaving a vehicle on a road for a reasonable time, although it amounts to an obstruction, does not amount to an unnecessary obstruction—*Salomon v Durbridge* (1956) 120 JP 231. A person who, without lawful authority or excuse, wilfully obstructs the free passage along a highway commits an offence and can be arrested [Act 1980/137]. Operating a mobile snack-bar in a lay-by was held to be a wilful obstruction of the highway—*Waltham Forest Council v Mills* [1980] RTR 201. A vehicle must not be driven on common land, moorland or other land not forming part of a road unless it is done within 15yds of a road for the purpose of parking the vehicle. A vehicle must not be driven on a footpath or bridleway. It is a defence to prove that the vehicle was being used for saving life, extinguishing fire or like emergency [Act 1988/34].

Parking a heavy commercial vehicle (i.e. a goods vehicle over 7.5 tonnes permitted maximum weight) on the verge of a road, on land between carriageways or on a footway is an offence. But it is a defence to prove that the vehicle was parked on a verge or footway (a) with the permission of a uniformed policeman, (b) to save life, fight fire or other like emergency or (c) to load or unload, could not be parked elsewhere to do so and was not left unattended [Act 1988/19, 20].

It is an offence to leave on a road a vehicle unattended by a licensed driver without stopping the engine (except for fire-engines, vehicles used for police or ambulance purposes or as long as they are not in a position or condition to endanger persons or property, vehicles with engine-driven ancillary equipment) and applying the parking brake [1078/86/107].

Whenever a vehicle is stationary on a road between sunset and sunrise it must, unless otherwise permitted by a uniformed policeman, be parked with its near-side against the edge of the road. There are exceptions which cover the operation of vehicles used in connection with building or demolition, repair of any other vehicle, removal of traffic obstructions, road repair or maintenance, laying or maintenance of gas, electricity, water or telephone services. Nor does the restriction apply to the use of one-way streets, parking places, hackney carriage stands and bus stops or to vehicles in use for fire-brigade, ambulance, police or defence purposes if its application would hinder the use of such vehicles [1078/86/101].

When a trailer is detached from its drawing vehicle, at least one wheel must be prevented from revolving by setting the brake, using a chain, chock or other efficient device [89].

No person must open, or cause or permit to be opened, any door of a vehicle on a road so as to cause injury or danger to any person [105].

When a vehicle is stationary its horn must not be sounded but this restriction does not apply to police, fire-brigade or ambulance vehicles, a reversing alarm or if the horn is a theft alarm, to summon assistance on a bus or is used in a case of danger due to the presence of another vehicle [99].

No waiting or parking is allowed on any main carriageway forming part of trunk roads as indicated by 'Clearway' traffic signs without authority from a police constable in uniform [1172/63/4]. In *Hawkins v Phillips* [1980] RTR 197 a slip road was held to be a main carriageway. Exceptions are vehicles used: in connection with building or demolition; for the removal of any traffic obstruction; for roadworks; for mains and other services; for fire-brigade, ambulance or police purposes; for postal vans; for the collection by or for a local authority of refuse or cleaning cesspools; a vehicle required to stop by law or to avoid an accident; and a vehicle prevented from proceeding by circumstances outside the driver's control [5]. A vehicle must not wait on a verge or lay-by adjacent to a clearway carriageway for the purpose of selling goods from the vehicle but exemption is made for selling and delivering to premises [6].

PARKING IN LONDON

Large areas in London have been designated special parking areas under Section 76 of the Road Traffic Act 1991. In these areas, parking and loading/unloading restrictions imposed by local authorities are no longer a criminal offence and neither are the general offences of parking on a cycle track or parking a heavy goods vehicle on a verge or footway [Act 1991/76(3)].

Parking restrictions are enforced against the vehicle owner—not the driver—by a penalty charge notice being attached to the vehicle by a parking attendant. Unpaid penalties are recoverable through the county court.

If a vehicle is stationary in a designated parking place and a parking attendant has reason to believe a penalty charge is payable he can fix a penalty charge notice to the vehicle or give it to the person appearing to be in charge of the vehicle [Act 1991/66(1)]. A penalty charge is payable, by the vehicle owner, if the vehicle has been left in contravention of an order relating to the parking place, if no parking charge has been paid or the vehicle has been left beyond the time paid for [66(2)]. The penalty charge notice must contain prescribed information [66(3)].

The procedure following the issue of a penalty charge notice is set out in Schedule 6 to the Act. If the penalty is not paid within 28 days the London authority can serve a notice to owner on the person who appears to have been the vehicle owner at the time. The notice must give prescribed information including that payment must be made within 28 days of service of the notice and representations can be made within those 28 days to the authority and, subsequently, to a parking adjudicator.

The (only) grounds for representation are:

a. the recipient was never the owner of the vehicle; had ceased to be the owner before the alleged contravention (he must give the name and address of the person to whom the vehicle was disposed of); or had become the owner after that date (he must give the name and address of the person from whom he acquired it);
b. the alleged contravention did not occur;
c. the parking had been done by a person in control of the vehicle without the consent of the owner;
d. the parking order is invalid;
e. the recipient is a vehicle hire firm and the vehicle was on hire at the time and the hirer had signed a form of liability for any penalty charge notice;
f. the penalty charge exceeds the amount applicable in the case.

The authority must consider the representation and any supporting evidence and serve notice on the person as to whether they accept the ground has been established.

Where the ground is rejected the authority must, in the rejection notice, state:

1. that a charge certificate may be issued unless, within 28 days, the penalty charge is paid or an appeal is made to a parking adjudicator;
2. indicate the power of an adjudicator to award costs against the person; and
3. describe the way in which an appeal must be made.

On an appeal, the parking adjudicator must consider the representations already made and any additional grounds within a. to f. above. The appeal procedure and the adjudicator's powers are contained in the Road Traffic (Parking Adjudicators) (London) Regulations 1993.

Where a notice to owner has been served and the penalty not paid within 28 days of the notice (or a notice of rejection of representations or notice of rejection of an appeal) the authority may serve a charge certificate to the effect that the penalty is increased by 50 per cent. Where such a certificate has been served and the increased penalty has not been paid the authority may, if a county court orders, recover the increased charge as if it were payable under a county court order.

Provision is also made for the attachment of an immobilisation device by a parking attendant to a vehicle illegally parked; for representations to be made to the authority against charges incurred; and for an appeal to a parking adjudicator against an authority's rejection of representations [Act 1991/69-72].

Pedestrian crossings

The driver of a vehicle must give precedence to a pedestrian who is within the limits of an uncontrolled zebra crossing [1524/71/8].

If the area of road at either side of a zebra crossing is marked with alternating diagonal white lines in the centre and edges of the carriageway that area is a 'zebra controlled area' [71/5]. The driver of a vehicle in a zebra controlled area who is travelling towards the crossing must not overtake:

(a) the nearest to the crossing of any moving vehicles, or
(b) the nearest to the crossing of any vehicles which have stopped to allow persons to use the crossing [10].

If a broken white line is marked across the carriageway, 1m from the crossing, the driver should stop at this line while giving precedence [5(2)]. In a one-way street a zebra crossing which is divided by a street refuge is treated as two crossings and a vehicle approaching one part of the crossing can overtake a vehicle which has stopped at the other part [11].

A vehicle must not stop in a zebra controlled area except

(a) to allow persons to cross the road or because it is illegal to overtake a vehicle stopped for this purpose,
(b) when prevented from going ahead by circumstances beyond the driver's control or by accident,
(c) when engaged on specified emergency, maintenance, building or repair work,
(d) if making a left or right turn, or
(e) a stage or express carriage picking up or setting down passengers having passed over the crossing [12, 14, 15].

Except in circumstances beyond the driver's control or to avoid an accident, a vehicle must not stop on a zebra crossing [9(1)].

When a red light is shown at a Pelican pedestrian crossing the driver of a vehicle must stop at the stop line or, if one is not visible, the first post carrying the traffic light [16/87/16]. When a flashing amber light is shown a driver must give precedence to anyone already on the crossing [17].

The area at each side of a Pelican crossing is marked with alternate diagonal white lines in the centre and edge of the carriageway in the same way as a zebra pedestrian crossing. This area is known as the Pelican controlled area and a driver must not cause his vehicle or any part of it to stop in that area [12], but a vehicle may stop in the controlled area if:

(a) a red light is showing,
(b) an amber flashing light is showing and precedence is being given to pedestrians,
(c) it is illegal to overtake another vehicle giving precedence,
(d) circumstances beyond the driver's control prevent him from proceeding,
(e) it is necessary to stop to avoid an accident,
(f) it is necessary to stop for a specified emergency, maintenance, building or repair work,
(g) the vehicle is making a left or right turn, or
(h) the vehicle is a public service vehicle (not on an excursion or tour) stopping to pick up or set down passengers and has passed the crossing [13, 14].

The driver of a vehicle in a Pelican controlled area who is travelling towards the crossing must not overtake (a) the nearest to the crossing of any moving vehicles, or (b) the nearest to the crossing of a stationary vehicle stopped by the red or amber lights [19].

A vehicle must not be stopped on the Pelican crossing except in circumstances beyond the driver's control or to avoid an accident [18].

Between 8am and 5.30pm a school crossing patrol wearing an approved uniform and exhibiting a prescribed sign can require the driver of a vehicle to stop at a place where children on their way to or from school, or from one part of a school to another, are crossing or seeking to cross the road [Act 1984/28(1)]. A driver must stop before reaching the crossing place, must not impede the crossing and must not put the vehicle in motion again while the sign is exhibited [28(2)]. Unless the contrary is proved, it is presumed that a sign is a prescribed sign, that a uniform is an approved uniform and that children are going to or from school or between schools [28(5)].

Quarry vehicles

A quarry vehicle must be equipped with a horn when used in a quarry and when such a vehicle is used in a quarry during the hours of darkness there must be provided sufficient artificial light, whether on the vehicle or not, to enable the vehicle to be used safely [168/70/3]. A quarry vehicle is described as a mechanically propelled vehicle, including plant, which forms part of the equipment of the quarry, but excluding pedestrian-controlled vehicles, motor cycles and vehicles for use on rails or a ropeway [2(1)].

A quarry vehicle or trailer with a tipping body must not be used unless devices are provided for preventing the body from collapsing when raised. The device can be on the vehicle but must be independent of the tipping mechanism [4(1)]. The quarry owner or manager must take steps, including the provision of stop blocks, anchor chains or similar devices, at places where a vehicle is tipped to prevent it causing injury by running away, falling or overturning [4(2)]. A person who uses a tipping quarry vehicle must use the safety devices provided [5].

A person in charge of a quarry vehicle must not leave it unless it is so placed or secured that it cannot accidentally move or be set in motion [6]. A person who drives a quarry vehicle in a quarry without due care and attention commits an offence [7]. A person must not drive a quarry vehicle unless (a) he is authorised to do so by the owner or manager and he is 17 years of age or (b) he is similarly authorised to receive driver-training and he drives under the close supervision of an authorised competent person [9(1)]. The owner or manager must ensure that when a learner drives a quarry vehicle prominent signs to that effect are shown at the front and rear of the vehicle [9(2)]. Overhead structures or cables which could obstruct a vehicle must be signed [10].

Reversing

A vehicle must not be reversed for a greater distance or time than may be requisite for the safety or reasonable convenience of the occupants of that vehicle or of other traffic on the road [1078/86/106]. Road rollers and other vehicles engaged on roadworks are exempt.

A driver who, after checking to the rear, reverses into a parked vehicle is not ipso facto guilty of careless driving—*Hume v Ingleby* [1975] RTR 502.

Road haulage international authorisations

For laden British haulage vehicles to enter or travel through most European countries an authorisation or permit is required. A limited number of authorisations are given by the Council of Ministers of the European Conference of Ministers of Transport, and, in relation to EC countries, under EC Regulation 881/92. The Department of Transport issues the permits or authorisations to British operators. To enable the Crown to charge for this service Section 56 of the Finance Act 1973 enables the Minister for Transport to make regulations fixing fees for issuing permits and ECMT and EC authorisations.

These regulations provide that the fees payable for ECMT and EC authorisations are £40 per year or £10 per quarter. The fee for a journey permit is £2 and for a period permit it is £20 per year or £5 per quarter. If a journey permit covers more than one return journey it is charged for at the rate of £1 for each return journey. The fee for a road-rail certificate or a special permit is £2 and for a Community removals authorisation it is £5 [1831/83, 2012/87, 2058/89 and 2646/91].

COMMUNITY AUTHORISATIONS

A community authorisation is required for any international carriage of goods by road for hire or reward by a goods vehicle registered in an EC country on a journey (a) between Member States, (b) from a Member State to or from a non-member country, (c) between non-member countries but which transit a Member State and (d) by an unladen vehicle in connection with the foregoing journeys [3077/92/3 & EC Regulation 881/92/2,3]. Until the Community has agreements with non-member countries, the EC Regulation does not apply to journeys subject to a bilateral agreement between a Member State and a non-member country [EC 881/92/1].

A person is entitled to be issued with a Community authorisation if he is the holder of an international operator's licence [3077/92/5]. In Great Britain the competent authority to issue authorisations is the Traffic Commissioner who issued the operator's licence and, in Northern Ireland, it is the Department of Environment [4].

The authority must issue the holder with the original of the authorisation which must be kept by the undertaking. It must also issue a number of certified true copies corresponding to the number of vehicles at the disposal of the holder. An authorisation must be made out in the haulier's name and cannot be transferred to anyone else. A certified true copy must be carried in the vehicle and be produced to police and traffic examiners [EC 881/92/5]. An authorisation must be issued for five years [6].

An authorisation must be withdrawn if the operator is no longer established in Great Britain or Northern Ireland; is no longer entitled to hold an international operator's licence; or has supplied incorrect information to obtain the authorisation. The competent authority may temporarily or partially suspend the certified true copies of an authorisation in the event of serious infringements or repeated minor infringements of carriage regulations [EC 881/92/8].

If an authorisation is withdrawn the holder must return it and all certified true copies within 7 days to the issuing authority. The holder must also return to the authority the number of certified true copies he requires if the number of vehicles at the disposal of the holder is reduced or the authority decides to suspend certified true copies [3077/92/9].

The holder of an authorisation must supply the authority with such information as he may reasonably require to decide whether the holder is entitled to retain the authorisation [10].

Where, due to death, liquidation, etc., a person is treated as the holder of an operator's licence (see page 237), that person will also be treated as the holder of the authorisation [11].

If a person entitled to an authorisation is refused one or has it withdrawn he can appeal to the Transport Tribunal or, in Northern Ireland, the Operator and Vehicle Licensing Review Board [3077/92/6].

Exemption from a Community authorisation is provided for:
1. carriage of mail as a public service;
2. carriage of damaged or broken-down vehicles;
3. carriage of goods in motor vehicles with a permissible laden weight, including any trailer, of not over 6 tonnes, or, a permissible payload not over 3.5 tonnes;
4. carriage of goods in motor vehicles as long as:
   a. the goods are the property of the undertaking or must have been bought, sold, let out on hire or hired, produced, extracted, processed or repaired by the undertaking;
   b. the journey must be to carry the goods to or from the undertaking or to move them inside the undertaking or outside for its own requirements;
   c. they are driven by employees of the undertaking;
   d. the vehicles must be owned by the undertaking, bought on deferred terms or hired (without contravening EC Directive 647/84); and
   e. carriage must be no more than ancillary to the activities of the undertaking.
5. carriage of medicinal products, appliances, equipment and other articles required for medical care in emergency relief, particularly natural disasters [881/92].

PERMITS

The International Road Haulage Permits Act 1975 enables the Secretary of State to make regulations providing that goods vehicles registered in the United Kingdom, trailers drawn by such vehicles and unattached trailers in the UK may not be used on international haulage or own-account transport unless a prescribed document is carried on the vehicle or by the person in charge of it. The Regulations now apply only to haulage and own-account journeys to Austria, including journeys passing through any part of Austria. A number of exceptions from the Regulations are provided and these follow the exemptions given in the bilateral transport agreements between Great Britain and Austria and in certain EC Directives [2234/75/4 & 3077/92].

If it appears to a traffic examiner that a prescribed document should be carried on a vehicle he may:

(a) require the driver to produce it and permit him to inspect and copy it;
(b) detain the vehicle for the above purpose;
(c) at any reasonable time, enter premises where he believes a vehicle to which the regulations applies is kept; and
(d) at any reasonable time, enter premises where he believes a prescribed document is to be found and inspect and copy any such document he finds there.[Act 1975/1(2)]

A driver who wilfully obstructs an examiner, or without reasonable excuse, fails to produce the required documents commits an offence [1(4)] as does any other person who wilfully obstructs an examiner acting under Section 1(2)(d) [1(5)].

If it appears to an examiner that the driver of a vehicle on an international journey has, without reasonable excuse, refused or failed to comply with a requirement under Section 1(2) he may prohibit the removal of the vehicle out of the United Kingdom [2(1)]. Written notice of the prohibition must be given to the driver specifying the reason for the prohibition, whether it applies absolutely or for a specified purpose and whether it is for a specified period or is indefinite. The prohibition has immediate effect [2(2)]. The prohibition may be removed by written notice when an examiner is satisfied that the vehicle is not being used on a journey to which the regulations apply or a prescribed document is carried on the vehicle [2(3)]. As soon as reasonably practicable after a notice has been given under Section 2(2) or (3) the examiner who gave it must take steps to inform the vehicle operator of its contents [2(4)]. A person who, without reasonable excuse, takes a vehicle out of the UK in contravention of a prohibition, or causes or permits such removal, commits an offence [2(6)].

The 'user of a vehicle' has the same meaning as in operators' licensing law [1(8)]. There is a rebuttable presumption that a vehicle which displays a licence or trade plates issued under the Vehicles (Excise) Act or corresponding Northern Ireland provisions is registered in the United Kingdom [1(6)].

An international road haulage permit is a document which it is an offence, with intent to deceive, to forge, alter, use, lend or allow to be used by another person. It is also an offence to knowingly make a false statement to obtain a permit. If a police officer or examiner has reason to believe an offence has been committed in relation to a permit he has power to seize the document [Act 1988/173, 174, 176].

The Goods Vehicles (International Road Haulage Permits) Regulations 1975 have applied the above rules to goods vehicles registered in the United Kingdom, trailers drawn by such vehicles and unattached trailers for the time being in the United Kingdom. Such a vehicle may not be used on a journey to which the Regulations apply unless an international road haulage permit issued by the Secretary of State for that journey and vehicle is carried on the vehicle or, in the case of a trailer, on the drawing vehicle or by the person in charge of it.

Sand, ballast and ready-mix vehicles

Before a road vehicle laden with ballast commences a journey the person in charge of it must be given a conveyance note containing prescribed particulars [Act 1985/Sch. 4(7)]. It must be produced to a weights and measures inspector if required [39]. The conveyance note must be handed to the buyer before the vehicle is unloaded or, if he is absent, left for him [Sch. 4(9)]. A vehicle carrying ready-mixed concrete mortar or concrete must also have with it a conveyance note when laden [Sch. 6(6)]. 'Ballast' includes sand, gravel, shingle, ashes, clinker, chippings (including coated materials), hardcore, aggregates and other materials known as ballast [Sch. 4(1)].

If the body of a vehicle is used as a cubic measure of ballast it must conform to specified calibration and marking requirements [Sch. 4(4)]. The body must not (a) have a false bottom, (b) have internal surfaces or projections which impede its discharge or (c) be constructed in a manner which facilitates fraud [1962/78/6(1)]. It must have four sides and a base and the angles between the base and sides and between adjoining sides must be 90 degrees, except if a body has one pair of sides longer than the others it may taper in width by up to 10 per cent and have its longer sides connected to the base by bevelled or curved sections (and the corners of the other sides reduced accordingly) provided the width of the base is not less than three-quarters of the width at the top [6(2) and 765/88]. The body has to be assembled in a permanent manner so that its form or volume cannot be changed in the course of trade, but sides may be hinged to swing outwards to facilitate discharge [6(3)].

The body must have a pair of metal calibration strips, one firmly attached in a vertical position on the inside of two opposing sides and near to the centre of the side. A strip must be attached by bolts or rivets and have a slot cut in the front to retain the head of a tee-bolt. The form the strip must take and the way it has to be sealed on to the body are prescribed [8].

A body with a maximum purported content of less than 4 cubic metres must have its calibration strips marked, in a specified way, to indicate quantities in every stage of 0.2 cubic metres up to its maximum content. If the content is 4 cubic metres or over the strip must be marked in multiples of 1 cubic metre with quantities of less than 1 cubic metre being marked in multiples of 0.2 cubic metres [7].

When a vehicle body is used as a measure its maximum content must be marked on its near-side [10]. When measuring ballast against a calibration mark the vehicle body must be filled in all parts and levelled off. If a person carrying out a measurement fails to level off the ballast when it is loaded or causes or permits a heaped load to be sent out he commits an offence [Sch. 4(5)]. These calibration and measuring requirements also apply to the body of a vehicle used as a measure for agricultural lime or salt, or inorganic fertilisers [Sch. 6(10)].

Seat belts—compulsory use

The Motor Vehicles (Wearing of Seat Belts) Regulations require every person of 14 years or more to wear an adult seat belt when he is (a) driving or riding in the front seat of a motor vehicle (other than a two-wheeled motor cycle with or without a sidecar), or (b) riding in the rear seat of a motor car or a passenger car [176/93/5].

A passenger car is a passenger vehicle with not more than eight seats in addition to the driver's seat and a maximum laden weight not over 3.5 tonnes [Act 1988/15 & 3105/92]. A rear seat is one which is not the driver's seat, a seat alongside the driver or a specified passenger seat [176/93/2(2)].

An adult belt is (1) a three-point belt or lap belt marked with a specified BSI or designated approval mark in accordance with the Construction and Use Regulations; (2) a seat belt or harness belt bearing a specified BSI number; or (3) a seat belt fitted in a relevant vehicle and is of a type approved in another EC Member State for use by persons over 13 years or of 150cm or more tall and corresponding legislation in that State would be met if the belt was worn by such a person [176/93/2(4)]. A relevant vehicle is a passenger car, a light goods vehicle or a small bus (all these vehicles are defined as not exceeding a maximum laden weight of 3.5 tonnes) [3].

A seat is regarded as provided with an adult seat belt if it is fixed in such a position that it can be worn by an occupier of that seat [2(6)] but a seat is not regarded as provided with an adult seat belt if the belt (a) has an inertia reel mechanism which is locked due to the vehicle being, or having been on a steep incline or (b) it does not comply with specified maintenance requirements (see page 186) [2(7)].

A seat belt does not have to be worn by a person who is:

(a) the holder of a medical certificate signed by a medical practitioner to the effect it is inadvisable on medical grounds to wear a seat belt or is a certificate to such effect issued by an authority under corresponding legislation in another Member State. (This exemption only applies if the certificate is produced to police at the time; at a police station within 7 days or as soon as reasonably practicable; or, if not produced, it was not reasonably practicable for it to be produced before proceedings were commenced—Act 1988/14);

(b) using a vehicle constructed or adapted for the delivery of goods or mail to consumers or addressees while engaged in making local rounds of deliveries or collections;

(c) driving while performing a manoeuvre which includes reversing;

(d) a qualified driver who is supervising a provisional licence holder who is making a manoeuvre which includes reversing;

(e) conducting a driving test and wearing a seat belt would endanger him or any other person;

(f) driving or riding in a vehicle while used for fire brigade or police purposes or for carrying a person in lawful custody;

(g) the driver of a licensed taxi while seeking hire, answering a hire call or carrying a passenger for hire or a private hire vehicle while carrying a passenger for hire;

(h) riding in a vehicle used under a trade licence for the purpose of investigating or remedying a mechanical fault in the vehicle;

(j) a disabled person who is wearing a disabled person's belt;

(k) a person riding in a vehicle in a procession organised by or on behalf of the Crown;

(l) a person riding in a vehicle taking part in a procession to mark or commemorate an event if it is one commonly or customarily held in that police area or notice of the procession has been given under the Public Order Act;

(m) a person driving the vehicle if the driver's seat is not provided with an adult seat belt; a person riding the front of a vehicle if no adult belt is available for him in the front of the vehicle; or a person riding in the rear of a vehicle if no adult belt is available for him in the rear of the vehicle.

[176/93/6].

Seat belts—compulsory use—children

A person must not, without reasonable excuse, drive a motor vehicle (other than a two-wheeled motor vehicle with or without a sidecar) on a road if a child under the age of 14 years is in the front of the vehicle not wearing a seat belt which complies with regulations [Act 1988/15(1) and 31/93/6].

The front of a vehicle is that part which is forward of a transverse plane passing through the rear of the driver's seat. No part of the upper deck of a vehicle will be regarded as being in the front of the vehicle [31/93/4].

The seat belt to be worn by a small child (i.e. not over 12 years and not over 150cm tall) in the front of a passenger car, light goods vehicle or small bus (none of which are over 3.5 tonnes maximum laden weight) must be:

(1) a child restraint marked with a BSI or designated approval mark which indicates it is suitable for his weight and either indicates it is suitable for his height or contains no height marking or

(2) a child restraint which would meet the law of another Member State if worn by that child in that State [5(1)(a),(2)]

If a small child is in the front of any other vehicle the child restraint must comply with (1) above [5(1)(b),(2)].

The seat belt to be worn by a large child (i.e. one who is not a small child but is under 14 years) must be a child restraint complying with (1) above or be an adult seat belt [5(1)(c),(2)].

Exempt from the requirement is—

(a) a small child aged 3 years or more if a child restraint for his height and weight is not available for him in the front or rear of the vehicle and he is wearing an adult belt;

(b) a child for whom there is a medical certificate. (The same rules regarding the issue and production of the certificate given in the preceding section on adult seat belts apply);

(c) a child under 1 year in a carry-cot if the cot is restrained by straps;

(d) a disabled child who is wearing a disabled person's seat belt;

(e) a child riding in a motor car first used before 1965 if the vehicle has no rear seat and, apart from the driver's seat, no seat in the vehicle has a seat belt appropriate for that child;

(f) a child under 14 years riding in a vehicle being used to provide a local bus service;

(g) a large child if an appropriate seat belt is not available to him in the front of the vehicle. The circumstances in which a seat belt is or is not available are specified [31/93/7 & Sch.2].

A person must not, without reasonable excuse, drive on a road a motor vehicle which has a seat belt fitted in the rear if there is also in the rear of the vehicle a child under the age of 14 years who is not wearing a seat belt which complies with regulations [Act 1988/15(3)].

A person must not, without reasonable excuse, drive on a road a passenger car if a child under 12 and less than 150cm tall is in the rear of the vehicle, no seat belt is fitted in the rear and a front seat is provided with a seat belt but is not occupied by anyone [Act 1988/15(3A)].

The preceding two paragraphs do not apply to—

(a) vehicles which are neither motor cars nor passenger cars;
(b) licensed taxis and licensed hire cars in which the rear seats are separated from the driver by a fixed partition;
(c) a small child aged 3 years or more if a prescribed child restraint for his height and weight is not available for him in the front or rear of the vehicle and he is wearing an adult belt;
(d) a child for whom there is a medical certificate. (The same rules regarding the issue and production of the certificate given in the preceding section on adult seat belts apply);
(e) a child under 1 year in a carry-cot as long as the carry-cot is retrained by straps;
(f) a disabled child who is wearing a disabled person's seat belt [176/93/9,10].

Securing crane gear

When a mobile crane is travelling on a road, any crane hook or similar 'implement' which is suspended from a crane or jib must be secured either to the main appliance or to some part of the vehicle so that it does not cause danger to any person on the vehicle or on a road [1078/86/108].

Skips

A builder's skip must not be deposited on a highway without permission of the highway authority [Act 1980/139(1)]. Where a skip had been deposited on a highway with permission but remained on the highway after the permitted period it was held in *Craddock v Green* [1983] RTR 479, to have been deposited without permission during the excess period. In giving permission the highway authority can impose conditions as to the siting of the skip, its dimensions, marking to make it easily visible, care and disposal of its contents, its lighting and guarding and its removal [139(2)]. In any case where permission is given the owner must ensure that the skip is properly lit at night; it is marked with owner's name and telephone number or address; it is removed when filled; and the authority's conditions are complied with [139(4)]. Where an offence is due to the fault of a person other than the owner that other person may be prosecuted even if the owner is not [139(5)]. It is a defence for a person charged under this section to prove that the offence was due to the fault of another and he could not prevent it [139(6)], but notice of the identity of the person responsible must be given to the prosecution 7 days before the hearing [139(7)]. A defence is provided for a person charged, under any other legislation, of failing to light a skip at night [139(8)]. If a person is charged with obstructing the highway with a skip it is a defence for him to prove that it was deposited in accordance with a permission [139(9)].

A builder's skip is described as a container to be carried on a vehicle and placed on roads for the storage of builders' materials, or the removal and disposal of builders' rubble, waste, household and other rubbish or earth. A person who hires a skip for more than one month is regarded as an 'owner' [139(11)].

Even though a skip may be deposited with permission, a highway authority or constable in uniform can require the owner to remove or reposition it or do so themselves [140(2), (4)]. A requirement by police must not be by telephone but by a policeman in uniform going to the offender—*R v Worthing Justices, ex parte Waste Management Ltd* [1989] RTR 131.

Similar provisions are in force in Scotland [Act 1984/85, 86].

Where any part of a builder's skip is on a highway (except a verge or footpath) each end of it must be marked with reflective markers of a specified design (shown in the accompanying diagram) [1933/84/3]. If a skip is placed sideways on the highway, the sides have to be treated as the ends [2(2)].

The markings must consist of two plates of equal size, the same shape and comply with British Standard AU 152:1970. The two plates have to be fitted to the end of the skip so that-

(a) each plate is as near to the skip's outer edge as its construction allows but the plate must not project beyond the edge;
(b) the inner edge of each plate is parallel to and the same distance from a vertical plane through the centre line of the skip;
(c) the upper edge of each plate is parallel to and the same distance from the upper edge of the end of the skip;
(d) no plate is attached to a lid or door unless a door is the only possible or convenient place it can be fixed;
(e) the upper edge of each plate is not more than 1.5m above the

ground not lower than the upper edge of the skip except that it may be lower where necessary due to the skip's construction [Sch. 2].

Markings must be kept clean and efficient and clearly visible for a reasonable distance to persons using the highway on which it is placed [4(1)]. The latter requirement does not apply to a marking on a skip door which is open for loading or unloading [4(2)].

The defences given in Section 139(5) to (7) of the Highways Act 1980 (mentioned above) are also available to persons charged with not complying with these requirements.

Identical requirements are in force in Scotland [642/86].

BUILDER'S SKIP MARKING

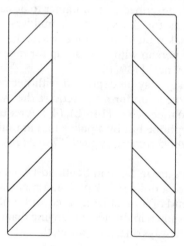

The shaded area must be of red fluorescent material and the un-shaded area of reflex reflecting material.

The width of each half of the marking shall be not less than 140mm nor more than 280mm.

The length of each half of the marking shall not be less than 350mm nor more than 700mm.

The angle of each stripe shall not be less than 40 degrees to the vertical nor more than 50 degrees to the vertical.

Each half of the marking shall have a minimum area of 980 square centimetres.

The breadth of each stripe shall not be less than 133mm nor more than 147mm [1933/84/Sch.1]

Sounding of horn

An audible warning instrument must not be sounded when a vehicle is stationary on a road, other than when danger arises due to another moving vehicle and it must not be sounded on a moving vehicle on a restricted road between 11.30 pm and 7 am [1078/86/99(1)]. But a reversing alarm may be sounded on a stationary vehicle which is about to move backwards and its engine is running [99(2)]. A reversing alarm must not be used on a vehicle other than a goods vehicle with a maximum gross weight of at least 2 tonnes; a bus; a refuse vehicle; engineering plant; or a works truck, and it must not be likely to be confused with the operating sound of a pedestrian crossing [99(3)]. No person may sound a gong, bell, siren or two-tone horn fitted to or carried on a vehicle [99(4)]. Regulations 99(1) and (4) do not apply to vehicles of specified emergency services if it is necessary or desirable to indicate the urgency of the vehicle's use or to warn other road users of its presence or where the instrument is sounded as an anti-theft device or to summon help on a bus [99(5)].

An instrument, other than a two-tone horn, may be used on a vehicle to inform the public that it is carrying goods for sale, provided it is used only for that purpose and, when on a restricted road, it is not sounded between 7 pm and 12 noon the following day [99(6)].

Speed plate

Low platform trailers and restricted speed vehicles which are voluntarily restricted to a speed lower than the legal maximum can benefit from concessions in the regulations dealing with tyre loads and speeds—see page 45.

But a vehicle displaying the double 'L' plate, prescribed for a low platform trailer, or anything resembling such a plate, must not be used at a speed exceeding 40mph.

And a vehicle displaying a '50' plate, prescribed for a restricted speed vehicle, or anything resembling it, must not be used at a speed exceeding 50mph [1078/86/100A].

Television sets

A person may not drive a motor vehicle on a road if he is in a position to see, whether directly or by reflection, a television or other cinematographic apparatus used to display anything other than information about the state of the vehicle, the location of the vehicle and the road it is on, the road adjacent to the vehicle, or to assist the driver to reach his destination. A television is a cathode ray tube which can display an image from a television broadcast, recording, camera or computer [1078/86/109].

Traffic signs and signals

A person driving a motor vehicle on a road must stop when required to do so by a constable in uniform [Act 1988/163]. Drivers must obey the directions of a constable engaged in the regulation of traffic [35] and a traffic warden in uniform so engaged [Act 1984/95(5) and 1958/70]. A policeman can stop or direct traffic for the purpose of a traffic survey but a traffic survey direction must not be used to cause unreasonable delay to a person unwilling to provide survey information [35(2), (3)].

Between 8am and 5.30pm when children are on their way to or from school and are crossing or seeking to cross the road, the driver of a vehicle must stop when a uniformed school crossing patrol exhibits the prescribed sign [Act 1984/28].

Drivers must comply with the red stop signal at traffic lights and signs indicating stop, give way, keep left, no entry, no 'U' turn, a bridge weight-limit, a mini-roundabout, a bus and cycle only route, a yellow box-junction and, where the sign is bordered by a red circle, a height limit. Where there is a green filter arrow at traffic lights a driver must not use that filter to go in a direction other than that indicated by the arrow. Drivers of large vehicles over 55ft long, 9ft 6in wide or 38 tonnes (or 32.5 tonnes where signed) must stop and telephone for permission before driving on to an automatic half-barrier level crossing [Act 1988/36 and 1519/94].

Where a road is marked along the centre with a continuous white line alongside a continuous or broken white line a vehicle must not stop (at either side of the lines) except to enable a person to get on or off the vehicle; to enable goods to be loaded or unloaded; to enable the vehicle to be used in connection with building or demolition, maintenance or repair work; vehicles used for fire, police or ambulance purposes; a vehicle required by law to stop, or to avoid an accident or in circumstances beyond the driver's control; if done with the permission of a uniformed constable; if stopping in a lay-by; or on a road with more than one traffic lane in each direction. When a continuous line is to the left of a broken or continuous line a vehicle must be driven so that the continuous line is on the right-hand side of the vehicle, except that a vehicle may cross or straddle the white line to gain access to a road or premises adjacent to the road; if it is necessary to do so to pass a stationary vehicle; owing to circumstances beyond the driver's control, to avoid an accident; to comply with the directions of a uniformed constable; or to pass a pedal cycle, horse or certain road maintenance vehicles, in each case not moving at a speed over 10mph [Act 1988/36 and 1519/94/26]. A warning arrow must be marked on the road surface before each section of continuous white line for the sign to be lawful—*O'Halloran v DPP* [1990] RTR 62.

The signs mentioned in the last two paragraphs are those to which the notice of intended prosecution requirement applies—see page 374.

In a traffic lights' prosecution evidence of a fact may be given by the production of a record produced by a prescribed device and a certificate as to the circumstances in which the record was produced [Act 1988/20]. A record produced or measurement taken by a prescribed device is not admissible unless the device is of a type approved by the Secretary of State and conditions relating to the approval are satisfied [20(4)]. A document is not admissible in evidence under these provisions unless, at least seven days before the hearing or trial, the defendant has been served with a copy of the document; and nothing in the document other than matters shown on a record produced by the prescribed device is admissible if the defendant serves a notice, not less than three days before the hearing or trial, on the prosecutor requiring the attendance of the person who signed the document [20(8)]. A device prescribed by the Secretary of State is one for recording by photographic or other image recording means the position of motor vehicles in relation to light signals [2843/92].

View to the front

No driver must be in such a position, when driving, that he cannot have proper control of his vehicle and cannot retain a full view of the road and traffic ahead [1078/86/104].

In *Simpson v Vant* [1986] RTR 247 a driver who had a sheepdog on his lap was held not to be in a position to have proper control of the vehicle and, since the dog could be regarded as a badly distributed load causing danger, licence endorsement was obligatory.

Weighbridges

Non-automatic weighing machines used for trade must be tested, approved and stamped by a weights and measures inspector [Act 1985/11 and 876/88/3].

A non-automatic weighing machine is one which requires an operator during the weighing process, especially to put loads on or take loads off the load receptor and to determine the results of the weighing process [876/88/2].

Non-automatic weighing machines used only as vehicle check-weighing machines and which bear a conspicuous notice to that effect are exempt these requirements [3(2)]. A vehicle check-weighing machine is one made available for use for trade only for checking compliance with vehicle and axle weight limits [2(1)].

Weighing equipment made available for public use, whether on payment or not, is treated as in use for trade [Act 1985/7(4)].

A person must not use for trade any non-automatic weighing machine for multiple weighing [876/88/4(7)]. Multiple weighing means determining the weight of a load by adding the results of more than one static weighing during which the load is only partially supported by the load receptor (e.g. weighbridge) [2(1)].

A non-automatic weighing machine must be erected so that during weighing, the load being weighed is stationary relative to the load receptor and supported only by the load receptor [26] and erected so that the operator can, from a single position, (a) see directly or with the aid of mirrors or closed-circuit television, the whole of the unladen load receptor, (b) operate the machine's controls and (c) obtain a weight reading [27].

An attendant at a public weighbridge, where a charge is made for weighing, must hold a certificate from a chief inspector of weights and measures that he has sufficient knowledge for the proper performance of his duties [Act 1985/18].

A public weighbridge attendant commits an offence if:

(a) without reasonable cause, he fails to carry out a weighing on demand;

(b) he carries out the weighing unfairly;

(c) he fails to provide a written statement of the weight;

(d) he fails to make a record of the time and date of the weighing and particulars of the vehicle and load sufficient to identify it;

(e) he delivers a false statement of weight; or

(f) he, or any person, commits a fraud in connection with any purported weighing [Act 1985/20].

Weighing for ro-ro ferries

Goods vehicles over 7.5 tonnes permitted weight have to be weighed before being loaded onto a ro-ro ferry, whether UK- or foreign-registered, carrying more than 12 passengers, leaving a UK port [1275/88/2, 270/89 and 568/89].

Weighing must take place in the port but in specified cases pre-determined weights and weights obtained outside the port are allowed.

Unless four conditions are met a 'qualifying cargo item' must not be loaded onto a ship

(a) sailing from a UK port to a non-UK port (including the Isle of Man and Channel Islands),
(b) sailing from a port in Britain to one in Northern Ireland, or
(c) sailing on specified routes serving the Scottish islands,

The conditions are:

(1) that the vehicle has been weighed in accordance with the Regulations;
(2) there are Ministry-approved arrangements at the port to prevent fraud by changing the load after weighing;
(3) a certificate of weight is supplied if the weighing takes place outside the port; and
(4) there are arrangements for retaining records of the weights at the port or on the ship [2(1)].

'Qualifying cargo items' are defined to include a goods vehicle, together with any trailer, with an actual or permitted weight over 7.5 tonnes and any other unit of cargo, except a bus, which exceeds 7.5 tonnes [1(3)].

Standards are prescribed for the weighing machine and it may be used only in accordance with any conditions specified by weights and measures and a person operating the machine (except a self-weigher) must have a certificate of competence [3(1)–(3)].

A self-weigher must incorporate, or be used under, approved arrangements to ensure that the identity of the item weighed is not falsified and instructions must be displayed near the machine on how it is to be used [3(4)]. A weighing machine outside a port used for these purposes must be certified for trade use [3(5)].

A vehicle or load must generally be weighed alone. But a trailer can be weighed with its drawing vehicle and a single load can be weighed with the carrying vehicle with, in either case, the weight of the drawing vehicle or carrying vehicle being subtracted from the total weight [4(1), (3)].

In such a case, the vehicle weight to be subtracted is

(a) that obtained by weighing in the port after the trailer or load has been removed;
(b) in the case of a motor vehicle drawing a trailer or carrying a single cargo item, either the weight obtained under (a) at the same port on a previous occasion or the 'mean operating weight' on a

certificate kept with the vehicle or retained, in original or copy, by the weighing manager;

(c) in the case of a trailer carrying a singly cargo item, either the weight obtained under (a) at the same port on a previous occasion or the unladen weight on a certificate presented at the time of weighing the cargo item or retained, in original or copy, by the weighing manager;

(d) in the case of a trailer carrying a single cargo item and drawn by a motor vehicle, the weights of the motor vehicle and trailer found under (b) and (c) above; or

(e) determined by a Ministry-approved method [4(4)].

The weight of an unladen vehicle may be taken as

(1) the weight obtained by weighing the same vehicle unladen at the same port on a previous occasion;

(2) in the case of a motor vehicle, or motor vehicle and trailer, the 'mean operating weight' on a certificate kept with the vehicle or retained, in original or copy, with the weighing manager;

(3) in the case of a trailer, the unladen weight on a certificate presented before loading or retained, in original or copy, by the weighing manager;

(4) in the case of a motor vehicle and trailer, the sum of the weights under (2) and (3); and

(5) that determined by a Ministry-approved method [4(5)].

The weight of a motor vehicle drawing a trailer, whether laden or not, may be taken, if the trailer has been weighed in the port with a different motor vehicle, as the sum of the combined weight of the outfit less the mean operating weight of the motor vehicle drawing the trailer onto the ship and which remains with it, and certificates of the mean operating weight of both motor vehicles are kept on the vehicles or retained by the weighing manager [4(6) and 270/89].

'Mean operating weight' is the overall weight of the unladen vehicle but including any loose tools and equipment, half of its maximum fuel capacity and a reasonable allowance for the driver [4(7) and 270/89].

A certificate of mean operating weight can be obtained by weighing (a) inside the port or (b) outside the port if the weighman is certified to operate a public weighbridge [4(8) and 270/89].

Subject to specified exceptions, the weighing of any qualifying cargo item must be made within the port of loading. The specified exceptions are vehicles or cargo items which have been customs' sealed; vehicles lawfully used over 38 tonnes, over 18m long or over 2.6m wide; and loads incapable of being weighed at the port due to their dimensions, weight or other physical characteristics [5(1)–(3)].

When a port weighbridge is unserviceable the DTp can approve the use of outside weighbridges or declared weights [5(4)].

Most offences against the regulations are committed by the ship owner, master or weighing manager of the weighing machine. But drivers can commit an offence if they fail to comply with the instructions on a self-weigh machine, supply false information or materially change the composition of a cargo item after weighing in the port without first arranging for it to be re-weighed [7(5), (7)].

It is a defence to a charge for a person to prove that he took all reasonable precautions and exercised all due diligence to avoid commission of the offence [9].

Weight markings

If a goods vehicle is fitted with a Ministry plate the vehicle must not be marked with any other weights except other plated weights, other weights required or authorised under the Construction and Use Regulations or weights authorised in other Regulations made for this purpose [Act 1988/64].

Any weight given on a vehicle's Ministry plate which must not be exceeded may be marked on either or both sides of the vehicle. The maximum permitted laden weight of a motor vehicle under the Construction and Use Regulations may be marked on either or both sides of the vehicle if it is less than the Ministry plated gross weight. The gross train weight permitted under the Construction and Use Regulations for a drawbar combination or articulated vehicle may be marked on either or both sides of the vehicle [1078/86/72].

The weights at which a vehicle manufacturer considers a vehicle can be used at a speed authorised under the Motor Vehicles (Authorisation of Special Types) General Order can be marked on a plate securely fixed in a conspicuous position on the vehicle [910/83].

Apart from agricultural vehicles, the unladen weight must be conspicuously marked on the outside of the nearside of a locomotive, a motor tractor and a registered bus [1078/86/71].

An unbraked trailer, other than one exempt brakes under Regulation 16(3), must have its maximum design gross weight conspicuously marked on the outside of the nearside of the vehicle [71]. For restrictions on the use of unbraked trailers see page 363.

Wheel clamps

Where a policeman finds a vehicle on a road parked in contravention of any prohibition or restriction under any enactment he may (a) fix an immobilisation device to the vehicle, or (b) move it to another place on the same or a different road and fix an immobilisation device to it [Act 1984/104(1)]. When taking such action a notice must be fixed to the vehicle indicating that the device has been fitted and specifying the steps to be taken to secure its release [104(2)]. A vehicle which has been fitted with a device may only be released by or under the direction of a policeman [104(3)] and must be released when the prescribed charge has been paid [104(4)].

The unauthorised removal of a notice or immobilisation device is an offence [104(5), (6)]. Though fitted with such a device a vehicle can still be removed under statutory powers [104(7)].

An immobilisation device is any device or apparatus, approved by the Secretary of State, designed or adapted to be fixed to a vehicle to prevent it being driven or put in motion [104(9)].

The above provisions do not apply to a vehicle which displays a current disabled person's badge and the vehicle is being properly used of to a vehicle at a parking meter bay as long as that use is not unauthorised [105].

The use of wheel clamps is authorised in the London Boroughs of Camden, Kensington and Chelsea, Hammersmith and Fulham, Westminster and in the City of London [1225/86 and 1746/89] and by parking attendants in special parking areas in London [Act 1991/69]—see pages 376 to 378

The charge for releasing a vehicle from a wheel clamp is £38 [386/92].

In *Lloyd v DPP* [1992] RTR 215 it was ruled that a motorist who cut off a wheel clamp attached to his car on private ground was properly convicted of criminal damage.

21 Vehicle excise licensing

Vehicle and Driving Licences Act 1969
Vehicle Excise and Registration Act 1994
Finance Acts 1982, 1983, 1984, 1985, 1987, 1988, 1989, 1991 and 1992
Visiting Forces and International Headquarters (Application of Law) Order,
   No. 1536/65
Motor Vehicles (Production of Test Certificate) Regulations, **No. 418/69**
Goods Vehicles (Production of Test Certificates) Regulations, **No. 560/70**
Road Vehicles (Registration and Licensing) Regulations, **No. 450/71**
Road Vehicles (Registration and Licensing) (Amendment) Regulations,
   No. 1865/72, 1089/75, 230/77, 1802/82, 814/84, 607/86 and **1364/94**
Motor Vehicles (Third Party Risks) Regulations, **No. 1217/72**
Motor Vehicles (International Circulation) Order, **No. 1208/75**
Road Vehicles (Registration and Licensing) (Amendment) (No. 2)
   Regulations, **No. 1177/86** and **1911/94**
Road Vehicles (Registration and Licensing) (Amendment) (No. 3)
   Regulations, **No. 2101/86**
Vehicle Licences (Duration of First Licences and Rate of Duty) Order,
   No. 1428/86
Recovery Vehicles (Number of Vehicles Recovered) Order, **No. 1226/89**
Recovery Vehicles (Prescribed Purposes) Regulations, **No. 1376/89**

Any person who uses or keeps on a public road any mechanically propelled vehicle (apart from one of an exempted class) for which an excise licence is not in force commits an offence [Act 1994/29(1)]. A person 'keeps' a vehicle on a road if he causes it to be on a road for a period, however short, when it is not in use there [62(2)]. An employer was held liable for using an unlicensed vehicle though he had not authorised his employee to use it on a road—*Richardson v Baker* [1976] RTR 56.

A public road is a road which is repairable at the public expense [62(1)]. High Court decisions on 'mechanically-propelled vehicle' are given on page 2.

The Vehicle Excise and Registration Act 1994 applies in Northern Ireland subject to modifications in various parts [Act 1994/67].

Exemptions

a. an electrically-propelled vehicle. A vehicle is not to be treated as electrically-propelled unless the electrical motive power is derived from an external source or from a storage battery which is not connected to any source of power when the vehicle is in motion;
b. a vehicle used on tram lines;
c. a vehicle not constructed or adapted for use, or used, for the carriage of a driver or passenger;
d. a fire engine. A vehicle constructed or adapted for fire fighting, salvage or both and used solely for the purposes of a fire brigade;
e. a vehicle kept by a fire authority when used or kept on a road for fire brigade service;
f. an ambulance. A vehicle constructed or adapted for, and used for no purpose other than, the carriage of sick, injured or disabled people to or from welfare centres or places where medical or dental treatment is given and which is marked 'ambulance' on both sides;
g. a vehicle kept or used by a health service body or a national health service trust;
h. a vehicle made available by the Secretary of State under the National Health Service Act and which is used on the terms on which it is made available;
i. a veterinary ambulance. A vehicle used for no purpose other than the carriage of sick or injured animals to or from places where veterinary treatment is to be given and which is marked 'veterinary ambulance on both sides;
j. a mine rescue vehicle;
k. a vehicle used solely for hauling a lifeboat and the conveyance of the necessary gear of the lifeboat being hauled;
l. a road construction vehicle used for conveying built-in road construction machinery, with or without materials used with that machinery;
m. a road roller;
n. a vehicle being used for clearing snow from public roads by means of a snow plough or similar device (whether or not forming part of the vehicle) or while going to or from the place it is to be used or while being kept for such use;
o. a vehicle made and used solely for conveying machinery for spreading materials on roads to deal with frost, ice or snow (with or without articles or materials for use with it);
p. a vehicle used solely within the area of a local authority by, or by persons under a contract with, the authority, for cleansing or watering roads or cleaning gullies;
q. a tower wagon used solely by, or by a person under a contract with,

a street lighting authority, for installing or maintaining materials or apparatus for lighting streets, roads or public places.

In *Anderson and Heeley Ltd v Paterson* [1975] 1 All ER 523 a platform truck fitted with a Hiab loader and used for carrying and installing street lighting columns was held not to be a tower wagon;

r. a vehicle not over 508kg unladen weight adapted and used or kept on a road for an invalid;

s. a vehicle being used, or kept for use, for the purposes of a disabled person if the vehicle is registered in that person's name and no other vehicle registered in his name is exempt duty on these grounds;

t. a vehicle (other than an ambulance) used for carrying disabled people by bodies recognised by the Secretary of State;

u. a vehicle used on public roads only in passing from land in the owner's occupation to other land in his occupation and for distances not exceeding a total of 6 miles in a calendar week. This exemption is only available where the licence applicant satisfies the Secretary of State that the conditions will be met;

v. a vehicle being used solely for submitting it by previous arrangement (at a specified time and date) for a compulsory test, bringing it away from such a test or during part of the test;

w. vehicles acquired by overseas residents and VAT zero rated;

x. Crown vehicles, but every such vehicle must carry a certificate of Crown ownership [450/71/24];

y. vehicles in the service of a visiting force or headquarters [1536/65/8(4)];

z. vehicles brought temporarily into Great Britain by persons resident outside the United Kingdom are exempt for three months [1208/75/5].

Mechanically-propelled vehicles, other than Crown vehicles, used exclusively on roads not repairable at the public expense or exempt duty under paragraphs (b), (d), (f), (i) and (m) above must be registered as though the owner were taking out a licence for the vehicle [450/71/25]. In relation to most other exempt vehicles, the vehicle owner must make annual declarations about the use of the vehicle [26].

Applications

An application for a vehicle licence can be dealt with at local vehicle licensing offices and an application should be made not more than 14 days before the licence is to have effect [450/71/4]. Head post offices can issue renewal licences within 14 days after the expiry of the last licence only if: (a) the application is made on the renewal notice

Form V11, (b) any change in ownership or address has been recorded in the registration document, and (c) no alteration has been made to the vehicle or change made in its use which could result in a different rate of tax being paid.

All applications, except for trade licences, must be accompanied by the appropriate certificate of insurance [1217/72/9] and, in the case of vehicles subject to test procedure and three or more years old, by the relevant test certificate or declaration [418/69/4], or, in the case of a goods vehicle over 30cwt unladen which requires a goods-vehicle test certificate, that certificate, a declaration or a certificate of temporary exemption [560/70/4].

The holder of a vehicle licence may surrender it at any time during its currency and apply for a refund of duty [450/71/5]. For each complete and unexpired month on the licence a refund, one-twelfth of the annual rate of duty for that licence is payable [Act 1994/19].

If a licence has been lost, stolen, destroyed, mutilated or become illegible the vehicle owner must apply for a duplicate. The fee is £3.50 but it is not payable if the Secretary of State is satisfied that the licence were lost in transmission from the issuing office, it were stolen with the vehicle or were a free licence issued to a vehicle exempt excise duty. If a registration book has been lost, stolen, destroyed or mutilated the vehicle owner must apply for a duplicate for which no charge is made [450/71/6 & 607/86].

Duration of licence

A vehicle licence may be taken out for any period of 12 months or for six months if the annual rate of duty is over £50 [Act 1994/3]. Duty on a licence for 12 months is payable at the annual rate and for six months at 55 per cent of the annual rate amount [4].

A first licence for a vehicle (other than one for a calendar year) may commence on the 10th, 17th or 24th day of the month in which it is issued subject to a prescribed charge being added to the 6 or 12 month rate of duty [Act 1994/3(3) & 1428/86].

A temporary licence lasting for 14 days may be issued pending the issue of a 6 or 12 month licence [Act 1994/9].

Rates of duty

Contained in Schedule 1 of the Vehicle Excise and Registration Act 1994 and are as follows:

GENERAL RATE—PART I

The annual rate of duty for a vehicle for which no other rate is specified is:

(a) a vehicle constructed before 1 January 1947   £70
(b) a vehicle not with (a)   £130

HACKNEY CARRIAGES—PART III

The annual rate of duty for a hackney carriage is as follows:

Seating capacity	Rate of duty
	£
Under 9	130
9 to 16	150
17 to 35	200
36 to 60	300
Over 60	450

[Sch. 1/3]

In calculating the seating capacity, 16in per person must be allowed in the case of continuous seats; otherwise the basis is one seat per person, not counting the driver's seat [450/71/42].

A 'hackney carriage' is a vehicle, other than a community bus, (a) standing or plying for hire or (b) bailed under a hire agreement by a person whose trade it is to sell vehicles or to bail or hire vehicles under hire agreements (other than hire-purchase) [Sch. 1/3(3)].

SPECIAL MACHINES—PART IV

The annual rate of duty on a special machine is £35 [Sch. 1/4].

Special machines are:

(a) tractors or agricultural engines. A tractor is either (i) an agricultural tractor or (ii) a tractor designed and constructed primarily for use off roads and is incapable by its construction of exceeding 25mph on the level under its own power
(b) digging machines designed, constructed and used for the purpose of trench digging or any kind of excavating or shovelling work which are used on public roads only for that purpose or for proceeding to and from such work, and when so proceeding do

not carry any load other than what is necessary for their propulsion or equipment

(c) mobile cranes used on public roads only, either as cranes in connection with work being carried on on a site in the immediate vicinity, or for the purpose of proceeding to and from a place where they are to be used as cranes and when so proceeding do not carry any load other than such as is necessary for their propulsion or equipment

(d) works trucks, being goods vehicles designed for use in private premises and used on public roads for carrying goods between two premises or between premises and a vehicle, or in connection with roadworks at or in the immediate vicinity of the site of the works.

(e) mowing machines

RECOVERY VEHICLES—PART V

The annual rate of duty for a recovery vehicle is £85 [Sch. 1/5].

A recovery vehicle is a vehicle which is either constructed or permanently adapted primarily for the purpose of lifting, towing and transporting a disabled vehicle or for any one or more of those purposes. It must not be used at any time for any purpose other than:

(a) the recovery of a disabled vehicle,

(b) the removal of a disabled vehicle from the place where it became disabled to premises for repair or scrap,

(c) the removal of a disabled vehicle from premises to which it was taken for repair to other premises for repair or scrap,

(d) carrying fuel and other liquids required for its propulsion, tools and other articles required for the operation of or in connection with its recovery equipment,

(e) carrying the driver or passenger of a disabled vehicle, and his personal effects, from the place where the vehicle is to be repaired or scrapped to his original destination,

(f) removing a vehicle from a road for police or a local authority, under their statutory powers, to a place they nominate,

(g) going to a place where the vehicle will be available for the recovery or removal of a disabled vehicle and remaining temporarily there, and

(h) proceeding from a place where the vehicle has been available for use, from recovering a disabled vehicle or from a place where the disabled vehicle has been removed for repair or scrapping [Sch. 1/5(3) & 1376/89].

Disregarded for the purposes of paragraphs (a) and (b) above are:

(i)   the carriage of persons or goods conveyed in a vehicle immediately before it became disabled,

(ii) repairing a vehicle at the place it became disabled or to which it had been taken for safety, and

(iii) drawing or carrying one trailer which had been carried or drawn by the disabled vehicle [Sch. 1/5(4)].

A recovery vehicle may not recover more than two vehicles at one time [1226/89].

In *DPP v Yates* [1989] RTR 134 it was held that a recovery vehicle towing a lorry and trailer by suspended tow was not a goods vehicle but was a locomotive and could draw two trailers. But in *DPP v Holtham* [1991] RTR 5 a similar vehicle was held, for speed limit purposes, not to be a locomotive but a goods vehicle.

The following High Court decisions relate to recovery vehicles when they were used under, and defined in, the trade licence law of the Vehicles (Excise) Act 1971. They remain relevant to the interpretation of the definition given above.

In *E Pearson & Son (Teeside) Ltd v Richardson* [1972] 3 All ER 277, [1972] 1 WLR 1152 it was held that an artic drawing unit kept for breakdowns and equipped with jacks and tow bar was a recovery vehicle. But in *Scott v Gutteridge Plant Hire Ltd* [1974] RTR 292 an articulated low loader fitted with a winch and carrying a defective tracked shovel was held not to be a recovery vehicle. The court did not decide the case on the construction of the vehicle but on the fact that the tracked shovel had been driven on under its own power and had not been raised by any apparatus.

In *Universal Salvage Ltd v Boothby* [1984] RTR 289 it was decided that a specialised breakdown vehicle (within EC Regulation 3820/85 but after also considering at length the definition of a recovery vehicle under the Vehicles (Excise) Act) was a vehicle specially built or adapted, and kept, for the purpose of going to the assistance of a broken-down vehicle and was generally capable of wholly or partly raising such a vehicle in order to effect its recovery by carrying or towing it. But the court held that a car-transporter trailer, the subject of that case, though equipped with winch and ramps for raising disabled vehicles, was not a specialised breakdown vehicle because it was not used for rendering assistance to individual broken-down vehicles but for carrying a number of vehicles from one destination to another. The use of a recovery vehicle to carry seven scrap cars was unauthorised, said the court in *Gibson v Nutter* [1984] RTR 8, because the reference to 'a disabled vehicle' in the Act was to be construed as one vehicle only, a decision which was affirmed in *Universal Salvage Ltd v Boothby* (above). But in *Kennett v Holding and Barnes Ltd* [1986]

RTR 334 it was held that a recovery vehicle could carry a disabled vehicle and tow a disabled vehicle at the same time.

In *Robertson v Crew* [1977] RTR 141 it was held that a car with its rotary arm removed was not a disabled vehicle and in *Squires v Mitchell* [1983] RTR 400, when ruling that a wartime Chevrolet truck being carried during renovation was not a disabled vehicle, it was said that a disabled vehicle is 'not only a vehicle which suffers from a significant disability but is a vehicle which has broken down because of that disability'.

VEHICLES USED FOR EXCEPTIONAL LOADS—PART VI

Motor vehicles used to carry, or draw trailers carrying, exceptional loads and authorised under a Special Types Order are taxable at an annual rate of £5,000 [Sch. 1/6].

An exceptional load is one which owing to its dimensions or total laden weight cannot be carried on a vehicle complying in all respects with the Construction and Use Regulations [Sch. 1/6(3)].

HAULAGE VEHICLES—PART VII

The annual rate of duty for a haulage vehicle is £100 for a showman's vehicle and £330 in any other case [Sch. 1/7].

A haulage vehicle (other than one to which Part IV, V or VI applies) is a vehicle constructed and used on public roads solely for haulage and not for carrying or having superimposed on it any load except such as is necessary for its propulsion or equipment [Sch. 1/7(2)]. In *LCC v Hays Wharf Cartage Co Ltd* [1953] 2 All ER 34 it was held that ballast blocks on a haulage vehicle were part of its equipment.

A showman's vehicle is a vehicle registered under the Act in the name of a person following the business of a travelling showman and which is used solely by him for the purposes of his business and for no other purpose [Act 1994/62(1)].

GOODS VEHICLES—PART VIII

A goods vehicle is a vehicle constructed or adapted for use and used for the conveyance of goods or burden for hire or reward or in connection with a trade or business [Act 1994/62(1)].

An unladen Land-Rover, taxed at the private rate, which was towing a trailer carrying goods was held to be used for 'conveyance of goods'. The court held that the Land-Rover was being used to convey goods from one place to another and it did not matter whether the goods were carried in the vehicle or the trailer—*James v Davies* [1952] 2 All ER 758.

In *Berkshire CC v Berkshire Lime Co (Childrey) Ltd* [1953] 2 All ER 779 the owners of vehicles constructed and used for spreading lime on farm land contended they were agricultural engines and subject to a lower rate of tax. But the court ruled that because they carried the lime from a quarry to the farmland they were also goods vehicles and duty had to be paid at the goods rates.

Two ex-army AEC Matadors fitted with a crane but no floor boards and used to load and draw trailers carrying felled timber were held to be haulage vehicles and not goods vehicles—*T.K. Worgan & Son Ltd v Gloucester CC* [1961] 2 All ER 301.

In *Booth v DPP* [1993] RTR 379 it was held that an unladen semi-trailer coupled to a tractor unit amounted to goods or burden on the tractor unit and the tractor should have been taxed at the goods rate.

Basic rate

The basic annual rate of duty is £150 and it applies to a goods vehicle:
(a) which has a plated gross or train weight over 3.5 tonnes but not over 7.5 tonnes;
(b) which has a plated gross or train weight over 7.5 tonnes but has that weight only by virtue of a maker's plate and the vehicle is not of a class prescribed by the Secretary of State;
(c) which is a tower wagon with a plated gross weight over 7.5 tonnes;
(d) which does not have a plated gross or train weight but has a design weight exceeding 3.5 tonnes [Sch. 1/8].

Drawbar trailers

If a rigid vehicle over 12 tonnes plated gross weight is used to draw a trailer with a plated gross weight over 4 tonnes and when drawn it is used for the conveyance of goods or burden the extra duty of £130 for a trailer not over 12 tonnes plated gross weight and £360 if over 12 tonnes is payable.

For this purpose a trailer does not include (a) an appliance for distributing loose gritting material on roads, (b) a snow plough, (c) a road construction vehicle, (d) a farming implement not constructed to carry goods and drawn by a farmer's goods vehicle, and (e) a trailer for carrying or making gas for propelling the drawing vehicle. [Sch. 1/17].

Rigid vehicles exceeding 7.5 tonnes

The annual rates of duty for a rigid goods vehicle with a plated gross weight over 7.5 tonnes is given in the following table in relation to the number of axles the vehicle is fitted with [Sch. 1/9].

Plated gross weight		Rate		
		2-axle	3-axle	4 or more axle
over tonnes	not over tonnes	£	£	£
7.5	12	290	290	290
12	13	450	470	340
13	14	630	470	340
14	15	810	470	340
15	17	1,280	470	340
17	19		820	340
19	21		990	340
21	23		1,420	490
23	25		2,160	800
25	27		2,260	1,420
27	29			2,240
29	31			3,250
31	32			4,250

Articulated vehicles

The annual rate of duty for a tractor unit with a plated gross train weight over 7.5 tonnes is shown in the following table according to its plated gross train weight, whether it has two axles or three or more axles and in relation to the number of axles fitted to the semi-trailer to be drawn by it [Sch. 1/11].

The definition of an axle includes a retractable axle [Act 1994/62(1)].

If a two-axled tractor unit is taxed for use with two- or three-axled trailers at a rate at least equal to the 26,000kg rate for a three-axled artic (i.e. £1,150) it can be used with a single-axled trailer without incurring extra tax as long as the total laden weight of the outfit does not exceed 26,000kg [Act 1994/16(2),(3)]

If a two-axled tractor unit is taxed for use with a three-axled trailer at a rate at least equal to the 33,000kg rate for a two-axled tractor with two-axled trailer (i.e. £2,450) it can be used with a two-axled trailer without incurring extra tax as long as the total laden weight of the outfit does not exceed 33,000kg [Act 1994/16(4),(5)].

Train weight of tractive unit		Rate for tractive unit with two axles			Rate for tractive unit with three or more axles		
Exceeding	Not exceeding	Any no. of semitrailer axles	2 or more semitrailer axles	3 or more semitrailer axles	Any no. of semitrailer axles	2 or more semitrailer axles	3 or more semitrailer axles
tonnes	tonnes	£	£	£	£	£	£
7.5	12	290	290	290	290	290	290
12	16	440	440	440	440	440	440
16	20	500	440	440	440	440	440
20	23	780	440	440	440	440	440
23	26	1,150	570	440	570	440	440
26	28	1,150	1,090	440	1,090	440	440
28	31	1,680	1,680	1,050	1,680	640	440
31	33	2,450	2,450	1,680	2,450	970	440
33	34	5,000	5,000	1,680	2,450	1,420	550
34	36	5,000	5,000	2,750	2,450	2,030	830
36	38	5,000	5,000	3,100	2,730	2,730	1,240
38	44	—	—	—	2,730	2,730	1,240

If a three-axled tractor unit is taxed for use with two-axled semi-trailers at a rate of duty at least equal to the 33,000kg rate for a three-axled tractor with single-axled semi-trailer (i.e. £2,450) it can be used with a single-axled semi-trailer without incurring extra duty as long as the total laden weight of the outfit does not exceed 32,520kg [Act 1994/16(6),(7)].

Farmers' and showmen's goods vehicles

The annual rate of duty for a farmer's or showman's goods vehicle with a plated gross or plated train weight not exceeding 3.5 tonnes or which has not such weight but a design weight not exceeding 3.5 tonnes is £85. If the weight is over 3.5 tonnes but not over 7.5 tonnes the rate of duty is £100 [Sch. 1/12(1),(2)].

If the plated weight is over 7.5 tonnes the rate of duty is that given above for rigid vehicles, drawbar trailers and articulated vehicles but the rates for a farmer's goods vehicle is 60 per cent of the rates given and for a showman's goods vehicle the rate is 25 per cent. But, the rate of duty for a showman's goods vehicle over 7.5 tonnes but not over 12 tonnes is £100 and the amount of trailer duty for a showman's goods vehicle is £80 [Sch. 1/12(3),(4) & (6)].

A farmer's goods vehicle is a goods vehicle registered in the name of a person engaged in agriculture and used on public roads solely by him for conveying the produce of, or articles required for, the agricultural land which he occupies, and for no other purpose (except that it may be used partly for private purposes) [Act 1994/62(1)].

Vehicles used by a contractor to cut and remove grass on farmland were not farmers' goods vehicles because the contractor did not 'occupy' the land—*Howard v Grass Products Ltd* [1972] 3 All ER 530, [1972] 1 WLR 1323. In *McKenzie v Griffiths Ltd* [1976] RTR 140 a vehicle used by a farmer to transport manure from a racing stable to a mushroom grower was held not to be a farmer's goods vehicle. In *Cambrian Land Ltd v Allan* [1981] RTR 109 carcass meat derived from animals reared by a farmer and being carried from a slaughterhouse to a butchers was held not to be produce of agricultural land.

Section 17(3) of the Act, however, authorises the licensee of a farmer's goods vehicle to carry the produce of or articles required for another farmer, provided that (a) the vehicle is so used only occasionally, (b) that the goods carried for another farmer represent only a small proportion of the total load carried and (c) that no payment or reward is made or given.

Down-licensing

The Secretary of State may make regulations to enable a person to apply for a vehicle to be licensed at its operating weight instead of its plated gross or train weight. Where a lower rate of duty is charged as a result the use of the vehicle would be subject to conditions to be prescribed by the Secretary of State [Sch. 1/13].

No regulations to provide for this down-licensing concession have been made.

Vehicles for conveying machines

A motor vehicle which is constructed for use and used for conveying a machine or contrivance and no other load except articles used in connection with the machine or contrivance and which (a) is not chargeable with duty under Part IV, V or VI and (b) has neither a plated gross weight or plated train weight, is chargeable with duty as if the machine or contrivance were burden even if it is built in as part of the vehicle [Sch. 1/14].

Private use

If a goods vehicle is used partly for private purposes, i.e. partly otherwise than for carrying goods for hire or reward or in connection with a trade or business, the annual rate of duty is the higher of the private rate and goods rate [Sch. 1/15].

Where goods rate duty has been paid and the vehicle is to be used to a substantial extent to carry the goods or burden of a particular person (whether the keeper or not) no extra duty is chargeable by reason of the vehicle being used to carry, without charge, employees of the user of the vehicle in the course of their employment [Act 1994/17(2)].

Exempted vehicles

The following vehicles are exempt goods rate tax but they are likely to be subject to excise duty at a different rate unless coming within the general exemptions:
(a) a motor cycle
(b) a special machine
(c) a recovery vehicle
(d) a haulage vehicle
(d) a vehicle which, though constructed or adapted for the conveyance of goods, is not used to carry goods for hire or reward or in connection with a trade or business [Sch. 1/16].

Plated weights

References in the Act to a plated gross weight of a goods vehicle or trailer are
a. in the case of a trailer which may lawfully be used without a Ministry plate, the maximum laden weight at which the trailer may lawfully be used in Great Britain; and
b. otherwise, the weight which is the maximum gross weight which may not be exceeded in Great Britain for the vehicle or trailer as indicated on the 'appropriate plate' [Act 1994/61(1)].

Plated train weight means the maximum gross weight which may not be exceeded in Britain by an articulated vehicle consisting of the vehicle and any semi-trailer it might draw as indicated on the 'appropriate plate' [61(2)].

An 'appropriate plate' is (a) a Ministry plate, (b) a plating certificate or (c) if (a) and (b) do not apply, a maker's plate [61(3)].

Change of use

If a vehicle is used in an altered condition or a different manner from that for which it was taxed, a higher rate of duty may become payable. For this to be so, however, the alteration (of condition or use) must be such as to satisfy all the conditions which bring a vehicle into that higher tax category [Act 1994/15 & 17(1)]. Notification of any such alteration must be sent by the vehicle owner to the Secretary of State along with the licence, registration book and extra duty [450/71/11].

Prosecutions

No proceedings may be brought in England and Wales or Northern Ireland for using or keeping an unlicensed vehicle, misuse of a trade licence or under-payment of duty except by the Secretary of State or by a constable with the approval of the Secretary of State [Act 1994/47(1)]. Those proceedings, or any under Regulations made under the Act, may be commenced at any time within 6 months of the date sufficient evidence to justify proceedings came to his attention, but no proceedings may be instituted more than 3 years after the commission of the offence [47(2)].

In Scotland summary proceedings may be instituted by the Secretary of State for any offence under the Act, except forgery, fraud, etc. [48(1)]. Summary proceedings may not be commenced for using or keeping an unlicensed vehicle, misuse of a trade licence, under-payment of duty, forgery or fraud more than three years after the commission of the offence [48(2)].

Proceedings instituted by the procurator fiscal on information received from the Secretary of State may be commenced at any time within 6 months of the date information came to the knowledge of the Secretary of State and, in any other case, at any time within six months of the date sufficient evidence to justify proceedings came to his attention [48(4)].

In any proceedings for using or keeping an unlicensed vehicle, misuse of a trade licence, making false declarations or supplying false or misleading information, the burden of proof will lie on the defendant if any question arises as to the number of vehicles used; the character, weight or cylinder capacity of a vehicle; seating capacity of a vehicle or the purpose for which a vehicle has been used [53].

Where a person is convicted of using or keeping an unlicensed vehicle and he was the keeper of the vehicle at the time of the offence, the court must order him to pay back duty at the rate of one twelfth of the annual rate for the vehicle in respect of each calendar month or part of a month in the relevant period. The relevant period is that ending with the date of the offence and beginning with (a) the date (if before the offence) the person notified acquiring the vehicle or, if later, the expiry of the licence last in force, or, (b) in any other case, the expiry date of the last licence in force or, if there has been no licence, the date the vehicle was first kept by the person convicted [Act 1994/30,31]. But if the person convicted proves that throughout any month or part of a month the vehicle was not kept by him or he has paid duty in respect of the vehicle for any such month or part of a month, whether or not on a licence, the back duty will be calculated as if that time were not included in the relevant period [31(5)].

In *Chief Constable of Kent v Mather* [1986] RTR 36 it was held that a court had no power to reduce the amount of back duty payable under this provision.

Registration marks and books

When a vehicle is licensed for the first time it is allocated a registration mark which must be displayed on it, and on any vehicle drawn by it, in a prescribed manner [Act 1994/23].

The registration mark must be exhibited at the front and at the rear of every mechanically propelled vehicle (except works trucks and agricultural machines), the size of lettering to be as prescribed [450/71/18]. These markings must be on a flat rectangular number plate or flat surface [Sch. 2/9]. Registration numbers on works trucks and agricultural machines can be either on both sides or on the back only [21]. In the case of invalid carriages and pedestrian-controlled vehicles, it is permissible to exhibit the front identification mark on both sides of the vehicle in a vertical position on a flat, unbroken surface or on both sides of the front mudguard [18(3)]. A motor cycle requires a number plate at the rear only [1089/75].

On vehicles first registered before 1 October 1938, the mark must be displayed in a vertical position and be 'easily distinguishable', but for vehicles registered for the first time on or after that date the mark, which must be 'easily legible', need not necessarily be vertical, but it must comply with the conditions as to visibility indicated in the diagram above [450/71/20]. A vehicle must be equipped with a rear registration plate lamp, see page 146.

When a trailer (including a broken-down vehicle) is drawn, the mark of the drawing vehicle must appear on the rear of the trailer except in the case of a trailer drawn by a vehicle travelling not more than 6 miles a week on a road or a special machine when the mark of another such vehicle owned by the same person may be displayed [22].

Number plates made of reflex reflecting material must be marked with the appropriate British Standard specification number, namely BS AU 145:1967.

Number plates of reflex reflecting material must be fitted on vehicles first registered on or after 1 January 1973, except vehicles over 3 tons unladen which are fitted with reflective rear markings; stage carriages; pedestrian-controlled vehicles; works trucks; agricultural machines; and trailers [1865/72].

The size and form of registration marks is contained in Schedules 2 and 3 of the Road Vehicles (Registration and Licensing) Regulations 1971.

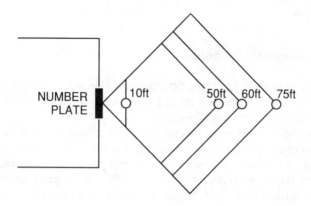

How the test of number plate visibility applies. The squares are the areas in which every letter and figure of the identification mark must be 'easily legible'. The square with the 50ft diagonal from the centre of the plate applies to the rear plates of motor cycles, pedestrian-controlled vehicles, and invalid carriages during the hours of darkness; the 60ft to the rear plates of motor cycles, pedestrian-controlled vehicles, and invalid carriages in daylight and to the rear plates of all other classes of vehicle at night: and the 75ft to both front and rear plates of all vehicles (except motor cycles, pedestrian-controlled vehicles, and invalid carriages) during daylight. The 10ft line is the *minimum* distance from which observations are to be made [450/71/18]. During the hours of darkness the rear number plate must be illuminated so that it is easily legible, in the absence of fog, in a square with a diagonal of 15m in the case of a motor cycle, invalid carriage or pedestrian-controlled vehicle or, in any other case, a square with a diagonal of 18m [19 & 814/84].

Registration marks must not be obscured or allowed to become not easily distinguishable [Act 1994/43] but it is a defence for a person to prove that he took all reasonable steps to prevent such an occurrence.

Before issuing a registration book for a vehicle the Secretary of State can require the vehicle to be produced in order to check that the particulars supplied by the owner are correct [450/71/8(1)]. The owner of a vehicle must produce the registration book when required, at any reasonable time, by a police officer or person acting for the Secretary of State [8(2)]. The Secretary of State can require a book to be surrendered to him for correction purposes [8(3)]. Except for persons authorised, it is an offence to deface or mutilate any registration book, or alter or obliterate any entry in it, or, except for a new owner entering his name and address in it, to make any entry or addition in the book [8(4)].

A registration mark can be transferred from one vehicle to another at a cost of £80 [9(4A), 230/77, 1802/82].

The Secretary of State can make any of the registered particulars (e.g. vehicle and keeper) available

(a) to a local authority in connection with a decriminalised parking contravention;

(b) to a chief officer of police; and

(c) on payment of a reasonable fee to be decided by the Secretary of State, to any person who can show he has reasonable cause for wanting the particulars [450/71/15 & 1364/94].

Licences

When a vehicle chargeable with duty under the Act is used or kept on a public road a licence must be displayed on it in the prescribed manner [Act 1994/33]. The licence must be in a holder to protect it from the weather [450/71/16(2)] and, in the case of a vehicle with a windscreen extending to the near-side, must be displayed on the near-side of the windscreen or, on any other vehicle with a driver's cab with a near-side window, on that window, or otherwise on the near-side of the vehicle in front of the driver's seat [16(3)].

It is an offence to alter, deface, mutilate or add anything to a licence or to display a licence so tampered with or on which the particulars have become illegible or the colour altered by fading. To exhibit anything which is intended to be or could be mistaken for a licence is also an offence [450/71/7].

Forgery and fraud

It is an indictable offence for a person to forge or fraudulently alter or use, lend or allow to be used any registration mark or document, hackney carriage plate, trade plate or licence [Act 1994/44]. Making a misleading or false declaration to obtain a licence and supplying false or misleading information is also an offence [45].

Trade licences

A motor trader or vehicle tester can apply to the Secretary of State for a trade licence. In the case of a motor trader the licence covers vehicles temporarily in his possession. In the case of a vehicle tester it covers vehicles submitted to him for testing and, in the case of a motor trader who is a manufacturer, it covers vehicles kept by him for research and development [Act 1994/11]. A trade licence cannot be used on more than one motor vehicle at a time, it can be used only for prescribed purposes and it does not authorise a vehicle to be kept on a road if it is not being used [12].

A motor trader is a manufacturer or repairer of, or dealer in, mechanically propelled vehicles and a person is regarded as a dealer if his business is mainly one of collecting and delivering mechanically propelled vehicles [62(1)]. A person who carries on a business of modifying vehicles (whether by fitting accessories or otherwise) prior to their first UK registration or of valeting vehicles is regarded as a motor trader [450/71/28A & 2101/86]. A disabled vehicle includes a vehicle which has been abandoned or is scrap [Act 1994/12(5)].

A trade licence may be taken out for one calendar year or for a period of six months beginning on the first of January or July or, in the case of a prospective motor trader or vehicle tester, for a period of 7, 8, 9, 10 or 11 months beginning on the first of any month other than January or July [Act 1994/13(1)].

The annual rate of duty is £55 for motor cycles and £130 for other vehicles. The rate for a six-month licence is 55 per cent of the annual rate [13(3),(4)].

A person may hold more than one trade licence [14].

A motor trader must not use a trade licence on a mechanically propelled vehicle on a road unless it is a vehicle temporarily in his possession in the course of his business as a motor trader [450/71/35(3)]

A motor trader must not use a mechanically propelled vehicle under a trade licence for a purpose other than a business purpose and one of the following purposes:

(a) for its test or trial or the test or trial of its accessories or equipment in the ordinary course of construction, modification or repair or after completion;

(b) for going to or from a public weighbridge for registration purposes;

(c) for its test or trial for the benefit of a prospective purchaser, and connected journeys;

(d) for its test or trial for the benefit of a person interested in promoting publicity in regard to it, and connected journeys;

(e) for delivering it to the place where the purchaser intends to keep it;

(f) for demonstrating its operation or that of its accessories or equipment when being handed over to the purchaser;

(g) for delivering it between parts of his own premises or premises of another motor trader;

(h) for going to or returning from a workshop in which a body or a special type of equipment or accessory is to be or has been fitted to it or in which it is to be or has been painted, valeted or repaired;

(i) for going from the premises of a motor trader to a place from which it is to be transported by train, ship or aircraft, or the reverse;

(j) for going to or returning from any garage, auction room or other place at which vehicles are usually stored or periodically offered for sale and at which the vehicle is to be or has been stored or is to be or has been offered for sale;

(k) for going to or returning from a place where it is to be or has been tested, or to a place where it is to be broken up or dismantled.

[450/71/35(4)]

For the purposes of paragraphs (a) to (k) above a motor vehicle drawing a trailer is deemed to be a single vehicle [35(2)].

Motor vehicles kept by a manufacturer for research and development can be used on a road under a trade licence for those purposes only [36].

A vehicle tester who is the holder of a trade licence may use the licence only for testing motor vehicles and trailers or their accessories or equipment in the course of his business as a vehicle tester [37].

A motor trader may not carry goods on a vehicle used under a trade licence except the following types of goods and only when on the authorised purposes specified:

(i) a load carried for testing or demonstrating the vehicle or its accessories or equipment and which is returned to the place of loading without having been removed from the vehicle, except for the last purpose or in case of accident or if the load is water, fertiliser or refuse, on a journey mentioned in (a), (c), (d) or (f) above;

(iii) a load built in as part of the vehicle or permanently attached to it;

(iv) parts, accessories or equipment to be fitted to the vehicle and tools for fitting them when on a journey mentioned in (g), (h) or (i) above;

(v) a load consisting of a trailer when the carrying vehicle is on a journey mentioned in (e), (h) or (i) above; or

(vi) in the case of a vehicle being collected or delivered when on a journey mentioned in (e) to (j) above, a load consisting of another vehicle used or to be used for travel from or to the place of collection or delivery. [450/71/38(1) and 1911/94].

The use of a vehicle which carried several container bases, only one of which was to be fitted to the vehicle, was held to be unauthorised in *Bowers v Worthington* [1982] RTR 400

A manufacturer's research and development vehicle used under a trade licence can carry only a load for testing the vehicle, its equipment or accessories and which is returned to the place of loading without having been removed from the vehicle (except for the last purpose or in case of accident), or a load built in or permanently attached to the vehicle [38(2)]. The same type of load can be carried on a vehicle being tested by a vehicle tester [39]. For the purposes of Regulations 38 and 39 an articulated vehicle is regarded as a single vehicle [38(3)].

The holder of a trade licence must not use a vehicle on a public road under the licence while carrying any person on the vehicle, or any trailer drawn, other than a person carried in connection with an authorised purpose [450/71/40 & 2101/86].

If the Secretary of State refuses an application for a trade licence made by a motor trader or vehicle tester the applicant is given 28 days in which to ask the Secretary of State to review his decision. In reviewing his decision the Secretary of State must consider any written representations made to him by the applicant [Act 1994/14(3) and 450/71/29].

If a licence holder changes his business name or address he must forthwith notify the Secretary of State and return the licence for amendment [450/71/30]. Trade plates issued with a trade licence must be displayed in the same manner as a normal registration mark and the plate carrying the licence must be at the front of the vehicle [33]. If a plate is lost or damaged the licence holder must apply for a replacement. A charge of £5.50 per plate is made where two are replaced at the same time and, in any other case, £6.50 for a front plate and £4.50 for a rear plate [31(3) and 1177/86]. It is an offence to alter, deface, mutilate or add anything to a trade plate or to display a trade plate which has been so tampered with. It is also an offence to display anything which could be mistaken for a trade plate [32]. Trade plates remain the property of the Secretary of State and must be returned when the holder ceases to hold a licence [31(2)].

22 Waste transport

Control of Pollution (Amendment) Act 1989
Environmental Protection Act 1990
Control of Pollution (Special Waste) Regulations, **No. 1709/88**
Collection and Disposal of Waste Regulations, **No. 819/88**
Controlled Waste (Registration of Carriers and Seizure of Vehicles) Regulations, **No. 1624/91**
Environmental Protection (Duty of Care) Regulations, **No. 2839/91**
Controlled Waste Regulations, **No. 588/92**

Registration of waste carriers

A person who is not a registered carrier of controlled waste must not, in connection with his business or with a view to profit, transport controlled waste to or from a place in Great Britain [Act 1989/1(1)].

Controlled waste is household, industrial or commercial waste. Waste includes any substance which constitutes scrap material or an effluent or other unwanted or surplus substance arising from the application of any process and any substance or article which requires to be disposed of as being broken, worn out, contaminated or otherwise spoiled [Act 1990/75]. Regulations prescribe types of waste which are to be, or not to be, regarded as household, industrial or commercial waste [588/92].

It is a defence to a charge of carrying controlled waste while not registered for a person to show:

(a) that it was carried in an emergency and notice was given, as soon as reasonably practicable afterwards, to the area waste regulation authority;
(b) that he neither knew nor had reasonable grounds to suspect he was carrying controlled waste and had taken reasonable steps to find out; or
(c) he acted under instructions of his employer [Act 1989/1(4)].

An emergency, in (a) above, means any circumstances in which, to avoid, remove or reduce any serious danger to the public, or serious risk of damage to the environment, it was necessary for the waste to be transported without the use of a registered carrier [1(6)].

EXEMPTIONS

Registration does not apply to:

1. transport between different parts of the same premises;
2. transport of waste imported into Great Britain to the place it is landed;
3. a waste collection authority, waste disposal authority or waste regulation authority. (Waste disposal contractors are not exempt);
4. the producer of the waste, unless it is building or demolition waste. This includes waste arising from works of construction or demolition, including preparatory works;
5. a charity or voluntary organisation;
6. a person who applied for registration before April 1992, while his application is pending or during the time allowed for appealing against refusal of registration   [Act 1989/1(2) and 1624/91/2]

THE REGISTER

A waste regulation authority must maintain a register of carriers of controlled waste which is open, at all reasonable hours, for inspection by the public free of charge. Copying facilities must be available at reasonable charges [1624/91/3].

A waste regulation authority is the London, Greater Manchester and Merseyside Waste Disposal Authorities and county or district councils or, in Scotland, an islands or district council [Act 1990/30(1)].

APPLICATIONS

Application for registration, or for renewal of registration, must be made to the waste regulation authority of the area in which the applicant has his principal place of business in Great Britain. If he has no place of business in Great Britain he can apply to any regulation authority [1624/91/4(1)].

An application must not be made while a previous application is pending or while the applicant is registered, but a renewal application can be made during the last six months of a registration's validity and a prospective partner of a firm can make an application even though the partnership is registered [4(2)].

The application form must conform to a type specified in the regulations and it can be obtained free from the regulation authority [4(7)(8)]. The form requires particulars of any conviction for using a vehicle without an operator's licence or for a specified waste dumping offence (prescribed offences), unless, in the case of an individual, it is a spent conviction.

The fee for consideration of an application is £95 [4(9)]. In its circular 11/91 the Department of Environment has advised that only one fee is payable for registration of a partnership but if a new partner joins the business he must pay the fee also.

When an authority accepts registration—or is directed to on appeal—it must allocate a registration number, specify the date registration commences and ends and enter the applicant's particulars in the register [6]. On registration the authority must issue the applicant, free of charge, with a certificate of registration and a copy of the register entry [6(3)]. A carrier can give written notice requiring the removal of his name from the register [Act 1989/3(2)].

RENEWAL

Registration lasts for three years and, no later than six months before the expiry date, the authority must notify the registered person of the expiry date and send him a renewal application form [1624/91/11(2)(3)]. The fee for consideration of a renewal application is £65 [4(9)].

When application for renewal is made in that six-month period registration will continue in force:

(a) until the application is accepted or withdrawn, or

(b) if the application is refused or the time allowed for re-registration has expired without it being made, during the appeal period or until the date the applicant indicates not making or abandoning an appeal [11(4)].

When the authority accepts renewal—or is directed to on appeal—it must amend its register and send the applicant, free of charge, a certificate and a copy of the register entry [12].

CHANGE OF CIRCUMSTANCES

A registered person must notify the regulation authority of any change of circumstance affecting the information in his entry in the register [1624/91/8(1)].

The authority must amend the entry, supply the carrier with a free copy of the amended entry and, if the change affects the information on the certificate of registration, supply a free copy of an amended certificate.

PARTNERS

A registration or renewal application relating to a business carried on by a partnership must be made by every partner completing an application form [1624/91/4(4)]. Registration of all the partners is made under one entry and one registration number is issued [6(2)].

Registration of a business carried on by a partnership ends if any of the partners ceases to be registered or if a person who is not registered becomes a partner [11(6)]. Registration is not affected if a person ceases to be a partner [11(7)].

CERTIFICATE OF REGISTRATION

The regulation authority must provide a registered person with copies of the registration certificate on payment of a reasonable charge [1624/91/9(1)].

Copies must be numbered, marked to show they are copies and show that they have been provided by the authority [9(2)].

A certificate and all copies must be returned immediately to the registration authority when registration ceases to have effect through expiry, cancellation by the operator, when an appeal against renewal refusal or revocation has been disposed of or an amended certificate issued [13].

REFUSALS

Refusal of registration or renewal can be made by a regulation authority but only if:

(a) the application procedure has not been followed, or
(b) the applicant; an employee; a company of which he was a director, manager or similar official; or, in the case of a company, a director, manager or similar official (referred to as relevant persons) has been convicted of using a vehicle without an operator's licence or one of the specified waste dumping offences and it is undesirable for the applicant to be authorised to carry controlled waste [Act 1989/3(5) & 1624/91/5].

In determining whether it is desirable for an individual to be authorised to carry controlled waste, the authority must, where a person in (b) above other than the individual has been convicted of a prescribed offence, have regard to whether the individual had been a party to carrying on a business in a way involving the commission of prescribed offences [Act 1989/3(6)]. If registration or renewal is refused the authority must give the applicant notice of the refusal and the reasons for its decision [1624/91/5(2)].

REVOCATION

A regulation authority can revoke a person's registration if he, an employee or other relevant person has been convicted of one of the prescribed offences and it is undesirable for him to continue to be authorised to transport controlled waste. The carrier must be informed of the reasons for the decision [1624/91/10].

Regardless of revocation, registration will continue in force until the expiry of the appeal period or until the date the applicant indicates not making or abandoning an appeal [Act 1989/4(7)].

APPEALS

An appeal to the Secretary of State for the Environment can be made against:
(a) refusal of an application for registration or renewal,
(b) revocation of registration, or
(c) failure to register an application within two months or, except for a renewal, such longer period as may be agreed between the authority and the applicant [Act 1989/4(1)(2)].

A notice of appeal must be in writing, state the grounds for it, be accompanied by relevant documents and a statement that the appellant wishes the appeal to be conducted by written representations or by a hearing [1624/91/15(1)]. At the same time the appellant must serve a copy of the grounds of appeal and how he wants the appeal conducted on the regulation authority [15(2)].

Notice of appeal must be given within 28 days of (a) being notified of refusal or revocation of registration, (b) where registration has not been made or refused, the end of the period allowed for registration, or (c) before a later date allowed by the Secretary of State [16].

An appeal hearing, which can be requested by either party or be directed by the Secretary of State, will be conducted by a person appointed by the Secretary of State [17(1)]. The person holding the inquiry will submit a report of his conclusions and recommendations (or reasons for not making any) to the Secretary of State [17(2)]. The Secretary of State must notify the appellant of his determination of the appeal, his reasons for it and, if a hearing was held, provide a report of the hearing [18].

PRODUCTION OF CERTIFICATE

If it reasonably appears to an authorised waste regulation officer or a policeman that controlled waste is being, or has been, transported by a person who is not a registered carrier he can:

(a) stop any person appearing to be, or to have been, engaged in the transport and require him to produce his or his employer's certificate of registration (or official copy of it) for transporting the waste and
(b) search any vehicle which appears to be, or has been, used for transporting that waste, test anything on it and take samples for test [Act 1989/5(1)].

Only police in uniform can stop a vehicle on a road [5(2)]
If the certificate is not produced at the time, the person concerned must produce it at, or send it to, the principal office of the regulation authority for the area in which he is stopped not later than 7 days after the day he was asked to produce it. A copy of the certificate can be produced if it was issued by the regulation authority [Act 1989/5(3) & 1624/91/14].

Intentionally obstructing an authorised officer or policeman or to failing, without reasonable excuse, to produce the certificate or copy is an offence [Act 1989/5(4)]. In the latter case the prosecution must show that the waste in question was controlled waste and the person transported it to or from a place in Great Britain [5(5)].

SEIZURE OF VEHICLES

A magistrate or, in Scotland, a sheriff can issue a warrant to a regulation authority for seizure of a vehicle if satisfied, on sworn information in writing, that there are reasonable grounds for believing:

(a) there has been an unlawful disposal of waste and the vehicle was used to commit the offence;
(b) proceedings for the offence have not been brought against any person; and
(c) the authority has failed, after taking prescribed steps, to find the name and address of the person using the vehicle at the time of the offence [Act 1989/6(1)].

The prescribed steps involve (a) attempting to trace the owner of the vehicle—or asking police to help in tracing the owner of a foreign-based vehicle—and (b) serving on the owner a notice requiring him to identify the user of the vehicle [1624/91/20].

Under the warrant, an authorised officer of a waste regulation authority or a policeman can seize the vehicle and its contents [Act 1989/6(2)]. Only police can stop a vehicle on a road and an authority's officer must be accompanied by police when seizing a vehicle [6(3)]. The warrant and person's authority must be produced if requested [6(4)].

A seized vehicle can be driven, towed or removed by any reasonable means and steps can be taken against the vehicle to facilitate its removal. A vehicle's contents can be separately removed to assist in removal of the vehicle, if there is good reason to store them in a different place from the vehicle or if their condition requires them to be disposed of without delay [1624/91/21]. Intentionally obstructing an authorised officer or policeman executing a warrant is an offence [Act 1989/6(9)].

RETURN OF VEHICLES

Unless it has been disposed of, property seized must be returned to a person who:

(a) produces satisfactory evidence of his entitlement to it and of his identity and address;
(b) when acting as agent of someone else, produces satisfactory evidence of his identity, address and authority to act for his principal and evidence of his principal's identity, address and entitlement to the property;
(c) where property is a vehicle and the person seeking its return purports to be its keeper or user, or agent of such person, produces the vehicle's registration document [1624/91/22(1)].

A person who establishes his entitlement to a vehicle will be treated as entitled to its contents except to the extent another person has claimed them [22(2)].

DISPOSAL OF VEHICLES

A regulation authority can sell, destroy or deposit at any place, seized property if:

(a) it publishes, in a local newspaper, a notice identifying the property and stating that it has been seized and will be disposed of;
(b) it serves a copy of the notice on a person thought to be the user of the vehicle, the police chief of the area concerned, DVLA and HP Information plc; and

(c) 28 days have passed since publication or service of the latest of the notices (and no obligation to return the property has arisen) or sooner if its condition requires it to be disposed of without delay [1624/91/23].

The proceeds of sale, less disposal costs, must go to a claimant who would have been entitled to the return of the property had it not been sold [25].

LIABILITY OF OTHERS

Where a person's offence is due to the act of default of another person, that other person can be convicted of the offence whether or not proceedings are brought against the first person [Act 1989/7(5)].

If a company is guilty of an offence due to an act or omission shown to have been done with the consent, connivance or negligence of any director, manager or similar officer, he too can be convicted of the offence. If a company's affairs are managed by its members, this provision applies to a managing member as if he was a director [7(6)(7)].

Unlawful deposit of waste

A person must not deposit controlled waste on any land, or cause or knowingly permit it to be deposited, unless the land is occupied by the holder of a waste management licence which authorises the deposit in question [Act 1990/33(1)].

Controlled waste is household, industrial and commercial waste [75] and regulations specify types of waste which are to be regarded as such and prescribe circumstances in which a waste management licence is not required [819/88 & 588/92].

It is a defence for a person to prove:

(a) he took all reasonable precautions and exercised all due diligence to avoid committing the offence;
(b) he acted under his employer's instructions and did not know and had no reason to suppose the deposit was illegal;
(c) the acts in question were done in an emergency to avoid public danger and, as soon as reasonably practicable, the waste regulation authority was informed [Act 1990/33(7)].

If an offence by a company is proved to have been with the consent, connivance or neglect of any director, manager or similar officer, he is liable to prosecution [Act 1990/157].

Special waste

A carrier of special waste must complete part of a prescribed consignment note, prepared by the waste producer, before removing it from the production premises to a place for disposal [1709/80/4]. Special waste is any controlled waste which (a) contains specified substances which make it dangerous to life or give it a flash point of 21 degrees Celsius or less or (b) is a medicinal product available only on prescription [2].

The carrier must give copies of the consignment note supplied to him by the waste producer to the disposer but retaining one copy, on which all parts have been completed, for himself [5(1)].

A register containing copies of all consignment notes relating to special waste he has transferred for disposal must be kept by a carrier. Consignment notes must be kept in the register for at least two years after the waste removal involved [13].

It is a defence to a person charged under these Regulations to prove that he took all reasonable precautions and exercised all due diligence to avoid the offence by himself or any person under his control. It is a defence to a charge under Regulations 4 or 5 for a person to prove he was not reasonably able to comply by reason of an emergency and copies of the consignment note were completed and supplied as soon as practicable after the event [16].

Hazardous waste international transport

A person who has possession or control of hazardous waste must not cause or permit it to be transported from Great Britain to another EC country or a third country unless prescribed formalities, including giving the carrier a copy of the consignment note, are complied with [1562/88/3-9]. Hazardous waste is special waste, defined above.

A carrier must not transport such hazardous waste in Great Britain unless it is accompanied by a completed copy of the consignment note or, in the case of non-ferrous metal, an EC uniform document [16(1)]. The carrier must not transfer the load to another person in Great Britain without endorsing the consignment note and retaining a photocopy of it or, in the case of non-ferrous metal, passing him copies of the EC uniform document [16(2)].

A carrier intending to transport hazardous waste (other than non-ferrous metal) from Great Britain for disposal in a third country, without transitting an EC country or Northern Ireland, must, before the consignment leaves Great Britain, endorse a copy of the consignment note, deliver it to Customs and Excise at the port of departure and keep a photocopy of it [17]. Copies of consignment notes required to be kept by the carrier must be retained by him for at least two years [18].

It is an offence for a carrier to contravene the regulations but it is a defence to prove that he took all reasonable precautions and exercised all due diligence to avoid the offence being committed by himself or any person under his control [28]. If an offence by a company is proved to have been with the consent, connivance or neglect of any director, manager or similar officer, he is liable to prosecution [29].

Duty of care

It is the duty of any person who imports, produces, carries, keeps, treats or disposes of controlled waste to take all measures, applicable to him in that capacity, which are reasonable in the circumstances:

1. to prevent the deposit or disposal of controlled waste otherwise that under a waste management licence and to prevent the treatment, keeping or disposal of controlled waste in a manner likely to cause pollution to the environment or harm to human health.
2. to prevent the escape of waste from his control or that of any other person;
3. on the transfer of waste, to secure-
   (a) the transfer is only to an authorised person or to a person for authorised transport purposes; and
   (b) a written description of waste which will enable anyone to avoid an unauthorised deposit of controlled waste and comply with the duty of care regarding the escape of waste is transferred [Act 1990/34(1)].

An authorised person is a waste collection authority, the holder of a waste management licence or disposal licence, a registered carrier of controlled waste, a waste disposal authority in Scotland or a person coming within specified exemptions [34(3)].

Authorised transport purposes are:

1. transport of controlled waste between different places within the same premises; and
2. transport to a place in Great Britain of controlled waste brought from an outside country and not having been landed in Great Britain until it arrives at that place [34(4)].

TRANSFER NOTES

When the written description of waste (in 3(b) above) is transferred a transfer note must be completed and signed by the transferor and transferee of the waste [2839/91/2(1)].

The transfer note must:

(a) identify the waste and its quantity; state whether it is loose or in a container; the kind of container; and the time and place of transfer;

(b) give the names and address of the transferor and transferee;

(c) state whether the transferor is the producer or importer of the waste;

(d) if the transfer is for an authorised transport purpose, specify which purpose; and

(e) state which category of person the transferor and transferee belong to. The categories are a waste collection authority; a waste disposal authority in Scotland; the holder of a waste management licence or a person exempt from holding one; or a registered carrier of controlled waste or a person exempt from registration. A registered carrier must give the name of the authority he is registered with and his registration number [2(2)].

The transferor and transferee must each keep a copy of the written description of waste and the transfer note for two years after the transfer. A waste regulation authority can, by written notice, require production and a copy of these documents within seven days [3,4].

If an offence by a company is proved to have been with the consent, connivance or neglect of a director, manager or similar officer, he is liable to prosecution [Act 1990/157].

23 Weight limits

Road Traffic Act 1988
Road Vehicles (Construction and Use) Regulations, **No. 1078/86**
Road Vehicles (Construction and Use) (Amendment) (No. 4) Regulations,
   No. 2016/92
Road Vehicles (Construction and Use) (Amendment) (No. 2) Regulations,
   No. 329/94

Goods vehicles

RIGID TRUCKS AND DRAWBAR TRAILERS

A rigid vehicle which is:

(a) a heavy motor car or motor car, or
(b) a composite or drawbar trailer, unless fitted with overrun brakes
    or drawn by a locomotive,

and which complies with the relevant braking requirements, is subject
to the gross weight limit given in Table No. 1 opposite [1078/87/75(1)].
If such a motor vehicle has twin tyres on every driving axle (other than
a steering axle) and every driving axle has road friendly suspension or
an axle weight not over 9,500kg, the vehicle's gross weight is given in
Table 2 [75(1)].

'Relevant braking requirements' are that the brakes of the motor
vehicle are maintained so that the efficiencies of the service and
secondary braking systems are (a) in the case of a vehicle first used on
or after 1 April 1983, 50 and 25 per cent when the vehicle is not
drawing a trailer or 45 and 20 per cent when a trailer is drawn, or (b)
in any other case, 50 and 25 per cent [3(2)].

Throughout this chapter 'road friendly suspension' is air suspension
or a suspension regarded as equivalent to air by EC Directive 7/92;
'air suspension' is a system in which at least 75 per cent of the spring

430

Table 1
Maximum laden weight of motor cars and heavy motor cars not fitted with
road-friendly suspension and trailers—none of them forming part of an
articulated vehicle

Number of axles	Distance apart of outer axles—m	Permitted laden weight kg
2	Less than 2.65	14,230
2	At least 2.65	16,260
2	At least 3 (goods vehicles only)	17,000
2	At least 3 (trailer only)	18,000
2	Trailer with two closely-spaced axles with distance between rearmost axle of drawing vehicle and foremost axle of trailer at least 4.2	18,000
3	Trailer with three closely-spaced axles with distance between rearmost axle of drawing vehicle and foremost axle of trailer at least 4.2	24,000
3 or more	Less than 3	16,260
3 or more	At least 3 but less than 3.2	18,290
3 or more	At least 3.2 but less than 3.9	20,330
3 or more	At least 3.9 but less than 4.9	22,360
3	At least 4.9	25,000
4 or more	At least 4.9 but less than 5.6	25,000
4 or more	At least 5.6 but less than 5.9	26,420
4 or more	At least 5.9 but less than 6.3	28,450
4 or more	At least 6.3	30,000

[Sch. 11, Part II]

effect is caused by an air spring; and an 'air spring' is a spring operated by air or other compressible fluid under pressure [75(4)(5)].

The weights in Tables 1 and 2 do not prevent a vehicle for which a plating certificate was in force immediately before 1 January 1993 from being used at the British legal gross weight limit shown in that certificate [75(3A)].

In the case of a vehicle, including a composite trailer, first used before 1 June 1973 and which comes within Table 1, the weight limits given there will not be taken to reduce its maximum laden weight below 14,230kg in the case of a four-wheeler; 20,330kg for a six-wheeler; or 24,390kg for a vehicle with more than six wheels [75(2)].

The maximum laden weight of a heavy motor car or motor car which does not come within Table 1 (e.g. does not meet braking criteria) is 14,230kg in the case of a four-wheeler; 20,330kg for a six-wheeler; and 24,390kg for a vehicle with more than six wheels [75(1)].

Table 2

Maximum laden weight of motor cars and heavy motor cars with a drive axle(s) fitted with twin tyres and road-friendly suspension and not forming part of an articulated vehicle

Number of axles	Distance apart of outer axles—m	Permitted laden weight kg
2	Less than 2.65	14,230
2	At least 2.65	16,260
2	At least 3 (goods vehicles only)	17,000
3 or more	Less than 3	16,260
3 or more	At least 3 but less than 3.2	18,290
3 or more	At least 3.2 but less than 3.9	20,330
3 or more	At least 3.9 but less than 4.9	22,360
3 or more	At least 4.9 but less than 5.2	25,000
3	At least 5.2	26,000
4 or more	At least 5.2 but less than 6.4	Distance in m between foremost and rearmost axles multiplied by 5,000kg and rounded up to next 10kg
4 or more	At least 6.4	32,000

[Sch. 11, Part IA]

A drawbar or composite trailer which does not come within Table 1 or the following paragraph and has less than 6 wheels is limited to 14,230kg maximum laden weight [75(1)].

The total laden weight of a trailer made before 27 February 1977 with no brakes other than overrun brakes and a parking brake must not exceed 3,560kg. But in the case of a trailer made on or after this date and which is fitted with overrun brakes, whether or not it is fitted with any other brake, the total laden weight must not exceed 3,500kg. This last limit does not apply to certain agricultural trailers [75(1)].

ARTICULATED DRAWING UNITS

The gross weight limits for a heavy motor car or motor car (other than an agricultural motor vehicle) which forms part of an articulated vehicle and complies with the relevant braking requirements are given in Table 3 opposite [1078/86/75(1)].

The maximum laden weight of a heavy motor car or motor car which does not come within Table 3 (e.g. does not meet braking or axle-weight criteria) is 14,230kg in the case of a four-wheeler; 20,330kg for a six-wheeler; and 24,390kg for a vehicle with more than six wheels [75(1)].

In the case of a vehicle first used before 1 June 1973 and which comes within Table 3, the weight limits given there will not be taken to reduce its maximum laden weight below 14,230kg in the case of a four-wheeler; 20,330kg for a six-wheeler; or 24,390kg for a vehicle with more than six wheels [75(2)].

Table 3
Maximum laden weight for heavy motor car or motor car forming part of an articulated vehicle

Number of axles	Spacing between outer axles m	Weight not exceeded by any axle kg	Permitted gross weight kg
2	at least 2.0	—	14,230
2	at least 2.4	—	16,260
2	at least 2.7	—	17,000
3 or more	at least 3.0	8,390	20,330
3 or more	at least 3.8	8,640	22,360
3 or more	at least 4.0	10,500	22,500
3 or more	at least 4.3	9,150	24,390
3 or more	at least 4.9	10,500	24,390

[Sch. 11, Part II]

ROAD TRAINS

Except for agricultural vehicles, the permitted maximum train weight of a drawbar trailer and the motor tractor, heavy motor car or motor car drawing it is as follows:

44,000kg – combined road/rail operation—see page 439

38,000kg – if the motor vehicle was first used on or after 1 April 1973; complies with relevant braking requirements; every driving axle (other than a steering axle) has twin tyres; every driving axle has road friendly suspension or no axle exceeds 8,500kg; and the combination has a total of 5 or more axles.

35,000kg – if the motor vehicle was first used on or after 1 April 1973; complies with relevant braking requirements; the combination has 4 axles and is being used for international transport.

35,000kg – if the motor vehicle was first used on or after 1 April 1973; complies with relevant braking requirements; every driving axle (other than a steering axle) has twin tyres; every driving axle has road friendly suspension; and the combination has 4 axles.

32,520kg – if the trailer (not within the above) has driver-operated

power-assisted brakes and the drawing vehicle is fitted
with a device to warn of a vacuum or air-pressure failure.
29,500kg – if the trailer was made on or after 27 February 1977, has
overrun brakes and the drawing vehicle was first used on
or after 1 April 1973 and it complies with the relevant
braking requirements.
24,390kg – if not within the above descriptions.
22,360kg – if either trailer or drawing vehicle is a track-laying vehicle.
[1078/86/76(1)].

ARTICULATED VEHICLES

Except for combined road/rail transport operations (see page 439), the
laden weight of an articulated vehicle, which complies with the
relevant braking requirements, is the lower of that given in Table 4
and Table 5 overleaf [1078/86/77(1)]. These Tables do not apply to
agricultural vehicles [77(2)].

Table 4
Maximum laden weight of articulated vehicle

Minimum axle spacing		Maximum weight
Motor vehicle with 2 axles m	Motor vehicle with 3 or more axles m	kg
2.0	2.0	20,330
2.2	2.2	22,360
2.6	2.6	23,370
2.9	2.9	24,390
3.2	3.2	25,410
3.5	3.5	26,420
3.8	3.8	27,440
4.1	4.1	28,450
4.4	4.4	29,470
4.7	4.7	30,490
5.0	5.0	31,500
5.3	5.3	32,520
5.5	5.4	33,000
5.8	5.6	34,000
6.2	5.8	35,000
6.5	6.0	36,000
6.7	6.2	37,000
6.9	6.3	38,000

In this table minimum axle spacing is the distance between the rearmost axle
of the tractor unit and the rearmost axle of the semi-trailer

[Sch. 11, Part III]

Table 5

Motor vehicle first used on or after 1 April 1973 and semi-trailer having a total of five or more axles	38,000kg
Motor vehicle with two axles first used on or after 1 April 1973 and a semi-trailer with two axles while being used for international transport	35,000kg
Motor vehicle with two axles first used on or after 1 April 1973 with every driving axle(s) (other than a steering axle) fitted with twin tyres and every driving axle(s) fitted with road-friendly suspension and coupled to a semi-trailer with two axles	35,000kg
Motor vehicle and semi-trailer with a total of four or more axles and not described above	32,520kg
Motor vehicle with two axles first used on or after 1 April 1973 with every driving axle (other than a steering axle) fitted with twin tyres and every driving axle fitted with road-friendly suspension and coupled to a semi-trailer with one axle	26,000kg
Motor vehicle with two axles and a semi-trailer with one axle not described above	25,000kg

[Sch. 11, Part IV]

If an articulated vehicle does not comply with the relevant braking requirements its permitted laden weight is 20,330kg if the trailer has less than 4 wheels and 24,390kg if it has 4 wheels or more [77(1)].

BOGIE WEIGHTS

The bogie weight limits in this section apply to motor vehicles which comply with the relevant braking requirements; trailers drawn by such vehicles; and agricultural motor vehicles, trailers and trailed appliances [1078/86/79(1)].

Where a vehicle described in Table 8 (page 437) has two closely-spaced axles the total weight transmitted by them to the road must not exceed the figure specified [79(2)]. Two axles are closely spaced if they are not more than 2.5m apart [3(8A)].

Where a vehicle described in Table 9 (page 437) has three closely-spaced axles the total weight transmitted by them to the road must not exceed the figure specified [79(3)]. Three axles are closely spaced if the outermost axles are not more than 3.25m apart [3(8A)].

Where a vehicle has four closely-spaced axles the weight transmitted by them to the road must not exceed 24,000kg [79(4)]. Four axles are closely spaced if the outermost axles are not more than 4.6m apart [3(8A)].

None of the above limits prevents (a) a vehicle first used before 1 June 1973 from being used at axle weights at which it could be used at if it came with item 5 of Table 7 and (b) a vehicle for which a plating certificate was in force immediately before 1 January 1993 from being used with an axle weight not exceeding the British legal axle weight limit shown on the certificate for that axle [79(5)].

AXLE WEIGHTS

Table 6

Heavy motor cars, motor cars and trailers which comply with the relevant braking requirements; agricultural motor vehicles, trailers and wheeled appliances; and, in items 1(b) and 2, buses

Item	Wheel criteria	Maximum weight kg
1	Two wheels in line where each wheel has a wide tyre or two tyres with centres not more than 300mm apart:	
	(a) if on the sole driving axle of a motor vehicle which is not a bus;	10,500
	(b) if the vehicle is a two-axled bus and weight is calculated under Regulation 78(5)	10,500
	(c) in any other case.	10,170
2	Two wheels in line but not coming within item 1.	9,200
3	More than two wheels in line:	
	(a) in the case of a vehicle made before 1 May 1983 if the wheels are on one of two closely-spaced axles	10,170
	(b) in the case of a vehicle made on or after 1 May 1983	10,170
	(c) in any other case	11,180
4	One wheel with no other in line:	
	(a) if it has a wide tyre or two tyres with centres not more than 300mm apart	5,090
	(b) in any other case	4,600

A wide tyre is a pneumatic tyre with an area of contact with the road at least 300mm wide [3(2)].

Table 7

Heavy motor cars, motor cars and trailers not within Table 6

5	More than two wheels transmitting weight to a strip of road at right angles to the length of the vehicle:	
	(a) less than 1.02m wide	11,180
	(b) 1.02m but less than 1.22m wide	16,260
	(c) 1.22m but less than 2.3m wide	18,300
6	Two wheels in line	9,200
7	One wheel where no other in line	4,600

[1078/86/78(1)(2)].

Table 8
Vehicles with two closely-spaced axles

Item	Description of vehicle	Total permitted weight of both axles—kg
1	Motor vehicle or trailer where the distance between the axles is less than 1.3m	16,000
2	Motor vehicle where distance between the axles is at least 1.3m or a trailer where distance between the axles is at least 1.3m and less than 1.5m, in either case not being a vehicle in 3 or 4 below	18,000
3	Motor vehicle where distance between the axles is at least 1.3m and every driving axle (other than a steering axle) is fitted with twin tyres and every driving axle has either road-friendly suspension or neither of them has an axle weight exceeding 9,500kg	19,000
4	Trailer with both axles driven from the drawing vehicle, fitted with twin tyres and either road-friendly suspension or neither has an axle weight exceeding 9,500kg	19,000
5	Trailer where distance between the axles is at least 1.5m but less than 1.8m	19,320
6	Trailer where distance between the axles is at least 1.8m	20,000

[Sch. 11, Part V]

Table 9
Vehicles with three closely-spaced axles

Item	Description of vehicle	Total permitted weight of both axles—kg
1	A vehicle in which the smallest distance between any two of the axles is less than 1.3m	21,000
2	A vehicle in which the smallest distance between any two of the axles is at least 1.3m and at least one of the axles does not have air suspension	22,500
3	A vehicle in which the smallest distance between any two of the axles is at least 1.3m and all three axles are fitted with air suspension	24,000

[Sch. 11, Part VI]

PLATED WEIGHTS

A person must not use on a road:
(a) a vehicle fitted with a maker's plate under Regulation 66, but for which no Ministry plating certificate has been issued, if any of the weights shown on the plate are exceeded;
(b) a vehicle for which a plating certificate has been issued, if any of the weights shown in column 2 of the certificate are exceeded;
(c) an agricultural trailed appliance fitted with a maker's plate under Regulation 68 if the plated maximum gross weight is exceeded [1078/86/80(1)].

In *Travel-Gas (Midlands) Ltd v Reynolds* [1989] RTR 75 it was held that Regulation 80(1) made it an offence to exceed each plated weight of a vehicle. It was also said that if there was no special culpability on the part of the driver, it would be wholly unnecessary to proceed against him as well as the vehicle owner.

The above restrictions do not apply:
a. to a vehicle for which a Schedule 10A or 10C plating certificate has been issued (i.e. an EC-type plate—see pages 260 and 262), the vehicle is being used on an international journey and none of the weights in column 3 of the certificate (EC maximum weights) is exceeded;
b. to the plated train weight of a motor vehicle where both a train weight and a maximum train weight are shown on its plating certificate, the vehicle complies with Schedule 11A (combined road/rail transport operations) and the maximum train weight in column 2 of the certificate is not exceeded [80(2A),(2B)].

If two or more axles are fitted with a compensator under Regulation 23 the sum of their Ministry plated weights must not be exceeded. If a plating certificate has not been issued, the sum of their maker's plated weights must not be exceeded [80(2)]. In *DPP v Marshall* [1990] RTR 384 it was ruled that charges for overloading compensated axles were correctly brought under Regulation 80(1) with Regulation 80(2) being only a qualification.

The weight limits in Regulations 75 to 79 do not permit a plated weight to be exceeded and vice versa [80(3)].

If, in any proceedings for a construction and use offence, a question arises as to a weight specified in a goods vehicle plating certificate and a weight of that description is marked on the vehicle (e.g. on a Ministry plate) it will be assumed, unless the contrary is proved, that the weight marked on the vehicle is the weight specified in the plating certificate [Road Traffic Offenders Act 1988/17(1)].

Combined road/rail transport operations

An articulated vehicle or a drawbar combination (comprising a heavy motor car and a trailer) can have a gross train weight up to 44 tonnes if engaged in a combined transport operation. This is defined as the transport of

(a) a bi-modal vehicle, i.e. a semi-trailer which can be used as a rail vehicle, or

(b) a receptacle at least 6.1m long designed for repeated carriage of goods and for transfer between road and rail vehicles (e.g. an ISO container),

on a journey where part is by railway on a network operated by British Rail or under a network licence; part is by road; and no goods or added to or removed from (a) or (b) between the beginning and end of the journey.

In the case of a drawbar combination, the motor vehicle and trailer must each be carrying a receptacle and, in the case of an articulated vehicle, it must be being used for the conveyance of a bi-modal vehicle or receptacle, in both cases, to a railhead from where it is to be transported by rail under a contract made before the journey began or transported from a railhead after rail transport. Rail transport does not include a piggy-back operation where the receptacle is carried on a vehicle which is itself carried on a rail wagon.

In the vehicle cab there must be a document specifying

a. in the case of a journey to a railhead, the railhead, the date the contract was made and the parties to it or,

b. in the case of a journey from a railhead, the railhead and the date and time the receptacle or bi-modal trailer was collected from the railhead.

DRAWBAR COMBINATION

The drawing vehicle must comply with braking efficiency rules; its driving axle(s) (not being a steering axle) must be fitted with twin tyres; and either the driving axle(s) must be fitted with road-friendly suspension or no axle must be over 8,500kg. The combination must have at least six axles and its total laden weight must not exceed 44 tonnes.

ARTICULATED VEHICLE

The tractor unit must comply with braking efficiency rules; its driving axle(s) (not being a steering axle) must be fitted with twin tyres; and either the driving axle(s) must be fitted with road-friendly suspension or no axle must be over 8,500kg. The tractor must have at least three axles and the articulated vehicle must have at least six axles. The distance between the rearmost tractor axle and the rearmost trailer axle must be at least 6.7m and the total laden weight must not exceed the following:

Minimum axle spacing—m	Maximum laden weight—kg
6.7	39,000
7.1	40,000
7.4	41,000
7.6	42,000
7.8	43,000
8.0	44,000

[1078/86/Sch.11A & 329/94]

Locomotives

The total laden weight of a locomotive must not exceed 20,830kg. But if each of its wheels is sprung and is fitted with a pneumatic or solid tyre the weight may be 22,360kg if it has less than six wheels; 26,420kg with six wheels; or 30,490kg with more than six wheels [75(1)]. Except for road rollers and four-wheeled locomotives first used before 1 June 1955, the axle weight must not exceed 11,180kg. On a four-wheeled locomotive first used before 1 June 1955, not more than three-quarters of its total weight may be on one axle [78(2)].

There are no weight limits for solo motor tractors since such a vehicle would become a locomotive if its weight, apart from fuel, loose tools, etc., exceeded 7,370kg.

The total laden weight of all trailers drawn by a locomotive must not exceed 40,650kg [75(3)].

Agricultural vehicles

An agricultural trailed appliance which is required to be fitted with a maker's plate must not exceed the maximum gross weight given on that plate [1078/86/80(1)(c)].

The total weight of an agricultural motor vehicle or a balanced agricultural trailer must not exceed the weight limit for a comparable rigid goods vehicle (see Table 1, page 431) except that an agricultural motor vehicle is restricted to a total weight of 24,390kg and a balanced agricultural trailer to 18,290kg. A balanced agricultural trailer is one where the whole of its weight is borne by its own wheels.

The total weight of an unbalanced agricultural trailer togetl the weight it imposes on the drawing vehicle must not 18,290kg. An unbalanced agricultural trailer is one where no than 35 per cent of its weight is borne by the drawing vehicle and the remainder is borne by its own wheels.

The total weight of an agricultural trailed appliance must not exceed 14,230kg [75(1)].

The total weight of an agricultural motor vehicle and any trailer or trailers it draws must not exceed (a) where an unbalanced agricultural trailer is drawn and the distance between the rearmost axle of the trailer and rearmost axle of the drawing vehicle does not exceed 2.9m, 20,000kg; or (b) in any other case, 24,390kg [76(1)].

Agricultural vehicles are also subject to the same bogie weight limits as normal goods vehicles, see page 435.

Buses

A bus is a motor vehicle constructed or adapted to carry more than 8 seated passengers in addition to the driver [1078/86/3(2)].

The gross weight and axle weight limits for a bus are given in Tables 1 and 4 on pages 431 and 434.

In the case of a vehicle first used on or after 1 April 1988, the weight is calculated when the vehicle is complete and fully equipped for service with (a) a full supply of water, oil and fuel; (b) a weight of 65kg for each person (including crew) in each seat and, where standing passengers may be carried, where each standing passenger may be carried, except that on a vehicle other than an articulated bus, the first four standees are disregarded; all luggage space outside the passenger compartment loaded at the rate of 100kg per cubic metre or 10kg per potential passenger, whichever is the less; and (d) any roof luggage area loaded at the rate of 75kg per square metre [78(5)].

In the case of a bus first used before 1 April 1988, weight is to be calculated when the vehicle is complete and fully equipped for service with (a) a full supply of water, oil and fuel; (b) weights of 63.5kg in each seating position and for each permitted standing passenger, except that on a vehicle other than an articulated bus, the first eight standees are disregarded [78(3)].

The weight of a bus (other than an articulated bus) coming within Regulation 78(3) may be calculated under Regulation 78(5) instead [78(4)].

The permitted maximum weight of an articulated bus is 27,000kg [75(1)].

The weight limits in Regulation 75 (Tables 1 and 2 on pages 431 and 432) do not apply to a two-axled bus if its laden weight as calculated under Regulation 78(5) does not exceed 17,000kg and the distance between its axles is at least 3m [78(6)].

Counting axles

Except for Regulations 26 and 27 (tyre mixing and maintenance), in counting the number of axles of a vehicle and the weight transmitted by any one axle, any number of wheels which rest within a strip of road surface 500mm wide at right angles to the length of the vehicle shall be counted as one axle [1078/86/3(8)], and, apart from those Regulations, two wheels will be regarded as one wheel if the distance between the centres of the areas of contact between the wheels and the road is less than 460mm [3(7)].

Where a four-wheeled vehicle exceeds front and rear axle weight limits and its gross weight limit three offences are committed— *J Theobold (Hounslow) Ltd v Stacy* [1979] RTR 411.

Defences

Section 41B(2) of the Road Traffic Act 1988 provides two defences to a person charged with contravening 'a construction and use requirement relating to any description of weight applicable to a goods vehicle'.

It is a defence to prove that when the vehicle was being used on a road it was going to a weighbridge which was the nearest available one to the loading place or the vehicle was going from a weighbridge after being weighed to the nearest point at which it was reasonably practicable to reduce the weight without causing an obstruction of the road. In *Lovett v Payne* [1980] RTR 103 it was held that 'nearest' meant nearest by road and not by a straight line on a map. In *Halliday v Burl* [1983] RTR 21 it was held that a weighbridge was 'available' even though it was cramped and vehicles entering or leaving created a risk to other road users.

The defence of proceeding to the nearest weighbridge is not available, it was ruled in *Hudson v Bushrod* [1982] RTR 87, in a prosecution for using a vehicle with a dangerously heavy load.

Where a limit is exceeded by not more than 5 per cent it is a defence to prove that the limit was not exceeded at the time of loading and that since loading no person has made any addition to the load.

In *Connolly v Lancashire County Council* [1994] RTR 79 the High Court ruled that tickets produced by a computerised weighbridge were not admissible in evidence, under Section 69(1) of the Police and

Criminal Evidence Act 1984, because there was no evidence that the computer was operating properly at the time in question.

In *R v Chelmsford Crown Court* [1990] RTR 80 it was ruled that a court should not have applied a rigid sentencing formula to a series of overloading offences. A formula is a justifiable base but in each case, even if there is only one offence, a court has to consider all the circumstances and apply well-known principles of sentencing.

Table 10

Community weights for vehicles on inter-state transport not yet in force in the UK but due to be implemented on 31 December 1998

Vehicle	*EC weight—kg*
Rigid truck with 2 axles	18,000
Lorry and drawbar trailer with four	36,000
Lorry and drawbar trailer with five or six axles	40,000
Artic with 4 axles:	
if trailer axles at least 1.3m apart	36,000
if trailer axles at least 1.8m apart, air suspension and double tyres ontractor drive axle	38,000
Artic with 5 axles or more	40,000
Artic with five axles or more (including a three-axled tractor) if carrying a 40ft ISO container on combined transport operation	44,000
Driving axle	11,500
Tri-axles	24,000

[EC Directive 85/3].

24 Visiting vehicles and drivers

Transport Act 1968
Road Traffic (Foreign Vehicles) Act 1972
Motor Vehicles (International Motor Insurance Card) Regulations, **No. 792/71**
Motor Vehicles (International Circulation) Order, **No. 1208/75**
Passenger and Goods Vehicles (Recording Equipment) Regulations, **No. 1746/79**
Goods Vehicles (Operators' Licences) (Temporary Use in Great Britain) Regulations, **No. 637/80**
Motor Vehicles (International Circulation) (Amendment) Order, **No. 1095/80**
Goods Vehicles (Operators' Licences) (Temporary Use in Great Britain) (Amendment) Regulations, **Nos. 37 and 527/81, 1832/83, 179 and 1835/84, 30/85, 1811/88, 2183/89** and **1191/90**
Motor Vehicles (Tests) Regulations, **No. 1694/81**
Goods Vehicles (Plating and Testing) Regulations, **No. 1478/82**
Road Transport (International Passenger Services) Regulations, **No. 748/84**
Road Vehicles Lighting Regulations, **No. 1796/89**
Motor Vehicles (International Circulation) (Amendment) Order, **Nos. 459/85, 993/89** and **771/91**
Motor Vehicles (International Circulation) Regulations **No. 610/85**
Road Vehicles (Construction and Use) Regulations, **No. 1078/86**
Motor Vehicles (Driving Licences) Regulations, **No. 1378/87**
Motor Vehicles (Driving Licences) (Amendment) Regulations, **No. 1602/93**

In this chapter are gathered together the various exemptions from British transport law given to vehicles and drivers from abroad which are temporarily in Great Britain. These exemptions benefit not only foreign residents but also British-based operators who draw foreign-based semi-trailers or who themselves have bases on the continent. Also described in this chapter are the additional law enforcement powers which relate only to foreign-based vehicles.

In most of the exemptions the terms Great Britain and United Kingdom are used, often in the same sentence. To avoid misunderstanding in such cases it is necessary to point out that Great Britain includes England, Scotland and Wales while the United Kingdom is England, Scotland, Wales and Northern Ireland. The Isle of Man and the Channel Islands are not in Great Britain or the United Kingdom.

Driver licensing

A person resident outside the United Kingdom who is temporarily in Great Britain and who holds:

(a) an international driving permit issued by a country outside the United Kingdom under the 1949 Geneva Convention or the 1926 Paris Convention; or
(b) a domestic driving permit issued in a country outside the United Kingdom; or
(c) a British Forces driving licence,

may, during the 12 months from his last date of entry into the United Kingdom, drive and be employed in driving in Great Britain a motor vehicle of a class authorised by his permit or licence, except a passenger-carrying vehicle or large goods vehicle, even though he does not hold a British driving licence. The reference to employment does not apply to the holder of a British Forces licence [1208/75/2(1), 993/89 and 771/91]. In the case of *Flores v Scott* [1984] RTR 363 it was ruled that a student from Mexico who intended staying in Britain for five years was not, from the moment he arrived in Britain, temporarily in Great Britain.

A person resident outside the United Kingdom who is temporarily in Great Britain and who holds:

(a) an international driving permit issued by a country outside the United Kingdom under the 1949 Geneva Convention or the 1926 Paris Convention; or
(b) a domestic driving permit issued in a country outside the United Kingdom,

may, during the 12 months from his last entry into the United Kingdom drive or be employed in driving in Great Britain any passenger-carrying vehicle or large goods vehicle even though he does not hold a British pcv or lgv licence [1208/75/2(2), 993/89 and 771/91].

A person resident outside the United Kingdom, who is temporarily in Great Britain and holds a British Forces (BFG) public service vehicle driving licence may, during the period of 12 months from his last entry into Great Britain, drive, and be employed in driving, any pcv if he is resident in another EC country, or, in any other case, a pcv brought temporarily into Great Britain and, in either case, if it is of a class authorised in the licence [1208/75/2(3), 993/89 and 771/91].

The above provisions do not authorise a person to drive vehicles in the United Kingdom if he is under the statutory minimum age (see page 86), but the minimum age of 21 years is changed to 18 years for a person, authorised above, who is not resident in the Community, the vehicle is not registered in an EC or AETR country or it is a goods vehicle for which the driver has a certificate of competence and it is brought temporarily into Great Britain [1205/75/2(4) and 993/89].

A member of a visiting force, a member of a civilian component of a visiting force and a dependent of any such member who, in each case, holds a driving permit issued in the sending country or by the visiting force can drive vehicles, other than an lgv or pcv, authorised by the permit in Great Britain without holding an ordinary British driving licence but he must comply with UK minimum age limits [1208/75/3(1), 3(3), 993/89 and 771/91].

The above provisions do not permit a person to drive a vehicle of any class if he has been convicted by a British court and is disqualified from holding a British ordinary driving licence [1208/75/2(5), 3(2) and 993/89].

The holder of a driving permit issued outside the United Kingdom or of a British Forces driving licence who becomes resident in Great Britain shall for five years after he becomes resident be regarded as the holder of a British ordinary driving licence as long as he is not disqualified from holding a British licence [1378/87/25(1) & 1602/93].

Those Sections of the Road Traffic Act 1972 which give a court and police power to require the production of a driving licence and prohibit the forgery and misuse of driving licences also apply to foreign permits and British Forces driving licences [1378/87/25(3)] and UK-issued permits [1095/80/8].

A person from abroad who becomes resident in Britain, or who is a visitor to Britain, and who holds a permit which enables him to drive in Britain for 12 months does not, during that period, if he takes out a British provisional licence, have to comply with the conditions attached to that licence, i.e. display L plates, be accompanied by a qualified driver or not draw a trailer [1378/87/9(5)].

Insurance

Where a motor vehicle specified in a valid insurance green card is used on a road by the visitor to whom the card was issued, or by a hiring visitor named in it, or any other person on their order or with their permission, the card will be treated as a policy of insurance meeting the compulsory third-party insurance requirements of Section 143 of the Road Traffic Act 1988. If a vehicle remains in the United Kingdom after the expiry date specified in the card then, as respects any time it is in Great Britain, the card will not be regarded as having ceased to be in force for the purposes of Section 143 by reason only of its expiry [792/71/5(1)].

For the purposes of the legal requirements relating to the production of a certificate of insurance to police or in case of an injury accident, a valid insurance green card will have effect as though it was a certificate of insurance [6(1)].

A visitor who applies for a road tax licence under the Vehicles (Excise) Act 1971 for a vehicle specified in a valid insurance green card in which he is named as the insured, may produce the card instead of an insurance certificate to the licensing authority as proof of insurance [8].

Vehicle excise duty (road tax)

A vehicle brought temporarily into Great Britain by a person resident outside the United Kingdom and which would otherwise be chargeable with vehicle excise duty under the Vehicle Excise and Registration Act 1994 is exempt from such duty for the same period that it is exempt from customs duty (normally three months for a commercial vehicle and six months for a private car) [1208/75/5 and 459/85].

A person resident outside the United Kingdom who brings a vehicle temporarily into Great Britain must, at any reasonable time he is required to do so, produce to a registration authority specified documents which have been issued for the vehicle. The documents are (a) a certificate of insurance or security or insurance green card; (b) a visitor's registration document; and (c) a registration card [610/85/4(1), (2)]. He must also produce a visitor's registration document at any reasonable time he is required to do so by a police officer or a person acting for the Secretary of State [4(3)].

A registration authority for these purposes is defined as the Royal Automobile Club, the Scottish Royal Automobile Club, the Automobile Association or the Secretary of State for Transport. A visitor's registration document is a registration certificate issued by a country outside the United Kingdom, a certificate under the 1926 Paris Convention issued outside the United Kingdom or a registration certificate issued by British or American authorities in Germany. A registration card is a document issued by one of the above registration authorities when it assigns a registration mark containing the letter Q to a vehicle [3(1)].

Under the international circulation arrangements the registration mark assigned to a visiting vehicle which is exempt from vehicle excise duty is:

(a) in a case where the driver holds a visitor's registration document which records a registration mark consisting only of Roman letters or ordinary European numerals or both, that registration mark; and

(b) in any other case, a registration mark containing the letter Q which is allocated to it by a registration authority [5].

When a Q registration mark is allocated to a vehicle the registration authority must issue to the person who brought it into Great Britain a registration card [6(1)]. The owner of the vehicle must produce the registration card when, at any reasonable time, he is required to do so by a police officer or by the Secretary of State. It is an offence to deface or mutilate a registration card or to alter, obliterate or add to any entries made on it [6(2)]. When a visiting vehicle for which a registration card has been issued is (i) sold or transferred; (ii) removed to a country outside the United Kingdom; or (iii) destroyed, the holder of the card must surrender it to a registration authority and state the reason for the transfer and, in a case of sale or transfer, give the name of the new owner and his address, if any, in the United Kingdom [6(3)].

A person who brings into Great Britain a visiting vehicle which is not exempt from vehicle excise duty must apply for a vehicle excise licence for it [7].

The vehicle's registration mark must be displayed at the front and back of the vehicle in the manner required under British law but, where a vehicle keeps its own national registration mark, it does not have to comply with the form prescribed for British registration marks and a front registration mark does not have to be displayed if it is not required in the vehicle's country of registration [8(1)].

At the back of a visiting vehicle which keeps the registration mark of its country of registration there must be exhibited a nationality sign indicating the country where the registration mark was issued. This requirement does not apply to a vehicle registered by British or American authorities in Germany [8(2)]. If a visiting vehicle draws a trailer a duplicate of the vehicle's registration mark must be displayed at the rear of a trailer. Except that where a visiting vehicle keeps its own registration mark and draws a trailer brought temporarily into Great Britain a registration mark issued to the trailer by a country outside the United Kingdom may be displayed instead of the registration mark of the drawing vehicle [8(3)]. At the rear of a trailer there must also be exhibited a nationality sign relating to the country (outside the UK) which issued the registration mark displayed on the trailer[8(4)].

A registration mark assigned to a vehicle under Regulation 5 (whether its own registration mark or a Q plate) becomes void when customs relief ceases to be given to the vehicle (three months for a commercial vehicle and six months for a private car) or, if the vehicle is sold or transferred during this period, at that earlier time. If a vehicle is used in Great Britain after the registration mark has become void it must be registered under the Vehicle Excise and Registration Act 1994 [8(5)].

Vehicle tests

The legal requirement for three-year-old cars, motor cycles and goods vehicles not over 1,525kg unladen weight to have a test certificate does not apply to a vehicle brought temporarily into Great Britain during the 12 months since its last entry. The exemption applies only to vehicles which display a registration mark assigned under Regulation 5 of the Motor Vehicles (International Circulation) Regulations 1985 (that is, the vehicle's own number or a Q plate) [1694/81/6(1)(j)].

Provided the above conditions are complied with, the requirement for mechanically propelled goods vehicles over 1,525kg unladen weight and over one year old to have a test certificate and a plating certificate does not apply during the 12 months since the vehicle's last entry into Great Britain [1478/82/Sch. 2].

Exemption is also made from the requirement that goods carrying drawbar trailers over 1,020kg unladen weight and semi-trailers, in either case over one year old, have a test certificate and a plating certificate. It applies to trailers brought into Great Britain and which have a base or centre in a country outside Great Britain from which the vehicle's journey is normally commenced, during the 12-month period following the vehicle's last entry into Great Britain [1478/82/Sch. 2].

Operators' licensing

Operators' licensing does not apply to foreign goods vehicles brought temporarily into Great Britain provided specified conditions are complied with. No such vehicle can remain in Great Britain more than 3 months, engage in transport between points within the United Kingdom and some part of the carriage of goods by the vehicle must take place outside the United Kingdom. Additional, and different, conditions apply in respect of vehicles from particular countries with which Britain has bilateral road transport agreements. The countries and conditions are contained in the Goods Vehicles (Operators' Licences) (Temporary Use in Great Britain) Regulations 1980 as amended.

An operator's licence is not required for a Northern Ireland or foreign goods vehicle used for carrying goods between EC member states:

(a) where the vehicle is
   (i)   loaded or unloaded at a place not more than 25 km from the coast of Great Britain and unloaded or loaded at a place not more than 25 km from the coast of another Member State but the straight-line distance between the two places (disregarding sea travel on a regular lorry-carrying ferry) not exceeding 100 km, or
   (ii) a motor vehicle or trailer drawn by a foreign goods vehicle having a gross weight limit not over 6 metric tons or a permissible payload not over 3.5 metric tons; or
(b) where the goods are
   (i)   required for medical or surgical care in emergency relief, or
   (ii) carried in security vehicles accompanied by guards, or
   (iii) refuse or sewage; or
(c) where the vehicle is being used on a journey for combined transport, as defined in EC Directive 106/92, and a specified document to that effect is carried on the vehicle;
(d) where the goods are carried in connection with the trade or business of the carrier and
   (i)   they belong to the carrier or have been sold, bought, let on hire or hired, produced, extracted, processed or repaired by the carrier;
   (ii) they are being carried to or from the premises of the carrier or otherwise for the carrier;
   (iii) the vehicle is driven by the carrier's employee; and
   (iv) the vehicle is owned by the carrier or he has it on hire-purchase, except when a replacement vehicle is used in case of breakdown.   [637/80/5]

An operator's licence is not required for a Northern Ireland goods vehicle for the carriage of goods loaded at one place in Great Britain and delivered to another place in Great Britain [4(2) and 1191/90] nor for a foreign goods vehicle used under a cabotage authorisation which is carried on the vehicle [6A and 1191/90].

Exemption from operators' licensing is also given to a vehicle used under an EC permit or an ECMT licence provided the permit or licence is carried on the vehicle or for removals carriage under an authorisation granted under EC Directive 269/1965 as long as the authorisation is carried on the vehicle [6 and 1832/83].

If a person resident outside the United Kingdom wishes to obtain an operator's licence for a motor vehicle or trailer brought temporarily into Great Britain he should apply to the Licensing Authority of the traffic area where the vehicle is landed [1208/75/6(1)].

The provisions of the Transport Act 1968 which deal with the grant and termination of operators' licences are modified to provide a simplified procedure in relation to foreign goods vehicles [637/80/34 and Sch. 5].

Public service vehicle licensing

A psv constructed to carry not more than 9 persons (including the driver) which is registered outside the United Kingdom and is brought into Great Britain for carrying passengers to Great Britain from outside the United Kingdom (or vice versa) and which remains in Great Britain for not more than three months is exempt from psv, operator and psv driver licensing and the requirement to have a certificate of initial fitness [748/84/7].

A vehicle for carrying more than 9 persons (including the driver) which is registered in an EC Member State outside the United Kingdom which provides a regular, shuttle or works service under Article 1, 2 or 6 of the EC Regulation 117/66 and is used in accordance with the relevant Council Regulations (see pages 332 to 337) is exempt from psv operator and psv driver licensing and the requirement to have a certificate of initial fitness [8].

A psv which is registered outside the United Kingdom but not in a Member State which is being used for the international carriage of passengers, in so far as the vehicle is used to provide a regular or shuttle service (as in Article 1 or 2 of EC Regulation 117/66) and is so authorised in its country of registration, is exempt from needing a certificate of initial fitness, or psv driver's licence and, instead of a psv operator's licence, there is carried on the vehicle an international passenger transport authorisation [9].

A vehicle for carrying more than 9 persons (including the driver) registered in an ASOR state (i.e. a party to the Agreement on International Carriage of Passengers by Road by means of Occasional Bus and Coach Services) or in an EC Member State outside the United Kingdom which is used to carry passengers

(a) on a closed-door tour under Article 2(1)(a) of ASOR or Article 3(1)(a) of EC Regulation 117/66,
(b) a laden and unladen return journey under paragraphs (1)(b) of these Articles,
(c) any other occasional service as described in paragraphs (1)(c) of those Articles,

and the vehicle is used in accordance with a passenger waybill carried on it, then the requirements as to certificate of initial fitness and psv driver licensing does not apply. And, in (a) and (b) above, where specified requirements are complied with, and in (c) above where an international passenger transport authorisation is carried on the vehicle, psv operators' licensing does not apply [10].

A psv registered in an ECMT state (i.e. a member of the European Conference of Ministers of Transport), other than an EC or ASOR state, which is brought into Great Britain carrying passengers for a temporary stay or in transit and does not remain more than three months, in so far as the vehicle is used to provide the type of service in (a), (b) or (c) above; the journey starts in an ECMT state and end in such a state or Great Britain; and the vehicle is authorised in its country of registration, the requirements as to certificate of initial fitness and psv driver licensing do not apply. And if, in the case of a service of type (a) or (b) a specified waybill is carried on the vehicle or, in the case of a service of type (c), an international passenger transport authorisation is carried on the vehicle, then psv operators' licensing does not apply [11].

A psv which is not registered in an EC, ECMT or ASOR state brought into Great Britain for carrying passengers for a temporary stay or in transit and who commenced the journey in the vehicle's country of registration or in Northern Ireland and which remains in Great Britain for not more than three months, in so far as it used to provide an occasional service of type (a), (b) or (c) above and is authorised in its country of registration, is exempt from the requirements as to certificate of initial fitness and psv driver licence and, as long as the vehicle carries an international passenger transport authorisation, from psv operators' licensing [12].

An international passenger transport authorisation is a licence, permit, authorisation or other document issued by the Secretary of State [748/84/Sch. 2].

An examiner, on production of his authority if required, may require the driver of a vehicle on an ASOR or Community regulated service to produce any authorisation, waybill or certificate required to be carried on the vehicle by virtue of the exempting provision. He may detain the vehicle for this purpose [16 & 17].

The PSV (Conditions of Fitness, Equipment, Use and

Certification) Regulations 1981 do not apply to a vehicle brought into Great Britain under the foregoing provisions [23].

Construction

A motor vehicle or trailer brought temporarily into Great Britain by a person resident abroad is exempt from specified construction requirements of the Road Vehicles (Construction and Use) Regulations 1986 provided it complies with:

(a) Articles 21 and 22(1) of the Convention on Road Traffic concluded at Geneva on 19 September 1949, and Part I, Part II (as far as it relates to direction indicators and stop lights) and Part III of Annex 6 to that Convention; or

(b) Paragraphs I, III, and VIII of Article 3 of the International Convention on Motor Traffic concluded at Paris on 24 April 1926.   [1078/86/4(4)]

The requirements which do not apply are those contained in the following Regulations—

Regulation

9(1)	—bus height	35	—speedometer
11	—overhang	36	—speedometer maintenance
12	—ground clearance		
13	—bus turning circle	36A	—coach speed limiter
13A, 13B	—lorry turning circle	36B	—lorry speed limiter
14	—articulated bus coupling	36C	—limiter sealers
15, 16	—brakes	37	—warning instruments
17	—brake pressure warning	38	—motor cycle stands
18	—brakes' maintenance	39	—petrol tanks
19	—application of trailer brakes	39A, 39B	—unleaded petrol
		41 to 44	—minibuses
20	—wheels compulsory	45	—power to weight ratio
21	—diameter of wheels	46	—seat belt anchorages
22	—springs	47	—seat belts
23	—compensator	48	—seat belt maintenance
24	—tyres	49	—rear underrun protection
25	—tyre loads		
26	—tyre mixing	50	—rear underrun protection maintenance
27	—tyre maintenance		
28	—tracks	51	—sideguards
29	—steering	52	—sideguard maintenance
30	—view to front	53A	—coach strength
31, 32	—glass	53B	—coach exits
33	—mirrors	54	—silencers
34	—wipers and washers	55 to 59	—noise limits

60	—radio interference	64	—spray suppression
	suppression	65	—spray suppression
61	—smoke		maintenance
62	—closets	66 to 69	—makers' plates
63	—wings	71	—unladen weight marking

The relevant parts of the Conventions referred to above are given at the end of this chapter on pages 458 to 467.

A foreign-based trailer brought temporarily into Great Britain is not subject to the requirements relating to rear under-run protection devices or sideguards [1078/86/49, 51]

Lights

Any vehicle which has a base or centre in a country outside Great Britain from which it normally starts its journeys is exempt from the need to fit lamps, reflectors and rear markings under the British law as long as a period of 12 months has not elapsed since the vehicle was last brought into Great Britain and the vehicle complies with the requirements as to lights and reflectors contained in the Convention on Road Traffic concluded at Geneva in 1949 or the International Convention on Motor Traffic concluded at Paris in 1926 [1796/89/5].

The relevant parts of the Conventions referred to above are given at the end of this chapter on pages 458 to 467.

Tachographs

In a goods or passenger vehicle to which EC Regulation 3821/85 applies there must be installed a tachograph which complies with that Regulation and the tachograph must be used in accordance with Articles 13 to 15 of that Regulation [Act 1968/97(1) and (6) and 1746/79]. These Articles are explained on pages 125 and 126.

Any record produced by the tachograph or any entry made on a record sheet by a crew member can be used in evidence—by the prosecution or defence—in any court proceedings for hours, records and tachograph offences [Act 1968/97B].

The statutory defences provided for persons accused of contravening the tachograph rules are given on page 131.

Extra prohibition powers

In addition to their general powers to enforce transport law (listed in the chapter Powers of Police, etc.) Department of Transport examiners and police have further powers which relate only to foreign vehicles and their drivers. They are contained in the Road Traffic (Foreign Vehicles) Act 1972. They apply to foreign goods vehicles and foreign public service vehicles.

A foreign goods vehicle is defined, for the purposes of this Act, as a goods vehicle which has been brought into Great Britain and which, if a motor vehicle, is not registered in the United Kingdom or, if a trailer, is drawn by a motor vehicle which is not registered in the United Kingdom and which has been brought into Great Britain [Act 1972/7(1)]. A foreign public service vehicle is defined as a public service vehicle which has been brought temporarily into Great Britain and is not registered in the United Kingdom [7(1)]. Section 1 of the Public Passenger Vehicles Act 1981 gives the circumstances under which a vehicle will or will not be regarded as a public service vehicle. They are explained on page 291.

The main prohibition provisions are contained in Section 1 and apply to a foreign goods vehicle or foreign public service vehicle where:

(a) an examiner exercises in relation to the vehicle or its driver any of the powers listed in Schedule 1 of the Act, or
(b) an authorised person exercises the powers he has under Sections 78 and 79 of the Road Traffic Act 1988 to weigh the vehicle. (These powers are given on page 265)

PROVISIONS CONFERRING FUNCTIONS ON EXAMINERS

Provisions	*Power conferred*
Section 99 of the Transport Act 1968.	To inspect and copy records and other documents required to be carried on goods and public service vehicles, to inspect tachographs and tachograph records.
Section 67 of the Road Traffic Act 1988	To test the condition of motor vehicles on roads.
Section 68 of the Road Traffic Act 1968	To inspect vehicles to secure proper maintenance.
Regulation 16 of the Road Transport (International Passenger Services) Regulations 1984	To require production, etc of documents required to be carried on certain passenger vehicles [Sch. 1]

If, in a case within paragraph (a) above (i) the driver obstructs the examiner, refuses or fails to comply with any legal requirement made by him or (ii) it appears to the examiner that there has been or there will be a contravention of specified laws, the examiner can prohibit the driving of the vehicle [1(2)].

The laws referred to above are specified in Schedule 2 of the Act and are as follows:

PROVISIONS RELATING TO VEHICLES AND THEIR DRIVERS

Provisions	*Effect*
Section 60 of the Transport Act 1968	To require users of certain goods vehicles to hold operators' licences unless exempted from doing so.
Sections 96 to 98 of the Transport Act 1968 and regulations and orders made under those sections and the applicable Community rules within the meaning of Part VI of that Act.	To limit driving time and periods of duty of drivers of goods and public service vehicles and to require the installation of tachographs and the keeping of records on such vehicles.
Section 40A of the Road Traffic Act 1988	To create offences of using motor vehicle or trailer in dangerous condition, etc.
Regulations under section 41 of the Road Traffic Act 1988.	To regulate the construction, weight, equipment and use of motor vehicles and trailers on roads.
Regulation 4 of the Passenger and Goods Vehicles (Recording Equipment) Regulations 1977.	To require the retention of records produced by recording equipment.
Section 99 of the Transport Act 1968.	To inspect and copy records, registers and other documents required to be carried on goods and public service vehicles and to inspect tachographs and their records.
Regulation 16 of the Road Transport (International Passenger Services) Regulations 1984	To require production, etc of documents required to be carried on certain passenger vehicles.
Regulation 19 of the Road Transport (International Passenger Services) Regulations 1980 and 1984.	To make it an offence to contravene certain requirements relating to international passenger services.

If, in a case coming within paragraph (b) on page 455 (i) the driver obstructs the authorised person or refuses or fails to comply with a requirement for the vehicle to be weighed or (ii) it appears to the authorised person that a weight limit on the vehicle has been or will be exceeded, the authorised person can prohibit the driving of the vehicle [1(3)].

Where an examiner or authorised person prohibits the driving of a vehicle on a road he can also direct the driver to remove it to a place and subject to such conditions as he specifies. The prohibition does not apply during such a removal immediately and it must give the reason for it and its extent [1(5)].

In the case of a goods vehicle a prohibition imposed for a supposed contravention of Section 40A of the Road Traffic Act 1988 (dangerous condition), construction and use or lighting Regulations may be made irremovable until the vehicle has been inspected at a heavy goods vehicle testing station [1(6)(a)]. A prohibition imposed on a goods vehicle in relation to its weight may be against driving the vehicle on a road until the weight has been reduced and official notification is given that it can continue [1(6)(b)]. The official notification must be in writing and given by an authorised person and may be withheld until the vehicle has been weighed to satisfy the authorised person that the weight has been reduced [1(7)].

A prohibition comes into force as soon as written notice of it has been given to the driver and continues till it is removed or a period specified in it expires [2(1)]. Where a prohibition notice has been given a written exemption for the use of the vehicle may be given (i) in the case of a prohibition imposed under Section 1(2) by an examiner and (ii) in the case of a prohibition imposed under Section 1(3) by an authorised person [2(2)].

An examiner or authorised person may remove a prohibition when satisfied that the circumstances leading to its imposition no longer exist and on doing so must give the driver written notice of the removal [2(3)]. But a prohibition which is made irremovable till the vehicle is inspected at a testing station cannot be removed till it has been inspected there [2(3A)]. A fee has to be paid for removal of a prohibition at a testing station [2(3B)].

If a person drives, or causes or permits to be driven, a vehicle on a road in contravention of a prohibition imposed under this Act he commits an offence. So also if he refuses or fails to comply within a reasonable time with a direction given under Section 1(4) to remove a vehicle [3(1)]. If a police officer in uniform suspects a driver of committing the offence he can detain the vehicle and direct a person to remove it to a specified place [3(3)]. Where a vehicle draws a trailer both vehicles can be detained [3(4)].

A vehicle can be detained until a police officer or the Secretary of State authorises its release on being satisfied that:

a. the prohibition has been removed or that no prohibition was imposed;
b. arrangements have been made to remove or remedy the circumstances leading to the prohibition;
c. the vehicle will be taken directly to a place from which it will be taken out of Great Britain;
d. it is no longer necessary to detain a motor vehicle or trailer which forms part of a vehicle combination which has been detained [3(5)].

A person who drives a vehicle in accordance with a direction under

Section 3(3) or who is in charge of the place where a vehicle is detained is not liable for damage to or loss in respect of the vehicle or its load unless it is shown he did not take reasonable care [3(6)].

An examiner may require (1) the driver of a foreign goods vehicle to produce a journey permit or own-account document (if the vehicle requires one) and (2) the driver of a foreign public service vehicle to produce a control document. If the driver refuses or fails to comply with the requirement the examiner can prohibit the use of the vehicle on a road. All the foregoing provisions relating to prohibitions then apply [4].

CONVENTION ON ROAD TRAFFIC CONCLUDED AT
GENEVA ON 19 SEPTEMBER 1949

Annex 6

Technical conditions concerning the equipment of motor vehicles and trailers in international traffic

I. BRAKING

(a) *Braking of motor vehicles other than motor cycles with or without sidecars*

Every motor vehicle shall be equipped with brakes capable of controlling the movement of and of stopping the vehicle in an efficient, safe and rapid way under the conditions of loading on any up or down gradient on which the vehicle is operated.

The braking shall be operated by means of two devices so constructed that, in the event of failure of one of the braking devices, the other shall be capable of stopping the vehicle within a reasonable distance.

For the purpose of this Annex, one of these braking devices will be called the 'service brake' and the other one the 'parking brake'.

The parking brake shall be capable of being secured, even in the absence of the driver, by direct mechanical action.

Either means of operation shall be capable of applying braking force to wheels symmetrically placed on each side of the longitudinal axis of the vehicle.

The braking surfaces shall always be connected with the wheels of the vehicle in such a way that it is not possible to disconnect them otherwise than momentarily by means of a clutch, gearbox or free wheel.

One at least of the braking devices shall be capable of acting on braking surfaces directly attached to the wheels of the vehicle or attached through parts not liable to failure.

(b) *Braking of trailers*

Every trailer having a permissible maximum weight exceeding 750kg shall be equipped with at least one braking device acting on wheels placed symmetrically on each side of the longitudinal axis of the vehicle and acting on at least half the number of wheels.

The provisions of the preceding paragraph shall be required, however, in respect of trailers if the permissible maximum weight does not exceed 750kg but exceeds one-half of the unladen weight of the drawing vehicle.

The braking device of trailers with a permissible maximum weight exceeding 3,500kg shall be capable of being operated by applying the service brake from the drawing vehicle. When the permissible maximum weight of the trailer does not exceed 3,500kg its braking device may be brought into action merely by the trailer moving upon the drawing vehicle (overrun braking).

The braking device of the trailer shall be capable of preventing the rotation of the wheels when the trailer is uncoupled.

Any trailer equipped with a brake shall be fitted with a device capable of automatically stopping the trailer if it becomes detached whilst in motion. This provision shall not apply to two-wheeled camping trailers or light luggage trailers whose weight exceeds 750kg provided that they are equipped in addition to the main attachment with a secondary attachment which may be a chain or a wire rope.

(c) *Braking of articulated vehicles and combinations of motor vehicles and trailers*

(i) *Articulated vehicles*

The provision of paragraph (a) of this Part shall apply to every articulated vehicle. A semi-trailer having a permissible maximum weight exceeding 750kg shall be equipped with at least one braking device capable of being operated by applying the service brake from the drawing vehicle.

The braking device of the semi-trailer shall, in addition, be capable of preventing the rotation of the wheels when the semi-trailer is uncoupled.

When required by domestic regulations a semi-trailer equipped with a brake shall be fitted with a device capable of stopping automatically the semi-trailer if it becomes detached whilst in motion.

(ii) *Combinations of motor vehicles and trailers*

Every combination of a motor vehicle and one or more trailers shall be equipped with brakes capable of controlling the movement and of stopping the combination in an efficient, safe and rapid way under any conditions of loading or on any up or down gradient on which it is operated.

(d) *Braking of motor cycles with or without sidecars*

Every motor cycle shall be equipped with two braking devices which may be operated by hand or foot, capable of controlling the movement of and of stopping the motor cycle in an efficient, safe and rapid way.

II LIGHTING

(a) Every motor vehicle other than a motor cycle with or without sidecar and capable of exceeding 20 km/h on the level shall be equipped with at least two white or yellow driving lights, fitted in front, capable of adequately illuminating the road for a distance of 100m in front of the vehicle at night time in clear weather.

(b) Every motor vehicle other than a motor cycle with or without sidecar and capable of exceeding 20 km/h on the level shall be equipped with two white or yellow passing lights fitted at the front of the vehicle and capable when necessary of adequately illuminating the road at night in clear weather in front of the vehicle for a distance of 30m without causing glare or dazzle to other road users whatever the direction of the traffic may be.

Passing lights shall be used instead of driving lights in all cases when the use of lights causing no dazzle or glare is necessary or compulsory.

(c) Every motor cycle with or without sidecar shall have at least one driving light and one passing light conforming to the provisions of (a) and (b) of this Part. However, motor cycles with an engine of a maximum cylinder capacity of 50cc may be excluded from this obligation.

(d) Every motor vehicle other than a motor cycle without sidecar shall be equipped with two white position (side) lights at the front. These lights shall be clearly visible at night time in clear weather at a distance of 150m from the front of the vehicle without causing any glare or dazzle to other road users.

The part of the illuminating surface of these lights furthest from the longitudinal axis of the vehicle shall be as near as possible to and in no case further than 400mm from the extreme outer edges of the vehicle.

Position (side) lights shall be shown at night time in all cases when the use of such lights is compulsory and at the same time as the passing lights if no part of the illuminating surface of the lamps of the passing lights is within 400mm of the extreme outer edges of the vehicle.

(e) Every motor vehicle and every trailer at the end of a combination of vehicles shall be equipped at the rear with at least one red light visible at night time in clear weather at a distance of 150m from the rear.

(f) The registration number displayed at the rear of a motor vehicle or a trailer shall be capable of illumination at night time in such a manner that it can be read in clear weather at a distance of 20m from the rear of the vehicle.

(g) The red rear light or lights and the light for the rear registration number shall be shown at the same time as any of the following: position (side) lights, passing lights or driving lights.

(h) Every motor vehicle other than a motor cycle without sidecar shall be equipped with two red reflex reflectors preferably of other than triangular form, fitted symmetrically at the rear and on opposite sides of the vehicle. The outer edges of each of these reflectors must be as near as possible to and in no case further than 400mm from the outer edges of the vehicle. These reflectors may be incorporated in the rear red lamps if these lamps comply with the above requirements. These reflectors shall be visible at night time in clear weather from a distance of at least 100m when illuminated by means of two driving lights.

(i) Every motor cycle without sidecar shall be equipped with a red reflex reflector preferably of other than triangular form, fitted at the rear of the vehicle, either incorporated in, or separate from, the rear red lamp and shall comply with the conditions of visibility mentioned under paragraph (h) of this Part.

(j) Every trailer and every articulated vehicle shall be equipped with two red reflex reflectors, preferably triangular in shape, fitted symmetrically at the rear and on opposite sides of the vehicle. These reflectors shall be visible at night time in clear weather from a distance of at least 100m when illuminated by means of two driving lights.

When the reflectors are triangular in shape, the triangle shall be equilateral, with sides of at least 150mm and shall be upright in position. The outer corner of each of these reflectors shall be as near as possible to and in no case further than 400mm from the extreme outer edges of the vehicle.

(k) With the exception of motor cycles, every motor vehicle and every trailer at the end of a combination of vehicles shall be equipped with at least one stop light at the rear showing a red or amber light. This light shall be actuated upon application of the service brake of the motor vehicle. If the stop light is red in colour and is either incorporated in, or associated with, the rear red light, its intensity shall be greater than that of the rear red light. The stop light shall not be required on trailers and semi-trailers when their dimensions are such that the stop light of the drawing vehicle remains visible from the rear.

(l)　When a motor vehicle is equipped with direction indicators, such indicators shall be one of the following:

(i)　a moveable arm protruding beyond each side of the vehicle and illuminated by a steady amber light when the arm is in the horizontal position,

(ii)　a constantly blinking or flashing amber light affixed to each side of the vehicle,

(iii)　a constantly blinking or flashing light placed at each side of the front and rear of the vehicle. The colour of such lights shall be white or orange towards the front and red or orange towards the rear.

(m)　No lights, with the exception of direction indicators, shall be flashing or blinking lights.

(n)　If a vehicle is equipped with several lights of the same kind, they shall be of the same colour and, except in the case of motor cycles with sidecars, two of these lights shall be placed symmetrically to the longitudinal axis of the vehicle.

(o)　Several lights may be incorporated in the same lighting device provided each of these lights complies with the appropriate provisions of this Part.

III　OTHER CONDITIONS

(a)　*Steering apparatus.*　Every motor vehicle shall be equipped with a strong steering apparatus which will allow the vehicle to be turned easily, quickly and with certainty.

(b)　*Driving mirror.*　Every motor vehicle shall be equipped with at least one driving mirror of adequate dimensions so placed as to enable the driver to view from his seat the road to the rear of the vehicle. However, this provision shall not be compulsory for motor cycles with or without sidecar.

(c)　*Warning devices.*　Every motor vehicle shall be equipped with at least one audible warning device of sufficient strength which shall not be a bell, gong, siren or other strident toned device.

(d)　*Windscreen wiper.*　Every motor vehicle fitted with a windscreen shall have at least one efficient windscreen wiper functioning without requiring constant control by the driver. However, this provision shall not be compulsory for motor cycles with or without sidecars.

(e)　*Windscreens.*　Windscreens shall be made of a stable substance, transparent and not likely to produce sharp splinters if broken. The objects seen through this substance shall not appear distorted.

(f)　*Reversing device.*　Every motor vehicle shall be equipped with a reversing device controlled from the driver's seat if the weight of the motor vehicle when empty exceeds 400kg.

(g) *Exhaust silencer.* Every motor vehicle shall have an exhaust silencer in constant operation to prevent excessive or unusual noise, the working of which cannot be interrupted by the driver while on the road.

(h) *Tyres.* The wheels of motor vehicles and their trailers shall be fitted with pneumatic tyres, or with some other tyres of equivalent elasticity.

(i) *Device to prevent a vehicle from running down a gradient.* When travelling in a mountainous region of a country where it is required by domestic regulations, any motor vehicle of which the permissible maximum weight exceeds 3,500kg shall carry a device, such as a scotch or chock, which can prevent the vehicle from running backwards or forwards.

(j) *General provisions.* (i) In so far as possible the machinery or accessory equipment of any motor vehicle shall not entail a risk of fire or explosion, nor cause the emission of noxious gases or offensive odours or produce disturbing noises, nor be a source of danger in case of collision.

(ii) Every motor vehicle shall be so constructed that the driver shall be able to see ahead, to the right and to the left, clearly enough to enable him to drive safely.

(iii) The provisions relating to braking and lighting shall not apply to invalid carriages which comply with the domestic regulations in the country of registration as regards brakes, lights and reflectors. For the purpose of this paragraph 'invalid carriage' shall mean a motor vehicle whose unladen weight does not exceed 300kg, whose speed does not exceed 30km/h and which is specially designed and constructed (and not merely adapted) for the use of a person suffering from some physical defect or disability and is normally used by such person.

INTERNATIONAL CONVENTION ON MOTOR TRAFFIC
CONCLUDED AT PARIS ON 24 APRIL 1926

ARTICLE 1

The Convention applies to road motor traffic in general irrespective of the object and nature of the transport, subject, however, to the special national regulations regarding public passenger transport services and public goods transport services.

ARTICLE 2

All passenger and goods-carrying motor vehicles running on any road to which the public have access, other than vehicles running on rails, are regarded as motor vehicles for the purposes of the present Convention.

ARTICLE 3

Every motor vehicle, in order to receive international authorisation to travel on any road to which the public have access, must either have been recognised as suitable for use on any road to which the public have access after an examination by the competent authority or by an association authorised by that authority or must conform to a type approved in the same manner. The vehicle must, in any case, fulfil the following conditions:

I. The motor vehicle must be equipped with the following:

(a) A strong steering apparatus which will allow the vehicle to be turned easily and with certainty.
(b) Either two systems of brakes, independent of each other, or one system of brakes with two independent means of operation, of which one means of operation will function, even if the other fails to function, provided that in all cases the system used is really effective and rapid in action.
(c) If the weight of the motor vehicle when empty exceeds 350kg, a mechanism by means of which the vehicle can from the driver's seat be made to move backwards under its own power.
(d) When the combined weight of the empty motor vehicle and the weight of the maximum load which it is officially declared to be capable of carrying exceeds 3,500kg, a special mechanism, such as can prevent, in all circumstances, the vehicle from running backwards, and in addition a reflecting mirror.

The controls and steering apparatus must be so placed that the driver can manage them with certainty and at the same time have a clear view of the road.

The machinery must be such as to work with certainty and disposed in such a way as to avoid, as far as possible, all danger of fire or explosion; as not to constitute any sort of danger to traffic and so as not to frighten or seriously inconvenience by noise, smoke or smell. The vehicle must be equipped with a silencer.

The wheels of motor vehicles and trailers drawn by them must be fitted with rubber tyres or with some other types of equivalent elasticity.

The distance between the ends of the hub-caps must not exceed the maximum width of the remainder of the vehicle.

II. The motor vehicle must carry:

a. At the front and the back, marked on plates or on the vehicle itself, the registration number which has been allotted to it by the competent authority. The registration number placed at the back as well as the distinctive mark referred to in Article 5 must be lit up as soon as they cease to be visible by the light of day.

In the case of a vehicle followed by a trailer the registration number and the distinctive mark referred to in Article 5 are repeated behind the trailer, and the regulation regarding the lighting of these marks applies to the trailer.

b. In an easily accessible position and in a form easily legible, the maker's name, chassis number and engine number.

III. Every motor vehicle must be fitted with an audible warning device of sufficient strength.

IV. Every motor vehicle travelling alone must, during the night and from sunset, be fitted in front with at least two white lights placed one on the right and the other on the left, and, at the back, with a red light.

For motor bicycles unaccompanied by a sidecar, the number of lights in front may be reduced to one.

V. Every motor vehicle must also be equipped with one or more devices capable of effectively illuminating the road for a sufficient distance ahead unless the two white lights prescribed above already fulfil this condition.

If the vehicle is capable of proceeding at a speed greater than 30km/h this distance must not be less than 100m.

VI. Lamps which may produce a dazzling effect must be provided with means for eliminating the dazzling effect when other users of the road are met, or on any occasion when such elimination would be useful. The elimination of the dazzling effect must, however, leave sufficient light to illuminate the road clearly for at least 25m.

VII. Motor vehicles drawing trailers are subject to the same regulations as separate motor vehicles in so far as forward lighting is concerned; the rear red light is to be carried on the back of the trailer.

VIII. In so far as the limits regarding weight and dimensions are concerned, motor vehicles and trailers must satisfy the general regulations in force in the countries in which they travel.

ARTICLE 4

With the object of certifying that every motor vehicle which has received international authorisation to travel on a road to which the public have access fulfills the conditions laid down in Article 3 or is able to fulfil them, international certificates are delivered on the model and according to the remarks contained in Annexes A and B to the present Convention.

These certificates are valid for one year from the date of their delivery. The written particulars which they bear must always be written in Latin characters or in so-called English script.

The international certificates delivered by the authorities of one of the contracting States or by an association authorised by them with the counter-signature of the authority give the right to travel freely in all other contracting States and are recognised therein as valid without further examination. The right to use the international certificate may, however, be refused if it is clear that the conditions laid down in Article 3 are no longer being fulfilled.

ARTICLE 5

Every motor vehicle, to receive international authorisation to travel on a road to which the public have access, must carry, in a visible position in the rear, a distinguishing mark consisting of from one to three letters written on a plate or on the vehicle itself.

For the purposes of the present Convention the distinguishing mark corresponds either to a State or to a territory which constitutes a distinct unit from the point of view of the registration of motor vehicles.

The dimensions and colour of this sign, the letters, their dimensions and their colour are given in the table contained in Annex C of the present Convention.

ARTICLE 6

The driver of a motor vehicle must possess qualifications which provide a reasonable guarantee of public safety.

In so far as international traffic is concerned, nobody may drive a motor vehicle without having received a special authorisation delivered by a competent authority or by an association authorised by it after giving proof of his competence.

This authorisation cannot be granted to persons of less than 18 years of age.

In order to certify, for international traffic, that the conditions laid down in the preceding article have been fulfilled, international driving permits are delivered on the model and according to the remarks contained in Annexes D and E of the present Convention.

These permits are valid for a year from the date of their delivery and for the categories of motor vehicles for which they have been delivered.

For the purposes of international traffic the following categories have been drawn up:

A   Motor vehicles of which the combined weight of the empty vehicle and the weight of the maximum load which it is officially declared to be capable of carrying does not exceed 3,500kg;
B   Motor vehicles of which the total weight, made up as above, exceeds 3,500kg;
C   Motor cycles with or without a side car.

The written remarks on international permits are always written in Latin characters or in so-called English script.

International driving permits delivered by the authorities of a contracting State or by an association authorised by them with the counter-signature of the authority authorise the holder, in all other contracting States, to drive motor vehicles which come within the categories for which they have been delivered and are recognised as valid, without re-examination, in all the contracting States. The right to use the international driving permit may, however, be refused if it is evident that the conditions prescribed in the previous article have not been fulfilled.

ARTICLE 8

The driver of a motor vehicle travelling in a country is bound to conform to the laws and regulations regarding traffic which are in force in that country.

An extract from these laws and regulations may be given to motorists on entry into a country at the office at which the Customs formalities are carried out.

Index